Educational Administration

Theoretical Perspectives on Practice and Research

Paula F. Silver
University of Illinois at Urbana-Champaign

HARPER & ROW, PUBLISHERS, New York
Cambridge, Philadelphia, San Francisco,
London, Mexico City, São Paulo, Sydney

1817

Sponsoring Editor: George A. Middendorf
Project Coordinator: Total Concepts Associates
Production Manager: Willie Lane
Compositor: Jay's Publishers Services, Inc.
Printer and Binder: R. R. Donnelley & Sons Company

Educational Administration: Theoretical Perspectives on Practice Research

Library of Congress Cataloging in Publication Data

Silver, Paula.
  Educational administration.

  Includes bibliographical references and index.
  1. School management and organization. 2. School management and organization—Research. I. Title.
LB2805.S588   1983   371.2   82-18730
ISBN 0-06-046161-6

EDUCATIONAL ADMINISTRATION

IN MEMORY OF
WILLIAM J. DAVIS

Contents

Preface

Discovering what theory is can be an exhilarating experience—like finding a special and exalted plane of existence, a rarefied, crystal-clear atmosphere where everything sparkles with the logic of pure abstraction. To grasp what theory is, beyond any mere definition, is to have a flash of insight about the nature of abstraction, a gasp of recognition that the words represent not mundane tangibles but inventions of the creative mind.

This book is an attempt to recreate for students the exhilaration of that discovery. I first experienced it as a graduate student at New York University in a required course on organization theory, in which each theory was treated as a separate and distinct system of thought. To the professors who organized and taught the material in that way—most particularly to Richard Lonsdale and Bryce Fogarty—I will always be grateful.

The book is intended for beginning and advanced graduate students of educational administration. It emcompasses 12 theoretical frameworks that appear to have profound relevance to practice and research in the profession of educational administration. Admittedly, the selection is a limited one, emphasizing sociology and social psychology more heavily than other behavioral or social science disciplines and stressing those theories that have already generated extensive research rather than more recent conceptualizations.

For beginning students the book can serve as an orientation to some of the most basic theoretical frameworks in the field of educational administration. Each theory is explained as a set of logically interrelated propositions, with the major constructs defined and some implications for practice explored. Each theory is associated with a simple image that is intended to evoke the theory in its entirety once the basic conceptualization is understood. A mastery quiz is provided, along with practical exercises, as a review of the basic terminology of each theory.

For more advanced students, including those about to undertake original research, the book can serve as a review and analysis of some of the most fundamental conceptualizations in the field of educational administration. Each theory is discussed *as* a theory, with some of its conceptual strengths and weaknesses examined and ideas for theory development suggested either explicitly or implicitly. For each new theory a synthesis of a representative sample of the empirical research is provided, and an extensive bibliography is offered as a good start on a review of the literature. In addition, practice-oriented questions are posed near the end of each theory chapter to suggest research topics that have the potential to contribute appreciably to the empirical knowledge in this field.

The book is intended to serve still another purpose beyond the education of graduate students who are about to embark (or have already embarked) on administrative careers. It represents the author's firm belief that what is needed to advance the field of educational administration to the status of a mature applied profession is the systematic use of theories to generate knowledge about the improvement of practice. By using schoolwide student achievement data in the cognitive, affective, and psychomotor domains as the criteria for assessing school principals' effectiveness, we can generate an extensive, codifiable body of knowledge about the effects of diverse administrative practices and, consequently, about how to improve administrative practice.

Most theoretical frameworks originating within the behavioral and social science disciplines bear important implications for administrative practice in schools. As a field of practitioners and researchers, however, we have not tested those implications systematically. By establishing a baseline set of criteria by which to assess administrative effectiveness—namely, student learnings in the affective and psychomotor as well as cognitive domains—we can readily apply the available theories to both descriptive and experimental tests in practice. Stated differently, the use of clear-cut, quantifiable, and socially endorsed criteria by which to judge administrative success (student outcomes in relation to stated goals) would enable the research community to determine systematically whether the practical implications of theories do in fact help to improve practice. Furthermore, the use of data on student outcomes of various types would facilitate the codification or systematic ordering and accumulation of knowledge in the field, since practice-oriented research findings would tend to cluster in relation to the types of administrative problems encountered with respect to student learnings.

Each theory in this book is examined in terms of its implications for administrative practices that are directed toward enhancing student learning outcomes. What is urgently needed is a body of research to test those (and other) implications and thereby to inform administrative practice in the future. At some point a central research facility might be founded, where theory-based and practice-oriented research data could be gathered from across the country and aggregated for in-depth analyses that cross the boundaries of individual theories. Such research would permit the identification of the interactive effects of many school variables and might thus lead to the development of more sophisticated theories. Until such a facility is established, however, there remains a tremendous need for studies to test the implications of individual theories for administrative practice. It is hoped that this book will stimulate such research, for the absence of demonstrably useful technical knowledge about how to enhance students' learning is one of the most serious shortcomings of the profession of educational administration.

Paula Silver

Part I
EMPIRICAL SCIENCE

Chapter 1
Theory in Relation
to Research and Practice

Why do people behave as they do? Have they been conditioned to respond automatically to certain stimuli—or are they unwittingly sublimat-
ing impulses to gratify the id? Are they moved by an external force—or
do they value particular objectives that they seek to attain? Are they
driven by needs—or do other people compel them? Or is there no explanation at all for human behavior?

What is an organization? Is it a pattern of relationships among people—or a random collectivity of organisms? Is it a social imperative for
survival—or an accident of history? Is it a locus of human growth—or a
constraint on personal freedom? Is it a product of natural evolution—or a
predetermined form of life? Or is it nothing in particular that can be
described?

These questions have no definitive answers. Perhaps all the options
are true to some extent. Perhaps some are true, or none. Perhaps nothing is *true* in the sense of having an eternal verity apart from people's
beliefs. Nevertheless, questions about human behavior and organizations
continue to be raised.

This book is about organizations such as schools and the way people behave in them. Although it does not offer the only possible answers to the questions posed here, it does provide some answers that have been generated in the tradition of empirical science. The scientific tradition of logical positivism demands that what counts as knowledge consists of sets of logically interrelated statements that can be verified through the processes of empirical research.

This chapter will explain briefly the nature of scientific theory as it relates to research and practice and will clarify the meanings of some specialized terms that are used throughout the book. The chapter serves as an essential background to the discussions of particular theories in later chapters.

EMPIRICAL THEORY

The Nature of Empirical Theory

The term *empirical theory* has been defined in a variety of ways by philosophers of science and by scholars in the academic disciplines. We shall approach the nature of empirical theory somewhat differently by defining it as:

A unique way of perceiving reality

An expression of someone's profound insight into an aspect of nature

A thought system that reaches beyond superficial experience to reveal a deeper dynamic than people usually perceive

A fresh and different perception of an aspect of the world we inhabit

To understand a theory is to travel into someone else's mind and become able to perceive reality as that person does. To understand a theory is to experience a shift in one's own mental structure and discover with startling clarity a different way of thinking. To understand a theory is to feel some wonder that one never saw before what now seems to have been obvious all along. This interpretation of the nature of theory does not sound very scientific. More formal definitions are dry, however, robbing theory of its beauty, its emotional significance, its importance in everyday life. A theory is a distinctive way of perceiving reality.

How do most of us usually experience reality? If we had no minds at all, we would probably experience a stream of raw sensations—nameless, undifferentiated visceral or sensory physical events. It is almost impossible to imagine such mindlessness, accustomed as we are to thinking, to naming and interpreting events. Nevertheless, these events constitute the concrete world, the raw materials of which experience is made.

CONCEPTS

During very early infancy we start learning words that represent raw experiences—names for things, verbs for actions, and all the modifications and relationships that make up our society's language. We learn to interpret concrete reality in a culturally acceptable way by assigning certain words to certain types of events. In brief, we learn concepts. A *concept* is a mental device for interpreting a unit in the stream of sensations we experience. A concept is a kernel of an idea, the smallest unit of analysis in the thought process. It is an abstraction that refers to an element in the concrete, experienced world. Concepts enable us to differentiate one event or sensation from another in the steady flow of events and sensations that constantly impinge on us. Concepts permit us to relate an event in the past to a similar one in the present or future. Virtually any word in our language—or any language—can represent a concept.

CONSTRUCTS

Most of us function at the level of concepts most of the time. We string them together in sentences and paragraphs to communicate what we are experiencing mentally and physically. Often, however, concepts cluster and merge into a higher-order unit of thought, a construct. For example, most of us share a concept of intelligence as a demonstration of the amount of knowledge one has, and a concept of age as the amount of time one has lived. The notion of intelligence quotient or IQ represents a merging of these two concepts: IQ refers to one's knowledge-in-relation-to-age. IQ is an example of a *construct*—a blending or combining of two or more concepts to form a new unit of thought. As the IQ example illustrates, a construct is further removed than a concept from concrete reality. Although a construct does not represent an element of reality that can be experienced directly, it does add richness and depth to the way we perceive reality. A construct is an abstraction referring to elements in the experienced world that cannot be perceived directly but are assumed to exist. A construct is a blend of concepts into a higher-order unit of thought.

Because we use language to communicate, and because the language is basically made up of concepts, a person who conceives of a construct may find it difficult to communicate that construct to other people. The word or phrase used to identify the construct might be one that is already in the language, and such words are usually associated with concepts rather than with constructs. Therefore, a new word is sometimes invented (for example, *id*, *ethos*, or *feedback*), or a symbol is used (for example, Σ, *P·E*, *V*) to represent the construct and to highlight the uniqueness of the conceptualization.

To recapitulate briefly, a concept is defined in this book as a mental representation of a unit of concrete experience. A construct is defined as a mental representation of a cluster or blend of concepts. A concept is somewhat abstract since it is one step removed from raw experience; a construct is even more abstract since it refers to a phenomenon that cannot be experienced directly. A construct is an invention—a merging of concepts in a unique way that adds richness to the meanings of the concepts.

PROPOSITIONS

On rare occasions an individual conceives of a pattern of relationships among several constructs and can articulate these relationships clearly, logically, and convincingly. This expression of relationships among constructs is called a *proposition*. A proposition thus represents a unique conceptualization of reality. It is an integration of constructs, which are blends of concepts, which represent events in the real world of experience.

The constructs in a proposition usually are uniquely identified with and integral to the particular proposition. That is, each construct in a proposition is generally a new, unique constellation of concepts; and the constructs are intrinsically interrelated in the context of the proposition. Because the constructs are new inventions, they must be defined and explained carefully so that others, who may have tended to think in terms of concepts or of different constructs, can grasp their meaning. The pattern of interrelationships among constructs must be described fully, both to clarify the constructs further and to convey their significance. In brief, a proposition is a statement of relationships between or among constructs.

THEORY

One proposition is usually insufficient to explain fully the creative thinker's new insight about an aspect of reality. Most often the complete articulation of this new insight requires a series of propositions that are logically related to each other. A set of logically interrelated propositions is called a *theory*. A theory, then, is an integrated set of propositional statements, each of which is an integration of constructs representing clusters of concepts pertinent to the world of human experience. Theory is the culmination of a highly abstract thought process whereby ideas are removed in successive stages from the world of immediate experience. Nevertheless, because of the logic of the thought process and the indirect linkage of constructs to concepts, theories are of profound significance for understanding the experienced world.

Once a theory has been expressed, it is often possible, through deductive logic, to recognize and state additional relationships among constructs that would be true if the theory itself is true. For example, theory omega might consist of two propositions: (1) A is greater than B; (2) B is equal to C. From this theory one might deduce that A is greater than C, even though this is not stated in the theory. This deductively derived statement is also called a *proposition*.

The meanings of the key terms used so far might be reviewed with the help of the ladder of abstraction depicted in Figure 1–1. Each rung represents a level of abstraction, and the levels proceed upward from the most concrete to the most abstract.

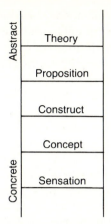

Figure 1-1   A Ladder of Abstraction in Perceiving Reality

Theory can now be defined more formally as:

"a set of interrelated constructs, definitions and propositions that presents
a systematic view of phenomena..." (Kerlinger, 1973:11).

"a set of interconnected propositions that have the same referent—the
subject of the theory..." (Argyris & Schön, 1974:4–5).

"a conceptualization—an orientation toward or perspective on phenomena
[which] forms the basis for [the] written or formal theory" (Reynolds,
1971:21).

Understanding Theory

The nature of theory might be clarified further with reference to a particular
theory that is not treated extensively in this book but is probably familiar to
most readers—Abraham Maslow's theory of motivation (Maslow, 1954). At the
most concrete level, this framework begins with events that people experience—a pang of hunger, for example, or an urge to talk, or a feeling of joy upon
discovering something. These sensations are direct experiences. One of
Maslow's basic insights is that these experiences represent needs—the need for
food, the need for company, the need for psychological growth. The specific
needs are fundamental concepts in this theory.

A further insight intrinsic to Maslow's theory is that all the diverse needs
people are said to have are classifiable within five categories or types. Thus the
theory is in part a typology of needs. The five types of needs Maslow identifies
are: physiological, security, affiliation, esteem, and self-actualization. Each of
these categories represents a construct—a constellation of concepts. For
example, the *physiological needs* construct incorporates the need for food, the
need for shelter, the need for warmth, the need for oxygen, and other
individual organismic needs.

These constructs (classes of needs) bear a specific relationship to each other in Maslow's theory. The physiological needs are the most fundamental and compelling; they must be gratified to some degree before security needs become salient. Likewise, the security needs must be gratified to some degree before affiliation needs emerge, and so forth throughout the sequence. In other words, the types of needs are *hierarchically* ordered, with physiological needs as the most essential and the first to emerge, and self-actualization needs as the least compelling and the last to emerge in salience. Since categories of needs are constructs, the statements of relationships among these categories are propositions.

This theory interprets needs as states of deficiency such that people strive toward wholeness or lack of deficiency be gratifying their needs. Motivation is viewed as a striving toward wholeness, and behavior as the attempt to gratify the type of need that is salient at the time of the behavior. The complete set of interrelated propositions, including those pertaining to relationships among need categories and those pertaining to motivation and behavior, constitute the theory of motivation as conceived by Abraham Maslow.

Maslow's theory has been described briefly here to illustrate how the ladder of abstraction relates to theories in general. Parts of this particular theory can be analyzed in terms of that ladder of abstraction, as in Figure 1–2.

As stated earlier, to understand a theory is to enter someone else's mind and become able to perceive reality as that person does. Understanding a theory requires effort. One must exert considerable effort to grasp fully the meaning of each construct as a new and unique unit of thought, an idea that has not previously been part of one's normal pattern of thinking. Because theories are abstract, understanding them requires more than simply memorizing the terms, their definitions, and their interrelationships. Understanding a theory entails stretching one's mind to reach for the theorist's meaning. It involves pondering the constructs and their definitions and interrelationships by recalling one's own experiences and trying to perceive and interpret them in the new way propounded by the theorist.

One can write "$E = mc^2$" without necessarily understanding the theory of relativity. Similarly, one can recite, "The five types of needs in order of prepotency are: physiological, security, affiliation, esteem, and self-actualization," without necessarily understanding Maslow's theory of human behavior. The reader must go beyond the mere definitions of terms in each theory and try to elicit a new and different way of construing reality. If at the end of any chapter in this book the reader has not yet understood the genuine freshness of the perspective, then either I have failed to communicate effectively the beauty and distinctiveness of the abstraction, or the reader has missed the significance of the terms. A theory is not a set of words and sentences to be memorized; it is a particular way of perceiving reality.

For educational administrators the reality to be perceived is in and around an educational unit of some sort—a grade level or department, a school or

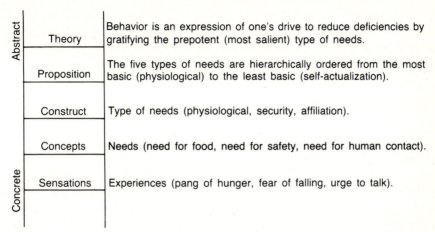

Abstract	Theory	Behavior is an expression of one's drive to reduce deficiencies by gratifying the prepotent (most salient) type of needs.
	Proposition	The five types of needs are hierarchically ordered from the most basic (physiological) to the least basic (self-actualization).
	Construct	Type of needs (physiological, security, affiliation).
	Concepts	Needs (need for food, need for safety, need for human contact).
Concrete	Sensations	Experiences (pang of hunger, fear of falling, urge to talk).

Figure 1–2   Maslow's Motivation Theory in Relation to a Ladder of Abstraction

school district, a state system or other educational organization. These units are the concrete realities inhabited by practitioners, the sources of raw experiences that ebb and flow continually. These realities can be perceived in many different ways, including those expressed in behavioral science theories. Theories drawn from the various behavioral science disciplines, if properly understood, can enhance both research and practice within these educational units.

THEORY IN RELATION TO RESEARCH

A theorist sets forth a perception of the nature of some aspect of reality in the form of clearly defined constructs and a set of propositions. The theory may be eloquently stated and convincing. When one recalls one's own experiences and learns to reinterpret them in terms of the theory, the theory may have the ring of truth; it may cast reality in a new light that seems to make sense.

People are often misled, however. They may believe firmly in a supposed law of nature that later has to be abandoned because it is no longer useful in understanding reality. The earth is not flat, after all, and the sun and planets do not revolve around the earth. Thus we need more than a belief that a theory makes sense, more than an intuition about the nature of reality. We need demonstrations, verification, proof that a theory does explain reality before we can accept it as truth. We need stronger evidence than merely our own individual perceptions that the generalizations in the theory do apply to real, concrete events. This is why we conduct research.

Much scientific research involves the collection and analysis of evidence for the purpose of determining the validity of a theory. A substantial portion of scientific research is also directed toward answering questions or solving problems in the world of experience. To understand the nature of scientific research, particularly in the deductive mode, we can start with our understanding of theory and move down the ladder of abstraction.

Conceptual Framework

A theory has been defined as a set of logically interrelated propositions. These propositions are generalizations that pertain to an infinitely broad array of particular situations or events. Since a study must confine itself to a sample of particulars, the context in which those particulars are being viewed must be explained at the outset. In other words, the theory being used as the basis for selecting the events to be studied must be described and linked logically to the particular problem being investigated. The theory serves to clarify the perspective or conceptual framework to be used as the foundation of the empirical study.

Hypothesis

As noted earlier, a proposition is a statement that is embedded in a set of interrelated statements (a theory) and that asserts a relationship between or among constructs. This suggests that the proposition of interest to a researcher is contained within the conceptual framework. In linking the abstract proposition to the specific study being conducted, the researcher converts the proposition into a statement of relationships between or among variables, factors to be studied empirically. This statement is called a *hypothesis*. For purposes of this book, a hypothesis can be defined as a transformation of a proposition from the general to the particular—a translation of abstract terms into terms that refer to specific, measurable instances.

We can draw on Maslow's theory again to illustrate this transformation of a proposition into a hypothesis. Statement A is a proposition that can be deduced from the theory related earlier:

A. People vary in the prepotency (salience) of their needs.

This statement can be converted into terms that refer to specific instances of reality, as in statement B:

B. Teachers within a school vary with respect to their prepotent (most salient) job-related needs.

The proposition (Statement A) refers to all people, all needs, and all settings in which needs can be gratified. The hypothesis (Statement B) refers to a particular class of people (teachers), a particular subset of needs (work-related), and a particular setting for need gratification (schools). In other words, hypotheses are generalizations, but they are less broadly general than propositions; a hypothesis refers to particular instances of phenomena rather than all instances of those phenomena. Each major term in a hypothesis relates to a construct in the proposition from which it was derived.

As noted earlier, a construct is a mental structure, a conceptualization of something that is not directly observable in nature. How, then, can we gather evidence to determine whether a hypothesis is true? To do so, we must transform the constructs in the hypothesis into terms that refer to more concrete experience, so that we can gather the relevant evidence. Thus the next step in conducting deductive research is to convert the constructs in the hypothesis into variables.

Variables

A variable is a quality or characteristic by which the individuals, groups, or things of interest differ from each other. Height and weight are examples of variables, as is need level. To demonstrate the conversion of a hypothesis into more concrete terms, we can transform Statement B (a hypothesis) into Statement C:

> C. Within schools there are differences among teachers in types of needs that are most important to them.

Statement C makes it clear that we are to examine the types of needs teachers have that are important to them within one or more schools. If the researcher were to find that teachers do differ in their need levels, the hypothesis would be supported.

Most hypotheses are more complex than Statement C. Usually the researcher seeks to confirm (or reject) a statement of relationships that are suggested by the theory. For example, Maslow's theory states that a type of need emerges only when lower-order needs have been sufficiently satisfied. This suggests a proposition: the salience of a particular type of needs implies gratification of lower-order needs. This proposition in turn suggests Hypothesis D:

> D. There is a direct (positive) relationship between the importance teachers within a school attribute to one type of needs and the degree of gratification of lower-order needs.

In this hypothesis the *perceived importance* of needs and the *gratification* of needs are the variables, the characteristics by which people differ. According to this hypothesis, as the importance of needs at one level increases, the gratification of needs at the next lower level increases. To test the hypothesis, the researcher would have to gather information about each variable. In order to gather the relevant information, however, the researcher must first operationalize the variables.

Operationalization

To operationalize a variable is to determine precisely how the information pertaining to that variable will be gathered. Will the researcher simply ask the people questions? observe from an unobtrusive place and take careful notes? use a device of some sort as a measuring gauge? Whatever the technique used, the researcher must be certain that the information being gathered does represent the variable in question.

To test the hypothesis in Statement D, one of the variables the researcher would have to operationalize is the perceived importance of needs. A device that includes all five types of needs and can be used to determine the most important type for each teacher would be needed. The researcher might decide to observe the teachers systematically after making a convincing case for inferring need importance from observable behavior. In this instance a form or protocol would have to be developed for recording all the behaviors as they are observed. Another researcher might decide to design a questionnaire whereby the importance of needs to respondents can be determined, or to use a questionnaire already in existence for that purpose. In this case the researcher would have to demonstrate that the questionnaire does validly and reliably measure what it purports to measure. Whatever information-gathering methods the investigator uses, a device of some sort is needed. The device for gathering information for research is called an *instrument*.

Instruments

Like a yardstick for measuring length or a thermometer for measuring temperature, a research instrument is a tool for measuring a variable. More precisely, an instrument is a tool for ascertaining the degree to which a characteristic is present or absent in the objects being studied. Instruments enable the researcher to assign a value to the units (individuals, groups, or things) under investigation. To test the hypothesis stated earlier (Statement D), the researcher would need one instrument to measure quantitatively the importance of needs to teachers, and another to measure degree of need gratification in quantitative terms. The information gathered in the context of research by means of research instruments is called *data*. One piece of information is a *datum;* several pieces of information are data. Instruments are constructed so that each part or *item* pertains to one specific instance of the variable being studied, and all the items in combination represent the variable in its entirety.

We have been proceeding down the ladder of abstraction in examining the deductive scientific research process. Now we can compare theory to research in terms of that ladder. As illustrated in Figure 1–3, each theory-related term has a comparable research-related term. The terms on the left side of the diagram are congruent with those on the right side, as shown by the arrows.

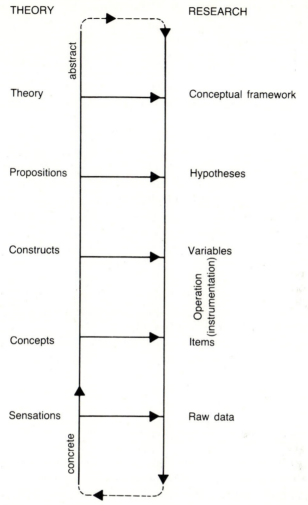

Figure 1–3   Theory and Research in Relation to a Ladder of Abstraction

Having decided on the instruments to be used in gathering data, the researcher must identify a sample of real units. In the case of the illustrative hypothesis, the units are teachers either within one school or in several schools (provided there are several teachers in each school, as Statement D is worded). The data are then gathered from the units in the sample and analyzed in ways appropriate for the hypothesis being tested.

The matters of sampling, instrumentation and scoring, and data analysis are too complex for treatment in this book. Readers should consult a good basic research textbook such as Kerlinger (1973), Good (1963), or Tuckman (1972) for further understanding of these issues. What is important in the context of this book is the realization that each empirical study cited is based on the researcher's thought process, which proceeds down the ladder of abstraction from the theory itself all the way to pieces of raw data. It should be noted also that in each empirical study cited in this book—whether the data were drawn from interviews, observations, existing documents, or questionnaires— instruments were used in gathering the data and interpreting it, and the data were analyzed to derive findings.

The *findings* of an empirical study are the results of analysis of the data at hand. The use of the findings to draw conclusions entails a progression back up the ladder of abstraction. The thought process in this progression goes something like this: the data were gathered by means of instruments that represent variables; if the variables relate to each other as predicted in the hypothesis, then the hypothesis is supported; if the hypothesis is supported, then the proposition from which it was deduced is also supported; and if the proposition is supported, then the theory of which it is a part is to some extent supported. Thus each piece of empirical research lends credibility to (or detracts credibility from) the theory to which it relates. Note that *support* and *nonsupport* are the appropriate terms. A theory cannot be proved or disproved—certainly not by any one study. The best a researcher can do is to render the theory more or less believable.

This cursory review of the scientific deductive research process has not examined the many variations that appear in the research literature or any of the distinctions among research designs. Its purpose is simply to orient readers to the research-related terminology used throughout this book.

THEORY IN RELATION TO PRACTICE

All people have theories about the things and events in their lives. People develop an immense number of generalizations in order to understand, predict, and control events. Without such generalizations and sets of generalizations, they would be unable to make sense of their experiences or to plan for the next moment, week, or year. Without conceptions of what things are, how things or people relate to each other, and why events transpire, it would not be possible to navigate through a day.

These personalistic theories can be assumed to be the foundations for individuals' actions. For example, a person who subscribes to a theory that eggs contain nutrients that are essential to the development of a sound body will buy eggs and serve them frequently, whereas another person—holding to the theory that eggs contain substances harmful to the body—will avoid them at the market and refrain from eating them. Educational administrators subscribe to many personalistic theories, developed in the course of living and practicing administration, that provide the foundations for their actions.

Theory and the Individual Practitioner

Practicing educational administrators generate many theoretical notions as they engage in practice, observe themselves and others, and think about their experiences. These sets of generalizations are seldom fully expressed, even to oneself; they usually remain at a tacit level (see Polanyi, 1967) as frameworks of which the individual is not even fully aware. If the administrator is asked why she reprimanded a teacher or sent a memo, some elements of her tacit theory might become explicit.

Argyris and Schön (1974) distinguish between tacit theories, which they call *theories-in-use*, and explicit theories, which they call *espoused theories*. They note that there is often a sharp discrepancy between one's espoused theories and one's actions. For example, an administrator might staunchly express the theory that teachers, as trained professionals, fully deserve high esteem and are best qualified to make decisions about classroom management. That same administrator, however, might observe the teachers without prior invitation, make judgments about their classroom management, and tell them how to change instead of learning from them the merits of the classroom procedures being followed. Chances are that the administrator in question holds to some theories-in-use that have never been articulated, even to herself.

Douglas McGregor (1960), who wrote extensively about business managers and administrators, highlighted the importance of theories-in-use in his discussions of Theory X and Theory Y. Administrators who subscribe to Theory X are guided in their actions by implicit or tacit generalizations such as: the employees are immature, lazy, and self-interested; they need to be coerced by threat or bribe to do a full day's work for a full day's pay. Other administrators, implicitly supporting Theory Y, are guided in their actions by tacit generalizations such as: the employees are mature individuals, hard-working and interested in making a contribution to the organization; they are to be appreciated, rewarded, and supported in their efforts. Clearly, Theory X and Theory Y would give rise to very different administrative actions.

Because theories-in-use are not verbalized but remain at an unconscious or preconscious level of awareness, they are often fragmentary and inconsistent, even mutually contradictory. As long as they remain tacit, they are inadequate bases for learning because the practitioner is unaware of the connections between the actions and their underlying generalizations. Argyris and Schön (1974) suggested that the practitioner can learn how to improve practice by bringing the theories-in-use into the light of conscious awareness in order to examine them for inconsistencies and use them as bases for experimentation in practice. In other words, individuals can test their own theories-in-use—once they become aware of these implicit frameworks—to discover whether they do in fact describe, explain, or predict events, or whether they need modification. Often the explanatory framework that best fits the events one experiences is actually contradictory to one's initial intuitions or tacit assumptions.

Scientific theories like those examined in this book differ in several respects from personalistic theories. First, their origins are external to the practitioner. Although each originated in the mind of an individual—the theorist—it is not an intrinsic part of the practitioner's world view. Second, scientific theories are coherent wholes that are internally consistent and logical. Instead of an assortment of unconnected or contradictory generalizations, each theory is a set of logically interrelated generalizations called propositions. Third, scientific theories are amenable to empirical validation or rejection. Because they are explicit, scientific theories can be tested by means of research. Even though the theorists are not always concerned with methods of verification, their products, as public statements, can usually be tested. Fourth, scientific theories are often counterintuitive. Many theories are actually contradictory to generalizations that practitioners make on the basis of limited individual experience. Because things are not always what they seem, counterintuitive theories often provide more comprehensive explanations than individuals' perceptions could yield.

Scientific theories, different as they are from personalistic and tacit theories, can nevertheless serve as foundations for practice. When an individual becomes aware of a scientific theory and comes to understand it fully as an explanation for some phenomenon or some pattern of events, that person can consciously and deliberately use the theory experimentally as a basis for action. With practice, the terminology of the theory will likely become a normal part of the practitioner's vocabulary and an integral part of the practitioner's world view, so that actions on the basis of the theory need no longer be intentional or deliberate.

The basic assumption underlying this book is that the theories presented (as well as other behavioral science theories that are not included) can enrich and expand administrators' perceptions and understandings of the realities in which they function. The perspectives presented here are not intended to supplant administrators' tacit frameworks developed through experience, but to supplement and complement them. They are presented not as absolute truths but as interesting and potentially useful ways of interpreting events in educational organizations. The readers are asked to reach for new insights in each theory, not to assume the theories are statements of what they knew all along. Without an awareness of the difference between the theory and intuition, readers will not be able to use the theory as a basis for changing their behavior.

Theory and the Profession of Administration

In all occupations the practitioners act on the basis of theories-in-use and standard procedures or technologies for getting the job done. This is true for every field of work from plumbing to selling goods to architecture to administration. Each established profession, however, also has a substantial body of explicit or scientific theories and an immense literature of theory-based, practice-oriented research.

A body of explicit theories offers several advantages for an occupational group. Since each theory represents a perspective for understanding or interpreting certain phenomena and includes a vocabulary for communicating about those phenomena, the practitioners within a profession have some insights or understandings in common and can communicate with each other about their understandings. Thus they can share their experiences in a language they all understand.

A literature of practice-oriented research based on theory also offers several advantages for an occupational group. Whereas individual practitioners might draw personalistic implications for practice from the various theories they know, the research literature can identify the best or most effective practices that have yet been devised. Furthermore, the individual practitioner can discover in the literature that some practices that seem promising on the basis of theory have unanticipated shortcomings or unintended side effects. Practitioners can also get ideas for improving practice by encountering methods and techniques in the literature that they might not have thought of themselves on the basis of the theoretical literature.

Professional practice is viewed in this book as action guided both by implicit or tacit theories (intuitions) and by explicit or scientific theories supported through empirical research. In other words, professional practice is viewed as both an art and a science. The set of theories in this book, intended as a supplement to intuitive insights, represents a portion of the body of theoretical literature for the profession of educational administration. What is propounded as an essential aspect of educational administration, if this field is to continue to develop as a profession, is an extensive program of practice-oriented research based on theory.

SUMMARY

The underlying theme of this chapter is that the knowledge base of a profession such as educational administration consists largely of theories that have been widely supported through research. A theory should be understood not only as a set of logically interrelated propositional statements, but also as a unique and compelling way of perceiving and interpreting an aspect of reality.

Theory rests at the apex of a so-called ladder of abstraction that proceeds from concrete experience to abstract conceptualization. At the most concrete level there is raw experience or sensation; in the act of perceiving, sensations are converted into concepts. Clusters of concepts are conceived as constructs; constructs can be related to each other in the form of propositions; and a full set of logically interrelated propositions is a theory.

In the conduct of deductive empirical research, the investigator proceeds down the ladder of abstraction in the interest of associating an abstract theory with concrete data. From a particular theory a proposition is selected and is translated into a testable hypothesis or statement of relationships between or among variables; each variable is then operationalized by means of an instrument of some sort to collect data. The data are then analyzed in a manner suggested by the hypothesis. The results of the data analysis are called findings; the findings, when considered in terms of a progression back up the ladder of abstraction, are used to draw conclusions pertinent to the theory with which the researcher started.

Theories are relevant to practice in several respects. They supplement individual administrators' repertoire of theories-in-use. They provide a common language whereby professionals can communicate with and learn from each other. Finally, in conjunction with practice-oriented deductive research, they can reveal effective techniques for solving the real problems that confront administrators.

REFERENCES

Argyris, C., & Schön, D. A. *Theory in practice: Increasing professional effectiveness.* San Francisco: Jossey-Bass, 1974.

Good, C. V. *Introduction to educational research: Methodology of design in the behavioral and social sciences,* 2nd ed. New York: Appleton-Century-Crofts, 1963.

Kerlinger, F. N. *Foundations of behavioral research,* 2nd ed. New York: Holt, Rinehart and Winston, 1973.

Maslow. A. H. *Motivation and personality.* New York: Harper & Row, 1954.

McGregor, D. *The human side of enterprise.* New York: McGraw-Hill, 1960.

Polanyi, M. *The tacit dimension.* Garden City, N.Y.: Doubleday, Anchor Books, 1967.

Reynolds, P. D. *Primer in theory construction.* Indianapolis, Ind.: Bobbs-Merrill, 1971.

Tuckman, B. W. *Conducting educational research.* New York: Harcourt Brace Jovanovich, 1972.

Part II
WHOLE
ORGANIZATIONS

Interest in the study and analysis of large organizations dates back to classical Egyptian and Greek societies, where the efforts of hundreds of workers had to be coordinated with the movement of equipment and supplies in constructing massive monuments and edifices. In the United States, however, the systematic study of organizations seems to have originated in 1931, with the publication of Mooney and Riley, *Onward Industry* (Scott, 1961). Since then the study of organizations in this country has evolved through several overlapping stages from what has been called the *classical* or *management science approach*, through a viewpoint designated the *human relations approach*, to the most recent orientation, called the *behavioral science approach* (Kelly, 1969).

An *organization* can be defined as "a social unit within which people have achieved somewhat stable relations...among themselves in order to facilitate obtaining a set of objectives or goals" (Litterer, 1963:5). Intrinsic to this definition are two aspects of organizations that have been of interest to students of organization: *structure* and *process*. The relative stability of relationships among people suggests a structure or pattern of some sort whereby the nature of the interpersonal relations can be specified.

The attainment of a set of objectives suggests that there are processes or actions undertaken in the course of organizational life. Organizational structure and process are the central point of interest in Part II of this book.

Organizational structure and its impact on the products of organizational life are explicated in Jerald Hage's axiomatic theory of organizations (Hage, 1965). To develop this theory, Hage reviewed and synthesized a large assortment of studies dealing with such structural features of organizations as complexity, centralization, formalization, and stratification. The structural characteristics of organizations are viewed as means for attaining objectives related to adaptiveness, production, efficiency, and job satisfaction. Since schools and school systems direct their efforts toward maximizing some or all of those outcomes, the theory seems to have some important implications for administrative practice in education.

Organizational processes are highlighted in the theory of systems in general and open systems in particular, as articulated by Ludwig von Bertalanffy (1968) and developed by Kenneth Berrien (1968). From a systems perspective, organizations can be seen as constantly exchanging energy and information with others in their environment. As a result, the subsystems that make up the organization are in constant interaction as they strive to accommodate the new inputs and produce the desired outputs. Thus organizations as open systems are perpetually in the process of evolving toward complexity. Understanding this process can help educational administrators to analyze their own organization's activities and possibly to rearrange them so as to increase student learning.

REFERENCES

Berrien, F. K. *General and social systems.* New Brunswick, N.J.: Rutgers University Press, 1968.

Bertalanffy, L. von. *General system theory: Foundations, development, applications.* New York: George Braziller, 1968.

Hage, J. An axiomatic theory of organizations. *Administrative Science Quarterly,* 1965, *10,* 289–320.

Kelly, J. *Organizational behavior.* Homewood, Ill.: Richard D. Irwin and Dorsey Press, 1969.

Litterer, J. A. (Ed.). *Organizations: Structure and behavior.* New York: Wiley, 1963.

Scott, W. G. Organization theory: An overview and an appraisal. *Journal of the Academy of Management,* 1961, *4,* 7–26.

Chapter 2
Organizational Structure

THE AXIOMATIC THEORY

Can an organization—a collectivity of people—have a structure?

One can easily contemplate the structure of a bridge, a building, a machine, or a living cell. In the case of such tangible physical entities, one thinks of structure as the nature and shape of the constituent parts and the relationships the parts bear to each other. But can a group of human beings be thought to have a structure in the same way?

The notion of structure as applicable to organizations has been of interest to scholars since the beginnings of the study of administration as a distinctive field of inquiry. The idea of organizational structure is analogous to the idea of the structure of a tangible physical entity. Since the focus of interest in organizations is people, the parts of the organization are the individuals it comprises, and the structure of the organization is the pattern of relationships among the people who constitute the organization.

It is important to bear in mind that organizational structure constructs, like other theoretical constructs, are highly abstract. Just as the notion of a geometric form, such as a triangle, can be imagined and diagramed though not directly perceived in reality, so the notion of organizational structure can be imagined and diagramed as the organizational chart though not directly perceivable in reality.

The early organization theorists, writing in the 1950s and earlier, conceived of many aspects of structure (pattern of relationships among people) in organizations. Some of their structural notions drew upon designations used in military organizations—line and staff relationship, chain of command, rank, span of control. More recent scholars, proponents of the behavioral science approach to the study of organizations, have drawn on theoretical frameworks such as bureaucracy theory (see Chapter 4) and system theory (see Chapter 3) for concepts such as hierarchy of offices, differentiation, and integration. A large body of literature about aspects of organizational structure has evolved.

In 1965 Jerald Hage published a synthesis of much of the research on aspects of the pattern of relationships among people in organizations. This synthesis was in the form of a concise set of logically interrelated generalizations based on much of the available theoretical and empirical literature about aspects of organizational structure. In addition, Hage drew on conceptual and research writings about organizational purposes, outcomes, or goals to generate statements about relationships between structural attributes of organizations and the outcomes of organizational functioning. The concise set of generalizations was presented in the form of 8 propositions or laws, called *axioms*, and 21 propositions, called *corollaries*, which were logically derived from 7 of the basic axioms (Hage, 1965). In brief, the structural characteristics of organizations—aspects of the pattern of interpersonal relationships—were regarded as the means whereby organizations accomplish the purposes or ends for which they were designed. In its simplest form, the means-ends relationships can be illustrated as in Figure 2-1.

THE ESSENCE OF THE AXIOMATIC THEORY

The ways in which the people in organizations are intended to relate to each other can be regarded as the organizational *means* whereby the organizations accomplish their purposes. The purposes or outcomes for which the organization was designed can be regarded as the organizational *ends*. Although this means-end continuum seems to imply that the structural properties (means) cause the outcomes (ends), it must be borne in mind that the ends might cause the means as well. That is, the particular purposes for which an organization is formed might well influence or constrain the particular structure that is established.

Both structure and outcomes have several dimensions. Drawing on the available theoretical and empirical literature, Hage (1965) specified four key dimensions of organizational structure and four key dimensions of organizational outcomes, which are defined and described in this section. On the basis

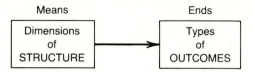

Figure 2–1   Relationship Between Organizational Structure and Organizational Outcomes

of the conceptual literature and research findings, the dimensions of structure can be expected to relate to each other and to organizational outcomes in specific ways.

Major Constructs in the Axiomatic Theory

ORGANIZATIONAL MEANS

Organizational means or structural attributes are dimensions of the pattern of relationships among people in organizations. This theory specifies four structural dimensions that characterize all organizations and represent aspects of the structural variations among organizations. These dimensions or properties are complexity, centralization, formalization, and stratification.

Complexity refers to the diversity of specializations of the employees in the organization and the expertise required to fulfill these specializations. Organizations differ in complexity. For example, according to this theory, a university would probably be more complex than a school district, in that the former encompasses a broader range of specializations and entails greater expertise for a relatively large proportion of the employees. By the same criteria, both a school district and a university would be more complex than, say, a large supermarket. Hage suggested number of occupational specialties in each organization and level of training required for the specialties as appropriate indicators of complexity.

Centralization refers to the extent to which decision making within the organization is done at the highest administrative level. An organization in which most decisions must be referred to a very high-level official is considered highly centralized, whereas one in which the heads of separate units, such as middle-management personnel, make many decisions is relatively *decentralized*. In centralized school districts, for example, the superintendent and her or his immediate subordinates make most of the decisions, whereas in relatively decentralized school districts the principals and their assistants make many decisions. Indicators of centralization would be the proportion of jobs that participate in decision making and the number of areas in which decisions are made by employees at each level in the organizational hierarchy.

Formalization, another name for standardization, refers to the relative absence or presence of latitude in doing the work. A highly formalized organization is one in which jobs are codified through job specifications, there are many written documents governing procedures, and there are rules for most contingencies. Whereas some schools have a formalized structure, with numerous standard operating procedures that are rigidly followed, others are much more flexible and informal. Hage suggests two indicators of formalization: the proportion of jobs that are codified (with complete written specifications) and the range of variation allowed within jobs.

Stratification refers to the number of status differences that exist among employees' jobs in the organization or the number of levels in the organizational hierarchy. In some school districts, for example, there are simply three status levels: the superintendent and associates, building principals, and staff members. These are so-called flat structures, with relatively little stratification. Other school districts of the same size might have central office divisions with assistants to the superintendent, directors and their assistants, coordinators, and managers overseeing particular functions. Such school systems have relatively "tall" structures or are highly stratified. Suggested indicators of stratification are differences in income and prestige among jobs and rate of mobility between low- and high-status jobs.

ORGANIZATIONAL ENDS

Organizational ends or outcomes of the organization's activities are of four types, all of which are relevant to all organizations. Specifically, organizations differ from each other in terms of the adaptiveness, production, efficiency, and employee job satisfaction they achieve in the course of their activities. All organizations accomplish these types of objectives to a greater or lesser degree, but they vary with respect to the amount of emphasis placed on each and the level of attainment in each area.

Adaptiveness or flexibility refers to the organization's responsiveness to changes in its environment. Adaptive school systems are dynamic organizations that change readily as new technologies emerge and as the community evolves. Relatively inflexible (or maladaptive) school districts, on the other hand, adhere persistently to one set of goals and procedures year after year, despite changes in their setting. Two indicators of adaptiveness suggested by Hage (1965) are number of new programs per year and number of new techniques introduced per year.

Production is a reflection of an organization's effectiveness in terms of the quality and quantity of outputs it generates. In business enterprises production is a function of the number and quality of units produced and of increases in volume per year without loss of quality. In education production is assessed in terms of number of students taught and amount of learning achieved, as well as increases in the number of students without decreases in learning and/or increases in the students' learning without increases in cost. Two suggested indicators of production are the number of units of output per time period and the rate of increase in units of output per time period.

Efficiency refers to the cost-effectiveness of the organization's operations.

In businesses efficiency refers to the lowest possible cost per unit of output. In education efficiency would be considered in terms of the per pupil expenditure in relation to students' learning outcomes. Suggested indicators of organizational efficiency are cost per unit of output for a given period and amount of idle or slack resources per time period.

Job satisfaction or morale refers to the employees' attitudes toward their organization and their work. Some executives and administrators are consistently attentive to the employees' feelings and do their best to maintain high morale, whereas others are relatively unconcerned with participants' feelings. Some suggested indicators of job satisfaction are employees' attitudes toward various aspects of their work and work setting (as measured by available instruments) and rate of employee turnover per year or rate of short-term absenteeism per unit of time.

These eight constructs—the four means attributes or structural properties and the four ends attributes or types of outcomes—are the basic components of the axiomatic theory of organizations. The remainder of the theory deals with the relationships among these constructs.

Relationships Among Constructs in the Axiomatic Theory

As noted earlier, the four attributes of organizational structure constitute a set of dimensions that describe the ways in which people are related to each other in order to achieve the organization's purposes. Just as a complete description of the structure of a physical object entails calibrations of the height, width, and depth of the object, so a description of an organization's structure entails consideration of the complexity, centralization, formalization, and stratification of the organization.

As means directed toward ends, the structural features of an organization would be expected to have some bearing on the outcomes or attainments of the organization. The relationships between means and ends are specified as Axioms (or propositions) I, II, IV, V, and VI, which follow. In addition, the structural attributes or means are related to each other in predictable patterns. These relationships are specified in Axioms III and VII.

The seven axioms take into consideration all eight of the major constructs in the theory. Therefore, it is possible to derive a complete set of propositional statements from the seven axioms by purely logical deductive means to generate a complete statement of the theory. For example, Axiom I states, "The higher the centralization, the higher the production." Axiom III states, "The higher the centralization, the higher the formalization." Straightforward logic indicates that the higher the formalization, the higher the production. These derived statements, which Hage (1965) called *corollaries*, are listed following the axioms.

The pairs of relationships specified in the major propositions (called *axioms* by Hage) are shown graphically in Figure 2–2, which is an expansion of the image presented earlier in this chapter. The solid lines indicate the relation-

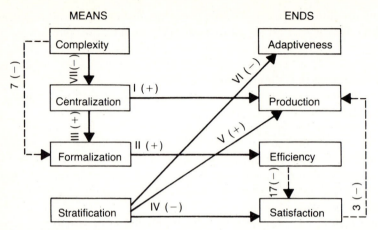

Figure 2–2 Relationships Between Organizational Means and Organizational Ends

ships stated in the axioms, and the solid arrows lead from the independent variables (means) either to the dependent variables (ends) or to other structural dimensions. The Roman numeral above each arrow indicates the number of the axiom being illustrated, and the plus or minus sign indicates whether the posited relationship is direct (+) or inverse (−). A direct relationship is one such that as one element increases, the other also increases; an inverse relationship is one in which one element decreases as the other increases. In Figure 2–2 some of the relationships specified in the corollaries are shown by arrows having dotted lines. Readers may wish to add dotted lines to indicate the corollaries not already represented in the diagram.

Major Propositions in the Axiomatic Theory

The axioms or major propositions constituting this theory, as stated explicitly by theorist (Hage, 1965:96), are:

I. The higher the centralization, the higher the production.
II. The higher the formalization, the higher the efficiency.
III. The higher the centralization, the higher the formalization.
IV. The higher the stratification, the lower the job satisfaction.
V. The higher the stratification, the higher the production.
VI. The higher the stratification, the lower the adaptiveness.
VII. The higher the complexity, the lower the centralization.

These seven axioms can be interpreted as meaning that organizations in which decision making is centralized are more likely than decentralized organizations to be highly formalized, relatively noncomplex, and highly productive and efficient. Similarly, organizations that are highly stratified (tall hierarchies) are more likely than less stratified organizations (flat hierarchies) to be highly productive but inflexible and to have less satisfied employees. An additional major proposition is:

VIII. Production imposes limits on the other seven elements.

From the first 7 axioms can be derived 21 corollaries, or logically deduced propositions, which have been enumerated by Hage (1965:96) as follows:

1. The higher the formalization, the higher the production.
2. The higher the centralization, the higher the efficiency.
3. The lower the job satisfaction, the higher the production.
4. The lower the job satisfaction, the lower the adaptiveness.
5. The higher the production, the lower the adaptiveness.
6. The higher the complexity, the lower the production.
7. The higher the complexity, the lower the formalization.
8. The higher the production, the higher the efficiency.
9. The higher the stratification, the higher the formalization.
10. The higher the efficiency, the lower the complexity.
11. The higher the centralization, the lower the job satisfaction.
12. The higher the centralization, the lower the adaptiveness.
13. The higher the stratification, the lower the complexity.
14. The higher the complexity, the higher the job satisfaction.
15. The lower the complexity, the lower the adaptiveness.
16. The higher the stratification, the higher the efficiency.
17. The higher the efficiency, the lower the job satisfaction.
18. The higher the efficiency, the lower the adaptiveness.
19. The higher the centralization, the higher the stratification.
20. The higher the formalization, the lower the job satisfaction.
21. The higher the formalization, the lower the adaptiveness.

These corollaries account for all pairs of relationships that were not included among the first 7 axioms. Table 2–1 displays all the pairs of relationships that are specified in the theory, with axiomatic relationships indicated by capital letters and derived relationships indicated by lower-case letters; the numbers of the axioms and corollaries are indicated in parentheses.

FURTHER DISCUSSION OF THE AXIOMATIC THEORY

The axiomatic theory is one of the relatively few frameworks that was originally written in explicitly propositional form. In this respect it is an excellent example of theory as a set of logically interrelated statements of relationships among constructs. Therefore, it is a good starting point for our examination of perspectives on organizations.

Like other theories, this one cannot simply be accepted as if it were a set of facts about the nature of organizations. All theories have their shortcomings as

Table 2–1 SUMMARY OF PROPOSITIONS AND COROLLARIES IN THE
AXIOMATIC THEORY OF ORGANIZATIONS

INDEPENDENT FACTORS	DEPENDENT FACTORS	
	MEANS	ENDS
COMPLEXITY	− CENTRALIZATION (VII) − formalization (7)	− production (6) + adaptiveness (15) + job satisfaction (14)
CENTRALIZATION	+ FORMALIZATION (III) + stratification (19)	+ PRODUCTION (I) + efficiency (2) − adaptiveness (12) − job satisfaction (11)
FORMALIZATION		+ production (1) + EFFICIENCY (II) − adaptiveness (21) − job satisfaction (20)
STRATIFICATION	− complexity (13) + formalization (9)	+ PRODUCTION (V) + efficiency (16) − ADAPTIVENESS (VI) − JOB SATISFACTION (IV)
PRODUCTION		+ efficiency (8) − adaptiveness (5)
EFFICIENCY	− complexity (10)	− adaptiveness (18) − job satisfaction (17)
JOB SATISFACTION		− production (3) + adaptiveness (4)

NOTE: The sign before each dependent factor indicates the direction of the posited relationship with the corresponding independent factor. + represents a positive or direct relationship; − represents a negative or inverse relationship.

well as their strengths. Questions can always be posed about the adequacy and accuracy of the perspective being propounded. In this section we shall consider briefly some of the questions that can be raised about the axiomatic theory. Specifically, we shall consider the type of perspective it represents, the close affinity of this perspective with bureaucracy theory, the particular set of relationships posited, and the measurement problems associated with this theory.

The Structuralist-Functionalist Perspective

Hage's axiomatic theory of organizations might be regarded as the epitome of what has been called the structuralist-functionalist perspective, which has been sharply criticized in recent writings about organizations in general and educational organizations in particular. The essence of the critique is that *structure* does not exist as an objective reality apart from the perceptions and enactments of people in the organization, and that the assumption that certain structures are functional for attaining goals is merely a rationalization for maintaining the status quo. For example, *centralization* is viewed in this theory as a structural attribute that is functional for increasing production and efficiency. The critique is that centralization is not an objectively real phenomenon and that the idea of centralization as increasing productivity serves as a rationalization for continuing to have some people dominate other people within the organization.

The criticisms of the structuralist-functionalist approach by phenomenological, hermeneutic, and neo-Marxist scholars are compelling. Critics point out, for example, that centralization (and other structural dimensions) are "socially constructed realities"; that is, each time an employee refers a decison to a higher authority, the employee is creating centralization by his or her own actions. Furthermore, the very assessment of the employee's act as the referral of a decision to a *higher* authority constitutes an interpretation of the act as centralization. Finally, employees do not have to refer decisions (or delimit what they do, or follow other people's rules, or take orders from anyone) for reasons that are objectively real; they do so usually because, even without thinking about it (that is, ideologically), they believe that they should and, sometimes, that they will be punished if they do not.

The position taken in this book is that aspects of organizational structure are highly theoretical constructs that can be useful for describing organizations systematically and comparatively but should not be taken as objectively real. The constructs pertaining to structure might be supplanted by other, more compelling theoretical abstractions in the future. Whether aspects of form (structure) are related to types of outcomes, and whether the structural characteristics are functional or dysfunctional, remain empirical questions to be addressed through research.

Bureaucracy Theory

The great sociologist Max Weber was deeply concerned with the types of questions posed here—why people exhibit certain behavior patterns in organizations and why they allow themselves to be dominated by others (Weber, 1946). His theory of bureaucracy, which is treated at greater length in Chapter 4, is an effort to address such questions.

Weber's theory influenced many theorists and researchers, including Jerald Hage, whose axiomatic theory might be considered a derivation of Weber's work. In fact, axioms I, II, and III and corollaries 1, 2, and 8 were explicitly drawn from Weber's writings. Because Weber specified dimensions of the structure of bureaucratic organizations, most theoretical and empirical writings about organizational structure refer to Weber's work. Several of the studies cited later in this chapter can be found in Chapter 4 as well.

Relationships Posited

A few issues pertaining to the contents of the theory itself merit special attention: the selection of structural features and their definitions; the specification of paired relationships; and the strong implication of causality.

As the reader now knows, Hage selected four structural properties of organizations for this theory, and he defined them in particular ways. Other theorists and researchers have disagreed both with the set of structural attributes and with the definitions and indicators of the attributes. For example, some scholars, following Weber, have identified five (Anderson, 1974); six (Hall, 1968); or more (Meyers, 1972) structural features. Whether the four constructs Hage selected constitute a necessary and sufficient set for describing organizations is not known.

Some scholars have disagreed with the definitions and indicators of the structural constructs. For example, Hage (1965:93) defines *complexity* in terms of specialization (horizontal differentiation) and level of training required (expertise); but others have defined complexity differently. Hall (1972), for one, defines complexity as horizontal differentiation, vertical differentiation (Hage's stratification), and spatial dispersion. Lawrence and Lorsch (1969), on the other hand, define complexity in terms of differentiation of tasks and integration of functions. The other major constructs also have varied definitions. In interpreting research on organizational structures, it is important that the reader understand the definitions and operationalizations of constructs as specified by the researchers.

Although the axiomatic theory specifies a comprehensive set of relationships between pairs of constructs, it does not include any considerations about multiple relationships. That is, two or more variables might have interactive effects on another variable that cannot be discerned simply by examining pairs of relationships. In addition, one of the variables might have a mediating effect on the relationship between two other variables. In fact, Blau and his colleagues (Blau, Heydebrand, & Stauffer, 1966) found that the level of staff professionalism (an aspect of complexity in Hage's framework) mediates the relationship between centralization and specialization (another aspect of complexity in Hage's theory). The exclusive attention to pairs of relationships is a serious limitation of the axiomatic theory.

The strong implications of causality inherent to this theory should also be highlighted. Although there are some theoretical reasons for assuming that structural properties cause given types of outcomes (that is, that means cause ends), there is very little evidence of causal directions. Most of the research on organizational structures has been of the descriptive-correlational type, with data all collected at one time and relationships between variables sought. If, for example, stratification is found to relate to production as predicted, one cannot infer from such findings that higher stratification was the *cause* of higher production; the reverse might be true, or other factors might have caused both.

Experimental research and time-lagged (longitudinal) studies can yield stronger implications of causality than do descriptive-correlational studies, but too few of these can be found in the published literature to warrant acceptance of the causal directions implied in this theory.

Measurement Problems

Like all theories, the axiomatic theory is beset by problems in operationalizing the constructs. In the research on organizational structure, the measurement debate has centered on *who* in the organization provides the information and *how* the data are gathered. In the set of studies conducted by the Aston group (for example, Pugh et al., 1963) and its followers (for example, Child, 1972; Holdaway et al., 1975; Mansfield, 1973), high-level officials were interviewed and organizational documents examined to generate data about each organization's structure. A shortcoming of this approach is that the researchers might discover what the executives intend as patterns of interpersonal relationships, but not what actually transpires at lower levels in the organizations.

Another approach to data gathering in research on organizational structure is represented by the studies done by Hall (1963), Hage and Aiken (1967), Bishop and George (1973), and others who distributed questionnaires to representative samples of employees occupying various levels in the organizational hierarchy. A problem with this approach is that the employees might not know what actually transpires in the organization (for example, they might think they are participating in the decision making, but their suggestions might actually be ignored), and their perceptions of structure might be colored by their attitudes toward the organization.

There is no simple solution to the measurement problems involved in testing this or any other theory. Research can neither prove nor disprove propositions; it can only suggest support or disconfirmation of theoretical statements.

In Support of the Axiomatic Theory

The issues explored in this section have been raised not to discredit the theory or to undermine its utility, but to underscore the problematic nature of theory in general and to encourage readers to examine their own assumptions and presuppositions about theory and research. Theories should not be accepted as gospel, since virtually any declarative statement about the nature of reality can be challenged in terms of its limitations and its verifiability. Rather, theories can be appreciated as high-level abstractions that provide systematic, coherent perspectives on some aspects of the world we inhabit.

The axiomatic theory of organizations is a clear and concise synthesis of many discrete studies and conceptualizations. It is a systematic, comprehensive framework for considering relationships between organizational structures and organizational goals. It offers a conceptual scheme for codifying a tremendous body of research on particular aspects of the relationships among people in organizations. Some of this research—a selected sample, since there have been so many studies of structural properties—is the subject of the next section.

RESEARCH RELATED TO THE AXIOMATIC THEORY

The research pertaining to organizational structures has been conducted in business, industrial, military, human service, and educational organizations. It is a diverse body of research using varied data-gathering techniques and numerous analytical methods. In summarizing these assorted studies, research in noneducational settings will be considered before that conducted in school settings. First, however, some of the widely used data collection tools will be reviewed briefly.

Instruments

As noted earlier, there is no one measure or set of instruments associated exclusively with the axiomatic theory. Typically, researchers have developed their own measurement techniques or have used one of several available measures of organizational structure. The most widely used of these are described in this section.

Hage and his colleagues (for example, Aiken & Hage, 1966; Dewar & Hage, 1978) used a questionnaire, of which many items are reported in Hage and Aiken (1967a: footnotes), completed by representative samples of employees at each hierarchical level in the organizations they studied. Each item is a statement that is answered with reference to a scale ranging from 1 (definitely true) to 4 (definitely false) or from 1 (never) to 5 (always). There are several items pertaining to each dimension of organizational structure. This questionnaire was not originally designed by Hage or his coauthors, however. It was initially developed by Richard Hall (1963) to operationalize the major constructs in bureaucracy theory.

A similar questionnaire, based on Hage's theory and relevant specifically to education, was developed by Bishop and George (1973) and called the Structural Properties Questionnaire (SPQ). As described in a 1973 article (Bishop & George, 1973), the SPQ consists of 54 statements that, like those used by Hall and by Hage, are answered on four-point scales. Although factor analyses of teachers' responses to the SPQ did not yield factors precisely congruent with Hage's constructs, the instrument holds promise for further development as a tool for testing the axiomatic theory.

A completely different measurement technique was used by Pugh and his colleagues in England to conduct the research that has come to be known as the Aston studies (for example, Pugh et al., 1968, 1969; Hinings & Lee, 1971;

Inkson, Pugh, and Hickson, 1970). This technique entails interviewing top-level executives about specific structural features of their organizations and quantifying the responses as specified in the original research. Written documents and organizational records are often consulted for verification of the oral responses or for completion of the data set. The items, which vary greatly in format and calibration, are described and listed in Pugh et al. (1968) and discussed extensively by Mansfield (1973). The definitions of terms and the indicators or operationalizations of constructs differ substantially from those of Hage, but the research findings are clearly relevant to tests of the axiomatic theory. Some research conducted in Canadian colleges and universities has yielded results similar to those of the Aston group (Holdaway et al., 1975).

Research in Varied Settings

Since the axiomatic theory was developed partly as a framework for organizing many research findings, we would do best to examine the related research in terms of each structural element individually. Thus this section treats complexity, centralization, formalization, and stratification sequentially. Research that is pertinent to the axioms and corollaries of the theory is treated first, and other relevant studies are then summarized. In these sections Roman and Arabic numerals in parentheses indicate the axioms and corollaries at issue.

COMPLEXITY

One proposition in the axiomatic theory states that complexity is inversely related to centralization (VII). The corollaries state that complexity is inversely related to production (6), formalization (7), efficiency (10), and stratification (13), but directly related to employees' job satisfaction (14) and organizational adaptiveness (15). Readers will recall that Hage (1965:93) defines complexity in terms of occupational specialization and required levels of training.

Support for the major proposition that complexity is negatively related to centralization of decision making can be found in several studies, including one that uses the written questionnaire method (Hage & Aiken, 1969) and some that employ the interview method (Child, 1972; Mansfield, 1973; Pugh et al., 1968). Blau and his colleagues also found professionalization of employees to be negatively related to centralization of authority in smaller public personnel agencies, but only in those larger ones that had a high administrative ratio (Blau, Heydebrand, & Stauffer, 1966).

Research findings related to the corollaries, however, have been consistently nonsupportive. For example, Blau (1968) found that greater professionalization of staff (complexity) was related to *more* numerous hierarchical levels (stratification), in contradiction to Corollary 13. Lincoln, Hanada, and Olson (1981) found that greater differentiation of jobs (complexity) was related to *less* satisfaction among Japanese employees, in contradiction to Corollary 14. The results of this study suggest that the employees' cultural heritage affects their feelings about aspects of organizational structure. Blau and his coauthors found greater differentiation of jobs (complexity) to be positively related to efficiency (Blau, Heydebrand, & Stauffer, 1966), which contradicts Corollary 10. Some studies have indicated that greater functional specialization (complexity) is positively related to formalization and stratification (Child, 1972; Pugh et al., 1968), which contradicts corollaries 7 and 13, respectively.

Other research has focused on external or contextual factors, such as size, that affect organizational structure. Larger organizations were found to have greater functional specialization (Blau, Heydebrand, & Stauffer, 1966; Mansfield, 1973; Dewar & Hage, 1978). Another contextual factor, degree of routineness of the work, was inversely related to the employees' levels of professional training (Hage & Aiken, 1969). The scope of the tasks performed was also related to the complexity of the organization (Dewar & Hage, 1978).

From the research related to organizational complexity, we can conclude that more complex organizations tend to be more decentralized, but also more highly stratified and more formalized. More complex organizations also seem to be more efficient, though less satisfying to employees. Organizational size and the nature of the work seem to have bearing on the complexity of the organization.

CENTRALIZATION

Three of the axioms in the theory pertain to the degree to which decision making is centralized in organizations. Greater centralization is posited to be related to higher production (I), greater formalization (III), and less complexity (VII). The relevant corollaries maintain that greater centralization is associated with greater efficiency (2) and stratification (19) but lower employee satisfaction (11) and less organizational adaptiveness (12).

Research supporting the inverse relationship between centralization and complexity, in support of the seventh axiom, has been summarized. Studies related to Axiom III have yielded inconsistent results. Greater centralization has been associated with lesser formalization in some studies (Pugh et al., 1968; Child, 1972) and with greater formalization in others (Hage & Aiken, 1967a). Mansfield (1973) found these two elements to be inversely related in large organizations but directly related in small organizations. Thus differences in samples and analytic techniques might account for the divergent research results, or size might be an intervening variable. On the other hand, Pennings (1973), who compared the Aston interview instruments with the survey questionnaire instruments for measuring both centralization and formalization, found the two types of measures to differ radically. It may be that the two constructs relate as posited in the theory when they are defined and operationalized as Hage intended. No studies of the relationship between centralization and production, as pertinent to Axiom I, were located.

There is little evidence relevant to the corollaries in the available research literature. Greater centralization was found to be associated with less stratification (Pugh et al., 1968; Child, 1972), in contradiction to Corollary 19; but it should be remembered that these Aston-type measures of centralization differed substantially from Hage's measures (Pennings, 1973). As posited in Corollary 11, however, greater centralization of decision making was found to be related to lower satisfaction or greater alienation (Aiken & Hage, 1966).

Several environmental or contextual factors have been found to be directly related to centralization. These include the routineness of the work (Hage & Aiken, 1969); the number of work sites the organization has (Pugh et al., 1969); and the organization's degree of dependence on external bodies (Pugh et al., 1969). Factors that have been associated with greater decentralization (that is, greater employee participation in decision making) include organizational size (Mansfield, 1973) and organizational age (Pugh et al., 1969).

In sum, the available research on correlatives of centralization appears more supportive than nonsupportive of the statements in the axiomatic theory, since the centralization and formalization variables in the disconfirming studies deviate substantially from the definitions given by Hage. Until further research demonstrates otherwise, we can assume that increased centralization of decision making relates to increased production, formalization, efficiency, and stratification, but decreased complexity, job satisfaction, and adaptiveness.

FORMALIZATION

Two major propositions in the axiomatic theory deal with the structural attribute of formalization. These assert that greater job codification and task standardization—both aspects of formalization—are associated with greater efficiency (II) and greater centralization (III). According to the corollaries, greater formalization is also associated with higher production (5) and greater stratification (9) but less complexity (7), adaptiveness (21), and job satisfaction (20). Organizations that are highly formalized are characterized by a lot of rules and regulations, standard operating procedures, detailed job descriptions, and rule-boundedness.

Few studies, apart from those already cited, deal directly with the relationships posited in the axioms. The contradictory findings bearing on formalization and centralization (III) have already been noted, and no studies of formalization in relation to organizational efficiency (II) have been found.

The search for studies relevant to the corollaries has been more fruitful, however. Several of these corollaries have been supported empirically. For example, greater formalization or standardization was found to be associated with greater stratification (Pugh et al., 1968; Hage & Aiken, 1967a; Child, 1972), as posited in Corollary 9. Formalization was also found to be negatively related to satisfaction (Aiken & Hage, 1966; Oldham & Hackman, 1981), as asserted in Corollary 20. However, as noted earlier, some evidence disconfirms the posited relationship between formalization and complexity in Corollary 7 (Pugh et al., 1968; Child, 1972). No studies linking formalization to production (5) or adaptiveness (21) have been located.

Research on the antecedent or contextual factors associated with formalization suggests that the degree of routineness of the work correlates directly with the organization's degree of formalization (Hage & Aiken, 1969). This finding is congruent with the work of Oldham and Hackman (1981), who found that characteristics of the work itself are better predictors of employees' motivation and satisfaction than are attributes of the organization's structure. Taken together, the studies suggest that organizational standardization relates to routinization of tasks, which in turn relates to employee dissatisfaction.

In summary, although the available evidence pertaining to the axioms is inadequate for drawing even tentative conclusions, the findings generally support the corollaries. Specifically, greater formalization in organizations appears to be associated with more numerous hierarchical levels and with greater routineness of tasks, but also with lower levels of job satisfaction among employees.

STRATIFICATION

The degree of stratification in an organization refers to the number of levels or layers there are in the hierarchy of authority. Some have referred to this attribute as the *tallness* or *flatness* of the organization. The three axioms dealing with this dimension maintain that greater stratification is associated with higher production (V) but lower job satisfaction (IV) and less adaptiveness (VI). The three relevant corollaries assert that stratification is positively related to formalization (9) and efficiency (16) but negatively related to complexity (13).

This aspect of organizational structure has attracted much attention in the research literature. With reference to Axiom IV, taller hierarchies have been found to have less satisfied personnel (Ivancevich & Donnelly, 1975). In Japanese firms in the United States, the height of the hierarchy was found to be positively related to job satisfaction for the Japanese employees but not for the Americans (Lincoln, Hanada, & Olson, 1981), further evidence of the effects of culture on employees' reactions to organizational structure.

The evidence related to Axiom V is far from conclusive. In one study individual salespersons' performance in terms of amount of sales was greater in flatter organizations (Ivancevich & Donnelly, 1975). On the other hand, productivity measures were found to be more thorough in taller organizations (Ouchi, 1977). In a very interesting experimental study using two tall groups and two flat groups of business administration students, Carzo and Yanouzas (1977) found that production in terms of profits and rates of financial return was higher in the taller groups. They also found in this study that the taller groups had significantly higher initial learning rates; this might contradict Axiom VI since it suggests that highly stratified organizations might be more adaptive than relatively flat ones, at least in initial responses to changes in the environment.

The available studies relevant to the corollaries have been cited in preceding sections on complexity and formalization. Of greater interest at this point might be the research on contextual factors related to stratification. Size, as might be expected, is one such factor, as it seems to relate positively to the tallness of the hierarchy (Ouchi, 1977; Blau, 1968; Dewar & Hage, 1978). Technology might be another such factor in that, although routineness of work was found to be unrelated to stratification in one study (Hage & Aiken, 1969), extent of computer automation was directly related in another (Blau, 1968).

In an especially interesting study of organizations in relation to their environments, Lawrence and Lorsch (1969) found that the nature of the environmental conditions (as perceived by top executives) has considerable bearing on the structure of the organization. They found that integrative structures tended to emerge in accordance with environmental complexity. Increasing stratification can be regarded as an increase in integrative mechanisms, since hierarchical levels serve to coordinate the activities of differentiated operational units.

In general, the empirical evidence tends to support the major theoretical propositions. Greater stratification seems to be associated with higher production and lower satisfaction, but with greater rather than less organizational adaptiveness. Stratification also appears to be related to organizational size, automation, and environmental complexity.

SUMMARY

The research reviewed in this section was conducted in business, industrial, and service organizations. Although no studies have been located that test the axiomatic theory in its entirety, numerous studies have supported parts of the theoretical framework. The research tending to disconfirm the axioms and their corollaries is generally in the areas of centralization and formalization, where the research methods of the nonsupportive studies deviated from Hage's definitions and indicators. The research results reviewed in this section and the next are summarized in Table 2–2.

Research in Educational Organizations

There have been fewer studies of structure in schools than in other types of organizations, and the majority of these have not been linked explicitly with the Hage formulations. Nevertheless, some evidence related to the axiomatic theory can be found. For the sake of variety, we shall consider this body of research in the order of the outcome or organizational ends variables: adaptiveness, production, efficiency, and job satisfaction.

ADAPTIVENESS

In a questionnaire study of almost two hundred school districts, Burnham found that the more innovative districts were characterized by greater differentiation among functional units (complexity) and greater integration of these differentiated units (stratification?). These districts also tended to be in

Table 2–2 SUMMARY OF RESEARCH FINDINGS RELEVANT TO ORGANIZATIONAL STRUCTURE

STRUCTURAL PROPERTIES	MEANS	ENDS	CONTEXT
Complexity	− *centralization** Blau et al., 1966 Hage & Aiken, 1967a Pugh et al., 1968 + centralization Mansfield, 1973 − stratification Blau et al., 1966 Child, 1972 Pugh et al., 1968 − formalization Child, 1972 Pugh et al., 1968 Holdaway et al., 1975	+ efficiency Blau et al., 1966 + output measurement Ouchi, 1977 − satisfaction (Japanese) Lincoln et al., 1981 + *innovativeness** Derr & Cabarro, 1972 + production Derr & Cabarro, 1972	+ size Blau et al., 1966 Dewar & Hage, 1978 Ouchi, 1977 − task scope Dewar & Hage, 1978 − routineness Hage & Aiken, 1969 + environment complexity Lawrence & Lorsch, 1969
Centralization	− *complexity** Blau et al., 1966 Hage & Aiken, 1967a Pugh et al., 1968 Mansfield, 1973 Child, 1972 − formalization Child, 1972 Pugh et al., 1968 Mansfield 1973 + *formalization** Hage & Aiken 1967a − stratification Child, 1972 Pugh et al., 1968	+ *alienation* (dissatisfaction)* Aiken & Hage, 1966 − *satisfaction** Miskel et al., 1979 Bishop & George, 1973	− size Mansfield, 1973 + size of parent organization Pugh et al., 1969 + routineness Hage & Aiken, 1969 − age of organization Pugh et al., 1969

Table 2–2 (*continued*)

STRUCTURAL PROPERTIES	MEANS	ENDS	CONTEXT

Formaliza-tion	− complexity
	  Pugh et al.,
	  1968
	  Child, 1972
	+ *centralization**
	  Hage &
	  Aiken,
	  1967a
	− centralization
	  Mansfield,
	  1973
	  Pugh et al.,
	  1968
	+ *stratification**
	  Pugh et al.,
	  1968
	  Hage &
	  Aiken,
	  1967a
	  Child, 1972
		+ *alienation* (dis-
		  satisfaction)*
		  Aiken &
		  Hage, 1966
		− *satisfaction**
		  Oldham &
		  Hackman,
		  1981
		+ satisfaction
		  Miskel et al.,
		  1979
			+ routineness
			  Hage &
			  Aiken, 1969
			− autonomy from
			  parent org.
			  Holdaway et
			  al., 1975

Stratifi-cation	+ complexity
	  Blau et al.,
	  1966
	  Child, 1972
	+ *formalization**
	  Pugh et al.,
	  1968
	  Child, 1972
	− centralization
	  Pugh et al.,
	  1968
	  Child, 1972
		+ *production**
		  Carzo &
		  Yanouzas,
		  1977
		  Derr &
		  Cabarro,
		  1972
		− sales (individ-
		  uals')
		  Ivancevich &
		  Donnelly,
		  1975
		+ output
		  measures
		  Ouchi, 1977
		− *satisfaction**
		  Ivancevich/
		  Donnelly,
		  1975
		− satisfaction (Ja-
		  panese)
		  Lincoln et
		  al., 1981
		+ initial learning
		  rates
		  Carzo &
		  Yanouzas,
		  1977
		+ innovativeness
		  Derr &
		  Cabarro,
		  1972
			+ size
			  Dewar &
			  Hage, 1978
			  Ouchi, 1977
			  Blau, 1968
			− environment
			  complexity
			  Lawrence &
			  Lorsch,
			  1969
			− automation
			  (computer)
			  Blau, 1968

*Findings supporting axioms or corollaries.

environments characterized by greater diversity and change (Derr & Cabarro, 1972).

PRODUCTION

In a case study of two equivalent school districts that were experiencing rapid changes in the composition of the student body, Cabarro found that student achievement was higher in the district characterized by greater differentiation of functions (complexity) and greater integration across functional units (stratification?). As reported by Derr and Cabarro (1972), this study and the one just cited support the Lawrence and Lorsch (1969) thesis that organizational differentiation and integration are effective organizational adaptations to highly complex environments.

EFFICIENCY

No studies directly relevant to this variable have been found in the education research literature. Many efficiency studies have been conducted—for example, studies of per pupil expenditure in relation to student achievements—but these have not generally taken organizational structure into consideration as a set of intervening variables.

One study that may be relevant, however, indicated that teachers' perceptions of the effectiveness of their schools were positively related to formalization, in terms of the presence of general rules for teachers, and to complexity, in terms of teachers' involvement in professional activities (Miskel, Fevurly, & Stewart, 1979).

JOB SATISFACTION

The largest body of relevant education research has dealt with this dependent variable. Teachers' job satisfaction was found to be positively related to formalization in terms of general rules for teachers but negatively related to centralization of decision making about curriculum and instruction (Miskel, Fevurly, & Stewart, 1979). Centralization has been of particular interest to education researchers. Conway (1976) found that teachers' satisfaction was related not to the absolute extent or frequency of their participation in decision making (decentralization) but to the degree of congruence between their preferred levels of participation and their actual participation. Both underparticipation (deprivation) and overparticipation (saturation) were dissatisfying. On the other hand, Barile found teachers' anxiety (dissatisfaction?) to be negatively related to school centralization of decision making (Bishop & George, 1973).

In another study, George and Bishop (1971) found that teachers' perceptions of the climate in their schools was influenced both by the school's structural properties and by the teachers' personalities. The researchers suggested that favorable climate perceptions—an indirect indicator of satisfaction—would result from a congruence or compatibility of organizational structure and individuals' personalities.

SUMMARY

Because of the small number of studies, the findings with respect to the axiomatic theory certainly cannot be regarded as conclusive. The studies cited here lend some support to Axioms II and V and Corollary 11 but tend to disconfirm Axiom VI and Corollaries, 6, 10, 15, and 20. Further research is needed before firm conclusions can be drawn.

In sum, the research in schools and school districts tentatively suggests that adaptiveness and production are positively related to complexity and stratification, that efficiency is positively related to complexity and formalization, and that job satisfaction is related positively to formalization but negatively to centralization or to teachers' desired levels of centralization.

The research summarized in this and the preceding section is tabulated in condensed form in Table 2–2. For each structural dimension the relevant correlatives, as found in the research, are listed with signs indicating the direction of the relationships and asterisks highlighting the predictions made in the axioms and corollaries. This table provides an overview of much empirical research dealing with organizational structure.

IMPLICATIONS OF THE AXIOMATIC THEORY FOR ENHANCING STUDENT LEARNING OUTCOMES

Schools have been called on to fulfill an ever expanding variety of functions for society as a whole and for its young people in particular. Reducing unemployment, furthering racial integration, reducing community health problems, and strengthening the moral fiber of the citizenry—these are only a few of the demands that various segments of society place on education systems.

Nevertheless, the primary function of schools and school systems remains the cognitive, affective, and psychomotor development of all young people. Therefore, the major professional obligation of all school administrators and other educators is to obtain and use the knowledge and skills required to maximize these types of school outcomes for all students.

The concluding section of each theory chapter in this book is devoted to an examination of the possible relevance of the theoretical framework in generating the knowledge needed to enhance student learning outcomes. In this chapter we face the question: Does the axiomatic theory appear to be useful for generating knowledge about how to improve students' cognitive, affective, and psychomotor achievements?

Several of the major propositions and corollaries from the axiomatic theory have bearing on student learning outcomes. One can regard school production as equivalent to the extent of students' gains in knowledge, attitudes, and skills. Efficiency can be interpreted as the lowest possible cost per student. Thus these ends can be considered separately with reference to school structural attributes.

Production

Theoretically, higher production is associated with greater centralization (I), greater stratification (V), and greater formalization (1), but less complexity (6). This suggests that in schools with relatively centralized decision making, numerous hierarchical levels, considerable job codification, and standardization of procedures, but with little differentiation of functions and relatively little professional training, student outcomes can be expected to be greater than in schools structured differently.

Within reasonable limits, some of these relationships make sense. Although advisory participation of faculty and students in the decisions that affect them is desirable, the administrator, who has the broadest view of the school and its environment, might be in the best position to make final decisions. School leaders can increase centralization without reducing participation by having faculty and student committees legitimately serve in an advisory capacity. Increased stratification can also have beneficial effects, as has been demonstrated in schools that have adopted a differentiated staffing pattern. In these schools, the most expert teachers have some supervisory and advisory authority over those less expert, so that the effective techniques of these so-called master teachers are more widely disseminated throughout the school.

In addition, clearly defining the various jobs in the school and establishing explicit procedures for dealing with routine matters, as in more formalized schools, can reduce confusion within a school and also reduce the time spent on duplication of activities and on trivial matters. In this way administrators can increase the time available for teachers to devote to the creative enterprise of educating children.

Efficiency

According to the axiomatic theory, school efficiency would be associated with greater formalization (II), greater centralization (2), and greater stratification (16), but with lower complexity (10). That is, the structural features associated with efficiency are the same as those associated with production. The administrator's role in furthering some of these aspects of school structure was discussed earlier. Reductions in school complexity might be desirable to the extent that they help to divest the school of nonessential functions and help to direct activities toward the educative functions.

Efficiency and production are considered to be positively related to each other in this theory (Corollary 8), and their association with similar structural attributes is congruent with this relationship. However, these two outcomes are thought to be inversely related to employees' job satisfaction (Corollaries 3 and 17). These corollaries are contradictory to some research findings and other theoretical propositions (see Chapters 13 and 14) that maintain that productivity is positively related to employee satisfaction. Therefore, some empirical questions arise that merit further research.

Since educational administrators can influence to some degree the structural characteristics of their schools or school districts, and since structure has a theoretical relevance to student outcomes, the axiomatic theory might indeed be an important framework for research designed to increase administrators' professional knowledge. Several questions remain to be answered through empirical research in schools. These include but are not limited to the following:

1. Is student achievement directly related to school centralization, formalization, and stratification, but inversely related to school complexity?
2. Are the different types of student outcomes—knowledge, attitudes, and skills—differentially affected by school structural properties?
3. Are students' learnings in the three domains negatively related to teachers' job satisfaction?
4. What other factors intervene in the relationships between school structure and student outcomes? For example, do students' personality or demographic characteristics or the type of school environment or the various subject areas affect in the means-ends relationships?

Answering such questions convincingly would entail careful and creative research strategies. They are important questions—perhaps crucial ones for generating knowledge about what school administrators can do to increase student learning.

MASTERY QUIZ

Test your own understanding and recollection of the axiomatic theory by completing the following statements *without reference* to the contents of the chapter or any of the diagrams. After completing all the items, check your answers in Appendix C, page 391.

1. In Hage's theory, the variable that is *not* a structural feature is:
   a. centralization.　　　　　　　　　c. efficiency.
   b. complexity.　　　　　　　　　　　d. formalization.
2. In the axiomatic theory, all of the following are pairs of structural properties *except:*
   a. stratification and　　　　　　　　c. formalization and
      centralization.　　　　　　　　　　centralization.
   b. centralization and　　　　　　　　d. complexity and
      production.　　　　　　　　　　　stratification.
3. The complete set of structural attributes, according to this theory, is:
   a. complexity—differentiation—stratification—formalization.
   b. centralization—formalization—satisfaction—complexity.

    c. efficiency—production—satisfaction—adaptation.

    d. stratification—centralization—complexity—formalization.

4. All of the following are ends in the axiomatic theory *except:*

    a. stratification.   c. production.

    b. satisfaction.   d. efficiency.

5. The ends in this theory include all the following pairs *except:*

    a. efficiency and job satisfaction.   c. job satisfaction and adaptiveness.

    b. production and formalization.   d. efficiency and production.

6. In all of the following *except one*, a means variable is paired with an ends variable:

    a. stratification—satisfaction.   c. production—formalization.

    b. centralization—efficiency.   d. efficiency—satisfaction.

7. Two indicators of complexity in Hage's theory are:

    a. differentiation and required training.

    b. required training and differences in prestige.

    c. prestige differences and job codification.

    d. horizontal differentiation and vertical differentiation.

8. Two indicators of formalization are:

    a. upward mobility and number of specializations.

    b. status differences and required training.

    c. rule-boundedness and job codification.

    d. number of specialties and participation in decision making.

9. The following statement that is *false* in terms of this theory is:

    a. Adaptiveness is indicated by the number of new programs per time period.

    b. Job satisfaction is indicated by the rate of employee turnover per time period.

    c. Production is indicated by the cost per unit of output.

    d. Efficiency is indicated by the amount of idle resources in a time period.

10. All *but one* of the following are true according to the axiomatic theory and corollaries of this theory. That one is:

    a. The higher the centralization, the higher the production.

    b. The higher the centralization, the higher the satisfaction.

    c. The higher the centralization, the higher the formalization.

    d. The higher the centralization, the higher the efficiency.

EXERCISES

1. The following diagram includes the four means constructs and the four ends constructs. The numbered arrows connect pairs of constructs. *Without reference* to the contents of this chapter or any of its diagrams, can

you indicate which relationships are positive (direct) and which are negative (inverse) according to the axiomatic theory? Try your hand by writing *positive* or *negative* on the lines corresponding to the numbers of the arrows. If you remember some relationships but not all, try to deduce those you don't remember from those you do. (*Note:* The arrows do not take into consideration all the posited relationships.) Answers can be found in Appendix C, page 391.

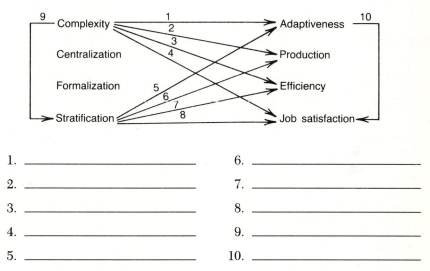

1. _____	6. _____
2. _____	7. _____
3. _____	8. _____
4. _____	9. _____
5. _____	10. _____

2. On scales of 1 to 10 (little structure to considerable structure), rate the school in which you now work or most recently worked in terms of *complexity, centralization, formalization,* and *stratification.* For each of these structural constructs, explain *why* you assigned the rating you did.

3. To reinforce your understanding of the propositions constituting this theory, review the axioms and corollaries listed in this chapter. For each of the 29 propositions, write a brief rationale explaining why the statement would be *true* of schools or school districts. The rationales can be brief, consisting of a sentence or two for each theoretical statement.

4. On scales of 1 to 10 (very poor to excellent), rate the school in which you now work or most recently worked in terms of its adaptiveness, production, efficiency, and employees' job satisfaction. For each of these that received a rating of less than 10, indicate how modifying some structural characteristics of the school might have improved the outcome. You may refer to the contents of the chapter in answering this question.

5. a. Using the definitions and indicators of the structural dimensions as a guide, create a questionnaire that could be completed by teachers to indicate the structural characteristics of their schools. Try to have at least four different questions for each indicator and to phrase your

questions so they can be answered on five-point scales as follows: 1 = never; 2 = rarely; 3 = sometimes; 4 = often; 5 = always. The higher scores should indicate greater structure.

b. Make copies of this questionnaire and have it completed by one or more teachers in each of two schools. Then tally the scores and make a tentative judgment as to which school is the more highly structured. This activity is intended as an introduction to the research process in terms of operationalizing constructs and interpreting data.

REFERENCES

Major Source

Hage, J. An axiomatic theory of organizations. *Administrative Science Quarterly*, 1965, *10*, 289–320.

Related Conceptual Literature

Anderson, B. D. An application of the bureaucratic model to the study of school administration. *Journal of Educational Administration*, 1974, *12*, 63–75.

Hall, R. H. The concept of bureaucracy: An empirical assessment. *American Journal of Sociology*, 1963, *69*, 32–40.

———.Professionalism and bureaucratization. *American Sociological Review*, 1968, *33*, 92–104.

———.*Organizations: Structure and process*. Englewood Cliffs, N.J.: Prentice-Hall, 1972.

Meyers, R. W. Bureaucratic theory and schools. *Administrator's Notebook*, 1972, *20*, 1–4.

Pugh, D. S.; Hickson, D. J.; Hinings, C. R.; Macdonald, K. M.; Turner, C.; & Lupton, T. A conceptual scheme for organizational analysis. *Administrative Science Quarterly*, 1963, *8*, 289–315.

Weber, M. Bureaucracy. In H. H. Gerth & C. W. Mills (Eds. and trans.), *From Max Weber: Essays in sociology*. New York: Oxford University Press, 1946, 196–264.

Related Research: General

Aiken, M., & Hage, J. Organizational alienation: A comparative analysis. *American Sociological Review*, 1966, *31*, 497–507.

Blau, P. M. The hierarchy of authority in organizations. *American Journal of Sociology*, 1968, *73*, 453–467.

Blau, P. M.; Heydebrand, W. V.; & Stauffer, R. E. The structure of small bureaucracies. *American Sociological Review*, 1966, *31*, 179–191.

Carzo, R., & Yanouzas, J. N. Effects of flat and tall organization structure. *Administrative Science Quarterly*, 1977, *22*, 178–191.

Child, J. Organization structure and strategies of control: A replication of the Aston studies. *Administrative Science Quarterly*, 1972, *17*, 163–177.

Dewar, R., & Hage, J. Size, technology, complexity, and structural differentiation: Toward a theoretical synthesis. *Administrative Science Quarterly*, 1978, *23*, 111–136.

Hage, J., & Aiken, M. Relationship of centralization to other structural properties. *Administrative Science Quarterly*, 1967a, *12*, 72–92.

———.Program change and organizational properties, a comparative analysis. *American Journal of Sociology*, 1967b, *72*, 503–519.

———.Routine technology, social structure and organizational goals. *Administrative Science Quarterly*, 1969, *14*, 366–376.

Hinings, C. R., & Lee, G. L. Dimensions of organization structure and their context: A replication. *Sociology*, 1971, *5*, 83–93.

Inkson, J. H. K.; Pugh, D. S.; & Hickson, D. J. Organization context and structure: An abbreviated replication. *Administrative Science Quarterly*, 1970, *15*, 318–329.

Ivancevich, J. M., & Donnelly, J. H. Relation of organizational structure to job satisfaction, anxiety-stress, and performance. *Administrative Science Quarterly*, 1975, *20*, 272–280.

Lawrence, P. R., & Lorsch, J. W. Differentiation and integration in complex organizations. In J. A. Litterer (Ed.), *Organizations*, vol. II; *Systems, control and adaptation*, 2nd ed. New York: Wiley, 1969, 229–253.

Lincoln, J. R.; Hanada, M.; & Olson, J. Cultural orientations and individual reactions to organizations: A study of employees of Japanese-owned firms. *Administrative Science Quarterly*, 1981, *26*, 93–115.

Mansfield, R. Bureaucracy and centralization: An examination of organizational structure. *Administrative Science Quarterly*, 1973, *18*, 477–488.

Oldham, G. R., & Hackman, J. R. Relationships between organizational structure and employee reactions: Comparing alternative frameworks. *Administrative Science Quarterly*, 1981, *26*, 66–83.

Ouchi, W. G. The relationship between organizational structure and organizational control. *Administrative Science Quarterly*, 1977, *22*, 95–111.

Pennings, J. Measures of organizational structure: A methodological note. *American Journal of Sociology*, 1973, *79*, 686–704.

Pugh, D.; Hickson, D. J.; Hinings, C. R.; & Turner, C. Dimensions of organization structure. *Administrative Science Quarterly*, 1968, *13*, 65–105.

———.The context of organization structures. *Administrative Science Quarterly*, 1969, *14*, 91–114.

Related Research: Education

Bishop, L. K., & George, J. R. Organizational structure: A factor analysis of structural characteristics of public elementary and secondary schools. *Educational Administration Quarterly*, 1973, *9*, 66–80.

Conway, J. A. Test of linearity between teachers' participation in decision making and their perceptions of their schools as organizations. *Administrative Science Quarterly*, 1976, *21*, 130–139.

Derr, C. B., & Cabarro, J. J. An organizational contingency theory for education. *Educational Administration Quarterly,* 1972, *8,* 26–43.

George, J. R., & Bishop, L. K. Relationship of organizational structure and teacher personality characteristics to organizational climate. *Administrative Science Quarterly,* 1971, *16,* 467–475.

Holdaway, E. A.; Newberry, J. R.; Hickson, D. J.; & Heron, R. P. Dimensions of organizations in complex societies: The educational sector. *Administrative Science Quarterly,* 1975, *20,* 37–58.

Miskel, C. G.; Fevurly, R.; & Stewart, J. Organizational structures and processes, perceived school effectiveness, loyalty, and job satisfaction. *Educational Administration Quarterly,* 1979, *15,* 107–118.

Chapter 3
Organizational Process

GENERAL SYSTEM THEORY

Let me have some feedback on this report when you've finished, okay?

We want everyone to have a chance for input before we make a decision.

What's the output of that department?

Systems terminology has become so much a part of everyday language that one can easily forget the highly theoretical origins of words like *input, output,* and *feedback.* Furthermore, we often speak of school systems, information systems, missile systems, and digestive systems as if they are intrinsically different; yet all these entities are called systems. Do schools, telephones, ICBMs, and digestive tracts have something in common that justifies calling them all systems?

Ludwig von Bertalanffy, a biologist with broad interests beyond his own discipline, was among the first to recognize that in such diverse fields as biology, psychology, mechanical engineering, physics, and sociology, scholars were developing generalizations that had striking similarities (Bertalanffy, 1968). More specifically, scholars were beginning to emphasize the importance of the relationships among parts of the phenomena being studied, whereas previously the emphasis had been on analysis of the parts individually.

In essence, this shift in emphasis was a realization that the whole is greater than the sum of the parts and a concomitant search for what it is that makes the whole exhibit basically different characteristics from those of the constituent parts. Drawing on developments in the various disciplines, Bertalanffy articulated a theory of systems in general to account for similarities in the functioning of such diverse phenomena as living organisms, machines, galaxies, and organizations.

THE ESSENCE OF GENERAL SYSTEM THEORY

General system theory is partly dependent on defining systems and their elements with sufficient generality for application to phenomena that are studied in the various physical and social sciences. Once a vocabulary of systems in general is established, it is possible to articulate lawlike statements that are pertinent to all systems.

Most broadly, a system can be defined as a complexity of elements standing in interaction (Bertalanffy, 1968:33). Moreover, systems exchange matter with their environments; that is, they import from and export to their surroundings (Bertalanffy, 1968:141). Thus, in its simplest and broadest terms, a system can be represented as in Figure 3–1.

Implicit in Bertalanffy's broad definition are the notions of a boundary that distinguishes the system from its environment and a purpose for the interactions among parts. Thus it is possible to develop an expanded definition of system and to elaborate the meaning and significance of each element in the definition as the major constructs of the theory.

Major Constructs in General System Theory

A *system* can be defined as "a set of *components* interacting with each other and a *boundary* which possesses the property of filtering both the kind and rate of flow of *inputs* and *outputs* to and from the system" (Berrien, 1968:14–15). Any time there are components interacting within a boundary, there is a system; and the system always requires inputs from the environment and always

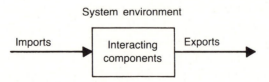

Figure 3–1   Basic Diagram of a System

produces outputs to the environment. Furthermore, the system's outputs are always, in some detectable characteristic(s), different from the inputs (Berrien, 1968:15). The discernible changes produced by the system can be regarded as the *purpose(s)* of the system. The italicized terms can be further defined and elaborated as follows.

COMPONENTS

Components of a system are the parts that interact with each other to fulfill the purpose(s) of the system. In a simple mechanical system such as a pair of scissors, the components are the two complementary cutting blades and the pin that joins them near the center. Note that the structure of each of the parts determines how they can interact with each other and that it is the interaction among parts that fulfills the purpose of altering a piece of paper or fabric. In a very complex system such as a school, the components are individual people (teachers, administrators, counselors) and individual pieces of material (books, film projectors, chalkboards). Again, the structure of each part—for example, the role of each person and the form of each piece of material—determines how the components interact, and it is the interaction among parts that fulfills the school's purpose(s) of changing the students in some discernible way(s).

Components can be defined more precisely as the *smallest meaningful units* that interact with each other to fulfill the purpose(s) of the system. Each blade of the scissors is in itself a system made up of molecules, which are its components; but since it is the blades joined by a linking pin that do the cutting, the blades and pin would be regarded as the components. Similarly, each teacher in a school is a system made up of individual living cells in interaction, but it is the whole teacher in interaction with other whole people and things that does the teaching; therefore, the teachers (and the other people and things) would be regarded as the components of the school.

BOUNDARY

The *boundary* of a system is the component that separates the system from its environment and filters the inputs to and the outputs from the system. The boundary may be a physical component such as the skin of an organism, the border of a country, or the casing of a machine; or it may be an intangible zone such as the outer limits of a social group. What is important is that the behavior of a component within a system differs from what that component's behavior would be outside the system. For example, a blade that could be part of a pair of scissors does not behave as such when it is not connected to a complementary blade via a linking pin. Similarly, the behavior of an educational administrator at home is different from that person's behavior in interaction with other components of the school. The boundary of a social system can be regarded as the outer limits of the role each person occupies.

Systems vary in the range of inputs that enter across the boundary and the rate at which inputs can enter or outputs leave the system. Some system boundaries are relatively impermeable, and others are highly permeable. In other words, systems can be described as relatively *open* or *closed*.

OPEN SYSTEM

An *open system* is one with a highly permeable boundary. Such a system imports many diverse elements at a rapid rate from its environment and uses those inputs for the interactions among components in the production of diverse outputs.

CLOSED SYSTEM

A *closed system* is one with a relatively impermeable boundary. Such a system imports few elements from its environment, and the inputs are relatively uniform in type. That is, few types of inputs can be used by the system for enabling the components to interact to produce the outputs, which are also limited in variety. The scissors system mentioned earlier is relatively closed, since only one type of input (a particular form of pressure from the fingers) will enable the components to interact to fulfill the system's purpose. One might hammer the scissors, heat them, or speak lovingly to them; but these potential inputs will not cause the components to interact to cut anything. An automobile is a somewhat more open system, since it imports gasoline, water, air, lubricants, electricity, and pressures from the human driver, and produces a variety of outputs (movement at varied rates and in diverse directions, light, sounds, and heat). A school, of course, would be among the most open of systems in terms of diversity and rate of inputs and outputs.

INPUTS

Inputs are all elements that enter the system across its boundary and cause or enable the components to interact or affect the ways in which the components interact in fulfilling the system's purpose(s). Although inputs can be relatively diverse or uniform, they can be classified as being of only two types, *energy* and *information* (See Buckley, 1967).

· *Energy Inputs. Energy inputs* are physical materials or forces imported to the system that enable the components to move and therefore to interact physically. Electricity, gasoline, water, food, and pressure are examples of energy inputs used by systems. As energy is used by the system, it is converted into heat, which dissipates throughout the system or is expelled to the environment, where it dissipates. That is, energy gets used up in a process called *entropy*, the randomization of molecules. The energy inputs to schools as systems include the fuel, electricity, air, and sunlight entering from the environment and the caloric energy the people bring (from the foods and beverages they ingest) that enables them to move about and speak.

· *Information Inputs. Information inputs* are signals that enter the system and indicate to the components how or when they are to interact. Information inputs include such signals as lights (for example, traffic lights), sounds (for example, alarm bells), announcements (for example, public address system messages), printed materials (for example, memoranda), and signs (for example, semaphore). Any signals the system receives that tell the system how or when the components are to interact are information inputs. The information inputs to schools would include students' actions and statements, community members' comments, legislative mandates, and central office directives—in short, all messages that affect the interactions among components.

Most often, the energy and information in a system's environment are in a form not directly useful to the system. These raw materials must be *encoded*, converted into a form that is useful to the system. For example, the food a person ingests is converted by the digestive system into a form that is useful to the individual cells. At another level of analysis, the food found in nature is converted by selecting, cutting, grinding, cooking, and other means to make it useful to the human organism as a whole. Similarly, the sounds and images (signals) in the environment are encoded by sorting, selecting, and interpreting to render them meaningful to the human recipient. This encoding is done by specialized parts of the system.

Another interesting feature of inputs is that often they cannot be used precisely when they are available from the environment, but they must be retained within the system until they are used. Energy inputs are retained in tanks, batteries, bins, or equivalent components called *storage* units. Information inputs are retained in libraries, files, minds, recorded tapes, or equivalent system components called *memory* units.

An additional noteworthy feature of inputs, both energic and informational, is that a minimal amount of input is required simply to sustain the system as such—to keep the components in such condition that they are able to interact—and that inputs beyond the minimum are required to enable the system to fulfill its purpose(s) and to grow. Katz and Kahn (1966) distinguish between *maintenance inputs*—those required simply to sustain the system—and *production inputs*—those used for growth and goal attainment.

OUTPUTS

Outputs are all the energy and information that a system expels to its environment or to adjacent systems. That which the system produces, either by design or incidentally, is its output. A system's output always entails altering the inputs (for example, consuming them in the process of doing work) and, often, altering something that is treated by the system. For example, a pair of scissors consumes the energy that the human user provides (thereby converting the energy to heat, which is an output); it also alters the fabric or paper that is processed by the system. The alteration in the paper or fabric is also an output of the scissors. A school consumes the energy and information it receives and, in so doing, alters the students who are "processed" by the school.

That which passes through the system and is changed in some way by the system is often called the *throughput*, although the changes in the throughput are the system's output. Vegetables diced by a food processor, paper going through a printing press, raw materials going through an assembly line, and a voice going through a telephone system are all examples of system throughputs; the changes in these throughputs are the respective systems' outputs.

In addition to performing the work of using inputs for purposeful interaction and transforming throughputs, systems always produce some energy and information other than those related to the system's purpose. These might be by-products of the interactions among components (for example, friction); or they might be outputs in excess of those useful to other systems (for example, oversupply). Nonuseful energy outputs are called *waste,* and nonuseful signal outputs are called *noise.*

Noting that human groups such as organizations have the dual purpose of affecting changes of some sort and fulfilling the psychological needs of the human components, Berrien (1968) distinguished between *Formal Achievement (FA)* and *Group Needs Satisfaction (GNS)* as the production outputs of social systems. FA is the successful completion of products or delivery of services that the group was intended to accomplish. GNS is the fulfillment of the human needs that are characteristic of the participants in the group.

Just as the inputs often need to be encoded for use by the system, so the outputs often need to be converted to a form useful to other systems in the environment. This conversion, called *decoding,* is done by the system itself before it expels its purpose-related outputs. Waste and noise are not decoded. A telephone system is a good example of the decoding mechanism. A voice is processed by the system in the form of electrical impulses or light waves, but before it is ejected from the system it is decoded into sound waves that are received by the listener as a voice.

PURPOSE

The *purpose* of a system is the function(s) the system performs in relation to adjacent systems or a larger system of which it is a part. For an artificial system such as a machine or an organization—that is, a system designed and created by people—the system's purpose is that which its designers intend to accomplish. For a natural system such as a living cell, an organism, or a galaxy—that is, a system that exists in nature rather than by human design— the system's purpose is regarded as the function(s) it serves for the larger system of which the particular system is a part. Some systems, like simple tools, may have only one or a few purposes. Others, like schools, may have a multiplicity of purposes, including constraining and socializing children; teaching children a variety of facts, attitudes, and skills; providing employees for businesses; and fulfilling various needs of staff members.

To summarize briefly, a system can be defined as a set of components interacting for a purpose within a boundary that filters inputs and outputs. The components of a system are its smallest meaningful parts that interact, and the system's inputs of energy, and sometimes information, enable or cause the parts to interact. The inputs enter the system across its boundary, which is relatively open (permeable) or closed (impermeable), and are encoded for use by the system. Excess inputs are retained in storage or memory until they are used to perform maintenance or production work. The system fulfills such purposes as transforming inputs and throughputs and, in some cases, gratifying human needs. At the same time the system produces nonuseful outputs called waste and noise.

Many systems are self-regulating or self-directing. They adjust themselves so as to fulfill their purposes of producing particular outputs. A furnace with a thermostat is an example of a self-regulating system, since it fulfills its purpose of maintaining a given temperature by turning itself on or off when the room's temperature falls below or rises above the specified temperature range. Self-regulating and self-directing systems adjust themselves by means of a process called *feedback*. This process entails drawing some of the system's outputs back into the system as information inputs so that possible discrepancies between intended outputs and actual outputs can be sensed. *Positive feedback* is information that there is no discrepancy, that the outputs are those intended. *Negative feedback* is information that a discrepancy exists, that an adjustment is needed in order to fulfill the system's purpose.

Most purposeful human behavior is dependent on the feedback process. The simple act of reaching for a cup of coffee, for example, entails the human system's output of an arm and hand movement, along with the visual feedback (input) that the hand is or is not moving in the right direction. When the movement is as intended, positive feedback is being received; if the hand veers off in a different direction or goes too far, negative feedback is received and the person can adjust the movement. Similarly, most animals as well as some plants and many machines depend on the feedback principle. Servomechanisms, self-guiding missiles, and some computers are examples of self-regulating machines requiring feedback mechanisms.

The terms associated with general system theory can best be reviewed by means of an expansion of the simple system diagram, as in Figure 3–2. The diagram and its technical labels might help to clarify how the language of system theory can foster communication across disciplines and can highlight the similarities among systems of all types.

Mention was made earlier of a simple system such as a pair of scissors and a complex system such as an organization. Systems vary considerably in their degree of complexity, depending on the number and diversity of components they comprise as well as on the groupings of components within them. Within each system the components cluster so as to fulfill purposes that are related to the purposes of the system as a whole. Thus there are *subsystems* and *suprasystems*.

SUBSYSTEM

A *subsystem* is a system that exists within a larger system. It is a set of components interrelating (within a boundary) for a purpose that relates to the purpose(s) of the larger system. In a human system, for example, there are

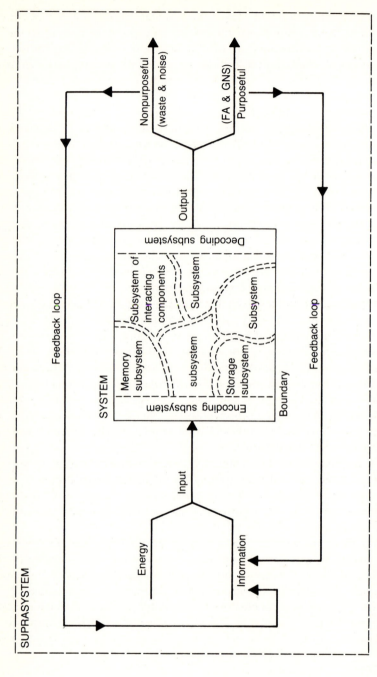

Figure 3–2 System Elements: An Expanded Model

56

circulatory, respiratory, digestive, reproductive, and other subsystems all made up of sets of living cells that are the components of human beings. In a school system there are instructional, administrative, and support service subsystems, all made up of people and things that are the components of school systems.

SUPRASYSTEM

A *suprasystem* is a larger system of which a particular system is a part. It is a set of systems interrelating (within a boundary) to fulfill a broad purpose that includes the purpose of the particular system. For example, a school can be regarded as a system; it has all the attributes of one. Nevertheless, the school exists within a larger system, a school district; and the school interacts with other schools to fulfill the purposes of the district as a whole. Thus the school is a subsystem with respect to the district, and the district is a suprasystem with respect to the school.

Another important feature of systems is that each one can exist in various *states* depending on the particular pattern of relationships among its components and the filtering condition of its boundary at a given point in time (Berrien, 1968:32). Two general states of systems are *equilibrium* and *disequilibrium*.

EQUILIBRIUM

Equilibrium is a state of stability or balance such that the inputs are processed as they enter the system and the components (or subsystems) are providing input to each other (in interaction) at a rate that enables processing as they are received. A burning candle in a draft-free room would be an example of a system in a state of equilibrium, since the oxygen input is consumed as it is received by the candle's components to yield a constant flame. As equilibrium pertains to machines, it is called *homeostasis*. As equilibrium pertains to open systems, it is called *steady state*. The steady state concept includes the growth and progressive differentiation that is characteristic of living phenomena; that is, the inputs are being received at a rate such that the organism can accomplish both growth and productivity.

DISEQUILIBRIUM

Disequilibrium is a state of instability or imbalance such that the inputs are being admitted too rapidly or slowly and with too much or too little diversity to be processed by the system. When a system is in a state of disequilibrium, some components (or subsystems) are overloading others. A burning candle in a drafty room is an example of a system in a state of disequilibrium: the oxygen input is being received too rapidly, and the flame falters or perhaps is extinguished. Insufficient input to the flame, as in a closed box, would also cause disequilibrium and perhaps extinction. Some disequilibrium is necessary for the growth and development of living systems, since it forces the components or subsystems to adapt to changes in the input. Too much disequilibrium, however, could result in the deterioration or extinction of the living system.

Relationships Among Constructs in General System Theory

The constructs that have been defined and illustrated in this chapter are all intrinsic to the definition of a system. As elements of one phenomenon, therefore, all the constructs are integrally related to and determined by each other. For example, the structure of the components determines the possible interactions among the components, and the components in interaction determine the boundary as well as what inputs can be used and what outputs can be produced.

The importance of the integral relationship of the elements to each other can be seen most clearly in open systems, where the components themselves are constantly changing in response to new signal inputs, including frequent negative feedback. As the components change, so do their interactions, boundaries and outputs; the open system grows, becomes more complex, and produces more varied outputs.

Major Propositions of General System Theory

One of the few system theorists to present general system theory in propositional form is Kenneth Berrien. He enumerated many propositions that are pertinent to social systems in particular. Most of these, which follow, can be found in his book, *General and Social Systems* (Berrien, 1968).

1. Initially, systems exhibit greater resistance to destruction than the subsystems or suprasystems that evolve subsequently. Later, the reverse may be true.
2. The state of a system is one determinant of the output.
3. Both signal and energy inputs are necessary for long-term survival.
4. Systems may produce useful or useless outputs as determined by the suprasystem.
5. Suprasystems select those outputs of their subsystems that are useful and reject useless outputs from their own subsystems.
6. Surviving systems are those in which useful outputs exceed useless outputs.
7. A critical proximity of components brought about by exogenous forces is a necessary but insufficient condition for system operations. (The components must be close enough, at least through communication media, to interact; but that is not enough to ensure that they will interact as a system.)

8. The near-steady functioning of systems is evidence of feedback. (Without feedback, systems would deviate further and further from the state or states that keep them producing the required output.)
9. Time is required in processing inputs to produce outputs. (All systems exist in real time and real space; their functioning is that of real physical matter.)
10. Storage may result from:
    a. excess maintenance inputs;
    b. relatively irreversible structural modifications caused by processing inputs. (Inputs that could be processed by the system in an earlier state might not be manageable by the system in a later state and might therefore be stored for use still later.)
11. Stored energies subsequently affect the processing of inputs.
12. Both storage and memories are necessary because of the imperfect matching of input-output flow from system to system.
13. The variability or limit of outputs is controlled by:
    a. the structure of the system components and boundary;
    b. a finite number of states the system can assume because of its components and boundary.
14. The capacity of a system is the range of its variability, which is limited as in item 13.
15. Organizations of systems develop toward greater complexity and emergent (new) characteristics.
16. Adaptation refers to those behavioral (interactional) and structural modifications within the life span of a system or across generations that are survival-extending. Adaptation is accomplished by blocking, dissipating, or neutralizing potentially harmful inputs.
17. Adapting systems develop toward greater rather than less stability.
18. Growth may be viewed as structural modifications initiated by some foreign input permitting the acceptance of maintenance inputs. (The alien input must be such that it can be sustained by the regular maintenance inputs of the system.)
    a. Growth is limited by the adaptation limits (see item 16) and memories of the system.
    b. Growth follows a plan embedded in substructures of the initial system and modified by localized specialization. (Open systems evolve well beyond their initial states, but the directions and extent of growth are constrained by initial states and environmental conditions.)
19. Learning may be viewed as structural modifications (memories) resulting from information inputs.
20. Suprasystems, though evolving out of their subsystems and hence dependent on them, gradually gain control over the subsystems.

(Once two or more independent systems become interactive, thereby forming a suprasystem, they become increasingly specialized and hence dependent on the suprasystem to provide inputs and absorb outputs.

These propositions require considerable thought in terms of individuals, groups, organizations, and perhaps entire societies as open systems for an understanding of how general system theory applies to a broad range of social phenomena.

FURTHER DISCUSSION OF GENERAL SYSTEM THEORY

Many people reject general system theory on the ground that it is too mechanistic a view of human beings. They view the theory as dehumanizing when applied to social phenomena in that it considers human groups to be in some ways similar to machines. Supporters of the theory, on the other hand, maintain that the open system construct—the notion of constant evolution, growth, and increasing complexity due to the perpetual flow in information and energy to and from the system—is not only an apt explanation of social phenomena but a liberating one as well. The theory suggests that receptivity to new information promotes cognitive growth to successive states of complexity and that only the filtering out or rejection of new information impedes such growth.

Others reject the theory on the ground that it views social phenomena as equivalent to natural phenomena, since social systems are seen as conforming to the same laws of nature as biological, botanical, geological, and planetary systems. These critics maintain that social groups and psychological beings are intrinsically different from natural entities in that they are social constructions and can be changed by the will or intent of the participants. The components of physical objects do not have a "will" and cannot change their systems by "intent"; nor do they "perceive" the systems in which they are located. Supporters of the theory, on the other hand, maintain that even though social groupings and organizations exist only insofar as they are perceived to exist by individual participants, and can be changed by participants, the dynamics of social grouping and of human perception itself are in keeping with the natural laws of open systems.

General system theory is fully in accordance with a scientific or positivistic approach to knowledge production. It fosters the seeking of constancies or predictable patterns in the flow of information and energy as forces bearing on systems, and it promotes the search for quantifiable factors in the relationships among parts. Moreover, the theory represents a holistic view of phenomena, a recognition that it is the nature of the relationships among parts rather than the nature of the parts themselves that makes each system unique.

Despite the strong implications of the theory for the logical-deductive scientific method, or what has come to be called the systems approach, there has been little empirical research on social phenomena to test the applicability of the theory directly. General system theory is so sweeping in scope that social science researchers have seldom attempted to test the theory in its entirety, although they have studied aspects of it, such as the feedback process. Greater effort seems to have been invested in generating middle-range theories within the broad general system perspective and in designing technologies for using this perspective in managing organizations. Social systems theory and conceptual systems theory, both of which are treated elsewhere in this book, are examples of middle-range theories derived from the broad general system orientation. Technologies such as Planning Programming Budgeting Systems or PPBS (Hartley, 1968), Program Evaluation and Review Technique or PERT (Miller, 1963) and cost-benefit analysis (Prest & Turvey, 1975) are examples of management strategies representing the general system perspective.

In using concepts and constructs from general system theory to interpret complex open systems such as schools, analysts often fail to make clear distinctions among the system elements. For example, some authors consider the inputs of schools to include the principal, materials, teachers, facilities, and students (for example, Lipham & Hoeh, 1974) or knowledge, values, goals, and money (for example, Owens, 1981). Such lists make it difficult to differentiate inputs, components, outputs, and purposes.

For the analysis of schools as systems, the recognition that input is of two types—information and energy—might help in clarifying the fact that it is not students in themselves but what students say and do that serves as information input. Similarly, it is not money in itself but the fuels (energy) and materials (information) purchased by money that serve as production inputs and the personnel salaries that serve as maintenance inputs. That is, money must be encoded by the system to provide useful inputs. It seems appropriate to regard teachers, administrators, and other staff members as human components of the school, since their knowledge, values, and needs are intrinsic to them as individuals. The actions and messages of school personnel, however, can be regarded as inputs. Similarly, the student body can be regarded as throughput (that which is processed by the system), although the students' actions and messages would certainly be information inputs.

A useful starting point for the analysis of schools as systems is the specification of the purposes of schools, which helps in recognizing the subsystem(s) designed to attain each purpose. If we assume that a school's purposes include advancing students' knowledge and skills (instruction), shaping students' attitudes and behavior (control) and satisfying staff members' needs, and if we acknowledge that all complex systems require maintenance (support service) and coordination (administrative service), then we can analyze a school as encompassing five subsystems, each made up of sub-subsystems, as in Figure 3–3. This diagram is not intended to be complete but is simply illustrative of a systems approach to understanding schools. Further analysis would entail specifying the inputs to and outputs from each subsystem, delineating the feedback mechanisms for each subsystem, and determining whether the outputs are in fact congruent with the overarching purposes of the school as a whole.

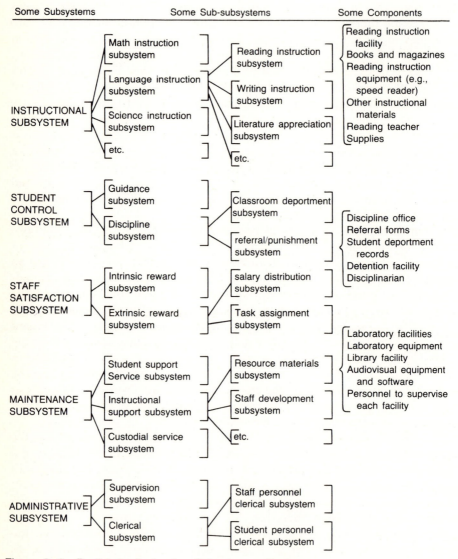

Figure 3–3   Partial Analysis of a School as a System

In sum, general system theory affords a *global* view of an immense variety of phenomena by providing a language abstract enough to pertain to highly divergent domains of inquiry. Although the theory has not been tested in its entirety with respect to human systems, it offers a *holistic* view emphasizing relationships among parts that is helpful in understanding organizations and interpreting organizational events. In addition, the theory represents a *process* view of social systems in that the total system and its constituent subsystems are seen as constantly evolving as they import energy and information, use these inputs purposefully, and export energy and information to their environments.

SOME IMPLICATIONS OF GENERAL SYSTEM THEORY FOR ENHANCING STUDENT LEARNING OUTCOMES

Recent research on the effects of schooling indicates quite consistently that the school a student attends makes a difference in that student's educational attainments. Schools with initially similar student populations vary greatly in the extent to which their students demonstrate the acquisition of knowledge and skills following attendance for a period of time (see, for example, Rutter et al., 1979). Therefore, it appears that there are school characteristics that account for differences in student accomplishments. Further, it is clearly within the purview of educational administrators to establish those school attributes that relate favorably to student achievements.

To this end it is incumbent on the field of educational administration as a whole to generate knowledge about what individual administrators can do to increase learning—to create an environment in which learning is maximized. Is the theory treated in this chapter a suitable one for generating such knowledge? Does general system theory provide a useful conceptual framework for research on how educational administrators can maximize youngsters' cognitive, affective, and psychomotor attainments in schools?

Although general system theory is a descriptive and explanatory framework dealing with how systems *do* function rather than with how they *should* function, the theory has profound implications for the analysis and possible redesign of existing systems. Theoretically, the outputs of a system are produced by the system, either by design or unintentionally. Thus, if the outputs are not useful to the suprasystem, the system must be redesigned or must fail to survive (see Galbraith, 1977). If a school is not producing outputs useful to the district, the community, or society as a whole, someone must reorganize its subsystems and control its inputs so as to produce more useful changes in the students.

A management technique that is representative of a systems approach to organizations and that has been found effective in the analysis and design of schools and other organizations as systems is Management By Objectives or MBO. As described by Migliore (1979), MBO entails specifying the purposes of the organization; identifying the particular objectives associated with each purpose or goal; establishing subsystems for attaining each objective and evaluating performance in relation to the goals and objectives; providing feedback to the appropriate subsystems so that adjustments can be made as necessary; and providing the inputs needed by each subsystem for maintenance and productivity. Implicit in the MBO strategy is the elimination of subsystems that are producing undesired outputs.

Many teachers in today's schools report that they know of no set of stated goals for their schools and no stated objectives for their particular units (grade, department, or class). Often, though by no means typically, there is a set of curriculum guidelines for subject areas, but there is likely to be no mandate that the curriculum be followed or monitoring to determine whether it is followed. In such circumstances teachers may establish their own implicit goals, or leaders within groups may establish implicit goals for their subsystems. These informal goals might be at some variance with the purposes of the school as a whole (see propositions 4 and 5 earlier). For example, a teacher might determine that orderliness is the major purpose of his class subsystem even at the expense of instructional purposes. A department head might decide that efficient use of the available instructional materials is a major purpose of her department, and instructional supervision might be underemphasized.

Many teachers in today's schools report that there is no testing program on a districtwide basis to assess students' cognitive attainments in all subject areas, although standardized tests of basic skills are used in many districts. Still rarer are periodic districtwide tests to assess students' affective or attitudinal attainments; and tests of motor skills such as balance and coordination, handling of basic tools, or performance of physical tasks are virtually never administered on a schoolwide or districtwide basis. In most schools the teachers, who may or may not have established their own goals, administer self-made tests as bases for feedback to themselves and to their students. In such circumstances the subsystem (class or department) can continue to drift unchecked from the overarching purposes of the school, since individualistic objectives may deviate from broader goals (see proposition 8) and since the teachers do not even get accurate feedback with respect to their own self-initiated goals. Teachers typically lack the expertise to develop valid and reliable tests of the domains they intend to measure; hence students' scores on teacher-made tests often do not accurately reflect their mastery of the content.

Many teachers indicate that they do not receive accurate periodic reports on their performance in the form of analyses of students' achievements on a class-by-class basis. When standardized tests are administered schoolwide or districtwide, teachers usually do not receive reports of their own students' gains in terms of class average gains (and standard deviations) in comparison to other teachers' class gains or average school gains at each grade level. Thus the output of the teacher as a system might be too limited or too diverse (see propositions 13 and 14) in relation to the school's purposes.

Furthermore, many teachers are not observed regularly; and those who are observed periodically often report that they do not receive useful or credible analyses of their performance (see propositions 15 and 19). In such circumstances teachers' patterns of behavior are permitted to deviate further and further from a desired pattern, since there is no feedback whereby they can adjust their performance (see proposition 18). Often a teacher's performance is permitted to deviate until a crisis of some sort erupts, by which time the extremely negative feedback might come too late for the teacher as a system to use as input (see propositions 14 and 16).

As many psychologists have noted, general system theory has profound implications for an understanding of the learning process and for the design of learning systems. These implications, particularly with respect to feedback loops and other input, pertain to teachers and administrators as well as to students (see Argyris & Schön, 1974). Without accurate and frequent feedback, teachers, supervisors, and administrators cannot adapt to the larger system's purposes through learning. An administrative technique for furthering staff learning—and student learning as a consequence—is the full implementation of an MBO plan for the school or for the district as a whole.

Although the implications of the theory for administrative practice are apparent, there is little empirical evidence to support the theory's utility in producing knowledge about schools. Some basic questions that merit further inquiry are:

1. For schools with similar student populations, is there a relationship between students' achievements and teachers' consensus on the goals of the school?
2. For schools in which the goals are stated and understood by staff members, is there a relationship between student learning outcomes and feedback to teachers?
   a. Do the *types* of feedback—that is, students' test scores, supervisors' ratings and comments, videotape recordings of instruction, students' assessments, or other forms of information to teachers about their performance—relate differently to student learning outcomes? If so, which is the most effective type of feedback?
   b. Does the *frequency* of feedback to teachers relate to their students' achievements? If so, what is the optimal rate of performance feedback to teachers?
3. Which teaching skills are modified by means of performance feedback?
   a. Are there particular types of feedback that are most effective for the acquisition of specific skills?
   b. Do teaching skills vary in the rate of feedback that is most effective?
   c. Do teachers' personality (or other) characteristics influence their receptivity to different types or rates of performance feedback?
4. Is there a relationship between the type or frequency of tests in schools and student learning outcomes by schools?

5. Do schools in which an MBO plan is implemented (without other major changes in personnel) exhibit significantly greater student achievements than those same schools exhibited before MBO implementation?

The questions posed here, and other pertinent ones deduced from the propositions of the theory, demand inventive research, some of it experimental in design. Pursuit of such inquiry is likely to indicate that general system theory is indeed a useful framework for producing knowledge about how administrators can improve students' cognitive, affective, and skill-related learnings.

MASTERY QUIZ

To test your mastery of the terminology associated with general system theory, indicate the letter of the best completion for each sentence below without reference to the preceding pages. The correct answers can be found in Appendix C, page 391.

1. The smallest interacting parts of a system are called:
    a. inputs.
    b. components.
    c. structures.
    d. feedback.
2. Signals that are received by a system are called:
    a. components.
    b. interactions.
    c. information input.
    d. entropy.
3. Two types of input to a system are:
    a. open and closed.
    b. information and entropy.
    c. homeostasis and steady state.
    d. energy and information.
4. The tendency of energy to become randomly distributed throughout a system is called:
    a. equilibrium.
    b. entropy.
    c. homeostasis.
    d. waste.
5. A system having a highly permeable boundary is called:
    a. a social system.
    b. an open system.
    c. a mechanical system.
    d. a closed system.
6. The return of some output to the system as input is:
    a. disequilibrium.
    b. interaction.
    c. entropy.
    d. feedback.
7. An interactive cluster of components within a system is called a:
    a. subsystem.
    b. memory.
    c. boundary.
    d. complex.
8. Two types of inputs to a system are:
    a. FA and GNS.
    b. waste and noise.
    c. memory and storage.
    d. production and maintenance.

9. Two types of outputs of a system are:
   a. homeostasis and steady state.
   b. components and interactions.
   c. waste and noise.
   d. storage and memory.

10. Something acted upon by the system but not part of the system is:
   a. goals and objectives.
   b. information and energy.
   c. system throughput.
   d. Formal Achievement and Group Needs Satisfaction.

EXERCISES

1. For further review of the terms associated with this theory, identify the best definition of each term in Column A by noting the appropriate letter drawn from Column B for the ten terms that follow. The answers are provided in Appendix C, page 391.

A	B
_____ 1. memory	a. material or force input
_____ 2. boundary	b. interacting components within an impermeable boundary
_____ 3. information	c. equilibrium
_____ 4. closed system	d. smallest interacting parts
_____ 5. noise	e. retention of signal inputs
_____ 6. Formal Achievement	f. satisfaction of members' needs
_____ 7. energy	g. transformation of inputs
_____ 8. encoding	h. signals
_____ 9. entropy	i. maintenance input
_____ 10. steady state	j. nonuseful signal output
	k. imbalance
	l. randomization of energy
	m. that which filters inputs
	n. waste
	o. accomplishment of system purposes
	p. storage
	q. set of interacting systems
	r. useless energy output

2. To demonstrate your full command of the specialized systems language, conceal all the terms in Column A, and state the word or phrase that best matches each of the terms in Column B.

3. For practice in analyzing systems, complete the following chart in the manner indicated:
   a. For the top portion select a subsystem of the human organism and

indicate in the appropriate columns some of its sub-subsystems, its
purpose, some inputs, and some outputs. Completions for the digestive
system have been provided for illustrative purposes.

b. Complete the lower portion of the chart by identifying three (3)
subsystems of a school as a system and by completing the columns as in
the upper portion. The subsystems you select may be but do not have
to be among those identified within the preceding chapter.

SYSTEM: THE HUMAN ORGANISM

SUBSYSTEM	SOME SUB-SUBSYSTEMS	PURPOSE(S)	SOME INPUTS	SOME OUTPUTS
digestive	*mouth, esophagus, stomach, intestine*	*convert food into nutrients*	*food, oxygen, enzymes*	*vitamins, minerals, carbon dioxide*

SYSTEM: A SCHOOL

SUBSYSTEM	SOME SUB-SUBSYSTEMS	PURPOSE(S)	SOME INPUTS	SOME OUTPUTS
			Energic: Informational:	FA: GNS:
			Energic: Informational:	FA: GNS:
			Energic: Informational:	FA: GNS:

4. Consider the 20 propositions listed within the preceding chapter. To demonstrate the relevance of general system theory to education, briefly illustrate each proposition with reference to a school or school district example. The first proposition might be illustrated as follows:

Within a science department (a system), a committee of teachers (subsystem) is appointed to develop science curriculum guidelines. At first the department is more stable than the committee; but if the committee members gain power and influence (because of their access to information and their communication network), the committee might ultimately unseat the department head and disrupt the department.

REFERENCES

Major Sources

Berrien, F. K. *General and social systems.* New Brunswick, N.J.: Rutgers University Press, 1968.
Bertalanffy, L. von. *General system theory: Foundations, development, applications.* New York: George Braziller, 1968.
Katz, D., & Kahn, R. L. *The social psychology of organizations.* New York: Wiley, 1966.

Related Conceptual and Technical Literature

Argyris, C., & Schön, D. A. *Theory in practice: Increasing professional effectiveness.* San Francisco: Jossey-Bass, 1974.
Buckley, W. *Sociology and modern systems theory.* Englewood Cliffs, N.J.: Prentice-Hall, 1967.
Galbraith, J. R. *Organization design.* Reading, Mass.: Addison-Wesley, 1977.
Hartley, H. J. *Educational planning—programming—budgeting: A systems approach.* Englewood Cliffs, N.J.: Prentice-Hall, 1968.
Lipham, J. H., & Hoeh, J. A., Jr. Systems theory. In *The principalship: Foundations and functions,* New York: Harper & Row, 1974, 19–47, chap. 2.
Migliore, H. *Long-range planning/MBO Migliore style.* Tulsa, Okla.: Oral Roberts University, 1979 (mimeo).
Miller, R. W. How to plan and control with PERT. In E. C. Bursk & J. F. Chapman (Eds.), *New decision-making tools for managers.* New York: New American Library, Mentor Books, 1963, 95–118.
Owens, R. G. Organizational theory and organizational behavior. In *Organizational behavior in education,* 2nd ed. Englewood Cliffs, N.J.: Prentice-Hall, 1981, 59–102, chap. 3.
Prest, A. R., & Turvey, R. Applications of cost-benefit analysis. In E. Mansfield (Ed.), *Managerial economics and operations research: Techniques, applications, cases,* 3rd ed. New York: W. W. Norton, 1975, 562–586.
Rutter, M.; Maughan, B.; Mortimore, P.; Ouston, M.; & Smith, A. *Fifteen thousand hours: Secondary schools and their effects on children.* Cambridge, Mass.: Harvard University Press, 1979.

Part III
POWER WITHIN ORGANIZATIONS

Power is an interpersonal phenomenon that exists whenever two or more people interact. It is ubiquitous in societies generally and in organizations in particular. It has been a subject of deep interest and intensive debate among sociologists and political scientists for decades. In school systems, as in other organizations, power affects people's behavior.

Despite the widespread recognition that power exists and the many attempts to study it scientifically, the phenomenon remains elusive and difficult to define (Wrong, 1979). Definitional problems include the issue of whether power resides within people or is attributed by others who could, if they wished, withdraw from the sphere of influence. Measurement problems include the issues of how to determine who the influential people are and how to assess whether or to what degree influence has occurred.

In an essay that has become a classic in the literature on power, French and Raven (1959) defined *power* as "influence on the person, P, produced by an agent, O, where O can be another person, a role, a norm, a group, or a part of a group" (p. 151). Their analysis of the bases of power emphasizes P's *perception* that O has the means and the ability to exercise influence. In other words, P *attributes* to O reward power, coercive power, legitimate power, referent power, and/or expert power— and P is influenced by that attribution.

The theoretical frameworks selected for Part III of this book are relevant to different aspects of the analysis French and Raven provided. The first of these frameworks, Max Weber's theory of bureaucracy (Gerth & Mills, 1958), focuses on legitimate power, that to which people accede because they believe deeply that others have the legislated right and obligation to exercise influence. The second of these frameworks, Amitai Etzioni's theory of compliance (Etzioni, 1975), deals both with the types of power used and with participants' orientations or attributions with respect to the uses of power. Both theories seem to have profound implications for the effective administration of schools.

REFERENCES

Etzioni, A. *A comparative analysis of complex organizations.* New York: Macmillan, Free Press, 1975.

French, J. R., & Raven, B. H. The bases of power. In D. Cartwright (Ed.), *Studies in social power*. Ann Arbor: University of Michigan, Institute for Social Research, 1959, 150–167.

Gerth, H. H., & Mills, C. W. (Eds. & trans.). *From Max Weber: Essays in sociology*. New York: Oxford University Press, 1958.

Wrong, D. H. *Power: Its forms, bases, and uses*. New York: Harper & Row, Colophon, 1979.

Chapter 4
Authoritative Power

BUREAUCRACY THEORY

Bureaucracy—to some, the word itself evokes a rush of unpleasant images: long lines of people waiting at clerks' desks; forms in quadruplicate with copies to every conceivable bureau; petty functionaries, callous and indifferent, citing rules from the company manual. Is there not a better way to administrate a massive enterprise?

We live in an era of rationality and efficiency. We expect people to have sound reasons for their actions. We assume goals, objectives, purposes, or motives for the things people do. Moreover, we expect people to approach their goals by the most direct and least costly means available. In contemporary Western society, to call an individual irrational or inefficient is to offend that person deeply.

These same values are reflected in the institutions and organizations that make up our society. According to Max Weber, these values are best represented in a bureaucratic form of organization. Stated differently, a bureaucracy is an organization that achieves the epitome of efficiency and rationality while at the same time resting on a bedrock of legitimacy. The image of a bureaucracy is perhaps best captured by a pyramidal form, as

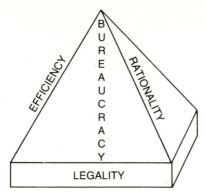

Figure 4–1   Basic Principles of Bureaucracy

illustrated in Figure 4–1, that is bounded by both efficiency and rationality and that stands firmly on a legal foundation.

THE CORE OF WEBER'S THEORY OF BUREAUCRACY

Max Weber was concerned with the issue of social dominance—with how a small number of individuals, particularly in government and industry, achieve dominance over huge numbers of people. Although he recognized that there are many bases of power, including coercion and persuasion, he was most interested in authority—the form of dominance that is contingent on voluntary obedience by others. He identified three types of authority, differentiated by the justifications recognized by leaders for exercising dominance and the reasons conceived by followers for obeying leaders' directives. These three types of authority are charismatic, traditional, and legal.

Charismatic authority is social dominance in which the leader's personal magnetism and exceptional attractiveness draws masses of followers. Charismatic leaders such as Mahatma Ghandi and Joan of Arc are viewed as embodying a compelling value that many hold dear. Often their influence is seen as divinely inspired.

Traditional authority is a form of dominance inherent in a position that is passed to individuals from one generation to the next. Traditional leaders such as monarchs and tribal chieftains are obeyed because persons in those positions have always been obeyed, regardless of the quality of their decisions.

Legal authority is a form of dominance created by legislation and upheld by the full legal machinery of the society. Legal authorities such as corporation officers and school administrators are obeyed because they have the legally mandated right and obligation to issue their directives.

The important feature of all three types of authority is that subordinates comply with their superiors' orders without questioning the legitimacy or desirability of those orders. That is, all three types of dominance are viewed by both the leaders and the followers as legitimate. If directives are questioned or challenged, some authority is lost; the leader might then have to resort to a different form of power to induce obedience (see Weber, 1963).

Each of these types of authority gives rise to a different type of organization. Charismatic authority currently is most prevalent in mass movements and voluntary associations. Such organizations often either dissolve when the leader dies or become routinized as members strive to retain the practices that evolved while the leader was alive. Traditional authority can currently be seen most distinctly in small family enterprises, those that have been founded by an individual and passed on to the oldest offspring. When these enterprises grow and become more complex, they tend to become more impersonal and competency oriented as they strive to compete in an open market. Legal authority characterizes government agencies and corporations, which are legal entities responsible to the state. Organizations in which legal authority is the predominant form of influence are called *bureaucracies*. They are stable structures bound by laws and routine operations. As this brief overview indicates, contemporary organizations tend to become bureaucracies. Although existing bureaucracies retain many traces of charismatic and traditional dominance, the primary mode of influence resides in the officials' legal authority.

In his analysis of historical developments across eras and cultures, Weber sought to identify those characteristics of legal structures that most sharply differentiate them from traditional or charismatic structures. He specified seven features of bureaucracies that, both individually and in interaction, maximize organizational rationality and efficiency. These features are: hierarchy of offices, rules and regulations, specialization of tasks, impersonality, written records, salaried personnel, and organizational control of resources.

Major Constructs in Bureaucracy Theory

The characteristics of bureaucracies are the key constructs associated with Weber's theory. These can be defined and illustrated as follows:

HIERARCHY OF OFFICES

Each administrative function in the organization is assigned an office, a position entailing a specified set of rights and responsibilities. These offices are arranged in pyramid form such that officeholders at each level are responsible to those at the next higher level and each office is associated with a particular status and degree of responsibility. Any person holding a particular office is subject to the rights and obligations pertaining to that position. In a school district, as the reader is well aware, the offices might include those of the superintendent, associate superintendents, assistant superintendents, division heads, directors, coordinators of particular programs, and building principals. The hierarchical ordering of offices within a district is usually depicted in the organizational chart of the district.

RULES AND REGULATIONS

There are routine procedures for dealing with recurring situations that affect each office in the organization, and there are standards of behavior for all participants. The standards that make up the rules and regulations of the organization are often printed in a manual. Generally speaking, they are unambiguous, reasonable, and limited in number so that all participants can learn them. In school districts there are typically rules and regulations pertaining to working hours, teachers' responsibilities, and student deportment.

SPECIALIZATION OF TASKS

All the work performed within the organization is divided among offices, and each office is associated with one type of work. This enables employees to become highly proficient at particular tasks and to acquire specialized training to enhance their expertise. Supervisory and administrative tasks are also performed by specialized officials. In schools, specialization is usually based on subject area, grade level, supervisory functions, and administrative tasks.

IMPERSONALITY

Interactions within the organization or between officials and clients are conducted uniformly in a nonindividualistic manner rather than with emotional overtones or personal biases. The rules apply to all individuals impartially, and decisions are based on efficient goal attainment rather than impulse or personal preferences. Emotional displays are out of place, and intimacy is discouraged. An example of impersonality in education might be the granting of child-care leave to all male and female staff members who qualify for it and request it; administrators' personal opinions and preferences would play no part in the decision.

WRITTEN RECORDS

All transactions, both within the organization and with clients, are recorded on documents that are filed and kept for future reference, for decision making, and for reporting to auditors. The relevant information is available as needed for all officeholders. It is probably unnecessary to mention the students' achievement, deportment, and attendance records and the teachers' personnel and evaluation records, all of which are endemic to education.

SALARIED PERSONNEL

The supervisory and administrative officers are full-time, salaried employees who depend on the organization for income. Their job is their major interest, their primary source of income, their means of career advancement, and their major locus for practicing the work for which they were specially trained. Schools often employ volunteers and part-time personnel to assume some delegated responsibilities, but the mainstay of the education system is the full-time, salaried staff.

CONTROL OF RESOURCES
Although the organization must acquire its resources from the external environment, the resources, once acquired, are controlled and allocated by the organization's officers. All the machinery, equipment, and supplies needed to meet the organization's goals are provided for employees by the organization, and outsiders may not determine how the resources will be deployed. Since schools are supported by taxes, school officials are financially accountable to the school boards. The board makes policy decisions only, however, and may not exercise administrative control over specific expenditures within the guidelines of the policy.

Relationships Among the Major Constructs in Bureaucracy Theory

As noted earlier, these characteristics of the pure bureaucracy are bounded by the principals of rationality and efficiency:

Rationality refers to the goal-directedness of the organization. Each activity undertaken within the organization is explicitly related to organizational goals; this goal-directedness provides the only legitimate justification for any pattern of actions. Although the goals of schools are often implicit rather than fully specified, the idea that an action is "best for the children" or "in the child's educational interest" is often invoked to support the rationality of a particular action.

Efficiency refers to the cost-effectiveness of the organization, where *cost* is the expenditure of organizational resources, and *effectiveness* is the organizations attainment of its goals. When alternative action plans are considered, the plan yielding the more favorable cost-benefit ratio is the one that can justifiably be pursued. In education a school district's efficiency would be a function of that district's per pupil expenditure in relation to the students' educational attainments. It should be recognized, however, that costs include not only dollars but also time, energy, and all other resources that are expended.

Each characteristic of the bureaucracy enhances the rationality and efficiency of the organization. For example, a hierarchy of offices ensures that decisions affecting the organization's operations are made by those in the best position to weigh all the relevant factors, and that once a decision is made it can be enforced by directives throughout the organization. Rules and regulations ensure that personnel are available to perform the required tasks as needed and that no one engages in behaviors that will endanger the equipment or other personnel or that will impede the performance of goal-related tasks.

In addition, each characteristic of the pure bureaucracy reinforces and

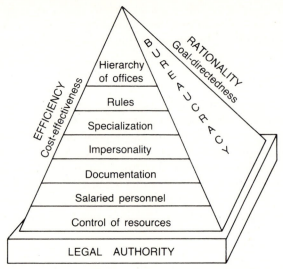

Figure 4–2   Characteristics of Bureaucracy as a Pure Type

facilitates implementation of the other features. For example, specialization of tasks enhances impersonality: decisions are based on expertise in task performance rather than whim, and each officeholder, having the requisite knowledge, makes objective decisions. Similarly, the practice of having salaried personnel facilitates organizational control of resources: each salaried employee becomes somewhat dependent on (and loyal to) the organization and therefore more willing to follow directives.

The characteristics of a pure bureaucracy are summarized in Figure 4–2, which emphasizes the pyramidal form of organization, the linkage to efficiency and rationality, and the legal foundation of bureaucratic authority.

Major Propositions in Bureaucracy Theory

Bureaucracy theory was not originally stated as a formal theory with an explicit set of propositions. Rather, it was presented by Weber in the context of a broad, sweeping analysis of organizations as they evolved historically (see Weber, 1964; Gerth & Mills, 1958; Wrong, 1970; Mouzelis, 1967). It is a grand theory, one of monumental proportions. Nevertheless, some propositions that make the empirical implications of the theory more readily apparent can be derived from Weber's description of bureaucracy as an ideal type.

1. Organizations based on legal authority (bureaucracies) are more efficient and more rational than are those based on charismatic authority or those based on traditional authority.
2. The more nearly an organization approximates a pure bureaucracy, the more efficient and rational that organization is.

3. The presence of any one characteristic of bureaucracy in an organization increases the likelihood that other characteristics of bureaucracy will be present in that organization.

FURTHER DISCUSSION OF WEBER'S THEORY OF BUREAUCRACY

Weber's theory of bureaucracy has been perhaps the most extensively examined, discussed, criticized, and researched of all theories in the literature of formal organizations. Because of its vast scope, it has attracted the interest not only of sociologists but also of political scientists, philosophers, social psychologists, and educators; of theorists as well as empirical researchers; of vociferous critics as well as staunch adherents. As a theory having global proportions, it has been subject to diverse and divergent interpretations. In this section we will not try to explore the full range of perspectives that scholars have brought to bear on Weber's theory. We will simply try to clarify some aspects of the theory, explore some of its research implications, and examine some of the criticisms of the theory.

The Ideal Type Method

First, the concept of bureaucracy as an ideal type should be emphasized. The phase refers to Weber's methodology, not his ideology. That is, having specified three types of authority, Weber proceeded to distill the characteristics of one type—the legal or bureaucratic type—as they might be imagined in their purest form. *Ideal* is used in the platonic sense to mean pure, but not necessarily desirable. In fact, Weber himself deplored the prevalence of bureaucratic organizations, although he saw them as inevitable in societies that were and are becoming increasingly technological.

An ideal type, of course, cannot exist in reality. It is a theoretical construct that exists only in someone's imagination. Thus purely bureaucratic organizations cannot be found in any real society. Any existing organization contains elements of charismatic authority and of traditional authority (as well as other types of power). One classifies an organization as charismatic, traditional, or bureaucratic on the basis of which form of authority predominates within the organization.

At this point a distinction should be made between authority and other forms of social dominance. *Power* can be defined broadly as the ability of a person or group to influence the actions of another individual or group despite the wishes of the others. One's influence over others' actions can be based on coercion, rewards, expertise, legislation, or personal magnetism (French & Raven, 1959). *Authority,* on the other hand, is one type of power—influence or dominance based on others' willingness to comply or cooperate. Whereas power might rest on force or threat or bribery, authority rests on others' willingness to obey. Weber's typology centers on three types of authority. Real organizations contain some elements of the various types of power in the exercise of influence; in a bureaucracy, however, almost all dominance would be based on authority—specifically, on legal authority.

Authoritative dominance is more efficient than other forms of power since authority requires little expenditure of resources to enforce obedience. Organizational participants accede to all directives within legitimate boundaries without resistance, question, or challenge. It is when requests or directives exceed these legitimate boundaries that nonlegal authority and other forms of power are likely to come into use. One major reason for the prevalence and stability of bureaucratic organizations is that, once participants have signed a legal contract of employment, they find it in their best interests to accede unquestioningly to all reasonable requests of superiors.

Empirical Research

Weber's theory of bureaucracy emerged at a time when legalistic forms of organization were just evolving in Western societies and existed side by side with other organizational forms such as traditional monarchies, feudal fiefdoms, guilds, and armies financed by wealthy landlords. In contemporary Western society virtually all government and corporate enterprises, as well as other organizations, have characteristics of bureaucracy to some degree. As Hills (1966) noted, Weberian bureaucracy theory is too blunt a tool for fine differentiations among contemporary organizations. Since almost all formal organizations in technologically advanced cultures can be considered bureaucratic, it has become necessary to distinguish among bureaucracies.

Empirical researchers have relied on many of Weber's characteristics of the pure bureaucracy to develop tools for distinguishing types of bureaucracies. The predominant approach in applying Weberian theory to empirical research has been to convert each characteristic of bureaucracies to a scale for measuring the extent to which that characteristic is present. Characteristics that would not have variance in modern society—such as full-time employment and organizational control of resources, features of virtually all formal organizations today—are not included in this type of analysis. Types of bureaucracies can then be distinguished on the basis of which characteristics are most prevalent and which are least in evidence. Alternatively, bureaucratic organizations can be differentiated on the basis of their degree of bureaucratization—the extent to which the characteristics, in combination, are present.

Criticisms of Bureaucracy

No discussion of Weber's theory would be complete without attention to some of the most salient criticisms of the theory itself and of bureaucratic organizations in society. Among other things, Weber has been criticized for his preoccupation with the functional aspects of bureaucratic characteristics without recognition of the dysfunctional aspects of those same features (Blau, 1970b). For example, although rules contribute to the organization's efficiency and rationality by reducing uncertainty and precluding individualistic actions that might be inappropriate, they also detract from efficiency and rationality by rendering the organization less responsive to unique circumstances and less able to benefit from the expertise of individual employees. Each of the attributes of the bureaucratic ideal type can similarly be shown to have dysfunctional as well as functional consequences with respect to efficiency and rationality (see Hoy & Miskel, 1978).

Another criticism that Blau (1970b) enunciated is Weber's disregard for the informal dimension of organizations—the fact that unofficial patterns of interaction always arise within organizations and that these nonlegitimized patterns influence individuals' behaviors as strongly as do official rules and directives. In another analysis of bureaucracy theory Blau (1970a) noted Weber's lack of clarity in identifying the sources of authoritative power and distinguishing it analytically from coercive power. Although obedience to legitimate directives is based on the widely shared belief that it is right and proper to comply, ultimately, as Blau pointed out, this belief is rooted in the state's coercive power to enforce obedience.

The bureaucratic form of organization has been criticized for its harmful effects on the people employed within bureaucracies and on the people served by them. In a fascinating analysis of the dysfunctions of bureaucracy, Robert Merton (1963) underscored the "trained incapacity" that bureaucracies induce in their employees. Officials become so imbued with the values of the organization and its rules and rituals that they become incapable of thinking for themselves or solving problems creatively. For many bureaucratic officials the rules supplant the organization's goals, and hapless clients can become ensnared in meaningless routines that have little bearing on their personal needs.

Clearly, bureaucratic organization is not ideal in the utopian sense, nor does Weberian theory account for the totality of organizational reality. No theory does this. This theory does provide an analytic framework for thinking about organizations and a conceptual basis for studying them empirically. As one ponders the deficiencies of the bureaucratic type of structure, one would do well to consider the debilitating effects of the traditional and charismatic types of organizations as well. Perhaps bureaucracy is after all the most effective form of organization yet devised.

RESEARCH RELATED TO BUREAUCRACY THEORY

Weber's theory of bureaucracy is surely among the most thoroughly studied of all behavioral science frameworks both in educational research and in organizational inquiry in general. This section reviews only a representative sample of the hundreds of studies conducted. After reviewing briefly a widely used measure of bureaucratic features, we will consider research in varied settings and then turn our attention to studies of schools and school systems.

Instruments

Although there are no empirical measurement tools associated with the original formulation of the theory, and researchers have used a wide variety of techniques—including case studies, interviews, and observations—for gathering data, an instrument developed by Richard Hall (1963) has been used extensively in diverse settings and adopted for research in education (Punch, 1970). This instrument facilitates the identification of different kinds of bureaucracies and different degrees of bureaucratization in contemporary societies.

The 62-item questionnaire comprises six scales, one for each major characteristic of bureaucracies as selected by Hall: hierarchy of authority, division of labor, system of rules, system of procedures, impersonality, and technical competence as the basis for hiring and promotion. The 10 or more items for each scale are five-point Likert-type items (response options ranging from "always" to "never") completed by several employees at different levels in each organization. Scores for each scale are averaged across respondents within each organization to ascertain that organization's degree of perceived bureaucratization on each dimension of bureaucracy.

This instrument can be used to differentiate types of bureaucracies on the basis of characteristics that are salient and nonsalient (that is, by developing profiles of organizations with different combinations of scale scores), as well as to examine factors that correlate with each characteristic of bureaucracy and to examine differences in perception among employees at different levels in the hierarchy. Hall (1968) also combined these scale measures in the form of a Guttman-type instrument to assess overall bureaucratization within organizations. Thus relationships between general degree of bureaucracy and other factors (such as professionalization, employee alienation, and organizational productivity) can be assessed.

Research in Varied Settings

Several strands of inquiry can be identified within the immense body of research on bureaucracies. Scholars have investigated relationships among the major characteristics, correlates of bureaucratization, and subtypes of bureaucracies and bureaucrats. These areas of research are reviewed briefly in this section.

RELATIONSHIPS AMONG CHARACTERISTICS

Several researchers interested in the Weberian proposition that the characteristics of bureaucracy are mutually reinforcing have studied the degrees of relationship among the major characteristics. In developing the perceptual instrument described earlier, Hall (1963) used random samples of workers in ten organizations. He found nonsignificant relationships among the six scales.

Blau and his colleagues also found independence of the individual characteristics of bureaucracy, although they noted interaction effects of combinations of variables (Blau, Heydebrand, & Stauffer, 1966). These studies tend to disconfirm the Weberian notion that bureaucratic elements vary together and reinforce each other.

On the other hand, Udy (1959), using data available in official records to determine the presence or absence of each of seven Weberian characteristics, found positive significant relationships within two clusters of variables but negative significant relationships between the two clusters. In this study of 150 organizations in nonindustrial societies, the so-called bureaucratic cluster (hierarchical authority, size of administrative staff, differential rewards) was negatively related to the so-called rational cluster (limited objectives, performance emphasis, segmented participation, compensatory rewards). Udy suggested that the informal structure found in most organizations—that is, the unofficial interaction patterns among employees—emerges when there is a clash between the bureaucratic and the rational aspects of the organization. Informal organization, then, may serve the purpose of reconciling contradictory pressures on the employees. Note that the clusters Udy designated rational and bureaucratic would both be bureaucratic in the Weberian scheme.

CORRELATES OF BUREAUCRATIZATION

An organization's degree of bureaucratization refers to the extent to which the characteristics of bureaucracy are prevalent. In studies of relationships between degree of bureaucratization and other organizational attributes, several relationships have been reported. Mansfield (1973), for example, found a weak but negative correlation between bureaucratization and centralization of decision making. The more bureaucratic the organization, the more decentralized the decision making, probably because the prevalence of rules and formal procedures ensures that appropriate decisions will be made at lower levels in the hierarchy. Both bureaucratization and decentralization were found to be related to organizational size in this study.

In a study of 252 public personnel agencies, Blau and his colleagues found that organizational size was directly related to functional specialization but not to other aspects of bureaucracy (Blau, Heydebrand, & Stauffer, 1966). The proportion of managers was positively related to staff professionalism, but centralization of decision making was negatively related to employee professionalism. These findings suggest that greater staff professionalism requires more managers to coordinate the professional specializations; on the other hand, less-professional staff members would be less capable of making important decisions.

Hall (1968) also studied professionalism, but in terms of the value orientations of staff members in 11 different professional and semiprofessional occupations. He found five of the six characteristics of bureaucracy to be negatively related to employees' feelings of autonomy, but technical competence as the basis for hiring and promotion was positively related to all the other aspects of professional orientation. In general, then, degree of bureaucratization seems to be negatively associated with employees' feelings of professionalism.

TYPES OF BUREAUCRACIES AND BUREAUCRATS

Some researchers have directed their attention to the correlates of bureaucratization or the relationships among characteristics of bureaucracy for purposes of developing subtypes of bureaucracies or workers within such organizations. Unlike the society of Weber's era, contemporary society is thoroughly permeated with structures of the more or less bureaucratic type. Therefore, subclassifications can be helpful in understanding today's culture.

The value orientations of employees in bureaucratic organizations can provide a fruitful approach to studying organizations. Leonard Reissman (1949), for example, interviewed 40 state civil service employees to gather information about their viewpoints. He was able to identify four types of bureaucrats: (1) the functional bureaucrat, who identifies herself or himself with the profession rather than the organization; (2) the specialist bureaucrat, who is profession-oriented but also identifies with the organization; (3) the job bureaucrat, the loyal and obedient organization-oriented worker; and (4) the service bureaucrat, who identifies with the clients and seeks to do public good. If one regards organization orientation as a vertical axis and profession orientation as a horizontal axis, as in Figure 4–3, the four types of bureaucrats can be depicted as occupying the four resulting cells.

Ben-David (1958), following similar interview procedures with 78 Israeli physicians, identified two of those types: the science-oriented physicians, who

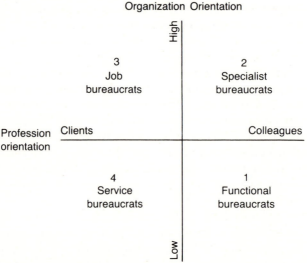

Figure 4–3 A Typology of Bureaucrats

would be equivalent to Reissman's functional bureaucrats; and the service-oriented physicians, who would be equated with Reissman's service bureaucrats. In this study the most bureaucratic medical services (large hospitals) had the greatest proportion of science-oriented doctors, whereas, as might be expected, the least bureaucratic services (private practice) had the greatest proportion of service-oriented doctors.

Also interested in the practice of medicine, Engel (1969) found that physicians in moderately bureaucratic settings had a greater sense of professional autonomy than did those in highly bureaucratic or nonbureaucratic service settings. She concluded that there is an optimal level of bureaucratization to foster autonomy among professional personnel.

The potential clash between legalistic and professional values of employees in increasingly professionalized bureaucracies has stimulated much research interest. Since studies have often indicated that the characteristics of bureaucracies form two unrelated clusters, Hoy and Miskel (1978) suggest a typology of bureaucracies based on two separate dimensions: the formal dimension, which they call bureaucratic (hierarchy, rules, standardization, impersonality); and the professional dimension (expertise, specialization). Thus they derive four subtypes of bureaucracies: the Weberian type (high formalism and high professionalism); the authoritarian type (high formalism and low professionalism); the professional type (low formalism with high professionalism); and the chaotic type (low formalism and low professionalism). Note how compatible this typology is with the Reissman (1949) typology described earlier.

SUMMARY

This review of the empirical research has been far from exhaustive. It has focused on the relatively large-sample empirical studies without reference to the classic case studies such as Gouldner's (1954) in-depth case analysis of industrial bureaucracies or Selznik's (1966) monumental study of the Tennessee Valley Authority, which are essential readings for students of organizations. The key findings of the research reviewed here are that the characteristics of bureaucracy tend to vary either independently (Hall, 1963) or in clusters (Udy, 1959; Hoy & Miskel, 1978), and that degree of bureaucratization is often but not always directly related to organizational size (Mansfield, 1973; Blau Heydebrand, & Stauffer, 1966) and inversely related to professional autonomy (Hall, 1968). Because of the divergence between organizational and professional values, researchers can identify subtypes of bureaucrats (Reissman, 1949; Ben-David, 1958) and of bureaucracies (Udy, 1959; Hoy & Miskel, 1978).

Research in School Systems

A substantial body of research in education has focused on school bureaucratization. Several studies have supported the notion that schools differ in their degree of bureaucratization (McKay, 1964; Punch, 1970; Bishop & George,

1973). Therefore, it is possible to examine school bureaucratization in relation to other important variables. This section is a brief overview of some correlates of educational bureaucratization, some types of educational bureaucracies, and socialization to the bureaucratic value system.

CORRELATES OF BUREAUCRATIZATION

An area that has attracted considerable attention is that of power and conflict in educational bureaucracies. Corwin (1965), for example, studied teachers' professional versus employee orientations in relation to conflict within schools. He concluded that teacher professionalization is a militant process involving the wresting of power both from administrators and from lay persons. This suggests that school systems might evolve from the authoritarian type to the professional type of bureaucracies but that conflict is intrinsic to this evolutionary process.

Moeller and Charters (1966) found, contrary to their expectations, that teachers' sense of power increased with school bureaucratization. In a study designed to replicate these findings, however, Meyers (1972) found that teachers' sense of power decreased as "degree of specialization throughout the system" increased; no other characteristics of bureaucracy were related to teachers' sense of power. The contradictory findings of these two studies suggest that there are other factors affecting teachers' sense of power.

One possibility is that the existence of teachers' unions, most prevalent in large and relatively bureaucratized districts, accounts for the differences in teachers' sense of power. However, Willower (1975) found that the strength of the teachers' collective-bargaining unit did not relate to the perceived distribution of power within school districts. Therefore, unionization does not seem to account for the discrepant findings noted here.

Another possibility is that the *type* of bureaucracy affects teachers' sense of power. Isherwood and Hoy (1973) found that in authoritarian bureaucracies teachers with professional values felt less powerful than did those with social values; in professional bureaucracies, however, teachers with organizational values felt less powerful than did the profession-oriented teachers. It seems that congruence between type of bureaucracy and employees' values accounts for some of the variation in employees' sense of power.

In a somewhat related study, Nirenberg (1977) found that teachers in alternative and traditional schools were equally professional in orientation but that traditional schools were more bureaucratic. Teachers felt significantly less powerful in the traditional schools than in the alternative ones, perhaps because the alternative schools were more like professional bureaucracies. It seems possible, as suggested by one study cited earlier (Engel, 1969), that there is an optimal level of school bureaucratization to foster teachers' professional autonomy; this optimum might vary in accordance with the teachers' degree of professional orientation.

The converse of participants' sense of power within organizations is their degree of *alienation* from the organization. Like sense of power, alienation has been studied extensively. Barry Anderson (1971a) found that students' sense of alienation from school was significantly related to their perceptions of school bureaucratization. Teachers and students differed considerably in their perceptions of school bureaucratization, however. Hoy and his coresearchers found that teacher esprit and teacher loyalty, which might be regarded as nonalienation, were positively related to participation in decision making but negatively related to hierarchy of authority, rule observation, and job codification (Hoy, Newland, & Blazovsky, 1977). Although both studies support the conjecture that school bureaucratization increases participant alienation, it is possible, again, that there is an optimal level of bureaucratization that fosters and facilitates individuals' participation in organizational life.

Other studies of student characteristics in relation to school bureaucratization have been conducted. Anderson (1971b) found that student socioeconomic status was strongly and inversely related to bureaucratic behavior control but not to bureaucratic status maintenance. Other demographic school characteristics such as school size, district size, and type of educational program had no significant bearing on degree of school bureaucratization. Anderson and Tissier (1973) found that school bureaucratization accounted for little of the variation in students' aspiration levels, but that student alienation (which increased with bureaucratization) in combination with type of educational program accounted for most of the variation in students' aspirations.

TYPES OF SCHOOL BUREAUCRACIES

As noted earlier, the clustering of the characteristics of bureaucracy enables scholars to identify subtypes of organizations that more or less represent the bureaucratic mode. The Isherwood and Hoy (1973) study mentioned earlier illustrates the use of a Hall-type instrument to identify subtypes of contemporary school bureaucracies. These researchers found two types of bureaucracies in their sample of seven secondary schools: authoritarian bureaucracies (high centralization, rule-boundedness, standardization, and impersonality); and collegial (professional) bureaucracies (high division of labor and technical competence). This study focused on bureaucratization as perceived by teachers.

The students, of course, are equally important participants in the education enterprise; their view of school structure thus merits attention. Anderson (1971b) identified two different clusters of characteristics in his study of students' perceptions: status maintenance and behavior control. Thus one can visualize four types of school bureaucracies with respect to the structuring of students' participation—high or low status maintenance combined with high or low behavior control.

SOCIALIZATION

The research findings in nonschool settings—that people tend to adopt the behavior patterns and value orientations of those in their organizations over time (Denhardt, 1968)—would suggest that employees in school bureaucracies become more bureaucratic as their tenure increases. For example, Bridges (1965) found that elementary school principals become more similar to each other in behavior patterns the longer they serve.

This supposition has not been supported consistently in education research. Scott (1978) found that superintendents with very long tenure—13 years or more in one position—were significantly more charismatic in their leadership style than were the less tenured superintendents. In a simulation study of Australian secondary school principals, Brennan (1973) found that the principals did not behave in a bureaucratic manner. Questions associated with the socialization process have been addressed by Brown (1978) and others, but they warrant considerably more research.

SUMMARY

Again, the research review provided here is not comprehensive, but is indicative of some strands of thought in the literature on school bureaucracies. Some important findings have been that school bureaucratization relates to teachers' sense of power (Moeller & Charters, 1966) but in complex ways probably contingent on the teachers' value orientations (Isherwood & Hoy, 1973; Nirenberg, 1977). Bureaucratization seems to relate directly to feelings of alienation for both students (Anderson, 1971a) and teachers (Hoy, Newland, & Blazovsky, 1977). Students' socioeconomic status and aspiration levels are apparently related to the degree of bureaucratization of the school (Anderson, 1971b; Anderson & Tissier, 1973). There has been little research on school bureaucratization in relation to student outcomes. We now turn to this issue.

IMPLICATIONS OF BUREAUCRACY THEORY FOR ENHANCING STUDENT LEARNING OUTCOMES

Public demands for accountability in education are still the order of the day. Accountability refers not only to the products of the education enterprise but also to responsibility for those products. Thus it is increasingly important that educational leaders attend to the results of schooling. Equally important is the development of knowledge that can help school leaders improve the products of education. Is bureaucracy theory a useful framework for generating knowledge about how to improve students' cognitive, affective, and psychomotor attainments?

Bureaucracy theory is directly concerned with the outcomes or products of large organizations. Theoretically, the more nearly an organization approximates the ideal bureaucracy characterized by Weber, the more efficient and rational it is. In education this would mean that goal attainment is most direct and most cost-effective when schools and school districts have the characteristics of bureaucracies.

Obviously, education systems do have many of the attributes of bureaucratic structure, as the research cited earlier indicates and as even a little experience in schools will verify. Many school systems, however, seem to lack a set of clear, explicit goals. Education often seems to have the accoutrements of bureaucracy without its raison d'être—a clearly stated purpose. Perhaps the functional aspects of the characteristics of bureaucracy can be clarified if one imagines a school district with unambiguous cognitive, affective, and psychomotor goals as well as a reasonably valid and reliable testing program for measuring the attainment of those goals throughout the district. In such a district each attribute of bureaucracy can be considered in terms of its functionality, and deviations from the bureaucratic mode can be seen as dysfunctional.

A logically ordered *hierarchy of offices* would ensure that each person in the district has a specific set of rights and responsibilities related to the goals, that each person has a higher authority to whom he or she can turn for advice and assistance in fulfilling the responsibilities, and that goal attainment is being monitored. When offices are not clearly delineated or when supervision is not related to the goals—as is so often the case in schools—confusion ensues: some goals are not addressed, or there is duplication of effort, or there is resentment about evaluation based on apparent irrelevancies.

Rules and regulations, if they are logically related to the goals, can conserve all the time and energy it would take to make decisions about frequently recurring events. If the rules are too numerous, vague, or unrelated to the organization's specified goals, they become difficult to enforce consistently; enforcement then becomes inequitable. On the other hand, without some rules that everyone understands, the school would constantly be adapting to diverse behaviors, leaving little time for goal attainment.

Specialization of tasks—for example, by subject, grade level, hierarchical position, or particular functions—enables staff members to become highly proficient in their areas by gaining expertise in a delimited domain. To the extent that such division of labor and its concomitant expertise are not present—for example, when department heads lack expertise in supervision, teachers instruct out of license, or an individual has too many diverse functions—students are denied access to the best knowledge and skill available for furthering their learning.

Impersonality in the enforcement of rules and the bestowing of rewards and penalties helps to ensure that goal achievement remains the primary focus of attention and that irrelevant factors are not considered. To the extent that there is favoritism, nepotism, or inequity of any sort, tremendous resentment is generated among those who do not advance, and people who are less than fully competent may occupy important offices. Goal attainment is hindered both by the diverted energies and by the inadequacies of office holders.

Written records are anathema to many educators who feel that they take up too much time. Nevertheless, if records are related to specific goals, they help in making educationally sound decisions, in pinpointing responsibility for successes and failures, and in maintaining equity for students and staff members. Furthermore, written records make it feasible to generate professional knowledge about teaching and administration. Without them every decision would entail a complete search for information from scratch, as there would be no organizational memory of what was done in the past.

Full-time *salaried staff* and organizational *control of resources* are so consistently characteristic of public schools that they require little discussion. Employees' dependence on the school system for their livelihood fosters loyalty to the system, willingness to abide by the rules, and motivation to gain expertise for career advancement. Control of resources make it feasible for the district to allocate those resources so as to maximize goal attainment.

Clearly, then, there are advantages associated with the existence of the attributes of bureaucracy. Some reflection on actual experiences in schools would probably indicate that it was the absence or inadequacy of bureaucratic elements, rather than excessive bureaucratization, that created the problems. Moreover, when the elements of bureaucracy are criticized in particular school systems, it is often their apparent irrationality—their lack of relevance to educational goals—that creates difficulties. Although excessive bureaucratization can make an organization too rigid to respond to changes, within reasonable limits, bureaucratization can be beneficial. Since school administrators can affect to some extent the degree of bureaucratization within their own organizations—and since the characteristics of bureaucracy seem to have some bearing on student outcomes—Weber's theory does seem to be a useful framework for generating knowledge to guide administrative practice. Some of the many empirical questions that remain to be answered in generating this knowledge are:

1. In districts or schools with equivalent goals, is there a relationship between the organization's degree of bureaucratization and the students' achievements?
2. Which of the characteristics of bureaucratic structure, if any, relate most consistently to student outcomes? Which types of student outcomes, if any, relate most consistently to school bureaucratization?
3. Is there a particular subtype of bureaucracy—Weberian, authoritarian, professional, chaotic (Hoy & Miskel, 1978:64)—in which the greatest student achievements are attained? Does the best type vary according to the demographic attributes of the student body?
4. In many schools having the characteristics of bureaucracy, the teachers and/or students do not perceive these features as rational (relevant to goal attainment). Is there a relationship between the perceived rationality of bureaucratic elements in schools and student achievements? If so, are students' perceptions or teachers' perceptions of rationality the better predictors of student achievements?
5. Most schools are either more or less bureaucratic than the participants would like them to be. Does the discrepancy between perceived and

preferred bureaucratization in schools relate to the students' learning outcomes? Are there particular elements of bureaucratization for which the discrepancies are most pronounced?

Despite the negative connotations of the word *bureaucracy,* the theory appears to have strong implications for the improvement of administrative practice. Studies directed toward discovering exactly what those implications are will not be easy, but they are clearly needed in the interest of learning what administrators can do to improve student outcomes.

MASTERY QUIZ

To test your own recollection and understanding of the preceding chapter, complete the following sentences by selecting the best option for each item below without reference to the contents of the chapter. The correct answers appear in Appendix C, page 392.

1. All but one of the following are types of authority in Weber's theory; the exception is:
   a. legal.
   b. traditional.
   c. expert.
   d. charismatic.
2. The type of authority on which bureaucracy is based is:
   a. legal.
   b. traditional.
   c. expert.
   d. charismatic.
3. Of the following, the term that does not refer to a characteristic of bureaucracies is:
   a. tradition.
   b. hierarchy.
   c. impersonality.
   d. specialization.
4. The term that refers to impartiality in decision making is:
   a. tradition.
   b. hierarchy.
   c. impersonality.
   d. specialization.
5. The term that refers to stratification of positions is:
   a. tradition.
   b. hierarchy.
   c. impersonality.
   d. specialization.
6. Of the following pairs of terms, the one that is not a set of bureaucratic characteristics is:
   a. regulations—documentation.
   b. specialization—hierarchy.
   c. resource control—impersonality.
   d. efficiency—rationality.
7. According to Weberian theory, the presence of impersonality tends to:
   a. reduce the number of rules.
   b. increase goal displacement.

     c. reduce organizational rationality.

     d. increase documentation.

8. Bureaucracy is, according to this theory:

     a. the most humanistic form of organization.

     b. the most rational form of organization.

     c. the most desirable form of organization.

     d. the most coercive form of organization.

9. In contemporary American society:

     a. bureaucracies are no longer prevalent types of organizations.

     b. traditional organizations cannot be found.

     c. there are various types of bureaucracies.

     d. charismatic authority is no longer used.

10. Critics of Weberian theory maintain that the characteristics of bureaucracy:

     a. are not present in organizations.

     b. tend to increase organizational rationality.

     c. tend to reduce organizational efficiency.

     d. do not include hierarchy of offices.

EXERCISES

1. This chapter has introduced several terms that might be new to readers. Test your understanding of the terminology by indicating for each term in Column A the letter of the most nearly synonymous term from Column B. Answers are in Appendix C, page 392.

A

_____ 1. traditional authority	_____ 6. impersonality
_____ 2. charisma	_____ 7. documentation
_____ 3. hierarchy	_____ 8. efficiency
_____ 4. office	_____ 9. rationality
_____ 5. specialization	_____ 10. bureaucracy

B

a. impartiality	j. division of labor
b. position entailing rights and obligations	k. greatest good for greatest number
c. goal-directedness	l. dominance based on persuasion
d. regulations	m. personal magnetism
e. written records	n. one's own best interests
f. dominance by right of inheritance	o. organization based on legal dominance
g. standardization	p. career orientation
h. expertise	q. formalization
i. cost-effectiveness	r. stratification

2. Select one of the studies cited in this chapter and find it in the library. After reading it carefully, outline the study by specifying the following elements:
   a. author and source (bibliographic reference).
   b. conceptual framework (1–3 sentences).
   c. hypotheses or research questions.
   d. sample (number and type of units of analysis).
   e. instrument(s) or data-gathering method.
   f. scoring and data analysis.
   g. findings (results of data analysis).
   h. author's conclusions(s).
   This "brief" can take only one or two pages if the outlining is concise enough.

3. Consider an organization in which you now work or recently worked in terms of its bureaucratization. For five of the characteristics of the pure bureaucracy (hierarchy, rules, specialization, impersonality, and written records), briefly describe the extent to which it is present and the extent to which it is absent in the organization. Then answer the following questions:
   a. In the Hoy-Miskel typology cited in this chapter, which type of bureaucracy is the organization you described? Explain.
   b. If you were in a position to change that organization, would you increase or decrease its degree of bureaucratization? Explain.

4. Based on your understanding of bureaucracy theory and of organizational life,
   a. generate three potentially testable hypotheses that can be deduced from this theory, and underscore all the variables in the hypotheses.
   b. select one of those hypotheses and think through how you might test it empirically. Jot some notes on your thoughts so that the research design can be discussed in class.

5. Select one of the questions posed at the end of the chapter and consider how one might conduct an empirical study to find an answer. More specifically, convert the question into one or more hypotheses and specify how one could operationalize each of the variables mentioned. If necessary, review Chapter 1 for the meanings of the technical terms.

REFERENCES

Major Sources

Gerth, H. H., & Mills, C. W. (Eds. & trans.). *From Max Weber: Essays in sociology.* New York: Oxford University Press, 1958.

Mouzelis, N. *Organization and bureaucracy: An analysis of modern theories.* Chicago: Aldine, 1967.

Weber, M. Bureaucracy. In J. A. Litterer (Ed.), *Organizations: Structure and behavior.* New York: Wiley, 1963, 40–50.

Weber, M. *The theory of social and economic organization* A. M. Henderson & T. Parsons, (Trans.). New York: Macmillan, Free Press, 1964.

Wrong, D. (Ed.). *Max Weber*. Englewood Cliffs, N.J.: Prentice-Hall, 1970.

Related Conceptual Literature

Blau, P. M. Critical remarks on Weber's theory of authority. In D. Wrong (Ed.), *Max Weber*. Englewood Cliffs, N.J.: Prentice-Hall, 1970a, 147–165.

Blau, P. M. Weber's theory of bureaucracy. In D. Wrong (Ed.), *Max Weber*. Englewood Cliffs, N.J.: Prentice-Hall, 1970b, 141–145.

Brown, R. H. Bureaucracy as praxis: Toward a political phenomenology of formal organizations. *Administrative Science Quarterly*, 1978, *23*, 365–382.

French, J. R. P., Jr., & Raven, B. The bases of social power. In D. Cartwright (Ed.), *Studies in social power*. Ann Arbor: University of Michigan Press, 1959, 150–167.

Hills, J. Some comments on James G. Anderson's "Bureaucratic Rules—Bearers of Organizational Authority." *Educational Administration Quarterly*, 1966, *2*, 243–261.

Hoy, W. K., & Miskel, C. G. Bureaucracy and the school. *Educational administration: Theory, research, and practice*. New York: Random House, 1978, 48–68, chap. 4.

Merton, R. K. Bureaucratic structure and personality. In J. A. Litterer (Ed.), *Organizations: Structure and behavior*. New York: Wiley, 1963, 373–380.

Related Research: General

Ben-David, J. The professional role of the physician in bureaucratized medicine: A study in role conflict. *Human Relations*, 1958, *2*, 255–257.

Blau, P. M.; Heydebrand, W. V.; & Stauffer, R. E. The structure of small bureaucracies. *American Sociological Review*, 1966, *31*, 179–191.

Denhardt, R. Bureaucratic socialization and organizational accommodation. *Administrative Science Quarterly*, 1968, *13*, 441–450.

Engel, G. V. The effect of bureaucracy on the professional autonomy of the physician. *Journal of Health and Social Behavior*, 1969, *16*, 30–41.

Gouldner, A. *Patterns of industrial bureaucracy*. New York: Free Press, 1954.

Hall, R. H. The concept of bureaucracy: An empirical assessment. *American Journal of Sociology*, 1963, *69*, 32–40.

Hall, R. H. Professionalism and bureaucratization. *American Sociological Review*, 1968, *33*, 92–104.

Mansfield, R. Bureaucracy and centralization: An examination of organizational structure. *Administrative Science Quarterly*, 1973, *18*, 477–488.

Reissman, L. A study of role conceptions in bureaucracy. *Social Forces*, 1949, *27*, 305–310.

Selznik, P. *TVA and the grass roots: A study in the sociology of formal organization*. New York: Harper & Row, Harper Torchbooks, 1966.

Udy, S. V., Jr. "Bureaucracy" and "rationality" in Weber's organization theory: An empirical study. *American Sociological Review*, 1959, *24*, 791–795.

Related Research: Education

Anderson, B. D. Bureaucracy in schools and student alienation. *Canadian Administrator*, 1971a, *11*.

————.Socio-economic status of students and school bureaucratization. *Educational Administration Quarterly*, 1971b, 7, 12–24.

Anderson, B. D., & Tissier, R. M. Social class, school bureaucratization and educational aspirations. *Educational Administration Quarterly*, 1973, *9*, 34–49.

Bishop, L. K., & George, J. R. Organizational structure: A factor analysis of structural characteristics of public elementary and secondary schools. *Educational Administration Quarterly*, 1973, *9*, 66–80.

Brennan, B. Principals as bureaucrats. *Journal of Educational Administration*, 1973, *11*, 171–177.

Bridges, E. M. Bureaucratic role and socialization: The influence of experience on the elementary principal. *Educational Administration Quarterly*, 1965, *1*,19–28.

Corwin, R. G. Professional persons in public organizations. *Educational Administration Quarterly*, 1965, *1*, 1–22.

Hoy, W. K.; Newland, W.; & Blazovsky, R. Subordinate loyalty to superior, esprit, and aspects of bureaucratic structure. *Educational Administration Quarterly*, 1977, *13*, 71–85.

Isherwood, G., & Hoy, W. K. Bureaucracy, powerlessness, and teacher work values. *Journal of Educational Administration*, 1973, *11*, 124–138.

McKay, D. A. An empirical study of bureaucratic dimensions and their relation to other characteristics of school organization. Unpublished doctoral dissertation, University of Alberta, 1964.

Meyers, R. W. Bureaucratic theory and schools. *Administrator's Notebook*, 1972, *20*, 1–4.

Moeller, G. H., & Charters, W. W. Relation of bureaucratization to sense of power among teachers. *Administrative Science Quarterly*, 1966, *10*, 444–465.

Nirenberg, J. A comparison of the management systems of traditional and alternative public high schools. *Educational Administration Quarterly*, 1977, *13*, 86–104.

Punch, K. Interschool variation in bureaucratization. *Journal of Educational Administration*, 1970, *8*, 124–134.

Scott, L. K. Charismatic authority in the rational organization. *Educational Administration Quarterly*, 1978, *14*, 43–62.

Willower, D. J. Relationships between teacher union strength and the distribution of influence attributed to hierarchical levels in school districts. *Peabody Journal of Education*, 1975, *52*, 150–154.

Chapter 5
Reciprocal Influence

COMPLIANCE THEORY

Societies and nations vary in many ways. They differ particularly in the kinds of social order they maintain—in the nature of the relationship between those who hold power and those who are subject to that power.

The recognition that in some nations the power holders rely on physical force, whereas in others they depend more on persuasion or material rewards, is insufficient to characterize a social order. The orientation of the populace to that power is equally important. A military dictatorship that is strongly supported by the citizens, for example, would be very different from a military dictatorship toward which the citizens were hostile and antagonistic; these two nations would have different types of social order.

Are organizations within one society also differentiated with respect to the relationship between the kind of power used and the orientations of those influenced by that power? In other words, do organizations have different kinds of "social order"?

People often think of social power as a one-way relationship: some have power and others are subject to it. Recently, however, theorists have come to recognize that power is a reciprocal relationship: power is

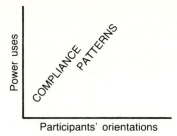

Figure 5–1   Compliance as a Blend of Power Uses and Participants'
Orientations

attributed to some individuals by people who are influenced by those
individuals. That is, one individual's intentions can influence the behavior
of others only to the extent that those others accede to that individual's
directives. *Social power* refers to a relationship, not a quality that some
have and others lack.

Amitai Etzioni (1961; 1975) emphasized this reciprocity in his analysis
of organizations, noting that they differ in the nature of this reciprocal
relationship. The organizational analogy of a societal social order is the
compliance pattern of the organization. Like a social order, a compliance
pattern is a relationship between the uses of power by high officials and
the perceptions or psychological orientations of those subject to control. It
must be emphasized that *compliance*, as the term is used in this theory,
does not refer to obedience, conformity, docility, or any other behavioral
response; it refers to a *relationship*. The interpretation of compliance as a
reciprocal relationship—as a blend of power uses and lower participants'
orientations—can be illustrated as in Figure 5–1, in which power and
orientations to it are depicted as separate axes, with compliance emerging
from the interaction between the two.

THE CORE OF COMPLIANCE THEORY

Organizations existing within societies have been classified in several ways on
the basis of various sets of attributes. One particularly useful system of
classification is based on compliance patterns (Etzioni, 1961; 1975). Thus
compliance theory is largely a *taxonomy*—a theoretical classification system or
typology—that offers insights about the nature and functioning of
organizations.

This taxonomy, as noted earlier, is derived from the merging of two key
elements: the *types of power* used by those in influential positions; and the
types of orientations toward that power held by persons in subordinate

positions. *Power* is defined as one person's ability to influence another person. *Power positions* are those offices or heirarchical levels having occupants who regularly have access to the means of influence. Those who are subject to influence by persons in power positions are the *lower participants*. The lower participants in turn have different types of orientations or attitudes toward the organization and its power uses; they have different types of *involvement* in the organization. Stated theoretically, then, the compliance pattern of an organization is a blend of the type of power used by those in power positions and the type of involvement lower participants have.

From the foregoing, it can be seen that the classification of organizations by compliance (or social order) depends on two subclassification schemes: a typology of power and a typology of involvement. Both of these are delineated in this section in order to specify the compliance taxonomy constituting the core of this theory.

Major Constructs in Etzioni's Theory of Compliance

POWER

Power has been defined as "an actor's ability to induce or influence another actor to carry out his [or her] directives or any other norms [she or] he supports" (Etzioni, 1975:4). The use of power entails the control of various means of influence; it entails granting or withholding rewards and punishments vis-à-vis those who are to be influenced. Power, then, is of different types, according to the means used to influence others' behavior. The three types specified in this theory are coercive, remunerative, and normative.

Coercive power is that in which physical force is used as the means of control. Coercive power might take the form of physical punishments such as the threat or actual application of beatings, confinement, starvation, and pain; or of physical rewards such as the granting of food, water, freedom of movement, and so forth. Custodial prisons and prisoner-of-war camps are the most striking examples of organizations in which coercive power is used; but it is well known that some holders of power positions in schools, hospitals, and mental institutions also resort to coercive power.

Remunerative power is that in which material resources are granted or withheld as the means of control. Remunerative power might take the form of material punishments such as salary cuts, reductions in fringe benefits or perquisites, and the withholding of contributions; or of material rewards such as tips, gifts, wage increases, services, and promotion (that is, access to more money). Profit-making businesses and households with domestic employees are relatively clear examples of organizations relying on remunerative means; but schools or class units operating on token economies, if the tokens are exchangeable for material goods, also employ remunerative power.

Normative power is that in which symbolic means are granted or withheld in the exercise of control. Normative punishments could include disapproval, withdrawal of acceptance, withholding of status symbols, and low ratings (if these are not tied to wages); normative rewards would include the granting of privileges, praise, status symbols, compliments, and high ratings (if these are not related to wages). Examples of organizations in which normative power is used are religious sects, professional associations, and some voluntary service organizations. Power holders in schools tend to use normative means as well.

A distinctive feature of Etzioni's power typology is that each type of power—coercive, remunerative, and normative—is a complete continuum with a positive and a negative end. Each type of power, in other words, can be used for both rewards and punishments. As Etzioni pointed out, organizations can be classified according to their power structure, taking into consideration which type of power is predominant, how strongly that power is emphasized, and which type of power constitutes the secondary means of control (Etzioni, 1975).

INVOLVEMENT

As noted earlier, *involvement* refers to the orientation of lower participants toward the organization and its uses of power. This orientation is both affective (emotional) and cognitive (evaluative); that is, involvement encompasses both feelings and thoughts. The lower participants are all persons who are affected or influenced by the power uses of those who have access to the means of power. On the one hand, the lower participants might be clients, such as patients in hospitals, inmates in prisons, students in schools, or recipients of welfare checks. On the other hand, the lower participants might be employees, such as orderlies and nurses in hospitals, guards in prisons, teachers in schools, and social caseworkers. All those who are subject to the will of others within the organization are lower participants, and their involvement is a function of both their attitudes or feelings and their reasons for being part of the organization. The three types of involvement, each with its affective and cognitive dimensions, have been specified in the theory as alienative, calculative, and moral.

Alienative involvement is an orientation characterized by intensely negative or hostile feelings and involuntary presence by the lower participants. Generally speaking, such groups as prisoners of war, political prisoners, and slaves can be expected to have alienative involvement in the organizations of which they are lower participants. Of course, some students are alienative in their involvement in schools; they are participants despite their own wishes, and they have hostile feelings.

Calculative involvement is an orientation characterized by neutral feelings (positive or negative, but not intense) and by an intention to gain material benefits by participation and obedience. In general, assembly line workers, domestic employees, salespersons who do not personally endorse their products, and unskilled service personnel would be expected to be calculative in their involvement; they are participants primarily for the money or material goods. Students who are attentive mainly because their school success will provide access to high-paying jobs can be regarded as calculative in their involvement in school.

Moral involvement is an orientation in which the participants' feelings are intensely positive and in which the reason for participation is a strong belief in the values for which the organization stands. Parishioners in church, loyal political party members, devotees of an art form, and followers of a gang leader generally have high moral involvement in their respective organizations. Students seeking enlightenment for its own sake would, of course, be morally involved in their schools.

A distinctive feature of Etzioni's involvement typology is that it incorporates both the cognitive and the affective elements of participants' orientations—both motives and feelings. Chances are that the lower participants within any one organization will be somewhat varied in their involvements and that individuals' involvements will shift to a degree from time to time. In each organization, however, there is a predominant type of participant involvement. Thus organizations can be classified according to the modal or typical involvement of lower participants or the particular mix of types of involvement that predominate.

To summarize, the taxonomy of organizational compliance incorporates two subclassifications: means of power and involvement of lower participants. The types of power, according to the means employed, are: coercive (physical), remunerative (material), and normative (symbolic). The types of involvement, according to affect and motive, are: alienative (involuntary), calculative (materialistic), and moral (idealistically committed). It is the blending or merging of these two typologies, however, that constitutes the essence of the compliance taxonomy, as will be explained in further detail.

Relationships Among Constructs in Compliance Theory

Having reviewed the subclasses of power and involvement, we can now consider the blending of the two typologies to generate a taxonomy of compliance patterns. As illustrated in Figure 5–2, an expansion of the earlier diagram, the three types of power combined with the three types of involvement yield nine patterns of compliance. Theoretically, then, there are nine types of organizations in terms of compliance patterns. Three of these types, however, are found more frequently than the other six. These are the congruent types (highlighted in capital letters in Figure 5–2)—organizations in which the kind of power used is appropriate for the kind of involvement lower participants have.

CONGRUENT COMPLIANCE TYPES

It would probably be possible through empirical research to locate some organizations of each compliance type, even the most unlikely. One striking example of incongruence is the Nazi prison camps in which, as described by Bettelheim (1943), the prisoners actually loved and identified with the very

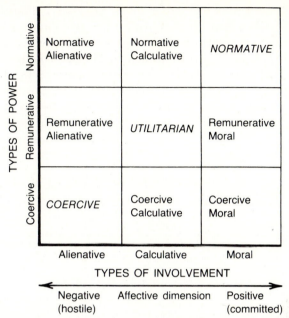

Figure 5–2   Compliance Patterns in Organizations: Nine Ideal Types

guards who brutalized them. At the opposite extreme of incongruence might be an innovative school for "incorrigibles" in which the teachers used only symbolic rewards in relating to students who were initially intensely hostile and antagonistic. Although examples of incongruence can readily be found, the most numerous and stable organizations are those having congruent power-involvement patterns. These organizations are called coercive, utilitarian, and normative.

Coercive organizations are those in which the power used is coercive (physical) *and* the lower participants' involvement is predominantly alienative (hostile).

Utilitarian organizations are those in which the power used is mainly remunerative (material) *and* the lower participants are mainly calculative (materialistic).

Normative organizations are those in which the power base is mainly normative (symbolic) *and* the lower participants' involvement is mainly moral (committed).

This classification of organizations on the basis of their compliance patterns can serve as a useful framework for the comparative analysis of organizations. It must be recognized, however, that the nine categories are ideal types. Organizations can be conceptualized in terms of pure or ideal compliance types, but in reality organizations are likely to be approximations of those types rather than unmitigated actualizations of any types. Existing organizations are likely to operate on the basis of a predominant type of power along with a secondary and perhaps even tertiary type of power. Similarly, the lower participants are likely to be characterized by a predominant type of involvement along with a secondary and perhaps a tertiary type.

Broad classification of all organizations can be done on the basis of primary power and modal involvement (nine types); more refined classification, however, would entail, within each major class, a subclassification based on secondary power and secondary involvement. Table 5–1 is an illustration of the range of categories that can be generated by the compliance taxonomy when secondary means and orientations are taken into consideration. The three

Table 5–1 TYPES OF ORGANIZATIONS IN TERMS OF PURE AND MIXED POWER AND INVOLVEMENT

COERCIVE ORGANIZATIONS	UTILITARIAN ORGANIZATIONS	NORMATIVE ORGANIZATIONS
*Coercive power Alienative involvement	*Remunerative power Calculative involvement	*Normative power Moral involvement
Coercive/remunerative power Alienative involvement	Remunerative/coercive power Calculative involvement	Normative/coercive power Moral involvement
*Coercive/remunerative power Alienative/calculative involvement	*Remunerative/coercive power Calculative/alienative involvement	*Normative/coercive power Moral/alienative involvement
Coercive/remunerative power Alienative/moral involvement	Remunerative/coercive power Calculative/moral involvement	Normative/coercive power Moral/calculative involvement
Coercive/normative power Alienative involvement	Remunerative/normative power Calculative involvement	Normative/remunerative power Moral involvement only
Coercive/normative power Alienative/calculative involvement	Remunerative/normative power Calculative/alienative involvement	Normative/remunerative power Moral/alienative involvement
*Coercive/normative power Alienative/moral involvement	*Remunerative/normative power Calculative/moral involvement	*Normative/remunerative power Moral/calculative involvement

*All types so marked are considered congruent.

congruent types alone generate 21 subtypes of organizations and the six noncongruent types would generate an additional 42 subtypes.

It is clear that the compliance taxonomy provides a basis for some sophisticated differentiation of organizations, which can then serve as a foundation for comparing organizations in terms of a broad range of other features—their effectiveness, their goals, their leadership styles, and their efficiency, among others. The core of the theory, however, is the taxonomy itself and the relationships intrinsic to it. These can be summarized as in the following propositions, all of which were drawn from Etzioni (1969).

Major Propositions of Compliance Theory

1. Organizations that differ in the *means of control* they apply also differ systematically in the *involvement* of their lower participants.
   a. Organizations applying *coercive* control generally have *alienative* lower participants.
   b. Organizations that apply *remunerative* means of control tend to have *calculative* lower participants.
   c. Organizations utilizing *normative* power typically have lower participants who are *moral* in their involvement.
2. Deviations from the congruence of power and involvement are unstable.
   a. Organizations tend to shift their compliance from incongruent to congruent relationships.
   b. Organizations that have congruent compliance patterns tend to resist factors pushing them toward incongruent compliance patterns.
   c. The three congruent types of organizations are found more frequently than the other six types. The congruent types are *coercive* (see 1a), *utilitarian* (see 1b), and *normative* (see 1c).

FURTHER DISCUSSION OF COMPLIANCE THEORY

Since the initial publication of this framework as a core taxonomy, compliance theory has been expanded to encompass many correlates of compliance patterns and to include some of the dynamics of social change. In this section we shall consider some of the expansions of the original theory—specifically, some of the correlates of compliance and some aspects of congruence and change. In addition, some related classification systems will be reviewed briefly in relation to the compliance taxonomy, and some measurement issues associated with this framework will be discussed. The unique strengths of this theory will be summarized in conclusion of this section.

Expansions of Compliance Theory

In the first and second editions of A *Comparative Analysis of Complex Organizations* (Etzioni, 1961; 1975), Etzioni examined the application of compliance theory to comparisons of organizations in terms of many aspects of their structure and functioning. Expansions on the core theory include analyses of organizational elites and their behavior patterns, participant activities and opinions, and environmental factors. Some of the major additions to the theory can be summarized in the form of propositions, as follows.

1. Organizations that have similar compliance structures tend to have similar *goals*, and organizations with similar goals tend to have similar compliance patterns:
   a. Organizations having a coercive compliance pattern generally have *order goals*—the segregation, the punishment, or even the elimination of deviants.
   b. Organizations having utilitarian compliance patterns generally have *economic goals*—the production of goods and services for those outside the organization.
   c. Organizations having normative compliance patterns generally have *culture goals*—the creation, preservation, and use of symbolic objects and the socialization of others to valuing the culture's symbolic objects.
2. Organizations that have congruent compliance structures are more effective and efficient in achieving their respective order, economic, and culture goals than are incongruent organizations.
3. Organizations that have different compliance patterns differ systematically in the frequency with which participants' *consensus* is likely to be found. Consensus refers both to lower participants' agreement with power holders and to agreement among lower participants:
   a. Coercive organizations most often have low participant consensus with respect to most organizational matters.
   b. Utilitarian organizations are typified by high participant consensus on procedural matters but low consensus in other areas.
   c. Normative organizations are generally characterized by high participant consensus, particularly with reference to ultimate values, goals, policies, and strategies for attaining goals.
4. The compliance patterns of organizations are associated with the *communication* flow within those organizations:
   a. In coercive organizations communication about *instrumental* activities is generally downward (from power holders to lower participants), whereas *expressive* communication is horizontal (among the lower participants).
   b. In utilitarian organizations *instrumental* communication tends to be both downward and upward, whereas *expressive* communication is usually horizontal.

c. Normative organizations are typified by horizontal *instrumental* communication (and relatively little instrumental activity), but *expressive* communication is typically downward (as from religious leader to congregation).

These generalizations and others pertinent to compliance theory were explored in considerable detail by the theorist himself (Etzioni, 1975) and by some empirical researchers. They are summarized for convenient reference in Table 5–2.

The theory has also been expanded with reference to analyses of sweeping social changes (see Etzioni, 1968). Skinner and Winckler (1969), for example, analyzed twenty years of modern Chinese history in terms of a compliance cycle model of social change. As Etzioni stated: "The main point is obvious: The more alienating usages of power [in a society] tend to split the societal units, increase the distances among the divisions, increase the instrumental or manipulative orientation, and lessen the opportunity for authentic leadership or participation—in short, decrease the possibility of an active society" (Etzioni, 1968:370). The notion of a tendency toward congruence has important implications for the dynamics of change, both within organizations and in entire societies. As noted earlier, the relationship between power and involvement is reciprocal. For example, an increase in coerciveness generates increases in alienation; by the same token, increasing alienation renders other power forms less effective and therefore increases coercive controls. Thus the compliance taxonomy can serve as a foundation for far-reaching organizational and societal analysis.

Related Classifications

Numerous theorists have developed classification systems for analytic purposes. Scholars have classified organizations, power bases, and participants' orientations, all for purposes of developing theories to describe, explain, or predict organizational realities. A few of these taxonomies and categorization schemes merit some consideration in relation to compliance theory.

One classification of organizations was generated by Blau and Scott (1962) on the basis of the primary beneficiaries of organizational activities. The four types of organizations they identified are: mutual benefit associations, business concerns, service organizations, and commonweal organizations (those serving the public at large). Although this classification in somewhat compatible with the compliance framework (see Hall, Haas, and Johnson, 1967), it does not have intrinsic implications for the interpretation of structural or dynamic aspects of organizational life. In this respect the Blau-Scott framework is more a flat classification scheme than a taxonomy.

Max Weber, whose theory of bureaucracies was discussed at length in Chapter 4, generated a taxonomy of the bases of legitimate power (authority). The reader will recall that the three types of power specified by Weber are

Table 5–2 SOME CORRELATES OF COMPLIANCE IN COMPLEX ORGANIZATIONS

COMPLIANCE	POWER	INVOLVEMENT	GOALS	CONSENSUS	COMMUNICATION	LEADERSHIP
NORMATIVE	Normative	Moral	Cultural	Generally: high	Instrumental: horizontal Expressive: downward	Instrumental: informal Expressive: formal
				Instrumental: high	Instrumental: down	Instrumental: formal
UTILITARIAN	Remunerative	Calculative	Economic	Expressive: low	Expressive: horizontal	Expressive: informal
COERCIVE	Coercive	Alienative	Order	Generally: low	Instrumental: downward Expressive: horizontal	Instrumental: formal Expressive: informal

charismatic authority, traditional authority, and legal authority (see Blau, 1970). As Etzioni noted, however, Weber was more concerned with business and governmental organizations than with the full range of social systems encompassed in the compliance framework (Etzioni, 1975). Furthermore, as Etzioni observed, coercive power, which is not part of Weber's taxonomy, is often viewed as legitimate by the lower participants—as in the case of police power, for example, or the control of mental patients (Etzioni, 1975).

Another taxonomy of the bases of power—a classic that is cited in most contemporary analyses of interpersonal influence—was developed by French and Raven (1959). This typology, based essentially on the kinds of resources that influential persons presumably can grant or withhold, specifies five types of power: coercive power (punishment), reward power (gratification), expert power (expertise), legitimate power (position or authority), and referent power (personal approval). In a sense this framework is richer than Etzioni's three-class framework, and its inclusion of expert power makes it particularly interesting for analyses of organizations. It is inconsistent, however, in that one class is exclusively negative (coercive), another exclusively positive (reward), and the remaining three either positive or negative. The latter three categories would probably be considered normative in Etzioni's scheme, but the former two are not compatible with the compliance typology.

A classification of lower participants' orientations was developed by William Gamson (1968) in conjunction with his theory of social conflict. This categorization is based on the degree of trust that the lower participants, called "potential partisans" in this theory, invest in the "authorities" to make equitable decisions. The three orientations toward authorities—alienated (great distrust), neutral (moderate distrust or trust), and confident (high trust)—are clearly compatible with the compliance involvement dimension (see Etzioni, 1975). In fact, *trust* can be interpreted as including both the cognitive and the affective aspects of participants' orientations, just as the involvement dimension does. Gamson's conflict theory is a compelling complement to the compliance framework and would be of particular interest to students of educational organizations.

Measurement Issues

Compliance theory, like all other theories, is associated with some problems of valid and reliable measurement. One such problem is related to the duality of the involvement dimension. As defined by Etzioni, involvement pertains both to *affect* (a continuum ranging from strongly negative to strongly positive) and to *cognition* or judgment (a categorical dimension). Whereas *alienative* describes a feeling, *calculative* and *moral* imply motives. Thus there is an intrinsic inconsistency that creates a measurement problem: Is involvement a continuous (ratio) scale construct or a nominal (categorical) construct? This is particularly significant in the middle range, since calculativeness may be compatible, but is certainly not synonymous, with mildly positive or negative feelings. In conducting studies to test this theory, researchers need to clarify which aspect of involvement they are measuring.

Another problem centers on the credibility of the sources of information. If the power holders are the research informants, as in a study by Hall, Haas, and Johnson (1967), one questions their ability to discern and reveal honestly the lower participants' orientations. If the lower participants are the subjects, as in most of the research, one questions the so-called halo effect—the tendency to rationalize responses or to perceive power uses in accordance with one's own positive or negative feelings. Perhaps the most convincing research strategy would be to have some lower participants report the power uses and other lower participants report their own orientations. This would be a legitimate research strategy for this theory, since the unit of analysis must be the organization as a whole or complete departments within an organization.

Unique Strengths of Compliance Theory

Despite some measurement problems and the fact that other taxonomies have been developed, the compliance framework is a powerful tool for understanding the dynamics of organizational life. First, as noted, it is a distinctive blend of two important elements: power and involvement. Second, it is a rich framework in that it permits the very refined differentiation of organizations that are superficially similar. Third, it includes explicit propositions that are readily amenable to empirical verification. Finally, it has strong implications for organizational design and the dynamics of change. Although this theory is seldom treated extensively in educational administration textbooks, it seems to be a compelling one, particularly for interpreting educators' practices.

RESEARCH RELATED TO COMPLIANCE THEORY

The most exhaustive and thoughtful review of the compliance research up to 1974 was conducted by Etzioni himself and reported in his 1975 book. Some of the studies he reviewed there and others conducted since then are summarized in this section. We shall consider first the empirical studies conducted in social spheres other than education and then those focusing on education specifically. Since there is no standard set of instruments associated with this theory, measurement techniques will be discussed when appropriate in conjunction with some of the studies.

Compliance Research in Varied Settings

Compliance theory has been tested empirically in a wide variety of organizations. Studies have focused either on the employees within the organization or on the clients subject to the organization's control.

EMPLOYEES

The tests of core propositions of the theory have generally been supportive of the congruence between supervisors' power uses and employees' involvement. For example, Mitzner (1968), in a study of over fifty diverse organizations, found that employees in the coercive organizations were the least committed to organizational values, whereas those in the normative organizations were the most strongly committed.

In a study of several different utilitarian organizations, Franklin (1975) found that more utilitarian power usage was associated with less committed staff. In these utilitarian organizations, normative power as a secondary means of influence was related to commitment for the white-collar employees but not for the blue-collar workers, whose involvement can be assumed to be more calculative. A related result was obtained by Miller (1967) in a study of research scientists in one normative and one utilitarian facility. The more remunerative the perceived power, the more negative the involvement. Since scientists can be assumed to be generally moral in their orientation toward scientific research, the use of noncongruent power seems to have generated negative attitudes.

In a study of a normative youth-oriented service organization shortly after a public crisis, Brager (1969) found that employees' organizational rank was directly related to their degree of commitment to the organization's values. Furthermore, the more positively involved (that is, morally committed) the lower participants were, the more strenuously they opposed the organization's utilitarian survival strategies, regardless of their degree of participation in the strategic decisions. Once again, the use of incongruent means seems to have generated adverse feelings.

CLIENTS

Many tests of the basic congruence proposition have focused on the lower participants who are served by the organization's employees. These studies have been quite consistent in their supportive findings. Thus, for patients in hospitals (Julian, 1968); inmates in prisons (Berk, 1966; Bigelow & Driscoll, 1973); and army recruits (Randell, 1968) more coercive power was associated with more negative involvement, and more normative power with more positive involvement. In one study army draftees were found to be significantly more negative toward their units than were high school students toward their schools, but the draftees were significantly more committed to the national defense (Randell, 1968).

Berk's interesting study of three different minimum-security prisons—one exclusively custodial, one having some treatment programs, and one rehabilitative—also tested and supported some other compliance hypotheses. At the custodial prison, the longer the stay and the more socially involved the inmates, the more negative their orientations. At the rehabilitation prison, longer term and greater social involvement were associated with more positive orientations. Furthermore, the custodial inmates chose more authoritarian, psychologically distant, and punitive informal leaders, whereas the rehabilitation prisoners chose more numerous, less authoritarian, and more accessible informal leaders (Berk, 1966). Julian (1966) also tested related hypotheses, this time in five hospitals. He found that communication blockage (both upward and downward) between patients and doctors was most frequent at the most coercive hospital and least frequent at the most normative hospital.

In sum, the core propositions have been consistently supported in the empirical research; several of the propositions constituting expansions of compliance theory have found support as well. The studies cited here, as well as many others, have been summarized and discussed extensively by Etzioni (1975).

Compliance Research in Schools, Colleges, and Universities

The relevant studies conducted in schools, colleges, and universities can be summarized in terms of the same two categories: research on faculty as the lower participants, and research on students as the lower participants.

EMPLOYEES
Only one investigation of faculty members was found that directly concerns a basic proposition in compliance theory. Schaupp (1971) found that in one school district the principals' power uses were generally congruent with the teachers' involvement; however, remunerative power was associated with negative involvement. As with the research scientists in the study cited earlier (Miller, 1967), the use of remunerative power with a basically morally involved group seems to generate negative feelings.

Some studies of staff in educational institutions have centered on relationships other than those suggested in the core propositions. Hodgkins and Herriott (1970), interpreting normative means of power as the principal's submitting teachers' suggestions to a faculty vote, found in accordance with their prediction that the higher the grade level, the less frequently this occurs. Since this report was based on a secondary analysis of data that had originally been collected for another purpose, there was no information about equivalent voting at the grade level or within departments in secondary schools.

In an examination of faculty in a university, Gamson (1966) found natural science professors to be more instrumental and less expressive in their interactions with students than were social science professors. These behavior patterns were interpreted as congruent with the cognitive goals of the natural science programs in contrast to the value (culture) goals of the social science programs.

On the basis of data collected from administrators in special education programs, Berjohn (1973) found a relationship between the degree of power-involvement discrepancy and the frequency of administrative problems, particularly in the areas of staff management, resource acquisition, and resource allocation. A follow-up study based on *staff* reports of power and involvement in relation to *administrators'* perceptions of problems would be an instructive contribution to the literature.

Warren (1968, 1969) used the French and Raven taxonomy as the conceptual framework for his study of teachers, but his findings seem relevant here. The responses of over five hundred teachers in 18 elementary schools were analyzed in terms of the types of peer groups present (job-specific, consensual, or diffuse); the degree of teachers' attitudinal and behavioral conformity; and the bases of power used by the principal. Warren's interesting findings include the following.

1. In nine of the schools, three or more of the five types of power were frequently used, whereas in two of the schools none of the power types was used much.
2. The broader the range of power bases used, the greater the teachers' overall conformity.
3. Behavioral conformity without attitudinal conformity was related to coercive power, whereas attitudinal conformity was related to the uses of referent, legitimate, and expert power, all of which would be considered normative in the compliance framework.
4. Coercive and legitimate power bases were associated with attitudinal conformity only when consensual peer groups were present, but referent power was associated with high attitudinal conformity regardless of the presence or types of teacher peer groups.

These two studies lend strong though indirect support to the compliance congruence proposition as well as to the consensus proposition.

An unusual study of administrative behaviors warrants mention here. As part of a broader project in developing taxonomies (Griffiths, 1969), Hencley and Chambers (1969) incorporated Etzioni's types of goals, power, involvement, and tasks to generate an 81-part classification system for sorting units of observable administrative behaviors. They then categorized the 90 "observable taxonomic units" that had been identified in the broader project (see Lutz, 1969) and found that 27 of the 81 theoretical categories were used. Since the sample of behavioral units was small and the dispersion of these units among categories relatively broad, the authors concluded both that the compliance taxonomy is a fruitful one for observational research and that important hypotheses about administrative behavior can be tested with this classification tool. The most frequent of the 90 administrative behaviors were classified as (1) order goals/normative power/calculative involvement/routine tasks and (2) economic goals/normative power/calculative involvement/routine tasks.

A body of research that is closely related to the compliance framework centers on teachers' orientations toward students. Using the 20-item Pupil Control Ideology (PCI) questionnaire (Willower, Eidell, & Hoy 1967) completed by teachers, researchers have found that teachers range from highly custodial to highly humanistic in their orientations toward students and that teacher custodialism is associated with a closed or repressive climate with respect to teachers' interactions with the principal (Hoy & Appleberry, 1970). As described by Hoy and Miskel (1978: 154), teachers having custodial orientations are likely to be found in schools characterized by high disengagement of faculty, low esprit among faculty, high principal aloofness, and low principal thrust. Although there is little research on teachers pupil control *behavior*, the PCI studies to date suggest that the principal's behavior sets a tone for the school that is reflected in teachers' ideologies regarding student control.

CLIENTS

The congruence proposition of compliance theory has been tested and to some extent supported in inquiries about student-teacher relationships. Sanders (1969), for example, found secondary school teachers' power uses to be congruent with students' involvement, as predicted from the theory. Of particular interest in this study is that the teachers in the nine schools provided the information on their power uses, and the students reported their own orientations; thus contamination of the variables was minimized. In a replication of this study, Zachary (1976) found the power-involvement congruence to exist only when the two vocational schools were removed from his 20-school sample. Further, the schools' goals were not congruent with their compliance patterns as predicted from the theory. The data suggested that the culture goals and order goals prevalent in the high schools are intrinsically incompatible.

In research using the PCI questionnaire described earlier, student alienation was found to be associated with teachers' control orientations. Both student normlessness and student sense of powerlessness were related to the degree of custodialism in teachers' viewpoints (Hoy, 1972).

An unusual test of the congruence proposition was conducted among doctoral students in eight different fields at one university. The authors reported that frequent coercive power and rare normative power used by faculty members were associated with students' alienative involvement, that normative and remunerative means of influence were used with roughly equal frequency, and that students were equally moral and calculative in their involvement (Azim & Boseman, 1975). Coerciveness and alienativeness, however, as Etzioni defined those terms, are inconceivable in a graduate program. Thus the instrumentation and interpretations in this study are questionable.

In sum, the compliance research in educational institutions, though limited in quantity and varied in quality, provides general support for the theory and confirms its usefulness as a framework for the analysis of schools. Clearly, additional research is needed before firm conclusions can be drawn.

Some important directions for further research are suggested in the next section.

IMPLICATIONS OF COMPLIANCE THEORY
FOR ENHANCING STUDENT LEARNING OUTCOMES

The issue of student discipline continues to be prominent in the education literature as well as in the popular press. This issue still occupies first place as an educational problem in public opinion surveys (for example, Gallup, 1980), at educators' professional development meetings, and in informal conversations. Without student discipline, the reasoning goes, education cannot take place.

In this book we are concerned with students' cognitive, affective, and psychomotor learnings and, in particular, with administrators' actions as they relate to those learnings. Thus we address the question of whether the theory treated in this chapter can be useful in generating knowledge about administrative effectiveness with regard to student achievement. Is compliance theory a potentially productive conceptual framework for generating knowledge about how administrators can have an active role in improving student learning outcomes?

To talk about student behavior in schools as a matter of student discipline is to direct attention toward the student as the originator and controller of her or his own actions. On this basis a body of literature has evolved concerning helping children learn to govern their own behavior, behavior modification techniques, and tactics for getting youngsters to conform to the teacher's preferences. To consider student behavior as a matter of compliance relationships, however, is to emphasize the reciprocity of student and teacher behavior and to bring to the fore the teacher's role in creating the social order of the school. Compliance theory maintains that the power holders—in this case, teachers and other school personnel—are at least equal partners in the establishment of a particular social order.

Teachers have available to them all three means of influence, which they use both punitively and rewardingly. In the coercive domain they can *and often do* punish by pushing or shaking children, twisting arms, paddling, confining children to a stimulus-free place, and standing over them in a threatening manner. Critical notes to parents and low grades can also be coercive punishments if the parents beat or confine their children on the basis of these messages from school. In the remunerative domain teachers can and often do punish by withholding privileges, withholding prizes or material tokens, and confiscating property. Here too, letters to parents and low grades can be remunerative means if the parents reduce allowances or curtail privileges as a result of these messages. In fact, to the extent that grades are treated as payments for conformity or deviant behavior or as the route to high-paying jobs, rather than simply as indicators of learning achievement, they are reduced from normative to remunerative means. In the normative domain teachers can and often do express disapproval, isolate, ridicule, and embarrass students, and withhold symbolic rewards such as stars, praise, or check marks.

The congruence proposition of compliance theory suggests that coercive punishment or reward generates intensely hostile feelings on the part of lower participants, whereas remunerative punishments or rewards only mildly affect attitudes, and normative punishment as well as reward might even generate positive feelings. For example, a teacher's slightly disapproving glance or an expression of disappointment might stir a youngster to greater commitment to the values of the highly respected teacher. Coercive punishment not only generates negative feelings but tends to supplant other means of punishment and reward as well; once used, coercive punishment is an ever present threat both to the individual so punished and to all others who have observed or heard of it. Remunerative punishment does not generally affect students' feelings much but does tend to foster goal displacement; students subject to this type of power often conform mainly for the sake of gaining, or at least not losing, material benefits and thus become calculative in their orientation toward school.

Just as teachers can affect students' involvement, students sometimes can affect teachers' uses of power to some extent. When students are alienated at the outset, normative and remunerative types of power are not fully effective means of influence. Thus some teachers, especially those who feel threatened by disobedience, resort to coercive control, thereby intensifying the already hostile feelings. Teachers are adults, however—people who are expected to have greater control of their own behavior than children do. Furthermore, as trained professionals, teachers are expected to behave rationally on the basis of knowledge rather than impulsively or instinctively. Teachers are usually in a position to change children's orientations, but children are less often in a position to change teachers' power uses or their own orientations.

Just as students' involvement is influenced by teachers' power, so teachers' involvement is influenced by supervisors' and administrators' power. Although some teachers are calculative from the start in their orientations toward schools—attracted by short hours, long vacations, tenure security, and so on— many, if not most, initially are morally involved: they are interested in helping children learn and committed to serving society at large. If these morally involved teachers are exposed to remunerative uses of administrative power, or if the reward and penalty system is based on student behavior control rather than student learning, they soon become calculative in their orientations. That is, if teachers are blocked in their efforts to advance students' learning, they often settle for the material benefits of a secure teaching job and sacrifice their idealistic aims. Similarly, if teachers are rewarded or penalized on the basis of their control of students' behavior, they will direct their energies primarily toward behavior control and tend to become coercive with students.

Thus the theory seems to have some clear implications for administrative action. First, uses of coercive power by teachers and other authority figures should be challenged as probably counterproductive, and the use of remunerative power should be minimized throughout the school. This suggests that administrators must become fully aware of the overt and covert means that teachers employ to influence youngsters and must encourage teachers to use appropriate normative means only. Second, since some teachers are unaware of the harmful effects of their power uses and of strategies for using normative power effectively, administrators should provide effective professional development programs. These should both clarify the harmful effects of coercion and remuneration and enhance teachers' skills in using normative power, especially normative rewards, effectively. Third, this administrative attempt to influence teachers' attitudes and behaviors must also be in accordance with compliance theory. That is, only normative means such as approval, status, growth opportunities, recognition, and the like (see Chapter 12) should be used by administrators in attempting to influence teachers' power uses with students. Finally, as the congruence between goals and compliance implies, the goals of the school should be unambiguously and exclusively cultural. Once any order goals (discipline) or economic goals (jobs or money) are introduced, they contaminate the culture goals (students' learning) that could prevail. In sum, it may well be that, instead of discipline being a prerequisite for learning, successful learning is a prerequisite for discipline.

These conjectures are, of course, primarily theoretical. There is little empirical evidence concerning the dynamic or causal aspects of the congruence between power and involvement or between goals and compliance. Some empirical questions remain to be answered through descriptive, longitudinal, and experimental research. These include the following:

1. Is there a relationship between the teacher-administrator compliance patterns of schools and the student-teacher compliance patterns?
2. In schools having similar student populations, is there a relationship between the student-teacher compliance relationship of the school and the students' learning outcomes? Do student-teacher compliance relationships differ in accordance with the racial, ethnic, or socioeconomic status of the student body?
3. In experimental situations with lower participants having similar attitudes initially, do coercive, remunerative, and normative punishment treatments relate to differential participant attitudes at the end of the experiment? If so, are the differences as predicted from compliance theory?
4. Within schools, what means of influence (coercive, remunerative, or normative) are used by those teachers whose students exhibit the greatest learning gains and by those whose students exhibit the fewest learning gains?

5. Can teachers, supervisors, and administrators learn to use normative power exclusively, without recourse to other means of influence? If so, what instructional strategies are effective in helping educators perfect normative behavior patterns?

Because of the salience of the discipline issue and the association in many people's minds between discipline and learning, compliance theory does seem to provide a promising direction for research. Carefully designed research conceptualized in terms of the compliance framework seems fruitful for producing knowledge about what administrators can do to enhance students' cognitive, affective, and skill-related learning.

MASTERY QUIZ

Without reference to any portions of the preceding chapter, complete each of the following sentences by writing the letter of the best completion on a piece of scrap paper. The correct answers are in Appendix C, page 392.

1. Of the following terms, the one that describes a type of power is:
   a. moral.
   b. utilitarian.
   c. calculative.
   d. remunerative.
2. Of the following terms, the one that describes a type of compliance is:
   a. moral.
   b. utilitarian.
   c. calculative.
   d. remunerative.
3. All but one of the following pairs of terms represent congruent power-involvement relationships. That one is:
   a. remunerative—calculative.
   b. cultural—moral.
   c. coercive—alienative.
   d. normative—moral.
4. The set of terms that refers to types of organizational goals is:
   a. coercive—remunerative—normative.
   b. economic—cultural—order.
   c. remunerative—utilitarian—calculative.
   d. alienative—calculative—moral.
5. All but one of the following are normative means of influence. The exception is:
   a. facial expressions.
   b. insulting remarks.
   c. gold stars.
   d. redeemable tokens.
6. Of the following terms, the one that is congruent with coercion is:
   a. remuneration.
   b. calculation.
   c. morality.
   d. alienation.

7. The pair of terms congruent with order goals is:
   a. normative—moral.
   b. remunerative—calculative.
   c. coercive—alienative.
   d. coercive—calculative.
8. The pair of terms congruent with culture goals is:
   a. normative—moral.
   b. remunerative—calculative.
   c. coercive—alienative.
   d. coercive—calculative.
9. Of the following punishments, the one that is coercive is:
   a. a harsh reprimand.
   b. a failing grade.
   c. a paddling.
   d. a dunce cap.
10. Of the following rewards, the one that can only be normative is:
    a. a high grade.
    b. a redeemable token.
    c. a smile.
    d. a complimentary note to parents.

EXERCISES

1. Ten organizations that were classified by Etzioni (1975:66–67) are listed. Assuming these organizations to be congruent types, indicate which compliance pattern is likely to prevail in each (coercive, utilitarian, or normative). The answers as specified by the theory appear in Appendix C, p. 392.

   _____ 1. farmers' organizations
   _____ 2. social clubs
   _____ 3. blue-collar industries
   _____ 4. prisons
   _____ 5. voluntary charity organizations
   _____ 6. colleges
   _____ 7. immigrant relocation centers
   _____ 8. concentration camps
   _____ 9. white-collar industries
   _____ 10. professional organizations

2. Recognizing that schools are primarily normative but varied in the degree to which they are purely normative, mixed, or incongruent types of organizations, think of a school or class situation that might fit each of the subcategories within the normative classification. See Table 5–1, column 3, for the seven subcategories. Write a brief vignette of three to five sentences to depict each. (*Note:* Recognizing that *schools* include military academies, elite prep schools, religion-affiliated education programs, two-

and four-year colleges, and prison training centers might help one conceptualize the compliance subtypes.)

3. Using compliance theory as the basis of your thinking, generate three testable hypotheses that you can deduce from the theory. For each hypothesis, identify all the variables for which data would be collected in an empirical study.

4. Analyze the school in which you currently work or recently worked in terms of compliance theory. Use the following questions as a guide to your analysis:
   a. Is it a congruent or incongruent type? Explain.
   b. Is it a pure or a mixed type? Explain.
   c. Could student achievement there be improved by increasing normative compliance relationships? If so or if not, explain.
   d. If you were (or are) the principal there, would you and could you increase the normative compliance relationships? If so, explain why and *how*. If not, explain why.

REFERENCES

Major Sources

Etzioni, A. *A comparative analysis of complex organizations.* Glencoe, Ill.: Free Press, 1961.

Etzioni, A. A basis for comparative analysis of complex organizations. In A. Etzioni (Ed.), *A sociological reader on complex organizations,* 2nd ed. New York: Holt, Rinehart and Winston, 1969, 59–76.

Etzioni, A. *A comparative analysis of complex organizations,* rev. ed. New York: Macmillan, Free Press, 1975.

Related Conceptual Literature

Bettelheim, B. Individual and mass behavior in extreme situations. *Journal of Abnormal Psychology,* 1943, 38, 417–452.

Blau, P. M., & Scott, W. R. *Formal organizations: A comparative approach.* San Francisco: Chandler, 1962.

Blau, P. M. Critical remarks on Weber's theory of authority. In D. Wrong (Ed.), *Max Weber.* Englewood Cliffs, N.J.: Prentice-Hall, 1970, 147–165.

Etzioni, A. *The active society: A theory of societal and political processes.* New York: Free Press, 1968.

French, J. R. P., Jr., & Raven, B. The bases of social power. In D. Cartwright (Ed.), *Studies in social power.* Ann Arbor: University of Michigan Press, 1959, 150–167.

Gallup, G. H. The 12th annual Gallup poll of the public's attitudes toward the public schools. *Phi Delta Kappan,* 1980, 62, 33–46.

Gamson, W. A. *Power and discontent.* Homewood, Ill.: Dorsey, 1968.

Skinner, G. W., & Winckler, E. A. Compliance succession in rural Communist China: A cyclical theory. In A. Etzioni (Ed.), *A sociological reader on complex organizations*, 2nd ed. New York: Holt, Rinehart and Winston, 1969, 410–438.

Related Research: General

Berk, B. B. Organizational goals and inmate organization. *American Journal of Sociology*, 1966, *71*, 522–534.

Bigelow, D. A., & Driscoll, R. H. Effect of minimizing coercion on the rehabilitation of prisoners. *Journal of Applied Psychology*, 1973, *57*, 10–14.

Brager, B. Commitment and conflict in a normative organization. *American Sociological Review*, 1969, *34*, 482–491.

Franklin, J. L. Power and commitment: An empirical assessment. *Human Relations*, 1975, *28*, 737–753.

Hall, R. M.; Haas, J. E.; & Johnson, N. J. An examination of the Blau-Scott and Etzioni typologies. *Administrative Science Quarterly*, 1967, *12*, 118–139.

Julian, J. Compliance patterns and communication blocks in complex organizations. *American Sociological Review*, 1966, *31*, 382–389.

Julian, J. Organizational involvement and social control. *Social Forces*, 1968, *47*, 12–16.

Miller, G. Professional in bureaucracy: Alienation among industrial scientists and engineers. *American Sociological Review*, 1967, *32*, 755–768.

Mitzner, M. An investigation of the relationship of prestige, compliance patterns and dogmatism to interpersonal perception of esteem in the chain of command of formal organization. Ph.D. dissertation, Emory University, 1968.

Randell, S. On some social influences of the military organization. In T. Agersnap (Ed.), *Contributions to the theory of organizations I*. Copenhagen: Scandinavian University Books, 1968, 58–74.

Related Research: Education

Azim, A. N., & Boseman, G. F. An empirical assessment of Etzioni's typology of power and involvement within a university setting. *Academy of Management Journal*, 1975, *18*, 680–689.

Berjohn, H. E. A study of special education district compliance patterns in Illinois. Ph.D. dissertation, Illinois State University, 1973 (Diss. Abstr. No. 73–22, 964).

Gamson, Z. F. Utilitarian and normative orientations toward education. *Sociology of Education*, 1966, *39*, 46–73.

Griffiths, D. E. (Ed.). *Developing taxonomies of organizational behavior in educational administration*. Chicago: Rand McNally, 1969.

Hencley, S. P., & Chambers, G. A. A taxonomy of organizational behavior based on compliance theory. In D. E. Griffiths (Ed.), *Developing taxonomies of organizational behavior in educational administration*. Chicago: Rand McNally, 1969, 94–127.

Hodgkins, B. J., & Herriott, R. Age-grade structure, goals and compliance in the school: An organizational analysis. *Sociology of Education*, 1970, *43*, 90–103.

Hoy, W. K. Dimensions of student alienation and characteristics of public high schools. *Interchange*, 1972, *3*, 38–51.

Hoy, W. K., & Appleberry, J. B. Teacher principal relationships in "humanistic" and "custodial" elementary schools. *Journal of Experimental Education*, 1970, *39*, 27–31.

Hoy, W. K., & Miskel, C. G. *Educational administration: Theory, research and practice.* New York: Random House, 1978, 151–160.

Lutz, F. W. The field study. In D. E. Griffiths (Ed.), *Developing taxonomies of organizational behavior in educational administration.* Chicago: Rand McNally, 1969, 26–62.

Sanders, I. R. Construction of instruments for measuring teacher control and student involvement and an empirical test of Etzioni's compliance relationships in public secondary schools. Ph.D. dissertation, Oklahoma State University, 1969 (Diss. Abstr. No. 70-21, 473).

Schaupp, F. W. Compliance patterns in a school system: A case study. Ph.D. dissertation, West Virginia University, 1971 (Diss. Abstr. No. 72-14, 059).

Warren, D. I. Power, visibility, and conformity in formal organizations. *American Sociological Review*, 1968, *33*, 951–970.

Warren, D. I. The effects of power bases and peer groups on conformity in formal organizations. *Administrative Science Quarterly*, 1969, *14*, 544–556.

Willower, D. J.; Eidell, T. L.; & Hoy, W. K. *The school and pupil control ideology* (Monograph No. 24). University Park: Pennsylvania State University, Educational Administration Department, 1967.

Zachary, R. A. The relationship between organizational goals and teacher-student compliance. Ph.D. dissertation, New York University, 1976.

Part IV
LEADERSHIP
IN ORGANIZATIONS

Leadership, whether it be directed toward nations, armed forces, informal groups, or large organizations, has been a topic of deep interest for centuries. It has engaged the attention of dramatists and poets, philosophers, historians, and politicians, among others. It is an inherent and perhaps inevitable feature of social interaction.

Social scientists have studied leadership extensively and from a variety of theoretical perspectives for the past several decades. Before 1960 most leadership research represented efforts to identify the key traits or personality characteristics of effective leaders. Because traits research failed to reveal a set of characteristics consistently associated with effectiveness, this approach was supplanted in the late 1950s by systematic analyses of the behavior patterns of persons in positions of leadership. Hundreds of studies conducted in the 1960s and 1970s have used this behavioral approach. In recognition of the fact that leaders' behavior patterns may change in accordance with the situations in which the leaders find themselves, however, scholars' attention has shifted most recently toward a situational or contingency approach to leadership research. The contingency perspective takes into consideration the interactive effects of a variety of factors, such as the leader's personality, her or his behaviors, the nature of the group, and the type of tasks performed. Although numerous studies are still conducted in the traitist and behavioral traditions, the contingency approach has captured the interest of most contemporary researchers.

Two of the prevalent approaches to leadership research are represented in this part. Chapter 6 focuses on leaders' behaviors as studied initially by scholars in the Ohio State University research program. Although the propositions are descriptive rather than explanatory, this framework offers important insights for school administrators. Chapter 7 examines a contingency approach to the analysis of leadership effectiveness. Important implications can be drawn for working with interactive groups in schools.

Chapter 6
A Behavioral Approach

THE LEADER BEHAVIOR FRAMEWORK

VIGNETTE NUMBER 1

At Piedmont Junior High School the department heads are assembled at the conference table where a meeting will begin at 10:00 A.M. The participants have their coffee or tea and note pads before them, and they are talking quietly. Two seats are empty—the one at the end of the table and one near the end of one side of the table.

At one minute before 10:00 the principal, Sandy Larchmont, enters briskly and takes the seat at the end of the table. "Well, good morning, all. I hope you are all well today," Larchmont says. "Perhaps we should get started, since I know you are all busy. Here's our agenda for this morning's meeting." A sheaf of papers is quickly passed around the table, and each person draws one sheet.

"As you know, the superintendent plans to launch a Management By Objectives plan for the district starting with a few pilot schools next year," the principal begins, "and I intend to have our school included in the initial group. I trust you all read the superintendent's memo and the plan for developing educational objectives that I worked out for our school."

At this point the door opens, and the late arrival closes it cautiously before hastening to the remaining empty seat. Larchmont nods a greeting to the newcomer while proceeding with the meeting. "Any problems with the time schedule I have worked out or the procedures for having your faculty members develop the objectives?"

... And so the meeting continues.

VIGNETTE NUMBER 2

At Hillcrest Middle School across town, a meeting of department heads will begin in about five minutes. The participants are milling about the staff lounge, some filling coffee cups while chatting, others riffling through books or notes. The principal, Curly Marlborough, is seated in one corner of the room in earnest conversation with a staff member. At 10:03 Marlborough glances around the room before saying, "Let's wait another few minutes to give Ev a chance to get here, since I know he's interested in this matter." Murmurs of assent follow this comment.

At 10:08 Marlborough suggests they begin. The staff members draw convenient seats into a rough approximation of a circle that includes Marlborough. "I'd like to know your reactions to the superintendent's memo about the projected Management By Objectives plan," the principal begins. "Any comments?"

Some discussion ensues, during which most of the participants have something to say. The general consensus is that the plan is a good idea and that the school should support it somehow.

Marlborough is about to speak when the door opens and Ev Johnson comes in. "Sorry I'm late," he offers, "but a conference with a parent ran longer than expected."

"No problem," Marlborough says. "Why not get yourself a cup of coffee and pull up a chair while we bring you up to date on the discussion."

Johnson settled, the meeting resumes with the principal's question: "Well, what do you see as the best way for us to proceed with the plan?"

... And the meeting continues, as we quietly exit.

Here we see two radically different examples of leadership as it can be exercised by a school principal. How would you describe the behavior of each principal? How might one capture the key differences between them? Which is the better leader?

Employees within an organization observe their supervisor's actions and reactions countless times in many different situations. Over a period of time they discern a pattern in the supervisor's behavior that tells them what to expect in future interactions. It would be difficult, however, for an outsider to learn how the supervisor behaves by asking one or several employees, since each has had different particular interactions with the leader and each is attuned to particular aspects of the leader's actions. Attaining a coherent impression of how the supervisor behaves might be difficult.

One important legacy of the leadership research work done at the Ohio State University in the 1950s is a conceptual framework for thinking about leaders' behavior patterns systematically. Like social psychologists before them, the Ohio State researchers found, through numerous empirical studies, that there are two major categories of actions by which any leader's behavior patterns can be described. These broad categories entail attending to the *system* and attending to the *individual people*. In other words, any job-related action in which a leader engages can be classified in one of these broad categories, as either primarily *system-oriented* or primarily *person-oriented*.

When one contemplates patterns of behavior, as opposed to individual actions, these broad categories can be viewed as independent dimensions of the leader's behavior. They are independent in that one class of behaviors does not necessarily affect the other. A leader may often perform system-oriented acts and may also perform person-oriented acts frequently. Knowing how often a leader engages in system-oriented actions does not help one predict the frequency of his or her person-oriented actions, and vice versa. If we imagine these two independent dimensions as intersecting at their midpoints, as in Figure 6–1, we can imagine four patterns of leader behavior.

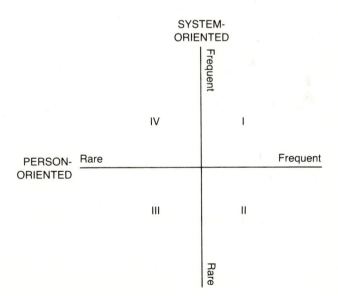

Figure 6–1   Four Styles of Leadership

In the upper right quadrant is the active leader whose actions are often system-oriented and often person-oriented. In quadrant II is the active leader whose behavior is often person-oriented but rarely system-oriented. In quadrant III is the inactive leader who rarely engages in either type of action. Finally, in quadrant IV, there is the active leader whose behavior is often directed toward the system but rarely toward the people in it. One could assign any leader a position somewhere in one of those quadrants by assessing the two key dimensions of that leader's behavior. We will return to the question of which behavior pattern is best later in this chapter.

THE ESSENCE OF THE LEADER BEHAVIOR FRAMEWORK

Numerous social psychologists—those studying small-group dynamics as well as those investigating work settings—have noted two key elements in interpersonal interactions. These dimensions of human interpersonal behavior have been given many names, such as the control dimension and the cathectic dimension (Brown, 1967); the instrumental dimension and the expressive dimension (Parsons, 1951; Bales, 1953); the nomothetic dimension and the idiographic dimension (Getzels & Guba, 1957); and the task-oriented and the relationship-oriented dimensions (Fiedler, 1967). In essence, actions can be seen as serving the dual purposes of getting things done and expressing feelings. In the leader behavior research, these two dimensions have usually been known as the *initiating structure* dimension and the *consideration* dimension, terms that have been associated with the leadership research program at the Ohio State University (Halpin, 1966). In this chapter, building on the work of Stogdill and Coons (1957) and Brown (1967), we have designated the task dimension *system orientation* and the relationship dimension *person orientation.*

According to the conceptual and empirical work of Ralph Stogdill, a leading member of the Ohio State research group, each of these major dimensions of behavior comprises six subsets of behaviors—six different categories of action that in combination yield each major dimension. In all there are 12 basic dimensions of leader behavior that can be subdivided into two broad categories.

Major Constructs in the Leader Behavior Framework

SYSTEM-ORIENTED BEHAVIOR

System-oriented behaviors are those directed primarily toward fulfilling the goals and accomplishing the tasks of the social system or organization. System orientation includes actions that are intended to clarify roles of the participants, establish patterns of interaction among the participants, specify and delineate the tasks to be accomplished, and focus participants' energies in the direction of organizational goals. Six categories of behavior make up the system orientation dimension of the leader's behavior pattern: production emphasis, initiating structure, representation, role assumption, persuasiveness, and superior orientation. As explicated by Stogdill (1963), these are defined and described as follows.

Production emphasis refers to those actions that are intended to increase the productive output of the group. This category includes such behaviors as encouraging overtime work and extra effort, pressuring people to work harder, and striving to surpass previous records of productivity.

Initiating structure refers to the establishment and clarification of roles and interaction patterns within the organization. It refers to those actions whereby leaders define their own role and let followers know what is expected of them. Initiation of structure includes such acts as scheduling the work that is to be done, assigning members of the group particular tasks, and establishing standards of performance.

Representation is the category of behaviors that entails acting as the spokesperson for the group. Such actions as publicizing the activities of the group, speaking up for the group at outside meetings, and furthering the group's interests with higher authorities are included in this category.

Role assumption refers to active exercise of the leadership position, as opposed to surrender of leadership to others. This category includes such actions as taking full charge in an emergency, exercising authority, making decisions about group members, and standing firm once a decision is made.

Persuasiveness refers to having firm convictions and convincing others of one's point of view. This class of behaviors includes such actions as explaining decisions convincingly, inducing others to cooperate, and influencing group members' attitudes.

Superior orientation includes those actions that serve to maintain cordial relations with superiors, exercise influence with them, and increase the leader's status within the organizational hierarchy. This category includes such behaviors as exercising influence with higher authorities, striving for promotion, and being friendly with superordinates.

These six types of behavior are aspects of the system orientation dimension of leader behavior. Each of the categories of action bears reference to the system as a whole more strongly than to the individual people within the system.

PERSON-ORIENTED BEHAVIOR

Person-oriented behaviors are those directed primarily toward satisfying the needs and preferences of the idiosyncratic individuals within the organization. This dimension of leadership refers to actions that are intended to express concern for and interest in the group members; to acknowledge their unique needs, talents and interests; to increase their comfort and satisfaction within the organization; and to support their individual growth and development. Six classes or categories of the leader's behavior constitute the person orientation dimension: tolerance of uncertainty, tolerance of freedom, consideration, demand reconciliation, integration, and predictive accuracy. As described by Stogdill (1963), these can be defined and illustrated as follows.

Tolerance of uncertainty refers to actions that show the leader's ability to accept postponement and indefiniteness without becoming anxious or upset. This category includes accepting delays, waiting patiently for the results of decisions, and showing calmness in the face of ambiguous situations.

Tolerance of freedom allows followers scope for their own initiative, decision making, and action. Behaviors such as encouraging independence in group members, respecting the competence and judgment of followers, and encouraging diversity are of this type.

Consideration is a category of behaviors that demonstrate the leader's regard for the comfort, well-being, status, and contributions of followers. Actions such as expressing friendliness and interest, consulting with group members and attending to their suggestions, and looking after the welfare of individual group members are included in this category.

Demand reconciliation is the class of actions that serve to reconcile conflicting demands on the leader's time and to reduce disorder within the organization. This category includes resolving complex problems efficiently, handling multiple details smoothly, and dealing with conflicting demands without becoming upset.

Integration is the type of action that serves to maintain a closely knit group and to resolve conflicts among participants. Behaviors such as settling intermember conflicts as they arise, maintaining a team spirit, and coordinating many individuals' interests at once are of this type.

Predictive accuracy is a set of behaviors that exhibit the leader's foresight and ability to anticipate outcomes. This category includes actions such as predicting problems and planning for them in advance, interpreting the trends of events correctly, and forecasting the outcomes of decisions.

These six types of behavior, all aspects of the person orientation dimension, are classes of action that bear reference to the people within the organization more strongly than to the organization as such.

Relationships Among Leader Behavior Constructs

As noted earlier, the two major classes of leader behavior—system-oriented action and person-oriented action—are independent of each other. At the same time, no individual action can be solely system oriented or solely person oriented. An interpersonal action can be directed primarily toward one or the other major factor, but it will always have some connotation of the other factor. Thus the categories of behavior defined here are predominantly but not exclusively either system oriented or person oriented.

Alan Brown (1967) has depicted this feature of the relationships among the major constructs in what he called a "circumplex model," as illustrated in Figure 6–2, an expansion on Figure 6–1. Figure 6–2 shows the two major dimensions of leader behavior intersecting at their zero points rather than at their midpoints. It illustrates the degree of relationship of each subcategory to both major dimensions. That is, if one were to drop a perpendicular line from any one point to both major dimensions—as illustrated by the dotted lines— one could see the extent to which that category relates to the system orientation dimension (the vertical axis) and the person orientation dimension (the horizontal axis). Note that when a straight line is drawn from the intersection of the two axes midway between the two major dimensions (that is, at a 45-degree

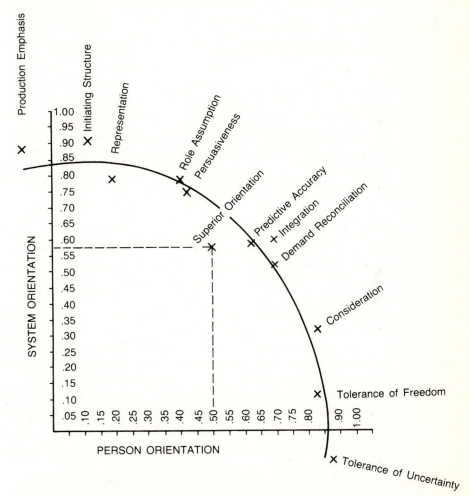

Figure 6–2   Relationships Between System Orientation Categories and Person Orientation Categories

angle to each), it separates the primarily system orientation constructs from the primarily person orientation constructs. Brown observed that the best line through all the points would be a quarter circle—hence, the *circumplex* model.

To summarize briefly, any job-related action undertaken by a person in a leadership position can be classified in one of twelve categories. Each of these twelve categories can in turn be classified into one of two major dimensions, depending on which it relates to most closely.

Major Propositions Associated with Leader Behavior

Since this is a descriptive rather than an explanatory framework, the key propositions are definitional. They assert the existence of particular phenomena and define the elements making up those phenomena.

1. Leaders' actions can be classified within two broad categories: system-oriented actions and person-oriented actions.
2. The system orientation category comprises six specific subcategories, as follows:
   a. System-oriented actions include production emphasis, initiating structure, representation, role assumption, persuasiveness, and superior orientation.
   b. These types of behavior range from the most predominantly system oriented to the least predominantly system oriented in the order listed in 2a.
3. The person orientation category comprises six specific subcategories, as follows:
   a. Person-oriented actions include tolerance of uncertainty, tolerance of freedom, consideration, demand reconciliation, integration, and predictive accuracy.
   b. These types of behavior range from the most predominantly person oriented to the least predominantly person oriented in the order listed in 3a.

On the basis of the circumplex model, Brown (1967) noted that the overall pattern of a leader's behavior can be defined by the relationship between the two major dimensions. Thus a person's *leadership style* (overall pattern) can be more system oriented than person oriented, more person oriented than system oriented, or a balanced combination of both, as represented in quadrant I of Figure 6–1 shown earlier. Brown called this balanced pattern of leadership a *transactional style*. Brown's insights suggest a fourth set of definitional propositions:

4. Leaders exhibit one of three styles in their pattern of behavior over time:
   a. Leaders who exhibit system-oriented action significantly more often than they engage in person-oriented action have a system-oriented style.

b. Leaders who exhibit person-oriented behavior significantly more frequently than they engage in system-oriented behavior have a person-oriented style.
c. Leaders who engage in system-oriented and person-oriented behaviors with approximately equal frequency have a transactional style.

Although this conceptual framework contains no explanatory propositions that would guide one's predictions about which leadership style is most effective, there is a substantial body of research to indicate that a highly transactional style—one characterized by very frequent system-oriented behavior and very frequent person-oriented behavior—is associated with most measures of effectiveness. Earlier we raised the question of which principal, Sandy Larchmont or Curly Marlborough, is the better leader. The vignettes were intended to portray Larchmont as having a system-oriented style and Marlborough as having a person-oriented style. If the brief episodes described were typical of the styles of the two leaders, chances are that each could benefit from some behavioral characteristics of the other.

DISCUSSION OF THE LEADER BEHAVIOR FRAMEWORK

The leader behavior framework highlighted in this chapter is a descriptive framework, not an explanatory theory. It lacks propositional statements about the relationships between leaders' behavioral styles and other phenomena, although it provides a comprehensive conceptual scheme for classifying both behaviors and leaders. This framework represents a highly empirical approach, entailing the development of instruments with which to describe and quantify leaders' behaviors. Therefore, many of the theoretical issues that have been explored in the leadership literature concern the nature and meaning of the measures that have been developed. Although one of the measures will be described in some detail later, the broader measurement issues can be explored briefly here. Another set of theoretical issues includes those associated with generating explanatory theories on the basis of the results of research in which leader behavior descriptions were used. We will consider these two types of issues—measurement issues and theory development issues—separately in this section.

Measurement Issues

One question posed by many of the scholars contemplating leader behavior is whether the two major factors, system orientation and person orientation, are in fact independent of each other (see Schriesheim, House, & Kerr, 1976; Lowin, Hrapchak, & Kavanagh, 1969; Wiessenberg & Kavanagh, 1972). In the early development of instruments to measure leader behavior, a statistical treatment called factor analysis was used to analyze pilot test responses and to select items that yielded two statistically independent clusters, which were called initiating structure and consideration (Halpin, 1966:86–90). In the empirical research using these instruments or variations of them, however, the two factors have often been found to be significantly related (see Schriesheim, House, & Kerr, 1976:304–305), sometimes positively and sometimes negatively. This has led researchers to question the independence of the factors and to analyze in detail the nature of the instruments used for assessing leaders' behaviors.

One feature of all of the measures developed in conjunction with the Ohio State leadership research program is that the questionnaire items call for some inferences on the part of respondents regarding the leader's intentions or the purposes of the leader's actions. That is, respondents do not indicate the frequency of specific observable acts, such as greeting a subordinate or inquiring after the subordinate's progress; instead, they indicate the frequency of a type of action, such as making subordinates feel comfortable or encouraging increased productivity. In other words, respondents are asked not for purely objective reports of their leader's behavior, but for interpretations of that behavior.

The distinction between objective and inferential items can be illustrated by means of one item of each type. A statement such as, "The principal speaks to each teacher individually as the teachers arrive at school," calls for an objective response: anyone could observe this action and report how frequently it occurs. On the other hand, a statement such as, "The principal is interested in all the teachers as individuals," calls for an interpretation on the part of respondents: the act of greeting teachers when they arrive may or may not indicate interest in the teachers as individuals. To report the extent of the principal's interest is to make assumptions about the principal's feelings.

Because of the inferential nature of so many of the items on the leader behavior description questionnaires, these instruments are subject to contamination by nonobjective factors, such as whether the respondents like or dislike the leader being described. A respondent's liking or disliking of the leader probably influences that respondent's interpretation of specific actions as socially desirable or undesirable. This element of nonobjectivity might explain some of the significant relationships found between the two statistically independent (orthogonal) factors in individual empirical studies.

Some of the measurement instruments developed in conjunction with the Ohio State research program are the Leader Behavior Description Questionnaire (LBDQ) to assess the initiating structure and consideration dimensions of leaders' behaviors (Hemphill & Coons, 1950); the Supervisory Behavior Description (SBD) to measure subordinates' descriptions of their supervisor's structuring and consideration (Fleishman, 1953); the Leadership Orientation Questionnaire (LOQ) to quantify the leaders' own attitudes regarding structuring and consideration leadership behaviors (Fleishman, 1953); and Form XII of the Leader Behavior Description Questionnaire (LBDQ-12) to assess twelve dimensions of the leader's behavior (Stogdill, 1963). These questionnaires, though somewhat similar and purported to operationalize the same constructs, have some differences that confound the research findings.

The discrepant research findings reported in the literature on relationships between the initiating structure and consideration dimensions stimulated Schriesheim and Kerr (1974) to examine the instruments and their related research findings in detail. They concluded that the measures developed by Fleishman (the SBD and its companion measure, the LOQ) include in their structuring dimension items related to leaders' punitiveness and authoritarianism—elements that are not a necessary part of structuring behavior. A review of the research, as summarized by Schriesheim, House, and Kerr (1976:304–305) indicates that studies using the SBD measure (Fleishman) have generally yielded negative but low correlations, whereas studies using the LBDQ (Hemphill and Coons) have generally yielded positive and high correlations between the two major dimensions. In another analysis of the research using these instruments, Schriesheim and Kerr (1974) concluded that the LBDQ-12 (Stogdill, 1963) has the best reliability and validity of the four measures mentioned. The point is that researchers examining leader behavior in relation to other variables should be fully aware of the differences among measures and should bear these differences in mind when interpreting their findings.

In a sense, the leader behavior measures might be considered analogous to a set of thermometers. A thermometer provides a measure of the extent to which something—in this case, heat—is present in a body of matter; but without a theoretical basis for interpreting the temperature found, the thermometer is of limited value. The leader behavior measures provide an indication of the extent to which something—in this case, initiation of structure and expression of consideration—is present in the leader's behavior pattern; but without a theoretical basis for interpreting the initiating structure and consideration scores, the measures are of limited value. Like a set of thermometers designed to measure temperatures of different entities (such as liquids, solids, or human beings), the leader behavior instruments measure somewhat different aspects of leadership behavior patterns.

Theory Development

Because of the limited utility of a measurement device in the absence of an underlying explanatory theory, several scholars have offered theories to explain or predict relationships between leader behavior and other phenomena. Most of the theoretical frameworks proposed have been derived from the sets of relationships observed in the leader behavior research.

Yukl (1971), for example, examined reported relationships between dimensions of leader behavior (consideration, initiating structure, and decision centralization) and the group's performance within the organization. He proposed that the leader's behavior patterns affect situational variables (subordinate motivation, task-role organization, and subordinate skill levels) that in turn affect the quality and quantity of subordinates' performance.

The work of Kerr et al. (1974) is another example of theory development based on reported research findings. These theorists focused their view of the research on relationships of leader behaviors to subordinates' performance and to subordinates' satisfaction. More specifically, they examined factors that have been found to moderate or influence the relationships between leader behaviors and those outcomes. Their conclusions were stated in the form of two major propositions:

> Proposition 1. The more subordinates depend on the leader to provide valued or needed services, the higher the positive relationship will be between leader behavior measures and subordinate satisfaction and performance (Kerr et al., 1974:75).
>
> Proposition 2. The more the leader is able to provide subordinates with valued, needed, or expected services, the higher the positive relationships will be between leader behavior measures and subordinate satisfaction and performance (Kerr et al., 1974:76).

These propositions were further explicated by means of ten hypotheses specifying aspects of subordinates' dependencies, needs, and values, as well as conditions of the leader's ability to provide the relevant services. Since this theory was generated as a synthesis of prior research findings, it merits further testing directed toward validation or modification.

Another of the theories developed on the basis of reported leader behavior (and other) research has been designated by House (1971) as the path-goal theory of leader effectiveness. This theory is closely identified with Vroom's expectancy theory of motivation (see Chapter 13) but incorporates the initiating structure and consideration dimensions of leader behavior in its propositional statements. In essence, the leader's *structuring* behavior is viewed as motivational to the extent that it clarifies for subordinates the best path to the goal of good performance; the leader's *considerate* behavior is viewed as motivational to the extent that it enhances the availability of extrinsic rewards for subordinates' efforts. House himself reported three studies in which numerous hypotheses deduced from the path-goal theory were supported (House, 1971); but the theory still requires further empirical testing in a variety of settings.

The leader behavior research has also stimulated the development of frameworks for the design of management training programs, of which the managerial grid approach (Blake & Mouton, 1964) is one of the best-known examples. The grid itself is a matrix derived from the two major leader behavior dimensions, as illustrated in Figure 6–3. The 9,9 cell of the matrix represents high task orientation as well as high relationship orientation; the 1,1 cell, by contrast, represents scant structuring in combination with little considerateness. Management trainees assess their own behavior in terms of the matrix and, after a week of workshop training, purportedly become more aware of and sensitive to the nature and impact of their leadership styles (see Bernardin & Alvares, 1976; Blake & Mouton, 1976). Thus the leader behavior framework and the measures associated with it have been useful in concep-

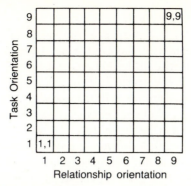

Figure 6–3   A Leader Behavior Matrix for Classifying Leadership Styles (Based on Blake & Mouton, 1964)

tualizing programs for the professional training of managers and in evaluating such training programs, as well as in theory development.

In summary, three theoretical frameworks based on research concerning leader behavior/organizational outcomes relationships have been proposed. These have centered on: (1) the leader's behavior patterns as the causes of situational factors that "cause" performance; (2) factors such as subordinates' dependencies and leaders' capacities that moderate the relationships between leader behavior and subordinate satisfaction and performance; and (3) the impact of leaders' behavior patterns on subordinates' work motivation. The bodies of research from which these theories emerged were studies using various related but not identical forms of leader behavior description questionnaires. Most of the background studies—and the theories evolving from them—have emphasized the initiating structure and consideration dimensions without reference to the subclasses of behavior that make up each.

The leader behavior theories and management training approach summarized here share the common feature of maintaining that both structuring and considerateness on the part of the leader enhance such outcomes as subordinate satisfaction and group productivity. In fact, the theories represent a common quest: they seek to explain why both system orientation and person orientation contribute to leader effectiveness.

RESEARCH ON LEADERS' BEHAVIORS

This review of the related empirical research centers first on the instruments that have been used to measure leader behavior, with special attention to the LBDQ-12, and then on studies that have been conducted in a variety of settings. The research in settings other than schools is examined first, and the research in educational institutions follows.

Instruments

As noted earlier, several descriptive measures of leader behavior were developed in conjunction with the Ohio State University leadership research program. These include the 30-item Leader Behavior Description Questionnaire (LBDQ; Hemphill & Coons, 1950; Halpin & Winer, 1957) the 48-item Supervisor Behavior Description (SBD; Fleishman, 1953), and a parallel 48-item Leader Orientation Questionnaire (LOQ) for measuring leaders' own attitudes toward leadership behavior (Fleishman, 1953). These three instruments, though differing slightly in item content, are scored for the two major dimensions of leader behavior, initiating structure and consideration.

The original LBDQ was later expanded to form the 100-item LBDQ–12 (Stogdill, 1963) for measuring the 12 dimensions of leader behavior specified earlier. For the 12 scales, 8 have 10 items each and 4 have 5 items each. Each item represents one of the 12 types of behavior; respondents, usually subordinates of the leader being described, indicate how frequently the leader exhibits each type of behavior on a 5-point scale ranging from "never" to "always." Usually each respondent's answers are scored by scales to yield 12 scores per respondent, and the scale scores of all respondents for each leader are averaged to yield 12 mean scores for each leader. The scale scores can then be combined for major factors by adding or averaging the relevant scale scores or by factor analysis to yield 2 scores per leader—one for system orientation and the other for person orientation. Both the instrument (Bureau of Business Research, 1962) and the manual for scoring it (Stogdill, 1963) are available from the Ohio State University.

The various versions of the leader behavior descriptions have been amenable to adaptations for diverse organizational settings and different groups of respondents. By means of slight changes in item wordings, the instruments can readily be used in industrial, military, educational, and other organizations; they can be used, also with slight modifications, for subordinates', superordinates' or self-report descriptions, as well as for descriptions of real and ideal leader behavior. Instrument scales and major factors have remained stable despite these slight changes, although a minimum of five subordinates' or superordinates' responses per leader is generally regarded as the best indicator of that leader's real behavior (Halpin, 1966). Analysis of the reliability and validity of the four leader behavior measures, provided by Schriesheim and Kerr (1974), indicates that the LBDQ–12 meets more of the criteria for excellence than do the other forms.

Leader Behavior Research in Varied Settings

Apart from the reports of instrument development (Fleishman, 1953; Stogdill, 1969; Stogdill, Goode, & Day, 1963, 1964), much of the leader behavior research literature focuses on relationships between leaders' behavior patterns and leaders' effectiveness. Other relevant bodies of research deal with factors that moderate the relationships between leaders' behavior and their effectiveness, with the effects of management training programs on managers' leader behavior patterns, and with personality characteristics associated with leaders' behaviors. These four areas of research are reviewed in this section.

LEADER BEHAVIOR AND LEADER EFFECTIVENESS

Effectiveness can, of course, be interpreted in a variety of ways. Three criteria of leader effectiveness that have been studied are group satisfaction, group productivity, and good performance ratings by superiors and subordinates.

The research consistently indicates that the leader's consideration (person orientation), as perceived by subordinates, relates to subordinates' job satisfaction (House, Filley, & Kerr, 1971; Hunt & Liebscher, 1973; Lowin, Hrapchak, & Kavanagh, 1969; Greene, 1975; Nealey & Blood, 1968; Schriesheim, House, & Kerr, 1976). Leader consideration is also inversely related to employee grievances and staff turnover, indirect indicators of dissatisfaction (Fleishman & Harris, 1962; Skinner, 1969).

The research is less consistent with regard to leaders' initiating structure (system orientation). Studies have found this dimension to be *directly* (positively) related to group satisfaction (Hunt & Liebscher, 1973; House, Filley, & Kerr, 1971; Schriesheim, House, & Kerr, 1976; House, 1971); *unrelated* to satisfaction (Greene, 1975; Lowin, Hrapchak, & Kavanagh, 1969); and *inversely* (negatively) related to satisfaction (Nealey & Blood, 1968; Fleishman & Harris, 1962; Skinner, 1969). It seems likely that both instrument variation and situational variation account for the inconsistent findings associated with leaders' initiating structure.

When leader effectiveness has been interpreted in terms of subordinates' performance or effectiveness ratings, the results have again been mixed. Some research indicates that both leader behavior dimensions relate directly to effectiveness (Fleishman & Simmons, 1970; Halpin, 1966; House, 1971). Other research demonstrates that leader structuring but not considerateness is related positively to effectiveness (Skinner, 1969). Some studies support the notion that leader considerateness but not structuring relates directly to effectiveness (Greene, 1975; Lowin, Hrapchak, & Kavanagh, 1969). To test the possibility that leaders experience conflicting expectations from superiors and subordinates, Graen and his colleagues studied behavior perceptions and preferences in relation to effectiveness ratings for both groups (Graen, Dansereau, & Minami, 1972). They found no conflict between the groups, although subordinates were found to value leader considerateness to a significantly greater degree than did superiors. It appears, then, that instrument variations as well as situational variations affect the relationships between leadership styles and leader effectiveness measures.

FACTORS MODERATING LEADER-FOLLOWER RELATIONSHIPS

The conflicting research evidence described here has led some researchers to seek variables that affect the magnitude and/or direction of relationships between leader behaviors and group performance or satisfaction. Some of the intervening variables that have been identified are employee independence from the organization (House & Kerr, 1973); the "group atmosphere" or quality of leader-member relations as perceived by the leader (Cummins, 1972); and job scope, task autonomy, role ambiguity, and intrinsic job satisfaction (House, 1971). Leader consideration has also been found to moderate the relationship between leader initiating structure and group performance (Cummins, 1971; House, 1971; Greene, 1975).

An unusual investigation of whether leader behavior causes or is caused by group performance and satisfaction was conducted by Greene (1975), who collected perceived leader behavior, subordinate satisfaction, and subordinate performance data at three times about one month apart. On the basis of cross-lagged analysis, he concluded that leader considerateness causes subordinate satisfaction, but that subordinate performance directly causes leader considerateness and inversely causes leader structuring. It seems that good group performance motivates the leader to behave more considerately, but poor group performance motivates the leader to initiate more structure. For highly considerate leaders, this structuring relates positively to subordinate satisfaction; but for nonconsiderate leaders structuring relates inversely to subordinate satisfaction.

EFFECTS OF MANAGEMENT TRAINING PROGRAMS

Professional development programs for practicing or prospective leaders are often intended to foster changes in the leaders' attitudes or behaviors. In evaluating the effects of two such programs, it was found that the participating leaders' attitudes supportive of consideration were increased (Hand & Slocum, 1972; Biggs, Huneryager, & Delaney, 1966), but that their support of initiating structure either remained unchanged (Hand & Slocum, 1972) or decreased (Biggs, Huneryager, & Delaney, 1966). Hand and Slocum, in their carefully designed study, also found changes in the behavior patterns of participants as much as two years after the training experience, with consideration having increased while initiating structure remained constant.

Bernardin and Alvares (1976), questioning the self-assessments associated with the managerial grid seminars (see Blake & Mouton, 1964, 1976), found no relationship between leaders' self-perceptions of behavior and their preferred conflict resolution strategies. This confirms several earlier research findings that self-reports of behavior and self-reports of attitudes about behavior do not relate systematically to others' perceptions or to any other variables (see, for example, Schriesheim & Kerr, 1974; Weissenberg & Kavanagh, 1972). It seems that leaders' self-reports are the least reliable source of data on leaders' actual (perceived) behaviors.

PERSONAL DETERMINANTS OF LEADER BEHAVIOR

Included among the leader characteristics found to be associated with behavior patterns are their levels of conceptual complexity (Streufert, Streufert, &

Castore, 1968) and their attitudes toward their least preferred co-worker, which might be another conceptual complexity measure (Rice & Chemers, 1975). The relatively complex (and more relationship-oriented) leaders seem to vary their behavior patterns in response to circumstances more than do the relatively simpler (and more task-oriented) leaders. Leaders' behavior patterns were also found to be affected by their need to express control (Biggs, Huneryager, & Delaney, 1966); and the assumption of the leadership role seems related to psychological dominance (Megargee, 1969).

The leader behavior research in industrial, military, and social service organizations can be summarized most concisely by noting that group satisfaction, group performance, and ratings of the leader are clearly related to consideration and probably related to initiating structure in complex ways. Although there are situational factors that affect the relationship between leader behaviors and group behaviors, and although the leader's behavior or behavioral variability appears related to some psychological characteristics, the leader's degree of overt considerateness seems amenable to influence by training. Few studies using the LBDQ-12 have examined in detail the differential effects of the subscales; instead, almost all the research has focused on the initiating structure and consideration dimensions of leader behavior.

Leader Behavior Research in School Settings

Educational administrators and supervisors have been studied extensively from the perspective of the leader behavior framework. Some of the earliest studies in education sought primarily to describe how educational leaders behave. Halpin (1955) and Evenson (1959) found that school administrators generally value consideration more highly than initiating structure and that there is little agreement between superordinates and subordinates about how the leader does behave. Educational leaders generally exhibit considerateness more frequently and structuring less frequently than do aircraft commanders (Halpin, 1955, 1959); and their self-descriptions do not coincide with others' descriptions of their behavior (Evenson, 1959).

Some research has been directed toward studying the effects of various leadership styles on faculty or school variables. Principals' consideration and initiating structure were found to be related to teachers' willingness to accept administrative directives (Kunz & Hoy, 1976), the structuring dimension being the more highly related to teachers' acceptance of directions. Principals' leader behavior was also found to be related to faculty consensus regarding satisfaction and school effectiveness (Brown & Anderson, 1967), with the consideration dimension being the better predictor in this case. Willower (1960) found that the relatively idiographic (person-oriented) principals in his sample perceived teachers as more professional than did the nomothetic (system-oriented) principals.

In an interesting experimental study of the effects of teachers' leader behavior on students' learning, Dawson and his colleagues found that the instructor's consideration behavior affected both the quantity and the quality of students' work, whereas the instructor's initiating structure behavior positively influenced only the quantity of student work (Dawson, Messé, & Phillips, 1972). In this study the instructor successfully replicated four different styles of leadership over a 10-week period, demonstrating that one's leader behavior pattern is subject to conscious control.

Leader behavior studies that included school administrators' personal characteristics have indicated that principals' sex and conceptual complexity affect their behavior patterns. In a study of 30 secondary schools, 15 of which were headed by women, the female principals were found to attain significantly higher representation, demand reconciliation, predictive accuracy, integration, and superior orientation scores, but lower tolerance of freedom scores than male principals (Morsink, 1969). Conceptually complex principals were perceived by their faculties to be more person oriented than their conceptually simpler counterparts (Silver, 1975; Burrus, 1979), with this behavior exhibited on five of the six LBDQ-12 subscales (Silver, 1975). System-oriented behavior was apparently not affected by conceptual complexity in either of these studies.

In sum, the research evidence seems to support Halpin's (1966) contention that both initiating structure and consideration are important behaviors for educational leaders. Table 6–1 summarizes the diverse findings reported in the leader behavior research. It lists the variables that were found to be related to leaders' structuring and considerate behaviors. The signs indicate the directions of the relationships found, with + representing a direct (positive)

Table 6–1 SOME CORRELATES OF LEADER CONSIDERATION AND INITIATING STRUCTURE

CONSIDERATION	INITIATING STRUCTURE
ANTECEDENTS	
Need to express control (0)	Need to express control (+)
Conceptual complexity (+)	Conceptual complexity (0)
Leadership style-LPC (+/−)	Leadership style-LPC (+/−/0)
Task structure (−)	Task structure (+)
Leader-member relations (+)	Leader-member relations (−)
GROUP AFFECT	
Faculty consensus (+)	Faculty consensus (+)
Employee satisfaction (+)	Employee satisfaction (+/−/0)
Zone of acceptance (0)	Zone of acceptance (+)
	Role clarity (+)
	Role ambiguity (−)
LEADER EFFECTIVENESS	
Group productivity (+)	Group productivity (+/−)
Grievances (−)	Grievances (+)
Employee turnover (−)	Employee turnover (+/−)
Leader proficiency (+/−)	Leader proficiency (+)
Organizational complexity (+)	

relationship and − indicating an inverse (negative) relationship. A zero (0) indicates that the relationship studied was found to be not statistically significant.

Figure 6–4 summarizes the research on variables that affect the relationships between leader behaviors and follower attitudes or performance. In this figure the signs in parentheses denote an increase in the degree of positive relationship (+) or a decrease in the degree of positive relationship (−). The dotted lines indicate which particular behavior-outcome relationship is affected by the moderating variables. In interpreting Figure 6–4 note that the variables in cell A (top, enclosed in dotted lines) have been found to intervene in the relationship between the leader's consideration and subordinates' job satisfaction. The negative sign beside *item a* indicates that the more the subordinates find the work to be intrinsically satisfying, the less relationship there is between leader consideration and subordinate job satisfaction. In other words, the more satisfying the work itself is, the less relevant the leader's considerateness is to employees' job attitudes. The positive sign beside *item b* indicates that the more certain or routine the work is, the greater the relationship between the leader's consideration and employees' job satisfaction. In other words, if the work itself is boring or routine, allowing for little initiative, then the leader's considerateness is an important factor in employees' job attitudes. The variables listed in cell B have been found to intervene in the relationship between leaders' initiating structure and employees' job satisfaction, and so forth.

IMPLICATIONS OF THE LEADER BEHAVIOR FRAMEWORK FOR ENHANCING STUDENT LEARNING OUTCOMES

Since the publication of the disheartening findings of the *Equality of Educational Opportunity* report (Coleman et al., 1966), numerous educational researchers have been striving to discover whether Coleman's conclusions were justified—whether schools in fact have little or no impact on student learning outcomes. Recent evidence seems to indicate that schools do make a difference and that the principal's behavior is one of the major factors influencing differential school effects, at least in urban elementary schools (Clark, 1980; Edmonds, 1979). Since few of the school effects studies have systematically examined principals' person orientation and system orientation in relation to student outcomes, however, we are left with a question about the viability of this framework for generating knowledge about the effects of principals on schools. Is the leader behavior description framework useful for producing knowledge about how administrators can enhance student learning outcomes?

Some closer examination of the two major dimensions of behavior and their constituent elements might help in resolving this question. We should note at the outset, however, that active and visible leadership in general is an

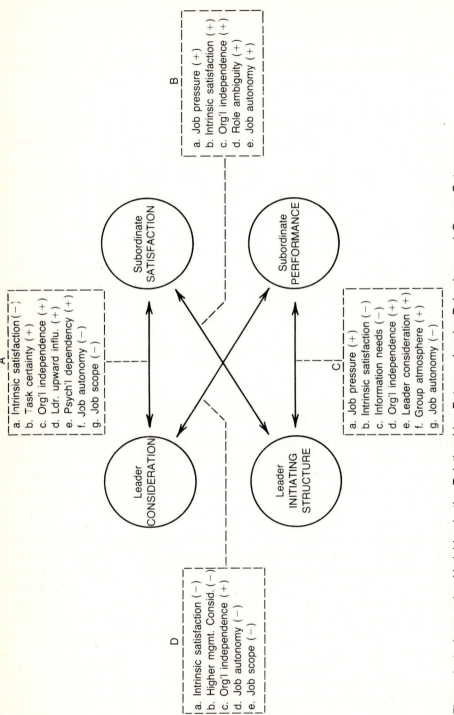

Figure 6–4 Intervening Variables in the Relationships Between Leader Behaviors and Group Outcomes

important key to either or both dimensions, since the leader behavior measures are based on how frequently each type of behavior is perceived to occur.

Person Orientation

Person-oriented leadership should not be confused with spinelessness or weakness, as some principals seem to believe (see Evenson, 1959), or with saccharine sweetness (Halpin, 1966). It is not a pro forma façade characterized by seasonal greeting cards to all staff members or by a routine, mindless "How're things?" every day. Rather, it is a sincere and genuine appreciation of the distinctiveness, the special competencies, and the unique needs of each individual. It is an intelligent, sensitive, and thoughtful understanding of the diverse capacities, talents, and interests of the group members that is not necessarily cloaked in smiles or glad-hand gestures.

The person orientation dimension, readers will recall, includes tolerance of uncertainty and tolerance of freedom, behavior patterns that would probably increase the teachers' professional autonomy, diversity, and independence of action in a school. If the teachers are highly skilled and aware of their special strengths, the principal's support of their independence would likely increase the extent to which unique teaching talents can be brought to bear on students' learnings.

The person orientation dimension also includes demand reconciliation and integration, behavior patterns that would probably increase the degree to which staff members can fulfill their own needs by means of school goal attainment. Principals who are accessible to teachers despite conflicting demands on their time can more readily respond to teachers' expressed professional needs. Similarly, principals who can invent original integrative solutions to problems of competing groups or individuals can more readily satisfy the professional needs of both parties in ways that are congruent with the school's goals.

This dimension also includes predictive accuracy, an ability to discern current trends and project them into the future as well as to plan for probable developments effectively. Principals exhibiting this capacity are likely to be able to prevent problems from arising through foresight and hence to be able to keep the organization functioning smoothly.

In sum, it appears that person-oriented leadership is a function of keen intelligence in combination with humaneness, rather than humanitarianism alone. There are logical reasons for believing that high person orientation on the part of the principal can indirectly enhance student learning outcomes.

System Orientation

System-oriented leadership, on the other hand, should not be confused with tyrannical authoritarianism, as some principals seem to believe (see Evenson, 1959), or with rigid, dogmatic dictatorship (Halpin, 1966). There is no inherent conflict between system-oriented and democratic leadership. Instead, system orientation implies a keen awareness of how to proceed toward a goal in orderly fashion, a deep understanding of the special talents and skills that will contribute to goal attainment, and a real commitment to the organization's goals. It suggests providing just enough structure and order to preclude chaos without oppressive restrictions or suppressive demands. System-oriented behaviors can well be facilitative and supportive without being at all punitive or confining.

The system orientation dimension, as described earlier, includes the initiation of structure, which can be interpreted as the creation of vehicles or channels whereby individuals' capabilities can best be expressed in the organizational context. Thus teachers with particular talents and interests are given a means to contribute to the school as a whole, and the school can benefit from individual members' strengths.

This dimension also includes production emphasis and persuasiveness, behavior patterns that include not only trying to increase or improve outcomes but also motivating others to contribute effort by convincing them of the desirability and feasibility of these outcomes through encouragement and persuasion of staff, rather than through inordinate demands.

Representation and role assumption, also aspects of system-oriented leadership, enhance the supportiveness of external groups and ensure that there is no leadership vacuum when decisions must be made. The principal who skillfully represents the interests of the school to higher authorities and to outside groups can substantially increase the material and symbolic resources available to the school for enriching instruction. Similarly, principals who see that decisions are made when necessary probably facilitate the smooth and uninterrupted functioning of professional staff.

Finally, superior orientation on the principal's part, like representation, can serve to increase the resources of the school and increase the rewards available to the teachers for performing well. Principals who have upward influence and are upwardly mobile might well be the best able to gather resources and to exercise autonomy within their own school.

The foregoing analysis seems to provide a logical basis for assuming that a high level of system orientation on the part of school leaders can indirectly affect student outcomes in a favorable direction. System-oriented leadership would have to be exercised in an intelligent and sensitive manner, however, if it is to enhance rather than ossify the school. It can serve to facilitate goal attainment without impeding gratification of needs for individual participants.

Needed Research

Although reason seems to indicate that both system orientation and person orientation of principals are related indirectly to student learning outcomes, empirical evidence is lacking. Some questions that remain to be answered through careful and inventive research are as follows:

1. Are there relationships between principals' leadership styles and their schools' student learning outcomes?
2. Which particular aspects of principals' leader behavior, if any, relate most closely to student outcomes of different types (that is, cognitive, affective, and psychomotor learning)?
3. Are there situational factors—such as teachers' attitudes and skills, school size or level, community locale, or student socioeconomic status—that affect relationships between principals' behavior patterns and student learning outcomes?

If research is generated to answer these and related questions, and if the presumed relationships are found to exist, then the prospects for improving school outcomes look excellent. There is some evidence to indicate that leaders' behavior patterns can be modified through training (Hand & Slocum, 1972) and that individuals can intentionally adopt particular behavior styles (Dawson, Messé, & Phillips, 1972). Therefore, leader training and selectivity in leader placement would be viable strategies for improving student learning outcomes. What remains to be done is the production of the relevant knowledge through extensive leader behavior research in schools.

MASTERY QUIZ

Try to select the best completion for each of the following sentences without reference to any of the preceding pages. The correct answers appear in Appendix C, page 392. If you can complete all ten correctly, you have indeed mastered the terminology of this descriptive framework.

1. The two major dimensions of leaders' behavior are:
   a. task orientation and system orientation.
   b. person orientation and system orientation.
   c. relationship orientation and person orientation.
   d. consideration and person orientation.
2. Of the following subcategories of behavior the one that is a type of system-oriented behavior is:
   a. consideration.   c. production emphasis.
   b. tolerance of freedom.   d. integration.
3. All but one of the following sets are pairs of system orientation terms. The exception is:
   a. initiating structure—role assumption.
   b. production emphasis—representation.
   c. demand reconciliation—consideration.
   d. persuasiveness—superior orientation.

4. The name for the category of actions that refers to organizing one's own time efficiently is:
   a. predictive accuracy.
   b. demand reconciliation.
   c. integration.
   d. role assumption.
5. Leadership actions that serve to strengthen the group's standing in the eyes of outsiders would be in the category called:
   a. representation.
   b. integration.
   c. predictive accuracy.
   d. consideration.
6. Of the following pairs of terms, the one that does not represent the person orientation factor is:
   a. tolerance of uncertainty—tolerance of freedom.
   b. predictive accuracy—consideration.
   c. demand reconciliation—integration.
   d. persuasiveness—superior orientation.
7. The name for the category of actions that serve to reconcile conflicting interests of groups within the organization is:
   a. demand reconciliation.
   b. persuasiveness.
   c. predictive accuracy.
   d. integration.
8. Those leadership actions that have the effect of making followers feel comfortable and respected belong in the category called:
   a. consideration.
   b. role assumption.
   c. persuasiveness.
   d. integration.
9. All but one of the following are sets of system orientation terms; the exception is:
   a. representation—role assumption—initiating structure.
   b. demand reconciliation—persuasiveness— production emphasis.
   c. superior orientation—persuasiveness—production emphasis.
   d. role assumption—persuasiveness—production emphasis.
10. Of the following groups of terms, the one that does not represent elements of a set is:
    a. demand reconciliation—consideration—tolerance of uncertainty.
    b. role assumption—initiating structure—integration.
    c. person-oriented—system-oriented—transactional.
    d. role assumption—representation—superior orientation.

EXERCISES

1. The 12 types of behavior that follow are those specified in this theoretical framework. Following them are 15 statements drawn from the LBDQ-12. Bearing in mind the definitions of the 12 categories (but without reference to the preceding pages), write on the line to the left of each item the name of the scale from which you think the statement was drawn. The correct answers appear in Appendix C, page 392.

Person Orientation	*System Orientation*
Consideration	Initiating structure
Tolerance of uncertainty	Production emphasis
Tolerance of freedom	Representation
Demand reconciliation	Role assumption
Integration	Persuasiveness
Predictive accuracy	Superior orientation

Note: Some of the following statements are worded negatively; they represent the opposite of what their category stands for.

1. _____ The leader gets along well with the people above her or him.

2. _____ The leader's arguments are convincing.

3. _____ The leader fails to take necessary action.

4. _____ The leader does little things to make it pleasant to be a member of the group.

5. _____ The leader speaks as the representative of the group.

6. _____ The leader accepts defeat in stride.

7. _____ The leader tries out his or her ideas in the group.

8. _____ The leader sees to it that the work of the group is coordinated.

9. _____ The leader gets things all tangled up.

10. _____ The leader takes full charge when emergencies arise.

11. _____ The leader is able to delay action until the proper time.

12. _____ The leader trusts the members to exercise good judgment.

13. _____ The leader urges the group to beat its previous record.

14. _____ The leader anticipates problems and plans for them.

15. _____ The leader can inspire enthusiasm for a project.

2. Regard each of the 12 categories listed in exercise 1 as a scale ranging from 1 (low) to 10 (high) so that the highest possible score for person orientation

or system orientation is 60. Then, bearing in mind the meaning of each scale, complete the following tasks:

    a. Assign the supervisor for whom you currently work (or recently worked) a score on each scale.

    b. By summing the scores for person orientation and for system orientation, specify the leadership style that supervisor exhibits.

    c. Using the same 12 scales, rate yourself in terms of your interactions with your subordinates (students, teachers, supervisors, or other administrators, depending on your position in the organization). Also, determine your own leadership style from these assessments.

    d. Consider what you think would be the ideal leader behavior for a person in your position, and assign a rating on each scale for the ideal leader.

    e. If there are discrepancies between c and d, how might you modify your own behavior (actions) in order to be more like your conception of an ideal leader?

3. To reinforce your understanding of Figure 6–4, consider the following intervening variables separately: Ad, Af, Bd, Cc, Ce, and Dd. For each of these, write a sentence stating what the diagram indicates and write a brief explanation (one or two sentences) of why that research finding seems logical.

4. Imagine that you have just become the principal of a school that has had a record of poor student performance on achievement tests and poor student attitudes regarding schooling and school property. Of course, you intend to bring about a dramatic change in the quality of the school. You plan to have a faculty meeting early in the year as the first step in bringing about the needed changes, and you intend to demonstrate from the very beginning of the year that you are a leader who would get a high score for system orientation and a high score for person orientation.

    List each facet of system orientation and each facet of person orientation down the left side of a page, leaving a few blank lines between items. Then beside each item write something you could do or say in conjunction with that first faculty meeting to demonstrate in an observable way the relevant type of behavior.

REFERENCES

Major Sources

Brown, A. F. Reactions to leadership. *Educational Administration Quarterly*, 1967, 3, 62–73.

Halpin, A. W. How leaders behave. *Theory and research in administration*. New York: Macmillan, 1966, 81–130.

Stogdill, R. M. & Coons, A. E. (Eds.). *Leader behavior: Its description and measurement.* Columbus, Ohio: Bureau of Business Research, Ohio State University, 1957.

Related Conceptual Literature

Bales, R. F. The equilibrium problem in small groups. In T. Parsons, R. F. Bales, & E. A. Shils (Eds.), *Working papers in the theory of action.* Glencoe, Ill.: Free Press, 1953, 11–161.

Blake, R. R., & Mouton, J. S. *The managerial grid.* Houston: Gulf Publishing, 1964.

Clark, D. L. An analysis of research, development, and evaluation reports on exceptional urban elementary schools. In *Why do some urban schools succeed?* Bloomington, Ind.: Phi Delta Kappa, 1980, 171–190.

Coleman, J. S.; Campbell, E. Q.; Hobson, C. J.; McPartland, J.; Mood, A. M.; Weinfeld, F. D.; & York, R. L. *Equality of educational opportunity.* Washington, D.C.: U.S. Government Printing Office, 1966.

Edmonds, R. Effective schools for the urban poor. *Educational Leadership,* 1979 (October), 15–24.

Fiedler, F. E. *A theory of leadership effectiveness.* New York: McGraw-Hall, 1967.

Getzels, J. W., & Guba, E. G. Social behavior and the administrative process. *The School Review,* 1957, 65, 423–441.

House, R. J. A path-goal theory of leader effectiveness. *Administrative Science Quarterly,* 1971, 16, 321–338.

Kerr, S.; Schriesheim, C. A.; Murphy, C. J.; & Stogdill, R. M. Toward a contingency theory of leadership based upon the Consideration and Initiating Structure literature. *Organizational Behavior and Human Performance,* 1974, 12, 62–82.

Parsons, T. *The social system.* Glencoe, Ill.: Free Press, 1951.

Stogdill, R. M. *Handbook of leadership.* New York: Free Press, 1974.

Yukl, G. Toward a behavioral theory of leadership. *Organizational Behavior and Human Performance,* 1971, 6, 414–440.

Related Research: General

Bernardin, H. J., & Alvares, K. M. The Managerial Grid as a predictor of conflict resolution method and managerial effectiveness. *Administrative Science Quarterly,* 1976, 21, 84–91.

Biggs, D. A.; Huneryager, S. G.; & Delaney, J. J. Leadership behavior: Interpersonal needs and effective supervisory training. *Personnel Psychology,* 1966, 19, 311–320.

Blake, R. R., & Mouton, J. S. When scholarship fails, research falters: A reply to Bernardin and Alvares. *Administrative Science Quarterly,* 1976, 21, 93–94.

Bureau of Business Research. *Leader Behavior Description Questionnaire–Form XII.* Columbus: Ohio State University, College of Commerce and Administration, 1962.

Cummins, R. C. Relationship of Initiating Structure and job performance as moderated by Consideration. *Journal of Applied Psychology,* 1971, 55, 489–490.

Cummins, R. C. Leader-member relations as a moderator of the effects of leader behavior and attitude. *Personnel Psychology,* 1972, *25,* 655–660.

Fleishman, E. A. The description of supervisory behavior. *Journal of Applied Psychology,* 1953, *37,* 1–6.

Fleishman, E. A., & Harris, E. F. Patterns of leadership behavior related to employee grievances and turnover. *Personnel Psychology,* 1962, *15,* 43–56.

Fleishman, E. A., & Simmons, J. Relationship between leadership patterns and effectiveness ratings among Israeli foremen. *Personnel Psychology,* 1970, *23,* 169–172.

Graen, G.; Dansereau, F., Jr.; & Minami, T. An empirical test of the man-in-the-middle hypothesis among executives in a hierarchical organization employing a unit-set analysis. *Organizational Behavior and Human Performance,* 1972, *8,* 262–285.

Greene, C. N. The reciprocal nature of influence between leader and subordinate. *Journal of Applied Psychology,* 1975, *60,* 187–193.

Halpin, A. W. How leaders behave. *Theory and research in administration.* New York: Macmillan, 1966, 81–130.

Hand, H., & Slocum, J. A longitudinal study of the effect of a human relations training program on managerial effectiveness. *Journal of Applied Psychology,* 1972, *56,* 412–418.

Hemphill, J. K., & Coons, A. E. *Leader behavior description.* Columbus: Ohio State University, Personnel Research Board, 1950.

House, R. J. A path-goal theory of leader effectiveness. *Administrative Science Quarterly,* 1971, *16,* 321–338.

House, R. J.; Filley, A. C.; & Kerr, S. Relation of leader Consideration and Initiating Structure to R & D subordinates' satisfaction. *Administrative Science Quarterly,* 1971, *16,* 19–30.

House, R. J., & Kerr, S. Organizational independence, leader behavior, and managerial practices: A replicated study. *Journal of Applied Psychology,* 1973, *58,* 173–180.

Hunt, J. G., & Liebscher, V. K. C. Leadership preference, leadership behavior, and employee satisfaction. *Organizational Behavior and Human Performance,* 1973, *9,* 59–77.

Lowin, A.; Hrapchak, W. J.; & Kavanagh, M. J. Consideration and Initiating Structure: An experimental investigation of leadership traits. *Administrative Science Quarterly,* 1969, *14,* 238–253.

Megargee, E. Influence of sex roles on the manifestation of leadership. *Journal of Applied Psychology,* 1969, *53,* 377–382.

Nealey, S. M., & Blood, M. R. Leadership performance of nursing supervisors at two organizational levels. *Journal of Applied Psychology,* 1968, *52,* 414–422.

Rice, R. W., & Chemers, M. M. Personality and situational determinants of leader behavior. *Journal of Applied Psychology,* 1975, *60,* 20–27.

Schriesheim, C. A.; House, R. J.; & Kerr, S. Leader Initiating Structure: A reconciliation of discrepant research results and some empirical tests. *Organizational Behavior and Human Performance,* 1976, *15,* 297–321.

Schriesheim, C., & Kerr, S. Psychometric properties of the Ohio State Leadership Scales. *Psychological Bulletin,* 1974, *81,* 756–765.

Skinner, E. W. Relationships between leader behavior patterns and organizational-situational variables. *Personnel Psychology,* 1969, *22,* 489–494.

Stogdill, R. M. *Manual for the LBDQ-Form 12: An experimental revision.* Columbus: Ohio State University, Bureau of Business Research, 1963.

————. Validity of leader behavior descriptions. *Personnel Psychology,* 1969, *22,* 153–158.

Stogdill, R. M.; Goode, O. S.; & Day, D. R. The leader behavior of corporation presidents. *Personnel Psychology,* 1963, *16,* 127–132.

————. The leader behavior of presidents of labor unions. *Personnel Psychology,* 1964, *17,* 49–57.

Streufert, S.; Streufert, S. C.; & Castore, C. H. Leadership in negotiations and conceptual structure. *Journal of Applied Psychology,* 1968, *52,* 218–223.

Weissenberg, P., & Kavanagh, M. J. The independence of Initiating Structure and Consideration: A review of the evidence. *Personnel Psychology,* 1972, *25,* 119–130.

Related Research: Education

Brown, A. F., & Anderson, B. D. Faculty consensus as a function of leadership frequency and style. *Journal of Experimental Education,* 1967, *36,* 43–49.

Burrus, D. D. The relationships of conceptual complexity of elementary school principals and teachers to the perceived leader behaviors of principals. Ph.D. dissertation, University of Tulsa, 1979.

Dawson, J. A.; Messé, L. A.; & Phillips, J. L. Effects of instructor-leader behavior on student performance. *Journal of Applied Psychology,* 1972, *56,* 369–376.

Evenson, W. L. Leadership behavior of high school principals. *NASSP Bulletin* (Publication of the National Association of Secondary School Principals), 1959, *43,* 96–101.

Halpin, A. W. The leader behavior and leadership ideology of educational administrators and aircraft commanders. *Harvard Educational Review,* 1955, *25,* 18–32.

————. *Leader behavior of school superintendents.* Chicago: University of Chicago, Midwest Administration Center, 1959.

Halpin, A. W., & Winer, B. J. A factorial study of the leader behavior descriptions. In R. M. Stogdill & A. E. Coons (Eds.), *Leader behavior: Its description and measurement.* Columbus: Ohio State University, Bureau of Business Research, 1957 (Monograph No. 88).

Kunz, D. W., & Hoy, W. K. Leadership style of principals and the professional zone of acceptance of teachers. *Educational Administration Quarterly,* 1976, *12,* 49–64.

Morsink, M. M. *Leader behavior of men and women secondary school principals.* Arlington, Va.: National Council of Administrative Women in Education, 1969.

Silver, P. F. Principals' conceptual ability in relation to situation and behavior. *Educational Administration Quarterly,* 1975, *11,* 49–66.

Willower, D. J. Leadership styles and leader's perceptions of subordinates. *Journal of Educational Sociology,* 1960, *34,* 58–64.

Chapter 7
A Situational Approach

CONTINGENCIES OF LEADERSHIP EFFECTIVENESS

At some time you may have served on a committee or team that just could not seem to get its job done without countless disruptions and delays. Perhaps at another time you worked with a group that functioned smoothly from start to finish and did a fine job. There is tremendous variation in the way groups function.

Groups have been studied from various perspectives for many years. Whereas some theorists and researchers have focused on group members, group interaction patterns, the nature of the tasks to be accomplished, or other features of the group situation, numerous scholars have emphasized the importance of the leadership of the group. Leadership research has also taken a variety of directions, usually emphasizing the personality traits of leaders, leaders' behaviors, or the types of situations in which leaders function (Stogdill, 1974). The unique perspective of the contingency theory of leadership effectiveness is its focus on the dynamic interaction between leader and situation as they both affect group performance.

Fred Fiedler is a theorist whose conceptualizations are based on a body of research that he himself conducted (Fiedler, 1967). His work centered on relationships among leaders' personality characteristics, aspects of the leader's group situation, and group productivity in a variety of interpersonal settings. He found that neither situational characteristics nor leader characteristics alone accounted for group productivity, but both elements in interaction did. As a result of extensive analyses of the research data, Fiedler developed a theory of leadership effectiveness that elucidates the dynamic interplay between leader and situation as both affect group performance.

The next time you participate in a team effort, you might be interested in analyzing your experience in terms of this contingency model. The important elements to bear in mind are the leader's personality and the group situation as they both, in interaction, affect the group's productivity. The pattern of relationships among these key elements can be depicted as in Figure 7–1.

THE CONTINGENCY THEORY
OF LEADERSHIP EFFECTIVENESS

Simply stated, the contingency theory of leadership effectiveness maintains that a group's success in accomplishing its tasks depends on the appropriate matching of leader and situation. Although the statement seems straightforward enough, it represents a unique perspective on two counts: first, the interpretations of groups, tasks, and leadership are distinctive, as will be clarified at the outset; second, the specific nature of the contingency is specified, as in the propositions presented later in this chapter.

A *group,* as treated in this theory, is a set of people who interact with each other and are dependent on each other for the accomplishment of tasks. As distinguished from sets of independent workers or sets of competing workers,

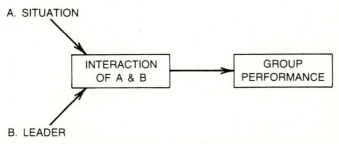

Figure 7–1   Dynamic Interplay of Three Theoretical Elements in the Contingency Theory

the groups relevant to this theory are *interacting* sets of people engaged in a task.

The *tasks* on which this theory focuses are specifically those activities that constitute the group's primary reason for being; other activities of the group are not relevant to the theory. For example, the tasks of a softball team are those associated with winning games; other activities, such as organizing parties or cleaning the locker room, are not tasks in the context of this theory.

Finally, *leadership* is regarded as an unequal power relationship in which one person, the leader, has more influence on group members' behaviors than any other group members have. The leader, as the person with responsibility for ensuring that the group's tasks are accomplished, requires a degree of influence over group members. Whether the leader is officially appointed, elected by the group, or simply regarded by group members as the leader, she or he wields more influence than others in the group.

With these definitions and delimitations in mind, we will examine the contingency model in detail. As expressed by Fiedler (1967), the theory states: the appropriateness of the *leadership style* for *maximizing group performance* is contingent on the *favorableness* of the *group-task situation*. Each of the italicized elements in this statement is a major construct in the theory.

Major Constructs in the Contingency Theory

LEADERSHIP STYLE

Leadership style is defined in terms of the underlying need structure that motivates the leader's behavior in various interpersonal situations. In this theory leadership style is a personality trait of the leader, a relatively enduring characteristic that is not directly observable; it is the pattern of needs that the leader seeks to fulfill in personal interactions. Theoretically, there are two basic needs that motivate leaders: the need for good relationships with other people and the need for successful accomplishment of tasks. Although all leaders (and other people) have both these types of needs, the dominance of one type of need over the other defines the leader's style as either relationship oriented or task oriented:

Relationship-oriented leaders are those in whom the need for good interpersonal relationships is dominant and the need for task accomplishment is secondary.

Task-oriented leaders are those in whom the need for successful task completion is dominant and the need for good personal relationships is secondary.

For both types of leaders, fulfillment of the dominant need results in increased feelings of self-esteem, satisfaction, and freedom from anxiety. If the primary need is fulfilled, then satisfaction of the secondary need enhances these feelings of well-being still further.

MAXIMIZING GROUP PERFORMANCE

Maximizing group performance refers to increasing group task completion toward its highest possible level, both quantitatively and qualitatively. In this theory the only tasks considered are those that the group was officially formed to accomplish; thus the degree of successful task completion by the group is the index of the leader's effectiveness.

GROUP-TASK SITUATION

The *group-task situation* is the interpersonal setting in which the leadership takes place. It is described in terms of the extent to which it facilitates the exercise of influence by the leader. Although many situational elements may facilitate or impede the leader's ability to influence the group members, three factors were identified by Fiedler as being particularly important—leader-member relations, task structure, and the leader's position power:

Leader-member relations can be defined as the quality of feelings group members have toward the leader—the degree of friendliness, cooperativeness, acceptance, supportiveness, and other feelings. This is considered the most important facet of the group-task situation.

Task structure refers to the degree to which the group's tasks are well defined. It includes the clarity of goals to members, the measurability of outcomes, the variability of procedures, and the specificity of solutions to problems. This is considered the second most important element in the group-task situation.

Leader's position power is the extent to which the leader's position itself enables the leader to exercise influence on group members. Position power includes status, authority, and reward or punishment power. It is the least important of the three factors defining the group-task situation.

All three of these factors are combined in describing the group-task situation.

SITUATION FAVORABLENESS

Situation favorableness is the composite of the three group-task situation factors. Each of these factors could be operationalized as a continuous variable, since each situation can range from very facilitating to very impeding in leader-member relations, task structure, and leader position power. Most often, however, each of these dimensions is divided at its midpoint to make assessments of the favorableness of the group-task situation. Thus three dichotomies are possible.

1. The leader-member relations are considered either good or moderately poor.
   a. Good: The group members have strongly positive feelings toward the leader.
   b. Moderately poor: The group members have rather negative feelings toward the leader.

2. The tasks performed by the group are either highly structured or low in structure.
    a. High: The group tasks are clearly defined in terms of goals, procedures, and outcomes.
    b. Low: The group tasks are ill defined in terms of goals, procedures, and outcomes.
3. The leader's position power in relation to the group is either strong or weak.
    a. Strong: The leader, by virtue of his or her office, has considerable influence; such leaders receive strong support from the organization and its higher authorities.
    b. Weak: The leader's position itself entails little influence; such leaders receive little or no official support from the organization as a whole.

When the three dimensions of the group-task situation are dichotomized in this way, the types of situations can be arranged in order of their favorability to the leader—that is, in the order of the extent to which they facilitate the leader's exercise of influence. The resulting eight types of group-task situations can be diagramed as in Figure 7–2.

By this analysis, any group-task situation can be assigned to an octant. For example, a situation in which leader-member relations are good, task structure is low, and position power is strong would fall in Octant III; this would be considered a favorable group-task situation. By contrast, a situation in which leader-member relations are moderately poor, task structure is low, and position power is strong would fall in Octant VII; that is considered a moderately unfavorable group-task situation.

Relationships Among Constructs in the Contingency Theory

At this point we can consider the statement of the theory and of the interrelationships among the major constructs. As noted earlier, the contingency theory states that the appropriateness of the leadership style for maximizing group performance is contingent on the favorableness of the group-task situation. This can be restated as follows: whether a relationship-oriented leader or a task-oriented leader is the more effective depends on the degree of favorability of the work setting.

In sum, the contingency theory emphasizes the notion that there is no particular leadership style that is most effective in all situations; rather, the effectiveness of one's leadership style is contingent on the work situation. One's leadership style, a personality trait, can be either relationship oriented or task oriented. Each group situation, having the three dimensions of leader-member relations, task structure, and leader position power, can be seen as having one of eight degrees of favorableness to the leader. The leader's effectiveness as a

Leader-member relations	Good	Good	Good	Good	Poor	Poor	Poor	Poor
Task structure	High	High	Low	Low	High	High	Low	Low
Leader position power	Strong	Weak	Strong	Weak	Strong	Weak	Strong	Weak
Octant numbers	I	II	III	IV	V	VI	VII	VIII
Favorableness	Favorable			Moderately favorable				Unfavorable

Figure 7–2 Group-Task Situations in Order of Decreasing Favorableness for the Leader (Based on Fiedler, 1967:34)

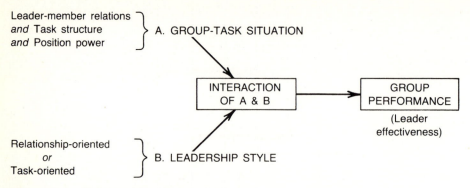

Figure 7–3   Relationships Among Constructs in the Contingency Theory of Leadership Effectiveness

leader, as gauged by the group's productivity, is a function of the match between leadership style and situation favorableness (see Fiedler, 1973). This contingency can be depicted by expanding on the diagram presented earlier, as in Figure 7–3.

Major Propositions of the Contingency Theory

The two major propositions associated with this theory are as follows:

1. *In favorable and unfavorable group-task situations, a task-oriented leadership style is the more effective style.* That is, groups in Octants I, II, III, and VIII tend to complete more tasks (or complete tasks better) with a task-oriented leader than with a relationship-oriented leader.
2. *In moderately favorable group-task situations, a relationship-oriented leadership style is the more effective style.* That is, groups in Octants IV, V, VI, and VII generally perform better with a relationship-oriented leader than with a task-oriented leader.

DISCUSSION OF THE CONTINGENCY MODEL OF LEADERSHIP EFFECTIVENESS

This theory has been widely acclaimed for its contribution to an understanding of why some leaders are more effective than others and why particular leaders are successful in some situations but not others. It suggests that leaders are motivated to act in particular ways to fulfill their needs and that in fulfilling their own needs leaders will enhance or impede group productivity. Although the specific behavior patterns of the leader cannot be predicted from the theory, the group's success is somewhat predictable from knowledge of the leader's style and the characteristics of the group situation. In using this theory for research or practice, however, one should bear a few of its unique features in mind.

First, as noted, the theory pertains only to interacting groups—those in which the product is a group effort and the members are interdependent. Groups in which members work independently (coacting groups) and those in which members compete with each other (counteracting groups) are not relevant to this theory. Thus, in a school, faculty committee success might be predictable from the theory, but individual teachers' success in advancing student learning would not be predictable, since the faculty is typically a coacting group, one with each member performing independently. Similarly, a class project's successful completion might be predictable from the theory if the teacher's leadership style and the students' feelings are known; but individual students' achievement would not be predictable, since students typically work independently within the classroom.

Second, the theory addresses the matter of leader effectiveness strictly in terms of accomplishment of the group's primary tasks—those that the group was constituted to perform. Other outcomes of group interactions, such as member satisfaction or friendship formations, are not explicitly treated in the theory. Thus in an educational setting the number of school newspapers produced by a student team might be predicted from leadership style and situation favorableness; but the esprit, morale, or climate of the team is not predictable. This theoretical focus on productivity is congruent with Likert's (1967) framework for analyzing managerial styles, in that informal or tangential outcomes of the employees' interactions are considered intermediate variables; only the organization's formal productivity is the measure of management success.

Another point that deserves mention is that the elements constituting the group-task situation are not completely independent of each other. Specifically, leader-member relations, task structure, and leader position power are conceptually interrelated. For example, the more definitively the tasks are structured, the easier it is for the organization to recognize and reward group success; therefore, increasing task structure has the effect of increasing the leader's position power. On the other hand, favorable attitudes toward the leader on the part of group members tend to reduce the leader's need to resort to the authority of office in influencing group members; thus improving leader-member relations reduces the need for position power. It is partly because of this interdependence of constructs that measurements of the three variables cannot simply be summed to yield a numerical description of the group-task situation. Instead, the dichotomization of variables, as described earlier, and the nominal classification of situations into eight categories are used to provide a rough approximation of their relative favorableness. Further empirical research would be needed on how the elements combine in various groups before a more refined quantification of situation favorability is possible.

A related issue that is not addressed explicitly by Fiedler is the logical interdependence between the leadership style and group-task situation constructs. To some extent leaders create the situations in which they find themselves. That is, it must be assumed that the leader's behavior with respect to establishing interpersonal relations, structuring tasks, and exercising influence shapes the group-task situation. Further, it must be assumed that the leader's style (needs pattern) motivated that behavior. Thus leadership style and group-task situation are not conceptually independent.

This construct interdependence might be further clarified with reference to a framework for considering power relationships. French and Raven (1959) noted that power is *attributed* to individuals in accordance with the power bases they seem to utilize; thus the leader's power is a function of group members' perceptions based on the leader's behavior patterns. French and Raven also identified the five bases of power as follows: reward, coercive, legitimate, expert, and referent. This suggests that *position power* is associated with the legitimate power base; *task structure* refers to the expert power base; and *leader-member relations* relates to the referent power base. In short, the constructs in the contingency model are conceptually interdependent.

Fiedler acknowledged that the three facets of situation favorableness do not constitute an exhaustive set (see Fiedler, 1966; Fiedler & Meuwese, 1963). Such group features as cohesiveness, heterogeneity, skill level, and longevity as a group would probably have impact on the leader's capacity to influence members, as would such external factors as resource availability and intergroup conflict. Some group characteristics are not a function of the leader's prior behavior patterns, whereas the characteristics mentioned in the theory do depend on the leader's past behaviors. In efforts to expand on the theory by identifying important characteristics of the group-task situation, a distinction should be made between the situational factors that are independent of the leader and those that are dependent on her or him.

To summarize, the contingency theory of leadership effectiveness is a useful tool for analyzing the productivity of some groups in relation to the leader's personality and work setting. The originality of this theory is in the dynamic interaction it posits among three key elements in organizational life—leadership style, group-task situations, and group productivity. Although the theory has been criticized on the grounds that its major constructs are not completely independent conceptually, it has yielded important insights about group processes and has generated an impressive body of empirical research. In using the theory to analyze ongoing events or to design research, its unique applicability to interacting groups and to task accomplishment should be kept in mind.

RESEARCH RELATED TO THE CONTINGENCY THEORY

Numerous studies have been conducted both in schools and elsewhere to test the viability of Fiedler's theory, and a substantial amount of support for the theoretical propositions has been obtained. Unlike many of the theories explicated in this book, the contingency model is associated with a particular set of instruments for operationalizing the major constructs. This section reviews first the research instruments associated with this theory and then a sample of the research both in varied settings and in schools.

Instruments

Since Fiedler (1967) reported on and provided copies of the instruments he used in his studies, researchers have generally used the same or similar measurement tools in their studies. The instruments are described briefly here in terms of the constructs they are intended to operationalize.

Leadership style is usually measured by an instrument of 16–20 items called the Least Preferred Co-worker (LPC) questionnaire (Fiedler, 1967:36–60). Each item is an eight-point scale on which the respondent rates the person with whom he or she least prefers to work on a joint project. Each item is a continuum representing a pair of adjectives by which the least preferred co-worker can be described, and the continuum ranges from the most negative rating (scored 1) to the most positive (scored 8). Each respondent's score for the LPC is the sum of ratings across all the bipolar adjective scales. The lower the score, the more task oriented the respondent; the higher the score, the more relationship oriented the respondent.

Fiedler and others have provided reliability and validity data on this instrument (Fiedler, 1967; Posthuma, 1970; Rice, 1978). The validity of the LPC as a measure of leadership style or of leaders' need structure has been questioned, however. Mitchell (1970), for example, believes this instrument might measure the leader's conceptual complexity (see Chapter 11), since it reflects the leader's differentiation of a co-worker's characteristics. This possibility should be considered in interpreting research findings.

Situation favorableness is determined by three measures, since this construct encompasses leader-member relations, task structure, and leader position power. First, *leader-member relations*, sometimes called group atmosphere, are measured by the Group Atmosphere Scale (GA), a ten-item instrument similar to the LPC in format. Each item is a bipolar adjective scale on which respondents rate their group from the most negative end of the continuum (scored 1) to the most positive (scored 8).

Fiedler (1967:32) indicated that respondents to the GA can be either the leader or the group members. If group atmosphere is treated as a function of group members' responses, then the leader's score is the mean of group members' scores. If the group atmosphere is measured by leader's responses, then what is being measured are the leader's perceptions of the leader-member relations—which might differ markedly from group members' perceptions. The practice of having group leaders complete both the LPC and the GA should be avoided, since both instruments might be measuring the leader's level of conceptual complexity.

Task structure can be measured by means of group members' responses on a four-item instrument for describing the decision verifiability, goal clarity, goal path multiplicity, and solution specificity of the group tasks. Each item is an eight-point scale ranging from the most structured to the most unstructured end of the continuum, and each respondent's score is the sum of ratings across the four items. The leader's score for task structure is the mean of group members' scores.

Position power of the leader can be measured by group members' responses to an 18-item Position Power Questionnaire (PP) on which respondents indicate whether each of the statements is true or false. Generally speaking, each "true" answer is scored 1 and each "false" answer is scored 0; but three of the items are assigned different weights (see Fiedler, 1967:22–25). The respondent's score is the weighted sum for all items, and the leader's PP score is the mean of group members' scores.

In published studies, researchers have frequently omitted this measure, assuming instead a particular degree of leader position power. In view of the types of items in the questionnaire, however—items that include all the types of power identified by French and Raven (1959)—this omission should be avoided.

Treatment of scores on these three measures usually entails dichotomizing each one by placing groups scoring above the mean for the sample in the upper half and those scoring below the mean in the lower half. By following the schema presented in Figure 7–2, groups are then placed in their appropriate octants.

Leader effectiveness must be interpreted, in the context of this theory, as a function of group accomplishment of formal tasks. Therefore, the measures of leader effectiveness will vary from one work setting to another—for example, number of games won, amount of money generated, number of machines assembled—but they should all be quantifiable measures of intentional group productivity.

The most usual procedure for testing hypotheses deduced from the theory entails partitioning the sample of groups into their appropriate octants and, within each octant, correlating leaders' LPC scores with group productivity scores. In this way the degree to which leadership style predicts or explains group productivity in each octant can be determined and the direction of the relationship established. By this type of analysis, the many studies conducted by Fielder as well as by other researchers have indicated that in favorable and unfavorable situations the correlation between leadership style and group effectiveness tends to be negative (the more task oriented the leader, the more productive the group); in moderately favorable or moderately unfavorable situations the correlations between leadership style and group productivity have tended to be positive (the more relationship oriented the leader, the more productive the group). The magnitudes of correlation have varied from study to study as well as from octant to octant.

Leadership Effectiveness Research in Varied Settings

Much of the reported research associated with this theory was designed to test its major propositions either through field studies or by means of laboratory experiments in which octants were replicated. Many, however, represent attempts to expand on the theory. This discussion will center on research to test the theory and research to expand the theory in sequence.

RESEARCH TO TEST THE THEORY

Of the studies designed to test hypotheses derived from the major propositions, Fiedler conducted by far the greatest number. In fact, he developed the contingency theory as a means of describing and explaining his findings in studies involving over eight hundred groups of such diverse types as bomber crews, athletic teams, and corporate employees. Several summaries of this research (Fiedler, 1967, 1970a, 1970b, 1971b, 1972) indicate that hypotheses based on the propositions have generally been supported, although the magnitudes of correlations within some octants have sometimes been small (not statistically significant) and some octants (specifically, Octants II and VI) have not been fully represented in the research. In his 1967 book Fiedler provided a concise overview of his earlier findings in the form of a diagram showing the average correlation between leader LPC and group productivity in each octant. This is reproduced as Figure 7–4.

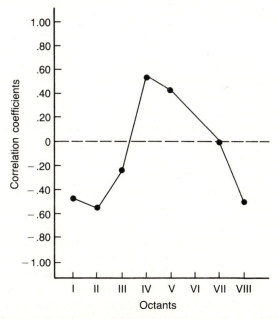

Figure 7–4   Average Correlations Between LPC and Group Performance in All Octants (Based on Fiedler, 1967:146)

As Figure 7–4 indicates, the average correlation coefficients, noted on the vertical axis, have been negative in Octants I, II, III, and VIII (the more task oriented the leader, the more productive the group), but positive in Octants IV and V (the more relationship oriented the leader, the more productive the group). In interpreting the diagram, the reader should bear in mind that these average correlations represent a wide range of actual correlations obtained in individual studies. In Octant III, for example, the actual correlations ranged from − .70 to + .85 in the 11 studies of groups in this octant; the average of this broad range of correlations was about − .35. In Octant I, on the other hand, the range of actual correlations for 8 studies was much narrower. It should also be noted that Octant VI was not represented by any studies and that the average correlation between LPC and group productivity in Octant VII was about zero.

A generalization that can be drawn from the findings in Figure 7–4 is that the contingency theory is clearly supported at the extremes of the situation-favorability dimension (Octants I, II, and VIII) and at the middle of this dimension (Octants IV and V). Research results in the transitional ranges—Octants III, VI, and VII—are less readily predictable, however.

Some further support for the theory was found in other field-based studies. Hovey (1974), for example, found that in college student groups with low task structure and low leader position power, the correlation between leader LPC and group *effort* was positive when leader-member relations were good (Octant IV) but negative when leader-member relations were poor (Octant VIII). When group product *quality* was the effectiveness measure, however, the theory was not supported. Hill (1969), in a study of interacting groups in a manufacturing company, found negative correlations between leader LPC and leaders' rated effectiveness in Octants II and VII and a positive correlation in Octant III, as predicted from the theory. In Octant VI, however, the direction of correlation was opposite to that predicted. Csoka and Fielder (1972), studying 171 military groups, found leader LPC and group effectiveness to be inversely related in Octants I, III, and VIII but directly related in Octant V, as predicted from the theory. Finally, Michaelsen (1973) found the predicted relationships in his study of 119 first-line production and maintenance supervisors.

Additional support for the contingency theory has been generated in experimental research. Rice and Chemers (1973), for example, in laboratory replications of Octants II, IV, VI, and VIII with groups of students, found correlations between leader LPC and group productivity in the directions predicted. Chemers and Skrzypek (1972) replicated all eight octants with groups of military cadets and found not only that correlations between leader LPC and group productivity were in the predicted directions, but also that the profile of these correlations was in close conformity with Fiedler's profile, as reproduced in Figure 7–4. Some contradictory evidence was obtained by Graen et al. (1970) and Graen, Orris, and Alvares (1971); but their conclusions are less convincing than those mentioned earlier because their measurement instruments and experimental conditions were less fully described in the research reports (see Fiedler, 1971a).

A weakness of the studies designed to test the theory is that the correlations found, though often in the predicted directions, were generally not statistically significant (Chemers and Skrzypek, 1972; Rice and Chemers, 1973; Hill, 1969; Hovey, 1974). This suggests two possibilities: first, that relationships between leader LPC and group productivity do exist beyond chance alone, but that the samples in each octant have been too small to demonstrate significance statistically; second, that leader LPC does influence group productivity as contingent on situations, but only to a relatively small degree. Although the .tradition has been to classify sample groups by octants for correlational analysis, it would be interesting to see whether significant differences in group productivity scores are predictable from different leadership-style/group-task situation combinations.

RESEARCH TO EXPAND THE THEORY
One of the perplexing features of the research associated with this theory is its reliance on the Least Preferred Co-worker instrument as a measure of leadership style. In essence, the construct validity of this instrument is in question. Fiedler initially considered leadership style, as measured by the LPC, to be a personality trait, with some leaders being oriented toward people and others toward tasks. Later he came to view LPC scores as an index of the leader's primary motivational patterns, with high-scoring leaders the more motivated to fulfill relationship needs and low-scoring leaders the more motivated to fulfull achievement needs. Other researchers have sought to clarify the issue by examining LPC scores in relation to cognitive styles and in relation to behavior patterns.

One of the proponents of the cognitive-styles interpretation is Mitchell (1970; Mitchell et al., 1970), who reported three studies of student groups. He found males' LPC scores to be significantly related to their scores on the List of Groups test, a measure of cognitive complexity that entails classifying information. Also, LPC scores predicted the types of information students would utilize in making judgments about group-task situations; specifically, high-LPC subjects were the most attentive to task structure and position power information and were the more discriminating of task information, whereas low-LPC persons were the more attentive to interpersonal information and the less discriminating of task information. Further evidence that the Least Preferred Co-worker is a cognitive measure was provided by Konar-Goldband, Rice, and Monkarsh (1979), who found that group performance influenced leaders' judgments of group atmosphere (leader-member relations) significantly more for low-LPC basketball captains than for high-LPC captains. Silver and Hess (1981) also found support for this conjecture in their finding that educational administration students' LPC scores were related to their object-sorting scores. On the other hand, Larson and Rowland (1974) found no relationships between LPC scores and cognitive complexity scores in their study of 177 business administrators and students. Although it seems reasonable to assume that leaders' ability to differentiate attributes of a co-worker, as on the LPC, reflects their ability to differentiate interpersonal stimuli in general, this assumption remains inconclusively justified.

Those who have examined leaders' LPC scores in relation to the leaders' behavior patterns have often found significant relationships that are moderated by circumstances. High-LPC leaders have been found to be more person oriented in behavior than low-LPC leaders under conditions of stress (Green, Nebeker, & Boni 1976; Larson & Rowland, 1973), unfavorability (Green & Nebeker, 1977), and low task structure (Chemers & Skrzypek, 1972). Conversely, low-LPC leaders were behaviorally more task oriented under adverse circumstances in these studies. Using a leader orientation measure other than the LPC, Michaelsen (1973) found that positive correlations between relationship orientation and pressure for production increased as situations increased in favorability. That is, the more favorable the group-task situations in this study, the greater the correlation between leaders' relationship orientation and leaders' pressure for production. These studies suggest that in favorable situations leaders attend to their secondary needs, whereas unfavorable or stressful circumstances cause leaders to revert to their primary needs (see Gruenfeld, Rance, & Weissenberg, 1969; Rice & Chemers, 1975).

Some of the research indicates that high-LPC leaders are the more sensitive to situational changes (Chemers & Skrzypek, 1972; Green & Nebeker, 1977) but that low-LPC leaders are the more popular (Rice & Chemers, 1973). In all, the research is convincing in its evidence that leaders' orientations (their LPC scores) relate to their perceived behavior patterns; but the relationship is a complex one, not a simple linear one.

Numerous studies have focused on other aspects of the theory. In exploring the relevance of the theory to coacting groups, Hill (1969) found correlations between leader LPC and supervisors' ratings of group effectiveness to be in the predicted directions for Octants I, III, V, and VII; but only that in Octant V was of a statistically significant magnitude. The theory was not useful in predicting the emergence of informal leaders (Rice & Chemers, 1973), since low-LPC individuals were almost invariably perceived to be both the emergent and the preferred leaders. Fiedler's contention that leader-member relations is the most important and position power the least important of the situational favorability dimensions was supported by Beach and Beach (1978) and by Mitchell (1970) in their studies of students' perceptions.

In an unusual experimental study of middle and upper management, Hunt (1971) found that low-LPC upper managers plus high-LPC middle managers got the best group productivity results, but that workers' satisfaction varied directly with upper managers' LPC scores. This study is especially interesting in that the upper managers had no direct communication with the workers.

To summarize, there is a substantial body of published research supportive of the theory's propositions and related hypotheses. Some noteworthy characteristics of the empirical studies are that they have relied almost exclusively on the Least Preferred Co-worker instrument as the measure of leaders' orientations, and that their samples almost invariably comprised male groups and leaders. Further research designed to operationalize the constructs in diverse ways, to identify other important dimensions of group-task situations, and to define situation favorableness more precisely might help to enrich the theory as well as to test its validity. Also, whether interactions involving female leaders and/or female group members conform to the same dynamic pattern remains a question worthy of further inquiry.

Leadership Effectiveness Research in School Systems

Most of the relevant research on education systems has been descriptive-correlational in design, using field-based groups as the study samples. Many of the studies were intended to test the contingency theory as a whole, but a few treated selected aspects of the theory.

RESEARCH TO TEST THE THEORY

The field studies designed to test the theory are somewhat inadequate because of omissions of variables, inappropriate effectiveness measures, or use of coacting rather than interacting group samples. In one study of eight departments in a business college, for example, Hopfe (1970) found no relationships between chairpersons' LPC scores and the productivity of faculty members. However, department faculties must be regarded as coacting groups rather than interacting groups; therefore, the theory cannot be expected to apply. Garland and O'Reilly (1976) found school principals' LPC scores to be unrelated to school climate. Climate, however, is a facet of situation favorability, not a group productivity measure; therefore, again, the theory cannot be expected to be applicable. In a study of teacher probation committees chaired by principals, Martin, Isherwood, and Lavery (1976) found the leadership-style/group-productivity correlations to be opposite to those predicted in the theory. However, these researchers failed to measure task structure or leader position power, and they used members' perceptions of effectiveness rather than a more objective assessment as the group productivity measure; therefore, support of the contingency theory would have been surprising.

One experimental study of teaching and learning was located (Reavis & Derlega, 1976) in which the teacher's style was found to be unrelated to students' learning in moderately favorable and unfavorable situations. In this study, however, leadership style was regarded as a behavioral variable rather than as a personality factor, and the validity of the experimental conditions was not established. Nevertheless, students were more satisfied with the person-oriented teacher in the moderately favorable situation and with the system-oriented teacher in the unfavorable situation.

RESEARCH ON ASPECTS OF THE THEORY

Some of the educational research reported in the published literature addresses specific aspects of the theory rather than the theory as a whole. In one descriptive study of 436 principals, Holloway and Niazi (1978) found principals' LPC scores to be unrelated to their self-reported propensity to take risks. In a study of administrators and teachers in 21 schools, Galfo (1975) found administrators' LPC scores to be unrelated to their self-reported behavior patterns. A study of 160 principals and the teachers in their schools revealed principals' LPC scores to be unrelated to teachers' perceptions of principals' effectiveness (Miskel, 1977).

This brief review of the research in school settings might lead one to conclude that the contingency theory of leadership effectiveness is not applicable to education systems. Alternatively, the major propositions of the theory may not have been tested adequately in school building, central office, or higher-education settings. There is an obvious need for well-designed, rigorous, inventive tests of the contingency model in education. In place of assumptions about leaders' degrees of position power or tasks' degree of structure, we need careful measures of all the variables. Instead of samples of coacting groups, we need samples of truly interactive or interdependent groups. Finally, to replace "opinionnaire" measures of group or leader effectiveness, we need objectively quantified measures of group-task accomplishment. Until such thorough research is conducted, we can reach no firm conclusions about the applicability of the contingency model to education.

IMPLICATIONS OF THE CONTINGENCY THEORY FOR ENHANCING STUDENT LEARNING OUTCOMES

Educational administrators have long confronted the problem of insufficient student learning. Vast numbers of school youngsters—particularly impoverished, minority, handicapped, and female youngsters—do not learn as much in as many subject areas as do the majority of white middle-class and upper-class males. It is essential that administrators become able to solve this problem as it manifests itself in their schools and school districts. It is also essential that researchers, in cooperation with administrators, produce the knowledge needed to solve this problem. Therefore, the key question throughout this book is: Does this theory appear useful in generating knowledge that would be helpful to school administrators in solving this overarching problem? Can the contingency theory of leadership effectiveness serve as a useful foundation for research and administrative practice related to student learning outcomes?

We can address this issue in terms of two types of relationships within educational organizations: those between administrators and teachers and those between teachers and students. In both cases our focus must be on interacting groups and their productivity.

Consider a situation in which a department chairperson convenes a group of teachers for the purpose of preparing a set of schoolwide mastery examinations, developing a well-articulated curriculum, or reviewing and attempting to resolve cases of individual student underachievement. Such a committee would probably constitute an interacting group, and the outcomes of its efforts would likely have some bearing, albeit indirectly, on student achievement. Again, consider a superintendent who appoints a committee of administrators to plan a year-long staff development program for teachers that will have some real impact on teachers' knowledge and skill. The administrator group also would probably be an interacting one, and its efforts can be seen as indirectly relevant to student learning. In both instances the contingency model might prove helpful in identifying the type of leader most likely to be effective.

Student learning on a schoolwide or districtwide scale is clearly an appropriate focus of attention for administrators, and student achievement or achievement gain scores would clearly be the measure most nearly congruent with Fiedler's concept of effectiveness. However, classroom instruction is typically directed toward students who are learning independently, even when total-class or homogeneous-grouping instruction is offered; and teachers typically perform independently in their classrooms. Thus faculties and student bodies would have to be regarded as coacting groups, and hence not relevant to the contingency model. On the other hand, when team teaching is fully implemented, teacher teams are ideally interacting groups. Similarly, when student group projects are under way or when student committees are functioning well, these sets of students are ideally interacting groups. In both types of situations the contingency model might ultimately prove helpful for determining in advance the most effective type of leader.

As noted earlier, the Least Preferred Co-worker instrument is intended to measure a motivational pattern of leaders, not their behaviors. In fact, LPC scores have been shown to be related to leaders' behaviors in a complex, situationally specific manner. As the research progresses and behavioral correlatives of LPC scores are more thoroughly identified, it might well become possible for school leaders to learn to behave in a manner that approximates that of the most effective leaders for each given situation, so as to improve group productivity. In publications for administrators Fiedler and others illustrated some uses of the contingency model for improving one's own management practices—uses such as diagnosing one's situation and one's own leadership style, matching leaders with situations, and modifying the situation and/or the leader's behavior (Fiedler, Chemers, & Mahar, 1976; Fiedler & Chemers, 1974; Chemers, 1969). These strategies might prove helpful in educational settings.

Although the contingency theory of leadership effectiveness seems to bear a logical, albeit indirect, relationship to student learning outcomes, there is little empirical evidence to demonstrate this relationship. Numerous questions remain to be answered. These might include the following:

1. Do the relationships posited in the contingency theory obtain for coacting groups as well as for interacting groups? More specifically, are students' achievements in the cognitive, affective, and psychomotor domains contingent on the matching of the principal's leadership style and the school's group-task situation in traditionally organized schools (that is, in schools in which teachers function individually in their classrooms)?

2. If the relationships among leadership style, group-task situation, and group productivity as posited in the contingency theory do not obtain, are there other patterns of relationship among the constructs that are pertinent to coacting groups? For example, is a particular leadership style on the part of the principal in conjunction with a particular faculty group-task situation related to student outcomes? Is task orientation on the principal's part best matched with moderate favorability of group-task situation for maximizing student outcomes?

3. In traditionally organized schools (that is, those having coacting faculty groups), which, if any, type of student outcomes—cognitive, affective, or psychomotor—relates predictably to the matching of principals' leadership styles and faculty group-task situations?

4. In schools utilizing a team teaching approach, are student learning outcomes in the cognitive, affective, and psychomotor domains a function of the appropriate matching of teacher–leaders' styles and teacher–group-task situations? Which type of student outcome, if any, is best predicted by the matching of teacher–leaders' personality and teacher–group situation? Note that the class rather than the school as a whole would be the unit of analysis in research designed to answer this question.

5. When student group projects are undertaken, is the quantity or quality of the work produced related to the matching of the student–leader's personality and the favorableness of the student–group-task situation, as posited in the contingency theory?

6. Do the relationships posited in the contingency model obtain when the major constructs are operationalized in ways other than those suggested by Fiedler? Are there aspects of group-task situations that were not highlighted by Fiedler but that are important factors in school situations?

Such questions suggest that the collection and analysis of information in accordance with the constructs of the contingency theory would be appropriate for generating knowledge that could eventually prove helpful in resolving problems associated with student learning. Such research would serve two important functions: it would resolve definitively the issues of whether and to what extent the theory is applicable to education, and it would contribute to professional knowledge about the school factors that affect student learning outcomes. The needed research requires ingenuity and careful analysis of all the relevant factors but holds promise for yielding important practical knowledge and theory development.

MASTERY QUIZ

Select the best completion for each of the following sentences, and jot your answer on a separate paper. Answers appear in Appendix C, page 392.

1. The type of groups on which this theory focuses is:
   a. coacting groups.   c. interacting groups.
   b. intersecting groups.   d. counteracting groups.
2. A person's leadership style refers to that person's:
   a. behavior patterns.   c. group-task situations.
   b. motivations.   d. leader-member relations.
3. The best measure of a production team's performance would be:
   a. the team members' rating of the leader.
   b. the extent to which the team sructures its tasks.
   c. the esprit of the team while working.
   d. the number of products produced by the team.
4. The three major constructs in the contingency theory are:
   a. group performance, leader effectiveness, and group-task situation.
   b. group performance, situation favorableness, and group productivity.
   c. group performance, leadership style, and situation favorableness.
   d. group productivity, leader-member relations, and leadership style.
5. The three important dimensions of group-task situations are:
   a. leadership style, task structure, and leader position power.
   b. task structure, leader position power, and goal specificity.
   c. leader position power, task structure, and leader-member relations.
   d. leader-member relations, leadership style, and task structure.
6. The order of importance of the significant aspects of group-task situations is:
   a. leadership style, task structure, leader position power.
   b. leader-member relations, task structure, leader position power.
   c. task structure, leader position power, leadership style.
   d. position power, task structure, leader-member relations.
7. The groups most likely to be productive, according to this theory, are:
   a. those with unfavorable situations and task-oriented leaders.
   b. those with favorable situations and relationship-oriented leaders.
   c. those with moderately favorable situations and task-oriented leaders.
   d. those with favorable situations and high-LPC leaders.

8. Highly relationship-oriented leaders are most likely to be effective in situations characterized by:
   a. good leader-member relations, high task structure, and high position power.
   b. good leader-member relations, high task structure, and low position power.
   c. moderately poor leader-member relations, high task structure, and high position power.
   d. moderately poor leader-member relations, low task structure, and low position power.
9. One of the theory's major propositions implies that:
   a. in favorable situations the relationship-oriented leader will be more successful.
   b. in unfavorable situations the high-LPC leader will be more successful.
   c. in moderately favorable situations the task-oriented leader will be more successful.
   d. in unfavorable situations the low-LPC leader will be more successful.
10. The research indicates that in stressful situations:
    a. high-LPC leaders will become more effective.
    b. low-LPC leaders will become more relationship oriented.
    c. high-LPC leaders will become more task oriented.
    d. low-LPC leaders will become more task oriented.

EXERCISES

1. For each of the following vignettes, indicate the octant in which you think it would fall and the leadership style most likely to be effective (print T for task oriented or R for relationship oriented). The intended answers appear in Appendix C, page 392.
   1. A teacher has divided his high school class into groups for preparing a unit project in social studies. The project can take the form of a written report, a scale model, or a multimedia oral-visual presentation. The groups select their own chairpersons for this six-week project.
      Octant _____
      Style _____
   2. The president of the student organization is working with a representative from each class to promote a raffle sale. The student representatives are not enthusiastic, since the money will be used to buy a new movie projector for the school's audiovisual department.
      Octant _____
      Style _____
   3. The English department chairperson, who is thought by the teachers to be rather petty and not highly competent, has assigned a group of

teachers the scoring of the short-answer portion of a districtwide English examination.

    Octant _____

    Style _____

4. In a physical education club each squad has elected its own captain to work with the squad in preparing for a close-order drill competition.

    Octant _____

    Style _____

5. The school principal, who is highly regarded by her faculty, has convened a committee of teachers to design a moral development program for the school.

    Octant _____

    Style _____

6. A well-liked principal is working with a group of volunteer students to prepare decorations for the senior class party. The decorations are to be paper cutout snowflakes and inflated balloons.

    Octant _____

    Style _____

7. Each principal in a district has been assigned the task of working with a voluntary committee of teachers to generate a set of affective goals and objectives for the school and to suggest strategies for attaining those goals and objectives. The desired number of objectives was not specified.

    Octant _____

    Style _____

8. A teacher who has often had discipline problems in his third grade class had opted to work with a group of underachieving students after school on improving their reading skills. Participating students are those who scored below grade level on the last reading examination, and oral reading followed by discussion is the instructional technique being used.

    Octant _____

    Style _____

9. An unpopular principal has assigned a group of teachers the task of grading a schoolwide multiple-choice examination during their free time for a period of three weeks.

    Octant _____

    Style _____

10. A teacher who is often avoided by his colleagues has been asked to select five or six teachers to help in preparing for a school arts and crafts festival. This will be the first time such a festival has been held in the school, and the festival coordinator is free to select those teachers whom he feels will be most efficient.

    Octant _____

    Style _____

2. Consider three group situations in which you were personally involved as a group member. Briefly describe each one in terms of its purpose, its leader-member relations, its task structure, the position power of its leader, and its degree of success in accomplishing its purpose. Conclude each description with your estimate as to whether the leader's style was the appropriate one for that situation.

3. Consider one group situation in which you were personally involved as the group leader. Using the contingency theory as your basis, describe what you did that made the group successful or what you could have done to make the group more successful.

4. Select one of the empirical studies that were mentioned in the section on leadership effectiveness research in school systems, and state one or more hypotheses that you think served as the foundation for that study. Then consider how one might best test that hypothesis or those hypotheses. Jot some notes on sampling, instrumentation, and data analysis so that you can discuss your research idea in class.

REFERENCES

Major Source

Fiedler, F. E. *A theory of leadership effectiveness*. New York: McGraw-Hill, 1967.

Related Conceptual Literature

Fiedler, F. E. *Personality, motivational systems, and behavior of high and low LPC persons*. Seattle: Organizational Research Laboratory, University of Washington, 1970a.

———. Personality and situational determinants of leader behavior. In E. A. Fleishman and J. G. Hunt (Eds.), *Current developments in the study of leadership*. Carbondale: Southern Illinois University Press, 1973.

Fiedler, F. E., & Chemers, M. M. *Leadership and effective management*. Glenview, Ill.: Scott, Foresman, 1974.

Fiedler, F. E.; Chemers, M. M.; & Mahar, L. *Improving leadership effectiveness: The leader match concept*. New York: Wiley, 1976.

French, J. R. P., & Raven, B. H. The bases of social power. In D. Cartwright (Ed.), *Studies in social power*. Ann Arbor: University of Michigan, Institute for Social Research, 1959.

Likert, R. *Human organization: Its management and value*. New York: McGraw-Hill, 1967.

Mitchell, T. R.; Biglan, A.; Oncken, G. R.; & Fiedler, F. E. The contingency model: Criticism and suggestions. *Academy of Management Journal*, 1970, *13*, 253–267.

Stogdill, R. M. *Handbook of leadership: A survey of theory and research*. New York: Free Press, 1974.

Related Research: General

Beach, B. A., & Beach, L. R. A note on judgements of situational favorableness and probability of success. *Organizational Behavior and Human Performance*, 1978, *22*, 69–74.

Chemers, M. M. Cultural training as a means for improving situational favorableness. *Human Relations*, 1969, *22*, 531–546.

Chemers, M. M., & Skrzypek, G. J. An experimental test of the contingency model of leadership effectiveness. *Journal of Personality and Social Psychology*, 1972, *24*, 172–177.

Csoka, L. S., & Fiedler, F. E. The effect of military training: A test of the contingency model. *Organizational Behavior and Human Performance*, 1972, 8 395–407.

Fiedler, F. E. The effect of leadership and cultural heterogeneity on group perform- ance: A test of the contingency model. *Journal of Experimental and Social Psychology*, 1966, *2*, 237–264.

———. Leadership experience and leader performance—Another hypothesis shot to hell. *Organizational Behavior and Human Performance*, 1970b, *5*, 1–14.

———. Note on the methodology of the Graen, Orris and Alvares studies testing the contingency model. *Journal of Applied Psychology*, 1971a, *55*, 202–204.

———. Validation and extension of the contingency model of leadership effectiveness: A review of empirical findings. *Psychological Bulletin*, 1971b, *76*, 128–148.

———. The effects of leadership training and experience: A contingency model interpretation. *Administrative Science Quarterly*, 1972, *17*, 453–470.

Fiedler, F. E. & Meuwese, W. A. T. The leader's contribution to task performance in cohesive and uncohesive groups. *Journal of Abnormal and Social Psychology*, 1963, *67*, 83–87.

Graen, G.; Alvares, K.; Orris, J. B.; & Martella, J. A. Contingency model of leadership effectiveness: Antecedent and evidential results. *Psychological Bulletin*, 1970, *74*, 285–296.

Graen, G.; Orris, J. B.; & Alvares, K. Contingency model of leadership effectiveness: Some experimental results. *Journal of Applied Psychology*, 1971, *55*, 196–201.

Green, S. G., & Nebeker, D. M. The effects of situational factors and leadership style on leader behavior. *Organizational Behavior and Human Performance*, 1977, *19*, 368–377.

Green, S. G.; Nebeker, D. M.; & Boni, M. A. Personality and situational effects on leader behavior. *Academy of Management Journal*, 1976, *19*, 184–194.

Gruenfeld, L. W.; Rance, D. E.; & Weissenberg, P. The behavior of task-oriented (low LPC) and socially-oriented (high LPC) leaders under several conditions of social support. *Journal of Social Psychology*, 1969, *79*, 99–107.

Hill, W. The validation and extension of Fiedler's theory of leadership effectiveness. *Academy of Management Journal*, 1969, *12*, 33–47.

Hovey, D. E. The low-powered leader confronts a messy problem: A test of Fiedler's theory. *Academy of Management Journal*, 1974, *17*, 358–362.

Hunt, J. G. Leadership-style effects at two managerial levels in a simulated organiza- tion. *Administrative Science Quarterly*, 1971, *16*, 476–485.

Konar-Goldband, E.; Rice, R. W.; & Monkarsh, W. Time-phased interrelationships of group atmosphere, group performance, and leader style. *Journal of Applied Psychology*, 1979, *64*, 401–409.

Larson, L. L., & Rowland, K. M. Leadership style, stress, and behavior in task performance. *Organizational Behavior and Human Performance*, 1973, 9, 407–420.

———. Leadership style and cognitive complexity. *Academy of Management Journal*, 1974, 17, 37–45.

Michaelsen, L. K. Leader orientation, leader behavior, group effectiveness and situational favorability: An empirical extension of the contingency model. *Organizational Behavior and Human Performance*, 1973, 9, 226–245.

Mitchell, T. R. Leader complexity and leadership style. *Journal of Personality and Social Psychology*, 1970, 16, 166–173.

Posthuma, A. B. *Normative data on the Least Preferred Co-worker Scale (LPC) and the Group Atmosphere Questionnaire (GA)*. TR No. 70–8. Seattle: University of Washington, 1970.

Rice, R. W. Construct validity of the Least Preferred Co-worker (LPC). *Psychological Bulletin*, 1978, 85, 1199–1237.

Rice, R. W., & Chemers, M. M. Predicting the emergence of leaders using Fiedler's contingency model of leadership effectiveness. *Journal of Applied Psychology*, 1973, 57, 281–287.

———. Personality and situational determinants of leader behavior. *Journal of Applied Psychology*, 1975, 60, 20–27.

Silver, P. F., & Hess, R. The stability of administrators' conceptual structures across interpersonal domains. *Educational and Psychological Research*, 1981, 1, 31–47.

Related Research: Education

Galfo, A. J. Measurement of group versus educational leaders' perception of leadership style and administrative theory orientation. *Journal of Educational Research*, 1975, 68, 310–314.

Garland, P., & O'Reilly, R. R. The effect of leader member interaction on organizational effectiveness. *Educational Administration Quarterly*, 1976, 12, 9–30.

Holloway, W. H., & Niazi, G. A. A study of leadership style, situation favorableness, and the risk taking behavior of leaders. *Journal of Educational Administration*, 1978, 16, 160–168.

Hopfe, M. W. Leadership style and effectiveness of department chairmen in business administration. *Academy of Management Journal*, 1970, 13, 301–310.

Martin, Y. M.; Isherwood, G. B.; & Lavery, R. E. Leadership effectiveness in teacher probation committees. *Educational Administration Quarterly*, 1976, 12, 87–99.

Miskel, C. G. Principals' attitudes toward work and co-workers, situational factors, perceived effectiveness, and innovative effort. *Educational Administration Quarterly*, 1977, 13, 51–70.

Reavis, C. A., & Derlega, V. J. Test of a contingency model of teacher effectiveness. *Journal of Educational Research*, 1976, 69, 221–225.

Part V
ORGANIZATIONS AS HUMAN CONTEXTS

The nature of the social environments that people inhabit in organizations is a topic of relatively recent interest in the social and behavioral sciences. Interest in individuals' social contexts was stimulated by the works of Kurt Lewin in the 1930s and 1940s (see Lewin, 1935, 1951). Lewin maintained that human behavior is a function of the individual's personality or needs in interaction with the social and psychological forces in that individual's environment. Interest in the description and analysis of environments as fields of forces affecting human behavior was thus triggered, and a body of literature on organizational climate emerged.

Since Lewin's time the scholarly work on organizational climate has taken a bewildering variety of directions. Conceptualizations of climate and its components have been diverse and only marginally interrelated. Research strategies have included field-based case studies, assessments of participants' perceptions, observations of objective features of organizations, and experimental manipulations of social variables (Forehand & Gilmer, 1964). At present no particular approaches to the study or interpretation of climate hold sway. In fact, the climate construct seems to have become fuzzier with the passage of time (James & Jones, 1974).

Nevertheless, interest in the topic remains keen, probably because of the acute sense one has on visiting several organizations that each has a unique and distinctive atmosphere that is almost tangible in its impact. In addition, the notion that one's environment strongly influences one's behavior has a compelling logic as well as a growing body of empirical support. Conceptual and empirical approaches to the study of the nature and effects of organizational climates are likely to proliferate until a convergence of orientations toward this elusive topic is achieved.

Two approaches to the study of climate, both pertaining primarily to schools, have been selected for this section of the book. Though representing divergent views of organizational climate, both perspectives have engendered widespread interest and attracted considerable research. The first of these, as examined in Chapter 8, is a descriptive approach developed by Andrew Halpin and Don Croft (1963). The focus in this framework is on principals' behavior patterns and teachers' behavior patterns as these combine to create school climates that are relatively open or closed as channels of communication. The second approach, as treated in Chapter 9, is a more direct outgrowth of Lewin's work mentioned earlier. This perspective, developed mainly by George Stern (1970), highlights the aspects of school environments that have bearing on individuals' psychological needs. Social forces that serve the expression or repression of human needs are identified. Both theoretical frameworks have important implications for administrative practice in school settings.

REFERENCES

Forehand, G. A., & Gilmer, B. von. Environmental variation in studies of organizational behaviors. *Psychological Bulletin,* 1964, 62, 361–382.

Halpin, A. W., & Croft, D. B. *The organizational climate of schools.* Chicago: University of Chicago, Midwest Administration Center, 1963.

James, L. R., & Jones, A. P. Organizational climate: A review of theory and research. *Psychological Bulletin,* 1974, 81, 1096–1112.

Lewin, K. *A dynamic theory of personality.* New York: McGraw-Hill, 1935.

Lewin, K. *Field theory in social science: Selected theoretical papers.* New York: Harper and Row, Torchbooks, 1951.

Stern, G. G. *People in context: Measuring person-environment congruence in education and industry.* New York: Wiley, 1970.

Chapter 8
The Description
of School Climates

You are a visiting dignitary in the Wunderkind School District and are being guided on a tour of this charming township's schools. During your first stop, at the Lake View School, you visit the faculty workroom and note that the many teachers there are busily completing forms of various sorts, grading papers, and preparing class materials. People seem to be engrossed in their tasks, and there is little conversation except for some questions asked of the principal when she enters the room.

At the Sea View School, your second stop, a visit to the teachers' lounge gives you a completely different impression. Here many of the teachers are chatting and bantering casually, while others seem to be planning a project together; the principal is conversing animatedly with a small group in the corner. A cheerful buzz of good humor permeates the atmosphere.

The two schools seem to represent opposite extremes, but the third stop on your tour affords yet a different impression. At Plainview School there are few teachers in the faculty room (actually a converted spare locker room); most are in their classrooms or out of the building. The few teachers in the room are individually occupied, one doing a crossword puzzle and another leafing idly through a magazine. The principal nods almost imperceptibly to the teacher as she enters the room and goes to the coffee pot, which is empty; they barely acknowledge her presence.

Your tour includes visits to the classrooms and other parts of the buildings, but in each school your initial impression, gleaned from the lounge, persists as you observe various features of the school. Obviously these schools are palpably different from each other in their atmosphere. Each seems to have a personality all its own. How can you articulate to your colleagues back home the unique impression each place conveys?

The tone, ambience, or atmosphere of an organization—the sense that a place has a quality uniquely its own—has come to be called the *climate* of the organization. To understand how the notion of climate has been conceptualized for empirical research, one can bear in mind the climate of a geographic region. Geographic climate results from the interaction of two important dimensions of nature: the atmospheric conditions such as prevailing winds, air pressure, and moisture; and the geological conditions such as latitude, altitude, topology, and ocean currents. The weather pattern or climate of a particular area is always a result of the blend of atmospheric and geographic conditions.

By analogy, the social climate of an organization can be viewed as a blend of two important dimensions of interpersonal interaction. Andrew Halpin and Don Croft conceived of the social climate of schools as a blend of two such dimensions: the principal's leadership and the teachers' interactions (Halpin & Croft, 1963). The group interactions of the teachers in a school might be regarded as analogous to the geographic contours of a region, and the principal's leadership style could be equated with the atmospheric conditions; in combination, the two result in a unique social texture in each organization, which has been called its climate. This merging of leader behavior and teacher behavior to yield organizational climate can be illustrated as in Figure 8–1.

THE CORE OF THE CLIMATE DESCRIPTION FRAMEWORK

The social climate of a school results from the reciprocal effects of the teachers' behavior pattern as a group and the principal's behavior pattern as a leader. Just as the group's characteristics can affect the ways in which the principal can exercise leadership, so the principal's behavior pattern can also affect the teachers' interpersonal interactions. Thus the reciprocal dynamics of leadership and group are viewed as the keys to identifying diverse school climates.

Four aspects of principals' leadership and four aspects of teachers' interactions were selected as the conceptual foundation for the analysis of school climates. These are defined and described in the next section. The eight

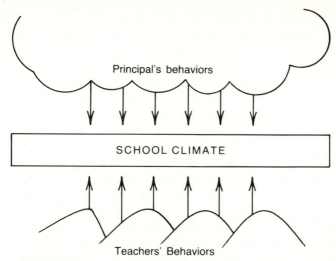

Figure 8-1   School Climate as a Blend of Principal Behaviors and Teacher Behaviors

aspects of social interaction are then combined to yield six distinctive climates that can be found in schools. As explained further in the section on relationships among constructs, the six types of climate range along a continuum from the most open climate to the most closed.

Major Constructs in the Descriptive Climate Framework

PRINCIPAL'S BEHAVIOR
This component of school climate pertains to the leader's style of interacting with the teachers. The way the principal behaves, as has been noted, influences the ways in which the teachers interact with each other and thus has considerable impact on the general atmosphere of the school. Four aspects of the principal's behavior that were identified as important by Halpin and Croft (see Halpin, 1966:152–154). These are aloofness, production emphasis, thrust, and consideration.

Aloofness refers to the psychological and physical distance from teachers that the principal typically maintains. Degree of formality is another way of interpreting this facet of the principal's behavior. Conducting faculty meetings as if they were business meetings, adhering to a tight agenda, establishing firm rules for teachers, and withholding the results of classroom visits are examples of aloofness on the principal's part. As Halpin (1966:151) noted, aloof behavior is universalistic rather than particularistic. Principals vary greatly in this dimension of their behavior, ranging from highly to not at all aloof.

Production emphasis refers to the degree of active supervision the principal typically exercises over staff. Degree of assertiveness in the supervisory role is another definition of production emphasis, which includes such actions as scheduling teachers' work, correcting teachers' mistakes, doing most of the talking, and seeing to it that teachers work hard. Strong production emphasis, in this framework, is associated with downward communication and insensitivity to teachers' reactions (Halpin, 1966:151). Principals differ in this aspect of their behavior, from being emphatic in supervision to paying scant attention to teachers' productivity.

Thrust pertains to the active, energetic role-modeling aspect of the principal's behavior. Personal drive and vigor are alternative interpretations of thrust. Arriving early and staying late, setting a good example by working hard, and being active and interested in new educational developments are all examples of high thrust. A leader characterized by high thrust does not expect teachers to give more of themselves than she or he does (Halpin, 1966:151) but sets a high standard for everyone. Principals may range from exhibiting high thrust to having virtually no thrust at all.

Consideration is a concern for staff members as individual beings; it is synonymous with kindness and humanitarianism. This dimension of leader behavior is exemplified by such actions as doing personal favors for teachers, helping them both in their work and in their personal lives, and standing up for the teachers' best interests. Considerate behavior is particularistic rather than universalistic. Principals vary greatly in this characteristic, ranging from highly considerate to not at all considerate.

These four dimensions of the principal's behavior pattern—aloofness, production emphasis, thrust, and consideration—are conceptually independent of each other. Knowing the principal's typical behavior with respect to one dimension does not help one to determine her or his behavior with reference to the other dimensions. One would have to assess all four aspects individually to derive a profile of the principal's behavior pattern.

TEACHERS' BEHAVIOR

This second major component of school climate is the pattern of interactions among teachers that evolves over a period of time. As noted earlier, the teachers' interactions can have considerable impact on the principal's behavior and thus can influence the general atmosphere of the school. The four dimensions of teachers' group behavior that make up this portion of the school climate framework are disengagement, hindrance, esprit, and intimacy.

Disengagement refers to the teachers' psychological and physical distance from each other and from the school as a whole. Teachers who are disengaged are "out of gear" with respect to the education process (Halpin, 1966:150). In a staff characterized by high disengagement, teachers bicker and criticize each other, form cliques, curry favor with the principal, annoy each other, and contemplate leaving. Disengagement can be regarded as the converse of cohesiveness. As the reader is probably well aware, schools vary greatly in this aspect of interpersonal life, with some having high teacher disengagement and others having little or no dissociation among teachers.

Hindrance refers to the burdensomeness of clerical tasks and responsibilities unrelated to teaching. In schools characterized by considerable hindrance teachers are overloaded with busywork (Halpin, 1966:150) and actually impeded in their teaching efforts by such requirements as paperwork, committees, reports, and routine duties. Hindrance, or "administrivia," is overwhelming in some schools and virtually nonexistent in others.

Esprit refers to the morale, spirit, and liveliness of the group of teachers. In schools characterized by high esprit, the teachers are cheerful and committed to education; they enjoy each other and are mutually respectful and helpful; they work energetically and are loyal to the school. As Halpin (1966:151) noted, the teachers in such schools are fulfilling their personal social needs at the same time as they are enjoying a sense of professional accomplishment. Schools vary in their levels of esprit; some are high in spirit, whereas others have hardly any esprit de corps at all.

Intimacy refers to the degree to which teachers share their private lives with each other and exchange confidences. Intimacy can serve to fulfill individuals' social needs without reference to the role demands of their job (Halpin, 1966:151). Schools that are characterized by high intimacy have teachers who socialize together outside school, visit each other's homes, discuss private matters deeply, and establish close friendships. In some schools the teachers' lives are like open books to each other, whereas in others the teachers rarely reveal their personal selves.

Like the four dimensions of the principal's behavior, the four facets of teachers' group behavior—disengagement, hindrance, esprit, and intimacy—are conceptually independent. Information about one aspect of the group's interactions yields no clues about the other aspects, but all are important features of the staff's interpersonal style.

A rough parallel can be noted between the dimensions of the leader's behavior and those of the teachers' behavior, as highlighted in Table 8–1. Each facet of the principal's behavior as an individual has an approximately equivalent counterpart in the teachers' behavior as a group. This is not to suggest that the pairs of characteristics occur simultaneously; that is not necessarily the case. For example, in one school having an aloof principal, the teachers might compensate for that remoteness by interacting cohesively with each other (as against a common enemy); in another school with an aloof principal the teachers might adopt equivalent behavior by becoming disengaged. Although all of the eight aspects of climate occur independently in reality, there is a conceptual linkage between the principal's behavior component and the teachers' behavior component in this theoretical framework.

Having specified the four elements of "atmospheric" conditions (princi-

Table 8–1 PARALLEL STRUCTURES OF THE TWO MAJOR COMPONENTS OF SCHOOL CLIMATE

PRINCIPAL'S BEHAVIOR	TEACHERS' BEHAVIORS
1. *Aloofness:* emotional and physical distance from the group.	1. *Disengagement:* emotional and physical distance from each other and the school.
2. *Production emphasis:* close supervision of tasks.	2. *Hindrance:* burdensome load of nonteaching tasks.
3. *Thrust:* energy, vigor, and drive as a role model; meeting both task and social needs simultaneously.	3. *Esprit:* energy, vigor, and drive as a cooperative group; meeting both task and social needs simultaneously as a group.
4. *Consideration:* concern for staff members as individuals.	4. *Intimacy:* concern for each other as individual people.

pal's behavior) and the four key elements of "geographic" conditions (teachers' behavior), we can now consider how these merge to form the prevailing "weather"—the climate—of the school.

Relationships Among Behavioral Constructs in the Descriptive Framework

As a result of their study of principals' and teachers' behavior patterns in a large number of elementary schools, Halpin and Croft (1963) found that six distinct profiles or configurations exist in schools. *Profile* here refers to a set of characteristics with respect to all eight aspects of interpersonal behavior as described earlier. The six profiles that were found in schools can be regarded as six distinctive *organizational climates.* These six climates, as they will be defined, described, and depicted, have been named: open climate, autonomous climate, controlled climate, familiar climate, paternal climate, and closed climate.

Open climate refers to an atmosphere characterized by high esprit and low disengagement on the part of teachers. They are not overburdened with paperwork, nor are they highly intimate, but they work well together to advance the interests of the school. The principal is highly energetic as well as considerate and not at all aloof; she or he does not emphasize production but works well with the faculty to advance the school. The major elements of an open climate are high esprit, low disengagement, and high thrust. The profile of a school with an open climate would look roughly like part A of Figure 8–2.

Autonomous climate describes an atmosphere of almost complete freedom for teachers to conduct their work and fulfill their social needs as they wish. Esprit and intimacy are relatively high, and there is little disengagement or hindrance. On the other hand, the principal, though a hard worker, is relatively aloof and lax with respect to supervision though considerate of teachers to an average degree. The profile of such a school would look

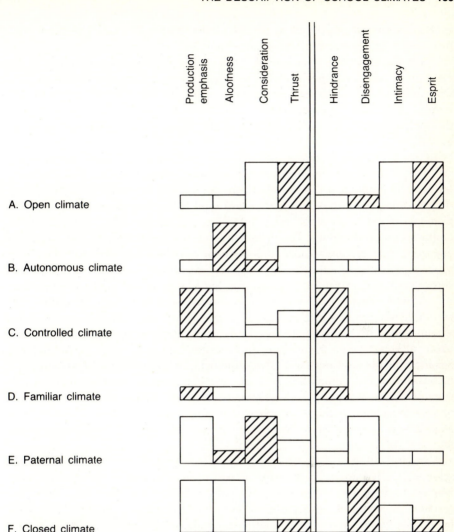

Figure 8–2   Graphic Profiles of Six School Climates

approximately like part B of Figure 8–2, with the most important elements being high aloofness and low consideration.

Controlled climate refers to an atmosphere of hard work at the expense of social life, although esprit is quite high. Teachers work and are committed to their job, but there is excessive paperwork and little personal interaction. The principal is dominating and directive but also aloof and not particularly considerate. The principal works hard enough to see that things run smoothly but is not a model of commitment or dedication. The profile of a school with a controlled climate, as depicted in part C of Figure 8–2, mainly features high production emphasis, high hindrance, and low intimacy.

Familiar climate describes an atmosphere of congenial sociability at the expense of task accomplishment. The teachers are disengaged with respect to work but intimate with respect to their personal lives. The principal, though highly considerate on a personal level and not at all aloof, does not emphasize productivity or supervise the work. In brief, the ambience is friendly but little gets done. The profile of such a school, illustrated as part D in Figure 8–2, centers on low production emphasis, low hindrance, and high intimacy.

Paternal climate denotes a social milieu in which the principal tries hard but is sadly ineffectual. The teachers are not overburdened with busywork, but they do not get along well together and tend to form competing factions. The principal is not at all aloof but is intrusive and unreasonable in terms of the emphasis on productivity. The principal is viewed as considerate and somewhat energetic but assumes more the style of a benevolent dictator than of a professional role model. The key features of a school with a paternal climate, shown as part E of Figure 8–2, are the low aloofness and high consideration.

Closed climate is the name for a social setting in which neither task accomplishment nor social satisfaction is prevalent. The staff is fragmented and disengaged. The teachers are overloaded with paperwork, and morale is at a nadir, although some friendships do form (perhaps as a psychological defense against a hostile environment). The principal in such a school is highly aloof and inconsiderate but demanding in a martinetlike manner. As Halpin (1966:181) suggested, the best prescription for such a school is radical surgery. The profile of a closed climate school, which would appear approximately like part F of Figure 8–2, is characterized especially by the low esprit, high disengagement, and low thrust present in the school.

In sum, there are six distinctive patterns of interaction that occur within schools. Each pattern represents a particular atmosphere or climate with respect to four aspects of the principal's behavior and four aspects of the teachers' behavior. The six patterns or profiles that have been found in schools have been designated open climate, autonomous climate, controlled climate, familiar climate, paternal climate, and closed climate.

As the names of the first and last types of climate suggest, the six configurations range along a continuum from the most open to the most closed in the order listed here. Openness, in this context, refers to genuineness and authenticity in interactions. Closedness, by contrast, refers to artificiality and inauthenticity. Openness also refers to the effective blending of personal needs with task accomplishment, whereas closedness implies the predominance of one at the expense of the other or, in extreme cases, the satisfaction of neither social needs nor professional role requirements. The arrangement of the six climates along a continuum from open to closed can be depicted as in Figure 8–3, an expansion of the diagram presented earlier as Figure 8–1. Typical principal behaviors and teacher behaviors are indicated, respectively, above

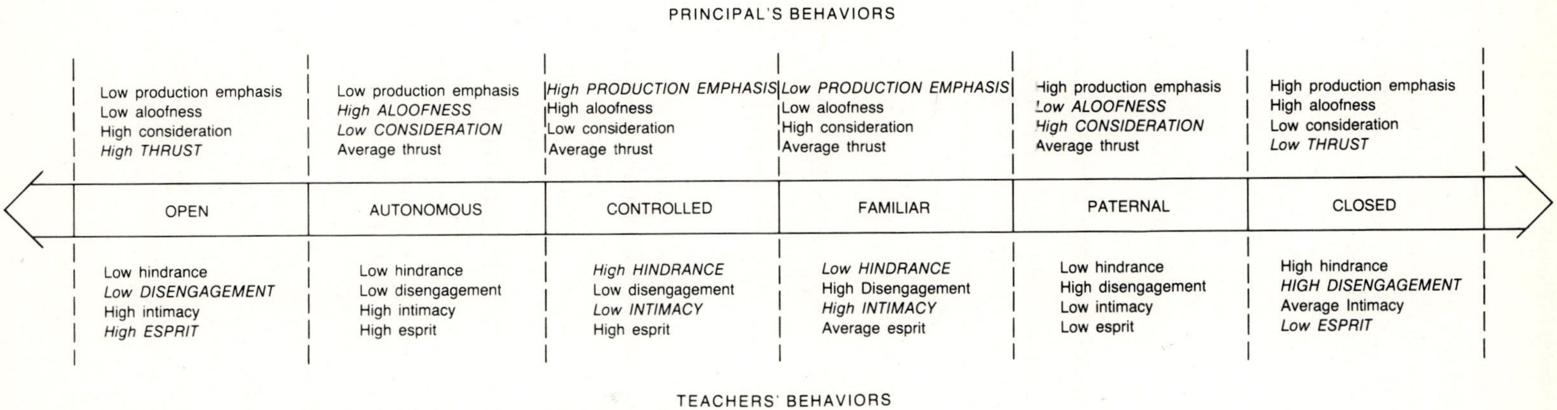

PRINCIPAL'S BEHAVIORS

OPEN	AUTONOMOUS	CONTROLLED	FAMILIAR	PATERNAL	CLOSED
Low production emphasis Low aloofness High consideration *High THRUST*	Low production emphasis *High ALOOFNESS* *Low CONSIDERATION* Average thrust	*High PRODUCTION EMPHASIS* High aloofness Low consideration Average thrust	*Low PRODUCTION EMPHASIS* Low aloofness High consideration Average thrust	High production emphasis *Low ALOOFNESS* *High CONSIDERATION* Average thrust	High production emphasis High aloofness Low consideration *Low THRUST*

OPEN	AUTONOMOUS	CONTROLLED	FAMILIAR	PATERNAL	CLOSED
Low hindrance *Low DISENGAGEMENT* High intimacy *High ESPRIT*	Low hindrance Low disengagement High intimacy High esprit	*High HINDRANCE* Low disengagement *Low INTIMACY* High esprit	*Low HINDRANCE* High Disengagement *High INTIMACY* Average esprit	Low hindrance High disengagement Low intimacy Low esprit	High hindrance *HIGH DISENGAGEMENT* Average Intimacy *Low ESPRIT*

TEACHERS' BEHAVIORS

Figure 8–3 School Climates on a Continuum from Open to Closed

and below the climates they represent; the most significant elements of each type of climate are capitalized.

A close examination of Figure 8–3 will reveal that the two sides of the continuum are like reflections of each other. Compare, for example, the open climate with the closed climate: for both principal and teachers, each dimension that is high in the open climate is low in the closed climate, and vice versa. The same relationship pertains in a comparison of the autonomous climate with the paternal climate: with the exception of hindrance, each facet of the one is reflected (opposite) in the other. Similarly, controlled climate and familiar climate are reflections of each other. Thus there is an approximate symmetry in the arrangement of climate types along the continuum.

Major Propositions Associated with Climate Descriptions

The climate framework treated in this chapter is a descriptive rather than an explanatory conceptualization. Therefore, the major propositions are definitional; they are statement-of-existence generalizations (Reynolds, 1971) rather than assertions about the dynamics of the climate phenomenon.

1. The climate of a school is a combination of the principal's behaviors and the teachers' behaviors.
   a. The four relevant aspects of the principal's behavior are aloofness, production emphasis, consideration, and thrust.
   b. The four relevant aspects of the teachers' interpersonal behavior are disengagement, hindrance, intimacy, and esprit.
2. The eight behavioral dimensions combine in various patterns to yield six distinctive climates that are found in schools. The six climates are open, autonomous, controlled, familiar, paternal, and closed.
3. The six climates range along a continuum from the most open or authentic to the most closed or inauthentic in the order listed in item 2.

DISCUSSION OF THE DESCRIPTIVE CLIMATE FRAMEWORK

The climate framework developed by Halpin and Croft must be regarded as a taxonomy or theoretical classification system that is comprehensive. All climate types are considered to be included somewhere along the open-closed continuum. Each of the six climates is regarded as an ideal type situated in specified positions along the continuum. In reality, each school approximates one of the pure types but probably deviates in some particulars. As a classification scheme this framework has been useful in categorizing schools and has been used for this purpose in numerous empirical studies. There are, however, some theoretical and empirical difficulties associated with this conceptualization. First, it is a cumbersome framework that contains some discrepancies and lacks parsimony. Second, the notions of openness and closedness are defined only vaguely and lack the sharp precision that good theory demands. At the operational level, researchers confront the difficult decision as to whether they are dealing with a categorical or a continuous variable. These issues are explored briefly in this section, which concludes with a summary of the strengths of this particular framework for analyzing schools.

Unwieldiness of the Climate Description Framework

This is a difficult conceptualization to learn. Students are asked to absorb at least four different dimensions of principal behavior, four different dimensions of teacher behavior, and six different climates. This is difficult enough in itself, since there is no explicit underlying rationale for selecting those particular aspects of behavior; to associate each climate with a particular profile is virtually impossible—and we have not even mentioned the factors yet. To complicate matters further, one dimension of behavior that was called teachers' behavior—namely, hindrance—does not seem to refer to teachers' interpersonal behavior at all, but to administrative demands instead. In brief, the framework lacks a clear underlying logic that would convince readers that these are in fact the existing climates and would enable readers to learn them readily.

Halpin (1966) hinted at a possible underlying conceptualization by referring to social needs, task accomplishment, and the effective blending of the two. If we think of instrumental action as task-oriented behavior and expressive action as person-oriented behavior (Bales, 1953), it becomes clear that the behavior dimensions specified in this framework almost but not quite conform to a parsimonious conceptualization, as illustrated in Figure 8–4. As shown in the diagram, both aloofness and disengagement refer to dissociation or emotional disconnectedness from the school. Both consideration and

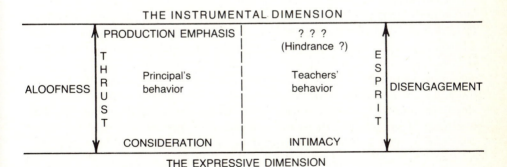

Figure 8–4   Instrumental and Expressive Behaviors as a Foundation for the Climate Framework

intimacy pertain to person-oriented behavior without reference to the tasks at hand. Both thrust and esprit pertain to the blending of social needs and task requirements. We encounter a problem in the task dimension, since hindrance takes the place of a set of teacher behaviors directed toward task accomplishment without reference to social needs. A conceptualization like that suggested here would encompass a complete set of principals' and teachers' behaviors and would enable researchers to study the social climate of schools without dependence on the one instrument associated with this theoretical framework. Stated differently, with a comprehensive theoretical foundation, scholars could study the phenomenon of climate rather than studying the schools' scores on a particular questionnaire.

Vagueness of Terminology

Associated with the difficulty of absorbing and integrating so many disparate elements is the problem of climate names that do not relate directly to the key elements of each climate. The titles do not evoke an awareness of the profiles underlying them. This is especially true of the two extremes, open climate and closed climate, since neither phrase has intrinsic connotations regarding any of the eight dimensions of behavior.

In using the terms *open* and *closed*, Halpin and Croft were drawing on Kurt Lewin's (1935) work on the structure of the mind (Halpin, 1966:170), which, the psychologist noted, can be relatively open (receptive to new information) or closed (rejecting of new information). Open-mindedness has been associated with "functional flexibility," whereas closed-mindedness is associated with "functional rigidity." The problem is that the aspects of interpersonal behavior that make up the six school climates do not have explicit bearing on the organization's receptivity to information from the environment or on the organization's adaptiveness to changing circumstances.

Halpin and Croft also related the notion of openness/closedness to authenticity or genuineness in interpersonal interactions (Halpin, 1966:203–224), though admitting that authenticity is a fuzzy concept (p. 204) and "a tricky concept" (p. 207). Unfortunately, the aspects of behavior that make up this climate framework do not explicitly indicate how open teachers and principals are in revealing their own personalities and perceiving each others' personalities. What the behavior dimensions do suggest indirectly is the extent to which channels of communication exist for improving the school. This is discussed at greater length in the concluding section of this chapter. With reference to channels of communication, one could consider schools to be relatively open or closed.

In brief, this climate framework could be strengthened considerably by naming the climates more consistently in accordance with their most salient behavioral features.

Operational Problems

As the reader has no doubt gathered, this climate framework is associated with a particular measurement instrument, which will be described in greater detail. Suffice it to say at this point that there are eight scales, one for each of the aspects of behavior just itemized. The dilemma a researcher confronts in using this device is whether to regard climate as a continuous variable or as a set of ideal categories.

In their research on elementary schools Halpin and Croft initially generated a pool of 1,000 items, which were completed by a pilot sample of teachers. The researchers then subjected the responses to a statistical treatment called factor analysis to determine which questionnaire items clustered together, and they refined the questionnaire so as to retain clusters and delete free-floating items. They repeated this process with several pilot samples of respondents successively until they were left with the eight clusters specified here. In other words, the refined instrument yielded eight first-order factors. The next step in the instrument development process was to assign the schools in their sample standardized scale scores (a score for each scale for each school), which they then subjected to another (second-order) factor analysis. The result was three second-order factors made up of high-loading scales, as follows (see Halpin, 1966:190):

Factor I: disengagement, esprit, thrust
Factor II: intimacy, production emphasis, hindrance
Factor III: consideration, aloofness

With the use of a computer, each school was then assigned a factor score for each of the three factors.

After these operations had been completed, the identification of six climates as ideal types was quite mechanical. A high score for Factor I but no other factors was considered the first category (open climate), and an exceptionally low score on Factor I but no other factors was considered the sixth category (closed climate). Factor III was the focus of the second and fifth categories: an exceptionally high score on this factor but no others was considered the second category (autonomous climate), and a relatively low score on Factor III but no other factors was named the fifth category (paternal climate). The middle two categories were based in a similar way on Factor II scores: a high Factor II score was considered the third category (controlled climate), whereas an especially low score on that factor signified the fourth category (familiar climate). Incidentally, this method of identifying ideal climates accounts for the symmetry along the climate continuum noted earlier.

We have not resolved, but in fact have exacerbated, the dilemma over whether climate is a categorical or a continuous variable. Factors are, by definition, statistically unrelated (orthogonal); therefore, statistically they cannot form one continuum. In this instance there are three continua. Scholars who are studying schools from the perspective of this climate framework need to determine in advance whether they are dealing with six distinct categories (types) of climate or whether they are concerned with a global concept measured along one continuum. Researchers have treated this operational problem in various ways, as will be illustrated further, with the result that aggregating the research findings is difficult, if not impossible.

Strengths of the Climate Description Perspective

To suggest that a conceptual framework has weaknesses is not to obviate its utility as a foundation for research or as a perspective for understanding schools as organizations. As noted frequently throughout this book, each theory has its shortcomings and its unique strengths as a way of thinking about reality.

The behavior description approach to climate treated in this chapter is one of the few conceptual frameworks pertaining specifically to schools rather than to organizations in general. In this respect it is uniquely applicable to education systems. Although the conceptualization and its instrumentation could be altered to apply to other organizations, this climate framework was conceived explicitly with schools in mind and might therefore capture a set of interpersonal qualities that are exclusive to education.

Another strength of this approach is that its focus is on observable behaviors rather than on less tangible constructs requiring inferences on the part of respondents. Furthermore, this framework is linked to a manageable instrument that is easily administered and quite quickly completed by respondents. Scoring is quite simple if total scores or scale scores are sought (though difficult if specific climates are to be identified).

Despite the fact that Halpin (1966:193–203) himself acknowledged that the instrumentation and the conceptual work were in their early stages of development, hundreds of researchers have seized on the questionnaire and used it as it appeared in 1966 or earlier without additional refinement. The climate framework, as indicated earlier, comes close to being a concise and compelling conceptualization dealing with instrumental and expressive interactions. If developed further by diligent researchers, this descriptive framework has the potential to evolve into an elegant explanatory theory about interpersonal behaviors in schools.

RESEARCH ON DESCRIPTIONS OF SCHOOL CLIMATES

We have alluded to a questionnaire that is intrinsic to this framework and its related research. This section describes the instrument and its scoring and reviews some of the descriptive research on school climates. The research review is divided into sections according to whether the studies treated climate as a single continuum, dealt with specific types of climate, or synthesized the findings of other research.

Instrumentation

The instrument used for all of the climate research related to this framework is the *Organizational Climate Description Questionnaire*, commonly known as the OCDQ, which was developed by Halpin and Croft (1963) for their study of schools (see Halpin, 1966:148–149). The OCDQ consists of 64 statements about principals' and teachers' behaviors in schools, and respondents indicate on a four-point scale for each item the frequency with which each behavior occurs in their own school (rarely, sometimes, often, or very frequently). The items, though appearing in mixed order in the questionnaire, represent eight scales of between six and ten items each. An accurate measure of school climate requires that all or most of the teachers (and possibly other staff members) respond. The responses are then grouped by schools to determine the average scale scores or total scores for each school. Some OCDQ validity data were provided by Andrews (1965), Halpin and Croft (1963), and Hall (1972).

As suggested earlier, the research question for which the OCDQ is used will determine to some extent the scoring technique applied. If one is interested in a global or general climate measure on one continuum, there are a few options: (1) compute all the average scale scores; inverse the scores of the negative scales (aloofness, production emphasis, disengagement, and hindrance); and sum across the eight scales; (2) reverse-score the negative items and sum across all 64 items; (3) as recommended by Appleberry and Hoy (1969), add the thrust and esprit scores for each school and subtract from that sum the disengagement score (readers will recall that these were the high-loading scales on Factor I).

If it is particular climates the researcher seeks, the scoring procedures are a bit more complex. In this case the options are: (1) submit the scale scores for the research sample to a factor analysis and, if there are three factors congruent with the Halpin-Croft factors, designate schools according to their highest or lowest factor scores; (2) develop a profile of scale scores for each school and assign schools to the climate category with the most nearly similar profile; (3) for each school compute the scale deviations from the norm for each type of climate, and classify the school according to the smallest deviation (this is similar to option 2 but more statistically sound).

The OCDQ is clearly much more manageable as a continuous measure than as a categorical one. Nevertheless, it has been used often in both ways for empirical research.

Research on Climate as a Continuous Variable

Several scholars have been interested primarily in the concept of openness (or closedness) and its possible relationship to other variables. In two such studies general openness of school climate was computed by summing the esprit and thrust scale scores and subtracting the disengagement score. Appleberry and

Hoy (1969), in a study of 45 elementary schools, found that school climate was related to teachers' orientations with regard to controlling students: the more open the school climate, the more humanistic the teachers' Pupil Control Ideology scores. In a related study Friesen (1972) compared a school that allowed students considerable independence of action with one that was much more controlling of students. He found that teachers in the former school perceived their own school's climate to be significantly more open than did those in the latter school; however, students completing a modified version of the OCDQ did not perceive a difference in general openness of climate. It appears, then, that teachers' esprit and disengagement, along with principals' thrust, relate to the degree of control students experience in school.

Using a modified version of the OCDQ to measure district central office climate as perceived by district administrators, Hughes (1968) found that the central office climates in innovative districts were significantly more like the open climate ideal type than were the climates in noninnovative districts. Analysis of the individual scale scores indicated that lower disengagement and higher esprit, both dimensions of Factor I, differentiated the innovative from the noninnovative districts.

In an unusual study of individual teachers' perceptions of school climate in relation to their expectations regarding changes in education, individuals' perceptions of the principals' thrust, consideration, and production emphasis were found to be directly related to optimism of expectations, whereas perceived hindrance was directly related to pessimism (Helsel, Aurbach, & Willower, 1969). From the teachers' point of view, the principal's behaviors but not the teachers' were related to anticipations of successful desired changes.

Another study of individuals' OCDQ scale scores indicated that teachers' perceptions of school climate are related to the combined effects of perceived organizational structure and individual personalities (George & Bishop, 1971).

Research on Climate as a Categorical Variable

The research on which this descriptive climate framework was based is a study of 71 elementary schools. Halpin and Croft (1963) identified the six prototypical organizational climates as described earlier and classified the schools in their sample accordingly. They found 17 open, 9 autonomous, 12 controlled, 6 familiar, 12 paternal, and 15 closed schools (Halpin, 1966:171–173). Note that this distribution does not approximate a normal curve, which suggests that what was measured was not a continuous variable (or that the sample was not representative of a normal population of elementary schools).

Some research has been conducted primarily for the purpose of verifying the validity and reliability of the OCDQ. In a study of teachers' OCDQ responses in 81 schools, Brown (1964) found that the first-order factor structure (the eight scales) was supported, but the second-order factor structure was not. Brown found that his three-factor solution differed substantially from the

Halpin-Croft factors and that a four-factor solution best accounted for variations in scale scores. Thomas and Slater (1972) also supported a four-factor structure in their study of Australian schools. Brown (1964) found schools having five of the six climates in his sample, but hybrid climates were also identified.

In another validation study, this one using 48 schools, Watkins (1968) found that faculty perceptions in 12 of the schools (one-quarter of the sample) were so varied that meaningful classification of those schools was impossible. When the remaining 36 schools were classified, it was found that black schools, secondary schools, and large schools were most often familiar, paternal, or closed (that is, having closed tendencies). Furthermore, secondary school teachers reported considerably more difficulty in answering the OCDQ than did elementary school teachers. These findings suggest that the questionnaire should be modified so as to be applicable to larger schools, where assistant principals and department heads may assume many of the functions that elementary principals in small schools perform.

The variations in teachers' responses, as found in the Watkins (1968) study, might suggest that members of informal groups would have more similar perceptions than total faculties would have. Heller (1964), however, found that this was not the case. Both for perceived climate and for preferred climate, informal groups were as varied in their perceptions as were total faculties. Wide variation in respondents' perceptions suggests that modification of the instrument toward more convergent responses would be desirable.

No studies were located in which the full climate typology was related to variations in other features of schools.

Reviews of the Climate Description Research

Several reviews of the OCDQ research have been undertaken in efforts to arrive at some generalizations about the antecedents or effects of school climate. Some *antecedents* of climate openness seem to be extensive experience on the part of principals and teachers (Cunningham, 1975) and higher student socioeconomic status (Brown & House, 1967; Cunningham, 1975), as well as relatively small school size (Cunningham, 1975) and elementary grade level (Mullins, 1976; Schwandt, 1978). Some *effects* of climate openness seem to be less student alienation, higher student morale, and fewer school dropouts (Mullins, 1976); greater innovativeness (Thomas, 1976); and greater job satisfaction on the part of teachers (Schwandt, 1978). There is some disagreement about the relationship between school climate and student achievement; Cunningham (1975) and Mullins (1976) concluded that climate openness was associated with higher student achievement; however, Schwandt (1978) maintained there was no clearly demonstrated relationship between school climate and student achievement.

Ross Thomas (1976), in a thorough review of the published and unpublished OCDQ research, noted the discrepant findings pertaining to teachers' and principals' personalities and to student achievements or achievement gains. He also observed with some disappointment that the OCDQ has declined somewhat in popularity since the enthusiasm of the late 1960s and early 1970s. Continued research effort, he emphasized, would be essential for the advancement of knowledge about education. Some research endeavors that would enrich the study of climate immensely are refinements of the OCDQ that would render it applicable to secondary schools (Carver & Sergiovanni, 1969); the establishment of national norms by means of a fully representative sample of schools; the development of a tight conceptual framework for the instrument; and the identification of correlatives of school climate.

IMPLICATIONS OF THE CLIMATE DESCRIPTION FRAMEWORK FOR ENHANCING STUDENT LEARNING OUTCOMES

The extent to which a student learns subject matter, skills, and attitudes in school is clearly a matter of the student's own commitment and the teacher's classroom skill—is it not? Then what bearing can the principal's behaviors vis-á-vis teachers and teachers' interactions with each other have on students' achievement in schools? Does the behavior description framework for studying school climate help us to learn what administrators can do to enhance student outcomes?

Although the research evidence on student achievement in relation to climate is mixed, there has been some support for the conjecture that climate affects student outcomes (see Thomas, 1976:453). A brief examination of the dimensions of behavior underlying the climate profiles might clarify why such a relationship, albeit an indirect one, should be anticipated.

The key administrative behavior pattern, readers will recall, is thrust—the energy and drive the principal exhibits as a role model for teachers. Principals who are in evidence in their buildings, observing what transpires, offering helpful suggestions, and mentioning new techniques at appropriate times, can certainly help teachers focus on their tasks and sharpen their professional skills. Aloofness, by contrast, would reduce the principal's knowledge of what is going on and would serve to discourage teachers from seeking advice and from offering suggestions; many of the exceptional techniques and creative ideas of outstanding teachers would thus be less likely to spread throughout a school that had an aloof principal. Genuine consideration for teachers could help in resolving problems that might interfere with teaching; it might also help teachers feel secure enough to share their teaching problems and seek advice honestly rather than withholding such information for fear of reprisals. In contrast, production emphasis, if exercised in a domineering or authoritarian manner, can generate resentment and stimulate the withholding of suggestions and personal information that could benefit the school as a whole as well as individual teachers. In brief, frequent sharing of information in the form of ideas, suggestions, advice, and problems can help individuals learn how to resolve their own teaching problems and facilitate the dissemination of the best practices throughout the school. To the extent that the principal's behavior fosters or impedes this communication, then, the climate of the school is related to the quality of instruction students receive.

As noted earlier, the key behavior pattern of teachers as a group is esprit—the energy, loyalty, and mutual supportiveness that teachers bring to the school. Esprit is expressed in terms of enthusiasm for school activities, commitment to helping students, and mutual respect among teachers—behaviors that are certainly visible to students and possibly infectious. In addition, high esprit implies teamwork and group action; in seeking the optimal solution to school problems or instructional problems, many heads are surely better than one. At the opposite extreme, disengagement refers to disinterest, dissociation, and disconnectedness of staff. Teachers in such a situation do not strive to improve their craft, do not seek advice from colleagues or welcome it when offered, and do not work together to solve problems. Thus there is relatively little learning, and teaching itself can be expected to suffer. Similarly, when hindrance is high, teachers are so overburdened with nonteaching paperwork and routine duties that they have little time, energy, or interest left for healthy developmental interaction. Finally, although intimacy may not seem particularly significant for professional development, it can be vitally important, since teachers who are close personal friends often confide their deepest professional experiences as well as their personal problems. Furthermore, teachers who have established an intimate relationship generate almost unlimited time for out-of-school social interaction and for sharing educational viewpoints, ideas, and plans—hence for growing professionally. In sum, it seems that for teachers' behaviors as well as the principal's, the various dimensions of climate relate to the extent to which good ideas are shared and educational problems resolved.

In terms of teachers' professional growth and development, it is clear that all the dimensions of school climate are likely to have some indirect impact on what students experience in the classroom and hence on the learning that takes place. How might an administrator affect a school's climate and move the school toward the open end of the continuum? Since the aspects of the principal's behavior are self-explanatory—suggesting that the change-oriented principal needs to be introspective and to adopt behavior patterns indicative of high thrust, high consideration, low aloofness, and low production emphasis—we will concentrate on teachers' group behaviors by offering some suggestions for increasing esprit and intimacy while reducing the hindrance and disengagement within a school.

To minimize *hindrance*, a principal could:

1. Assign as much of the paperwork as possible to clerical staff. Through both automation and carefully designed procedures, principals can relieve teachers of much of the attendance, reporting, and record-

keeping labor associated with schooling in general and funded programs in particular.

2. Assign as much of the paperwork as possible to volunteers by drawing on parents, senior citizens, service organizations, and college students. Some schools have successfully implemented a "class parent" plan to relieve some of the clerical, instructional, and extracurricular load of teachers.

3. Assign many of the routine duties to volunteers or to responsible students. Such responsibilities as yard, cafeteria, and corridor supervision; audiovisual equipment distribution; library assistance; and chaperoning activities can well be assumed by interested citizens. Students could benefit immensely from having opportunities to volunteer their help.

In an effort to improve *esprit,* a principal could:

1. Invite recommendations and suggestions from faculty regarding improvements of the school—and implement those suggestions to the fullest extent possible.

2. Appoint faculty committees, preferably on a volunteer basis, to generate solutions to problems that the teachers themselves have identified—and abide by the recommendations of these committees to the fullest extent possible.

3. Institute a variety of school projects that can attract public attention and serve as vehicles for building school pride. Such events as science or craft fairs, theatrical and musical performances, student publications, and athletic demonstrations—all organized by groups of teachers with students—can both build school spirit and increase teachers' interpersonal interaction.

4. Provide time and an attractive, functional workplace for teachers to pursue group ventures. The time can be made available by means of carefully planned large-group instruction and the use of adult volunteers. The space might require creative imagination and ingenuity but is worth some effort and expense if it enhances teachers' cooperative effort.

5. Express appreciation and recognition, both formally and informally, to those who invest themselves to further school activities.

To reduce *disengagement* if it is present, the principal could:

1. Try some or all of the foregoing strategies for increasing esprit.

2. Confer with the teachers individually to learn what might engage their interest in the school. It is important that the suggestions of the more alienated or disinterested teachers be adopted if at all possible, particularly if the implementation would involve the individual who made the suggestion.

3. Initiate several faculty social activities, perhaps planned by a committee, for bringing teachers together in pleasant, nonthreatening situations. Parties, picnics, bring-a-dish suppers, and sports competitions
can sometimes be vehicles for reaching disengaged teachers informally.

4. Arrange a retreat for a weekend or longer so that teachers, away from
the school and from home distractions, can air their differences, invent
solutions to problems, and plan for the future.

The key to increasing *intimacy* is ample informal interaction that can
blossom into close personal friendships. To increase the likelihood of such
developments, all of the foregoing suggestions are recommended. In addition,
the principal could:

1. Provide a comfortable, attractive eating facility for teachers. Early-
morning snacks, coffee breaks, lunches, and after-school refreshments
help to foster informal interaction. At such times teachers may discover
common interests that can serve as the core of personal friendships.

2. Implement a staff development program, planned and organized by
teachers, designed to bring teachers together in an informal setting for
personal growth and learning. After-school sessions could be followed
by social events so that the interaction stimulated in the workshop can
be extended to more personal domains.

The social atmosphere or climate of a school cannot be changed overnight
or by token gestures or halfhearted attempts. Such change requires a sincere
concern, a receptivity to information both critical and complimentary, and a
persistent commitment to improvement despite obstacles. Additional suggestions for improving school climate are offered in Brown (1965), Halpin (1967),
and Miklos (1965).

Having considered some strategies for opening the communication
channels among teachers and between teachers and the principal, and having
examined the potential relevance of climate to student learning, we are still
confronted with the question of whether school climate does in fact affect
student outcomes. As Schwandt (1978) remarked following his review of the
climate research, there has been virtually no research on climate as an
intervening variable—that is, on how climate affects the relationships between
other important variables. Some of the empirical questions that merit further
investigation are:

1. For schools that are similar with respect to size, grade levels, and
student demographic characteristics, is the openness of the climate
related to student outcomes? Is one particular type of climate
associated with the greatest student gains?

2. Does school climate relate differentially to students' cognitive, attitudinal, and skill achievements? For example, is one type of climate
associated with the greatest content learning and recall, another type
with the highest student self-respect and enthusiasm for school?

3. Can principals who remain with their schools over time effectively change the school's climate by intent? If so, which strategies are most effective in moving a school's climate toward the open end of the continuum?

4. Are there different types of climate that are associated with high achievement for different student populations? For example, do low-SES (socioeconomic status) students fare best with one type of climate, middle-SES students with another? Do college-bound students do best with one type of climate but vocationally oriented students accomplish more with another type?

Because of the implications of climate for teachers' professional growth and development, it seems most likely that school climate has a profound though indirect impact on student learning outcomes. By means of carefully designed and creative studies, we can discover whether this is in fact the case.

MASTERY QUIZ

Try to complete each of the following sentences without referring to any of the preceding pages. The correct answers appear in Appendix C, page 392. If you can complete all ten items correctly, you have truly mastered this difficult framework.

1. The two major components of this climate framework are:
   a. teachers' behavior patterns and students' behavior patterns.
   b. teachers' behavior patterns and principals' behavior patterns.
   c. principals' behavior patterns and students' behavior patterns.
   d. principals' behavior patterns and principals' personality characteristics.

2. Of the following terms, the one that is not a dimension of the principals' behavior is:
   a. consideration.   c. thrust.
   b. disengagement.   d. production emphasis.

3. The pair of terms that does not pertain to principals' behavior is:
   a. production   c. thrust—consideration.
      emphasis—consideration.   d. aloofness—production
   b. controlled—familiar.   emphasis.

4. All but one of the following refer to teachers' behaviors; the exception is:
   a. esprit.   c. intimacy.
   b. disengagement.   d. thrust.

5. Of the following pairs of terms, the one that represents the best match between an aspect of the principal's behavior and an aspect of the teachers' behavior is:
   a. esprit—disengagement.   c. controlled—
   b. disengagement—   paternal.
      aloofness.   d. aloofness—production
                                           emphasis.

6. The set of terms below that does not represent parts of a set is:
   a. controlled—familiar—paternal.
   b. esprit—intimacy—hindrance.
   c. thrust—production emphasis—consideration.
   d. autonomous—disengagement—intimacy.
7. Of the following terms, the one that does not refer to a type of climate is:
   a. considerate.
   b. familiar.
   c. open.
   d. autonomous.
8. The one of the following pairs of terms that does not pertain to types of climate is:
   a. open—closed.
   b. autonomous—paternal.
   c. esprit—thrust.
   d. controlled—familiar.
9. The sequence below that represents the best ordering of types of climate is:
   a. open—autonomous—controlled—familiar—paternal—closed.
   b. open—familiar—closed—paternal—autonomous—controlled.
   c. open—paternal—controlled—autonomous—familiar—closed.
   d. open—familiar—autonomous—paternal—controlled—closed.
10. The type of climate that is most nearly the opposite of autonomous climate is:
    a. controlled climate.
    b. open climate.
    c. paternal climate.
    d. familiar climate.

EXERCISES

1. On eight scales of from 1 (low) to 10 (high), rate the school in which you now work or recently worked in terms of the four principal behaviors and the four teacher behaviors. Then:
   a. Make a graphic representation of the school's climate as you perceive it.
   b. Determine which type of climate the school most nearly represents.
   c. If the school is not in the open climate category, suggest five (5) actions the principal could take to enhance the climate.
2. Interview five (5) classmates or colleagues who work in different schools regarding the relevant principals' and teachers' behaviors. Then:
   a. Classify the five schools in terms of the climate types they best represent.
   b. Determine which of those schools you would most like to work in, and explain why.
3. Analyze the case description (Appendix A, pages 383–387) from the perspective of this climate framework. In developing your case analysis, follow an outline such as this:
   a. State the theory briefly, and then state the case problem in terms relevant to the theory.

b. Discuss each major construct from the theory with reference to the case situation, emphasizing the relevance of this element to the problem as a whole.

c. Explain how the problem can be resolved or could have been prevented by a leader who knew this theory thoroughly.

An example of a theory-based case analysis following this outline is provided as a guide in Appendix B, pages 000–000.

4. Consider a school that is faced with a problem of extensive and repeated vandalism as well as thefts of school property. Select three (3) of the climates featured in this theoretical framework, and for each one invent a vignette or story of two or three paragraphs to describe how the school staff (principal and teachers) would respond to this problem. Your product will be three stories, each one representing a particular school climate.

REFERENCES

Major Sources

Halpin, A. W. The organizational climate of schools, *Theory and research in administration*. New York: Macmillan, 1966, 131–249.

Halpin, A. W., & Croft, D. B. *The organizational climate of schools*. Chicago: University of Chicago, Midwest Administration Center, 1963.

Related Conceptual Literature

Bales, R. F. The equilibrium problem in small groups. In T. Parsons, R. F. Bales, & E. Shils (Eds.), *Working papers in the theory of action*. Glencoe, Ill.: Free Press, 1953, 11–161.

Brown, A. Two strategies for changing climate. *The CSA Bulletin* (Publication of the Canadian School Administrators Association), 1965, *4*, 64–80.

Halpin, A. W. Change and organizational climate. *Journal of Educational Administration*, 1967, *5*, 5–25.

Lewin, K. *A dynamic theory of personality*. New York: McGraw-Hill, 1935, 194–238.

Reynolds, P. D. *A primer in theory construction*. Indianapolis, Ind.: Bobbs-Merrill, 1971.

Related Research

Andrews, J. School organizational climate: Some validity studies. *Canadian Education and Research Digest*, 1965, *5*, 317–334.

Appleberry, J. B., & Hoy, W. K. The pupil control ideology of professional personnel in "open" and "closed" elementary schools. *Educational Administration Quarterly*, 1969, *5*, 74–85.

Brown, R. J. Identifying and classifying organizational climates in twin city area elementary schools. Ph.D. dissertation, University of Minnesota, 1964 (Diss. Abstr. No. 65–7324).

Browne, A. F., & House, J. H. The organizational component in education. *Review of Educational Research*, 1967, *37*, 399–416.

Carver, F. D., & Sergiovanni, T. J. Some notes on the OCDQ. *Journal of Educational Administration*, 1969, *7*, 78–81.

Cunningham, P. A survey of selected research on the Organizational Climate Description Questionnaire. Ph.D. dissertation, Temple University, 1975 (Diss. Abstr. No. 75-28, 271).

Friesen, D. Variations in perceptions of organizational climate. *Alberta Journal of Educational Research,* 1972, *18,* 91–99.

George, J. R., & Bishop, L. K. Relationship of organizational structure and teacher personality characteristics to organizational climate. *Administrative Science Quarterly,* 1971, *16,* 467–475.

Hall, J. W. A comparison of Halpin and Croft's organizational climates and Likert and Likert's organizational systems. *Administrative Science Quarterly,* 1972, *17,* 586–590.

Heller, R. W. Informal organization and perceptions of organizational climate of schools. Ph.D. dissertation, Pennsylvania State University, 1964 (Diss. Abstr. No. 64–13, 403).

Helsel, R. A.; Aurbach, H. A.; & Willower, D. J. Teachers' perceptions of organizational climate and expectations of successful change. *Journal of Experimental Education,* 1969, *38,* 39–44.

Hughes, L. W. "Organizational climate"—Another dimension in the process of innovation? *Educational Administration Quarterly,* 1968, *4,* 17–28.

Miklos, E. School climate and program development. *The Canadian Administrator,* 1965, *4,* 25–28.

Mullins, J. Analysis and synthesis of research utilizing the Organizational Climate Description Questionnaire: Organizations other than elementary schools. Ph.D. dissertation, University of Georgia, 1976 (Diss. Abstr. No. 77–12, 408).

Schwandt, D. R. Analysis of school organizational climate research 1962–1977: Toward construct clarification. Ph.D. dissertation, Wayne State University, 1978 (Diss. Abstr. No. 78–16, 082).

Thomas, A. R. The organizational climate of schools. *International Review of Education,* 1976, *22,* 441–463.

Thomas, A. R., & Slater, R. C. The OCDQ: A four factor solution for Australian schools? *Journal of Educational Administration,* 1972, *10,* 197–208.

Watkins, J. F. The OCDQ—An application and some implications. *Educational Administration Quarterly,* 1968, *4,* 46–60.

Chapter 9
School Climates
as Social Forces

THE NEEDS-PRESS FRAMEWORK

The atmosphere, tone, or ambience of an organization permeates the entire organization and colors everything that happens there. Each organization seems to have a distinctive personality. This pervasive quality has been called the *climate* of the organization. Like the weather all around us, the climate of an organization is an important aspect of the context in which individual actions occur.

Organizational climate has been conceptualized in a variety of ways. Climate has been an elusive notion, difficult to define precisely or measure scientifically. Nevertheless, if one visits a number of schools, it is apparent that each has a special quality manifested in the sensations one feels while walking through the building.

One of the most interesting approaches to the study of organizational climate is that introduced by George Stern (1970, 1971) as an outgrowth of earlier work in the field of psychology. Stern conceived of the climate of an organization as the social context in which each individual's personality is expressed or repressed in varying degrees. The social context, as a relatively enduring pattern of actions and interactions of people within the organization, constitutes a set of social forces or pressures on each individual; these pressures may be either congruent or discrepant with the personalities of particular individuals.

Stern's primary emphasis is on the systematic description of the social forces inherent to organizations, especially schools. By virtue of the relatively sensitive measuring device developed by Stern and his colleagues, it is possible to specify the pattern of interpersonal pressures peculiar to each organization. To understand the conceptualization of climate as a pattern of social forces, however, it is necessary to review earlier conceptualizations of social behavior as a function of personality and environment in interaction.

THE THEORY OF CLIMATE AS SOCIAL PRESS

Kurt Lewin, a psychologist who became deeply interested in field theory as it applies to the discipline of physics, developed a theory of human action that is analogous to physical theories of the behavior of matter. Just as the behavior of physical matter is a result of the dynamic interplay of forces within (such as energy) and forces from without (such as gravity), so human behavior can be viewed as the dynamic interplay of forces within individuals (such as drives) and forces from the environment (such as social norms). In *A Dynamic Theory of Personality*, Lewin (1935) set forth a complex theoretical framework in which the individual is seen as inhabiting a "psychological space" made up of forces that act on the internally produced drives of the individual. The book provides the theoretical background for Lewin's classic formulation, $B = f(P \cdot E)$, where B = behavior, P = personality, and E = environment. That is, behavior is a function of the interaction between the personality and the environment.

Among the numerous scholars whom Lewin's work influenced was the psychologist Henry Murray. Murray (1938) interpreted the Lewinian concept of internal and external forces as *needs* and *press*, respectively. He identified a set of 30 forces that constitute the individual's psychological needs or internal forces. These same forces have environmental counterparts that act as social press or external forces. Individuals' behaviors could thus be viewed as the result of the dynamic interplay between psychological needs and analogous dimensions of environmental press, as illustrated in Figure 9–1.

The 30 forces specified by Murray as making up both internal and external influences on behavior are displayed and defined in Table 9–1. It is important to study these forces and their meanings since they provide the foundation or taxonomic base of the work on organizational climate to follow.

As explained by Stern (1962a), the 30 forces enumerated by Murray represent "organizational tendencies [within individuals] that appear to give unity and direction to personality" (p. 703). Since internal states or needs cannot be observed directly, they must be inferred from actions performed by

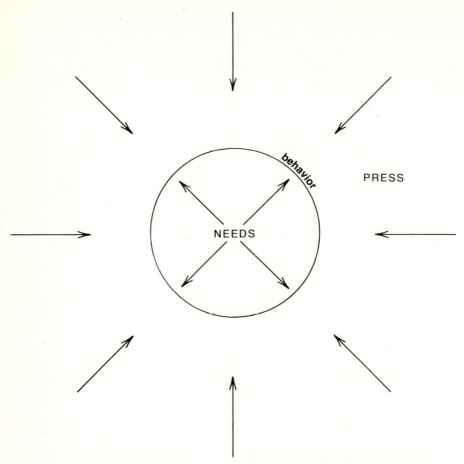

Figure 9–1   Behavior as the Interplay Between Personality Needs and Environment Press

the individual or from responses to projective psychological tests. One such test that has been used widely in psychological research is the Activities Index (Stern, 1962a:704n), which is described later in this chapter.

Like needs, social press cannot be observed directly. Stern defined press as "a property or attribute of an organizational setting which facilitates or impedes the efforts of the individual to satisfy his [or her] need strivings" (Steinhoff & Bishop, 1974:38). The types of press acting on individuals in an organizational setting can be inferred either from the interactions among people and observed features of the setting or from responses to perceptual questionnaires completed by a representative sample of people within the organization. By combining the questionnaire responses of many people within the organization, one can glean the group's perceptions of the types of press

Table 9–1 DIMENSIONS OF PERSONALITY AND ENVIRONMENT

1. ABASEMENT   ASSURANCE

Abasement = self-depreciation: ready acknow-
ledgement of inadequacy: self-degradation.
Assurance = self-confidence

2.   ACHIEVEMENT

Achievement = surmounting obstacles and attaining a
successful conclusion to prove one's worth; striving
for success through personal effort.

3. ADAPTABILITY   DEFENSIVENESS

Adaptability = public acceptance of criticism, advice,
assistance.
Defensiveness = resistance to suggestion, guidance
and advice; concealment or justification of failure.

4.   AFFILIATION

Affiliation = gregariousness; group-centeredness;
friendly associations with others (as opposed to
detachment, unsociableness).

5. AGGRESSION   BLAME AVOIDANCE

Aggression = disregard for the feelings of others, as
manifested in hostility.
Blame avoidance = denial or inhibition of
aggressiveness.

6. CHANGE   SAMENESS

Change = variable or flexible behavior.
Sameness = repetition and routine behavior.

7. CONJUNCTIVITY   DISJUNCTIVITY

Conjunctivity = organized, purposeful, or planned
activity.
Disjunctivity = uncoordinated, disorganized
self-indulgence.

8.   COUNTFRACTION

Counteraction = persistent striving to overcome
difficult, humiliating or embarrassing experiences or
failures.

9. DEFERENCE   RESTIVENESS

Deference = respect for authority; submission to the
opinions and preferences of others perceived as
superior.
Restiveness = noncompliance; insubordination;
rebelliousness; defiance of authorities.

10. DOMINANCE   TOLERANCE

Dominance = ascendancy over others by assertive
control.
Tolerance = nonintervention; forbearance; acceptance
of others.

Table 9–1 DIMENSIONS OF PERSONALITY AND ENVIRONMENT (*continued*)

11.   EGO ACHIEVEMENT

Ego achievement = self-dramatizing, idealistic social action; active or fantasied dominance through sociopolitical activity.

12.   EMOTIONALITY   PLACIDITY

Emotionality = intense, open expression of feelings.
Placidity = stolidness, restraint, control, or constriction.

13.   ENERGY   PASSIVITY

Energy = high activity level; intense vigorous effort.
Passivity = sluggishness or inertia.

14.   EXHIBITIONISM   INFERIORITY AVOIDANCE

Exhibitionism = self-display; attention seeking.
Inferiority avoidance = shyness, embarrassment, or self-consciousness; avoidance of the attention of others.

15.   FANTASIED ACHIEVEMENT

Fantasied achievement = daydreams of success in achieving public recognition; hopes of fame, power or distinction.

16.   HARM AVOIDANCE   RISK TAKING

Harm avoidance = fearfulness: excessive caution in situations that might result in pain, injury, illness, or death.
Risk taking = careless indifference to danger; provocative disregard for personal safety; thrill seeking.

17.   HUMANITIES SOCIAL SCIENCES

Humanities social sciences = symbolic manipulation of social objects or artifacts through empirical analysis, reflection, discussion, and criticism.

18.   IMPULSIVENESS   DELIBERATION

Impulsiveness = rash, spontaneous, or impetuous behavior.
Deliberation = care, caution, or reflectiveness.

19.   NARCISSISM

Narcissism = egotistical preoccupation with self; erotic feelings about one's own body or personality.

20.   NURTURANCE

Nurturance = supportiveness of others by providing love, assistance, or protection.

21.   OBJECTIVITY   PROJECTIVITY

Objectivity = detached, nonmagical, unprejudiced thinking.
Projectivity = autistic, irrational, paranoid, or otherwise egocentric perceptions and beliefs; superstition.

Table 9–1 (*continued*)

22.	ORDER	DISORDER

Order = compulsive organization of the immediate physical environment; preoccupation with neatness and detail.
Disorder = habitual confusion, disarray, or carelessness.

23.	PLAY	WORK

Play = pleasure seeking; pursuit of entertainment.
Work = persistently purposeful, serious, task-oriented behavior.

24.	PRACTICALNESS	IMPRACTICALNESS

Practicalness = useful, tangibly productive applications of skill in crafts, social affairs, or commerce.
Impracticalness = a speculative, whimsical, or indifferent attitude toward craft, social, or commercial affairs.

25. REFLECTIVENESS

Reflectiveness = contemplation; preoccupation with private psychological, spiritual, esthetic, or metaphysical experience.

26. SCIENCE

Science = symbolic manipulation of physical objects through empirical analysis, reflection, discussion, and criticism.

27.	SENSUALITY	PURITANISM

Sensuality = sensory stimulation and gratification; voluptuousness; hedonism; preoccupation with aesthetic experience.
Puritanism = austerity; self-denial; abstinence; frugality.

28.	SEXUALITY	PRUDISHNESS

Sexuality = erotic heterosexual interest or activity.
Prudishness = restraint; denial or inhibition of erotic impulses.

29.	SUPPLICATION	AUTONOMY

Supplication = dependence on others for love, help, protection.
Autonomy = detachment; independence; self-reliance.

30. UNDERSTANDING

Understanding = intellectualization; problem-solving analysis, theorizing, or abstraction as ends in themselves.

prevailing in the organization. One such questionnaire that has been widely used in organizational research is the Organizational Climate Index (Stern, 1962b), which is described in some detail later in this chapter.

Once the 30 scale scores of the Organizational Climate Index have been computed and the average scale scores within each organization have been determined, the scores can be subjected to a statistical technique called *factor analysis* in order to identify clusters of closely related scales. Although the Activities Index responses can also be factor analyzed, the Organizational Climate Index factors are of primary importance here, for they represent the major dimensions of social press within organizations.

Factor analyses of the scale scores of the Organizational Climate Index (henceforth called the OCI) have often yielded six factors, each of which includes several scales from the 30-scale questionnaire. When the factor scores for each organization are computed, these can again be subjected to factor analysis to determine how the factors cluster or interrelate. This second-order factor analysis has typically yielded two second-order factors, each of which includes several of the first-order factors. Both types of factors—the first-order factors based on scale scores and the second-order factors based on factor scores—have been named in accordance with the concepts they encompass. They constitute some of the major constructs of the needs-press climate theory.

To recapitulate briefly, behavior in a social setting is a result of the interaction between two types of forces: the internal forces or personal *needs* characteristic of the individual and the external forces or environmental *press* characteristic of the social setting. Just as there are patterns of individual needs that constitute each personality, so there are patterns of environmental press that constitute each organization's climate. The organizational press or climate either facilitates or impedes the gratification of individual participants' needs.

The climate of an organization such as a school can be described most generally in terms of two broad dimensions: development press and control press. *Development press* is a pattern of social forces that tend to facilitate the fulfillment of individuals' psychological growth needs. This has been called an *anabolic* or growth-enhancing force. *Control press*, on the other hand, is a pattern of social forces that tend to foster the inhibition of personal expression and the denial of gratification of individuals' psychological growth needs. This has been called a *catabolic* or growth-impeding force. These two broad dimensions and their constituent parts will be defined and described in greater detail.

Major Constructs in the Needs-Press Theory of Climate

DEVELOPMENT PRESS

Development press is a cluster of social forces that, in combination, foster the self-realization and personal development of individual participants (Steinhoff & Bishop, 1974:40). In organizations characterized by a strong development press, participants are helped to support, satisfy, and enhance their growth needs. The five major forces constituting development press within organizations are intellectual climate, achievement standards, practicalness, supportiveness, and orderliness. Each of these can be defined and described, as adapted from Owens (1970), in the following manner.

Intellectual climate is a social pressure to engage in intellectual activity, to be socially active, and to be personally effective. Organizations having a strong intellectual climate are those perceived as high in *humanities and social sciences* (17), and *science interests* (26) as well as high in *reflectiveness* (25), *understanding* (30), *fantasied achievement* (15), *sensuality* as opposed to puritanism (27), *ego achievement* (11), *exhibitionism* as opposed to inferiority avoidance (14), and *change* as opposed to sameness (6). Note that the terms in italics refer to the scales that were originally identified by Murray (see Table 9-1). The numbers in parentheses indicate the scale numbers as listed in Table 9-1.

In schools having a strong intellectual climate press, one would find much activity associated with the arts and sciences. Such schools would probably feature musical and theatrical performances, art and science exhibits, and political activism. Students would have many opportunities to gain recognition for their personal accomplishments in a variety of different spheres of activity (see Stern, 1963a).

Achievement standards press is a social force to achieve success by dint of hard work, perseverance, and commitment to the goals of the organization. Social settings that have high achievement standards are those with high scores in *counteraction* (8), *energy* as opposed to passivity (13), *achievement* (2), *emotionality* as opposed to placidity (12), and *ego achievement* (11).

In schools characterized by a strong achievement standards press, one would expect to find active participants (teachers and/or students) busily engaged in challenging pursuits and deriving delight from success or disappointment (but not ego damage) from lack of success. This setting is considerably more task oriented and less exhibitionistic than the one depicted previously.

Practicalness is a social pressure to be realistic and at the same time friendly. Organizations that are highly practical receive high scores for *practicalness* as opposed to impracticalness (24), and *nurturance* (20). People in such settings are helped and encouraged in their strivings toward realistic objectives.

In a school characterized by a strong practicalness press, students and teachers would emphasize realistic goals and the applicability of knowledge and skills to the workaday world. Fantasies would be discouraged, but much support would be given for the pursuit of useful knowledge and skills. Emphasis would be placed on vocational and applied knowledge rather than on intellectuality or knowledge for its own sake.

Supportiveness press is a social force to respect the integrity of individuals while at the same time gratifying their dependency needs. Organizations that are high in supportiveness press are those having high scores for *assurance* as opposed to abasement (1), *tolerance* as opposed to dominance (10), *objectivity* as opposed to projectivity (21), *affiliation* (4), *conjunctivity* as opposed to disjunctivity (7), *supplication* as opposed to autonomy (29), *blame avoidance* as opposed to aggression (5), *harm avoidance* as opposed to risk taking (16), and *nurturance* (20).

One can imagine the participants in schools with a strong supportiveness press as mutually sympathetic and gently encouraging to those individuals who tend to experience insecurity in social settings. Courtesy, conventionality, and group cohesiveness would likely be common features of such sheltering environments. Deviance, individuality, and creativity would be discouraged, but positive reinforcement would be amply available for sociable behavior.

Orderliness press is a social force to be orderly, systematic, and respectful of the organization's hierarchy of authority. Organizations that are characterized by strong orderliness press are those receiving high scores for *order* as opposed to disorder (22), *narcissism* (19), *adaptability* as opposed to defensiveness (3), *conjunctivity* as opposed to disjunctivity (7), *deference* as opposed to restiveness (9), and *harm avoidance* as opposed to risk taking (16).

Schools that have a strong orderliness press are likely to have standard operating procedures to govern participants' behavior in most circumstances. Good deportment, neatness, and respect for authority would be emphasized; and individuals would tend to submerge themselves in the group.

In sum, organizations in which high development press is the dominant climate are those featuring intellectual climate, achievement standards, practicalness, supportiveness, and orderliness. Schools or other organizations that are *not* characterized by such behavior patterns can be said to have low development press.

CONTROL PRESS

Control press is a cluster of social forces that, in combination, impede the self-realization and personal development of individual participants by inhibiting or restricting expressiveness and spontaneity (Steinhoff & Bishop, 1974:40). The three major dimensions of control press within organizations, as specified by Owens (1970:187) are reflected intellectual climate, reflected achievement standards, and impulse control. These can be defined and described, after Owens, as follows:

Reflected intellectual climate, which is equivalent to antiintellectualism, is a social pressure to behave in ways counter to those characteristic of an intellectual climate. Since this factor is a reflection (the converse) of the intellectual climate factor, organizations characterized as antiintellectual are those having *low* scores for *humanities and social sciences* (17), *science* (26), *reflectiveness* (25), *understanding* (30), and *fantasied achievement* (15); they would be characterized by *puritanism* as opposed to sensuality (27), low *ego achievement* (11), *inferiority avoidance* as opposed to exhibitionism (14), and *sameness* as opposed to change (6).

One can imagine a school with a strong reflected intellectual climate as peopled by passive and unexcited teachers and students. Nothing much happens or changes there. It is a stultifying atmosphere, lacking in exploration, curiosity, and activity. Questioning is discouraged or subtly punished, and individual achievements go unrecognized in this routinized setting.

Reflected achievement standards press is a social pressure *not* to attain success for achievement. As a reflection or inversion of the achievement standards force, this pressure is indicative of *low counteraction* (8), *passivity* as opposed to energy (13), *low achievement* (2), *placidity* as opposed to emotionality (12), and *low ego achievement.*

Schools' with a high reflected achievement standards press have environments that are stagnant and inactive. No one does much of anything, and individuals are actively discouraged from rocking the boat. Those few who do seek learning or who achieve some success are ridiculed and punished for their deviance, as a cowering, herdlike behavior pattern is valued in this setting.

Impulse control press is a social force to restrain one's individuality and conform to organizational restrictions. Organizations that are high in impulse control press are those characterized by *work* as opposed to play (23), *prudishness* as opposed to sexuality (28), *blame avoidance* as opposed to aggression (5), *deliberation* as opposed to impulsiveness (18), *placidity* as opposed to emotionality (12), and *inferiority avoidance* as opposed to exhibitionism (14).

In a school having a strong impulse control press, the students and teachers would be excessively cautious and would welcome regimentation as a protection against unexpected challenges. People would work hard, but at routine tasks; and there would be little personal pleasure or expressiveness when the job is done since what lies ahead is only another tedious task.

To summarize, organizations in which strong control press is the dominant climate are those featuring antiintellectualism, low standards for achievement, and high control of impulses. Schools or other social settings that are not characterized by these features can be said to have low control press.

Relationships Among Major Constructs in the Needs-Press Theory

As noted earlier, the theoretical constructs were derived from factor analyses, first of the scale scores and then of the first-order factor scores. The latter type of factor analysis—that is, second-order analysis of factor scores—has indicated that the order of importance or order of relevance of the factors to the major dimensions of development press and control press is as listed here. Thus, with reference to development press, the constituent constructs in order of significance are: (1) intellectual climate, (2) achievement standards, (3) practicalness, (4) supportiveness, and (5) orderliness. With reference to control press, the constituent constructs in order of importance are: (1) reflected intellectual climate, (2) reflected achievement standards, and (3) impulse control. What this means is that a high score for intellectual climate contributes more to high development press than does a high score for achievement standards or any of the other constituent factors. Nevertheless, all the constituent factors have some degree of influence on the development press dimension.

The two major dimensions of organizational climate, development press and control press, have been found to be statistically unrelated. To the extent that these factors are independent, each organization can be regarded as having a degree of development press and a degree of control press. This can be depicted as in Figure 9–2, which shows the major dimensions as orthogonal (perpendicular) axes.

Although these factors are statistically independent, two of the three control press constructs are reflections or inversions of important development press constructs. Therefore, organizations could not logically appear in the upper right quadrant (high development press and high control press). Research has indicated that schools are distributed among the other three quadrants, as indicated by the shaded area in Figure 9–2 (after Owens, 1981:202).

At this point let us summarize the needs-press framework as it has been explicated up to now. Organizations are viewed as social settings in which the fulfillment of individuals' psychological growth needs is either facilitated or

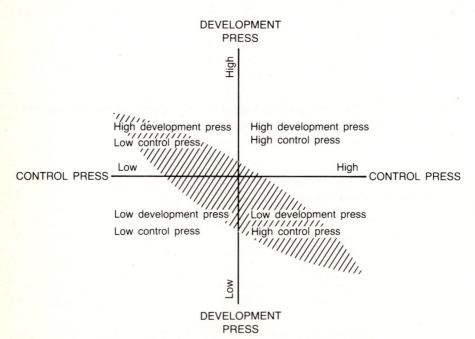

Figure 9–2 Quadrants Resulting from Independent Development Press and
Control Press Factors (Based on Owens, 1981:202)

impeded. The organization is viewed as the individuals' environment, a source of forces or pressures that act on the individuals' needs and thereby contribute to shaping their behavior. These forces, called *press*, can be classified within two broad categories (development press and control press) and eight narrower categories, each of which represents an important construct in the theory. The relationships among the major constructs and their impact on needs and behavior can be depicted as in Figure 9–3, an expansion of the diagram

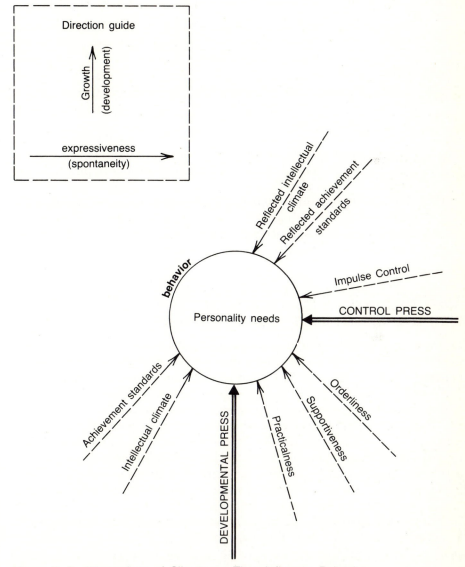

Figure 9–3   Dimensions of Climate as They Influence Behavior

presented earlier. In this figure arrows in an upward direction represent forces toward intellectual growth, and arrows toward the right represent forces toward emotional expressiveness. The leftward direction of the control press arrow is indicative of forces toward the suppression of expressiveness.

Major Propositions in the Needs-Press Climate Theory

Although this theory was not stated in propositional form by Stern or other theorists, some generalizations can be inferred from the theoretical literature.

1. Participants in organizations characterized by high development press exhibit more psychological growth (fulfillment of psychological growth needs) than do those in organizations characterized by low development press.
2. Participants in organizations characterized by high control press exhibit less psychological growth than do those in organizations characterized by low control press.
3. The fulfillment of psychological growth needs is related to the following dimensions of the organization's climate, in descending order of importance: intellectual climate, achievement standards, practicalness, supportiveness, and orderliness.
4. The repression or inhibition of psychological growth needs is related to the following dimensions of the organization's climate, in descending order of importance: reflected intellectual climate or antiintellectualism, reflected achievement standards or low expectations, and impulse control.

SOME THEORETICAL ISSUES ASSOCIATED WITH THE NEEDS-PRESS CLIMATE FRAMEWORK

One very attractive feature of the needs-press framework for viewing organizational climate is that it is associated with a sophisticated theory about human behavior—namely, Lewin's field theory. With further research this climate framework might reveal subtle differences among organizations that nevertheless could have great impact on human development.

Factorial studies of organizational climate and descriptions of the types of press found in various organizations have dominated the climate literature related to this theory. However, there also has been some research on the need patterns of organizations' members. In addition, some factor-analytic research has been directed toward identifying configurations of need and press factors in organizations such as colleges and universities.

One shortcoming of the needs-press model is its preponderantly empirical foundation and the fact that the major constructs are derived from factor analysis. Another problem is that it has not generated much research in which the three essential elements of Lewin's field theory—personality (needs), environment (press), and behavior (action)—are drawn together.

Need Factors

Readers will recall that one set of 30 scales is used to measure both psychological needs of individuals and environmental press of organizations. Just as group responses to the Organizational Climate Index have yielded clusters of scales when subjected to factor analysis, so individuals' responses to the needs measure, the Activities Index, have yielded clusters of scales. Stern (1970:47) found that individuals' needs tend to be grouped in about 14 clusters and that these in turn form 4 major groupings, some of which overlap. The groupings of first-order factors (scale clusters) are depicted in Figure 9–4 (after

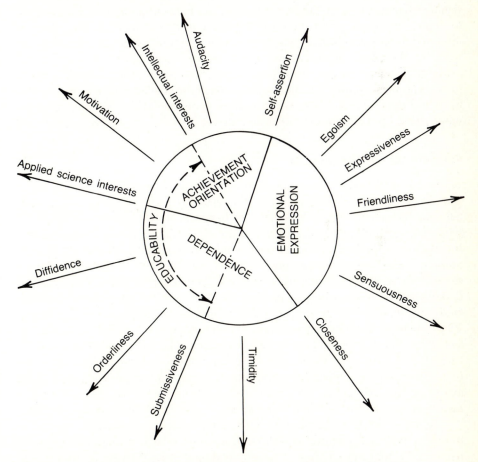

Figure 9–4 The Factors Representing Clusters of Personality Needs

Stern, 1970:49–52). It can be seen here that the factors are distributed in a complete circle. Thus they appear to represent a total personality. Note that the upward arrows represent intellectual development drives, and the generally rightward arrows represent emotional expression drives. The second-order personality factors found in Stern's research are:

1. *Achievement orientation:* strong ego strivings directed toward success or personal accomplishment.
2. *Dependence:* submissive and socially controlled behavior.
3. *Emotional expression:* social participation and spontaneity.
4. *Educability:* a combination of intellectuality and submissiveness.

Although these psychological need factors (personality constructs) are not of immediate relevance to one's understanding of organizational climate, they might be of interest to students and of importance in further research on schools. The need factors and press factors can be combined, as in Figure 9–5, to depict the needs-press theory of behavior in its entirety. As this figure is intended to indicate, individuals' achievement orientation needs are congruent with (in the same direction as) a school's development press. Emotional expression needs, on the other hand, oppose or clash with a school's control press. The need factor that Stern called *educability* includes both achievement need and dependence scales and therefore appears midway between achievement drives and emotional constraint drives.

Factor-Analytic Foundation

The fact that the major constructs in this theory have been derived from factor analysis poses some dilemmas. First, the factor structure of the Organizational Climate Index and its variants has not been absolutely consistent across all types of organizations or for all researchers. For example, Owens reported one set of first-order factors based on a study of inner-city schools (Owens & Steinhoff, 1969) in his earlier book (Owens, 1970:187) and a slightly different set of first-order factors in his later book (Owens, 1981:200). Steinhoff and Bishop (1974:39) reported yet another set of first-order factors based on their study of departments of educational administration (also see Kight & Herr, 1966). In brief, the OCI and its variants do not seem to exhibit the degree of factor stability that would best facilitate research. The common elements of the three factor structures mentioned here are intellectual climate and achievement standards as aspects of development press and impulse control as an aspect of control press. It appears that further work on the OCI as a measurement tool is needed to establish firmly the dimensions of climate.

Another dilemma associated with factor-analytic research arises in the interpretation and naming of factors. Researchers have a tendency to apply names that conform to their own expectations, perspectives, or biases; the factor names given may not fully capture the scale or item contents of the

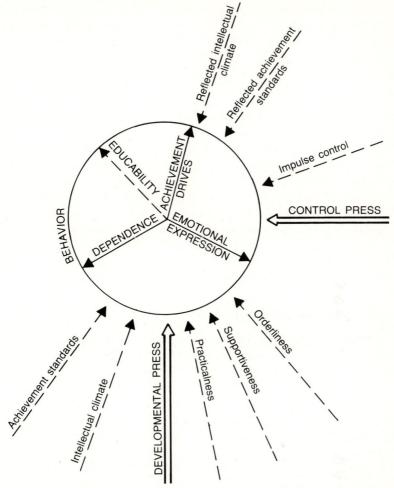

Figure 9–5 Combined Need and Press Factors as They Influence Behavior

factors in question. In the case of this climate framework, a discussion of any first-order factor can serve to illustrate the point. The first factor to emerge from factor analysis of the OCI includes scales pertaining to fantasied achievement, sensuality, ego achievement, exhibitionism, and change, as well as those pertaining to humanities and social sciences, science, reflectiveness, and understanding. It would seem that this factor could have been named *inner-directedness press*, *active curiosity press*, or *confidence press* as well as *intellectual climate*.

It is important in understanding this theory of climate to have a thorough grasp of the constituent parts of each factor, including an awareness of the items on the scales that make up each factor, in order to understand the meaning of each construct within the context of the theory. Intellectual climate, for example, has a meaning in the context of this framework that departs considerably from the dictionary definition or everyday connotations of the term.

Research Gaps

The heuristic value of a good theory rests on its usefulness for predicting regularities that will occur in reality. Although the needs-press framework has explicit implications for predicting individuals' behavior within organizations, few researchers have attempted to relate observable behaviors to participants' needs and organizational press. Much of the empirical research associated with this theory has focused on descriptions of the climates of diverse organizations and on analyses of the measurement instruments, but little has been directed toward predicting or explaining aspects of behavior. Whether this reflects a shortcoming of the theory or a limitation within the scholarly community is uncertain, but the fact remains that the heuristic value of the theory continues to be questionable until its relevance to behavior is demonstrated.

Strengths of the Needs-Press Model

The concept of organizational climate, ambiguous and intangible as it may be, is a compelling one. It relates to sensations we have all had when visiting different schools or even different classrooms within one school. Of the many attempts to capture and quantify the elusive atmosphere of an organization, the needs-press framework is among the most interesting because of its roots in an important explanatory theory. This approach to the study of climate is the only one with the potential for linking personality and environment systematically and explicitly to behavior. Further, its foundation in 30 dimensions of personality that are theoretically sound holds the promise that it will permit the identification of very fine distinctions among organizations.

RESEARCH RELATED TO THE NEEDS-PRESS THEORY OF ORGANIZATIONAL CLIMATE

Because this theory of organizational climate was developed with educational institutions specifically in mind, it has generated a large body of research in schools of various types. The sample of studies reviewed in this section is subdivided into sections according to the level of education studied. Following an overview of the measurement tools most closely identified with this theory, a summary of the research in colleges and universities is provided. This section concludes with a synthesis of the relevant studies conducted in secondary schools and some generalizations that can be inferred from the research findings.

Instruments

Like several of the theories examined in this book, the needs-press framework for studying organizational climate is associated with specific measurement instruments. The two instruments of greatest importance are the Organizational Climate Index to measure organizational press and the Activities Index to measure individuals' needs (see Stern, 1958; 1963b).

The Organizational Climate Index (OCI) is a 300-item questionnaire made up of 30 scales having ten items each. Each item is a statement about an event or behavior pattern that might occur within the organization of interest. Some of the items refer to relatively objective or readily observable patterns, whereas others require more subjective judgments (McFee, 1961). Respondents indicate whether each statement is true or false; and the responses are scored, usually by computer, so that the 30 scale scores for each individual can be computed easily. The individuals' scores within each organization are then combined to yield average scale scores for each organization in the sample. As described earlier, those scale scores are then subjected to factor analysis, first to derive first-order factor scores (based on sets of scales) and then to derive second-order factor scores (based on sets of factors). Persons considering using the OCI for research should contact the Psychological Research Center at Syracuse University in New York State for information about obtaining and scoring the instrument.

Several variations of the OCI have been developed over the years, with items reworded to apply to particular types of organizational settings. For example, the College Characteristics Index or CCI (Stern, 1958) was the first of the environmental press measures developed (Pace & Stern, 1958). Later, the High School Characteristics Index or HSCI was designed. The OCI, a general climate measure useful in a variety of types of organizations, was the last of the set to appear (Stern, 1970:14–15). In addition, there are shorter versions of these instruments available—forms that require much less response time and are easier to score but that afford less refined differentiation among organizations. Some researchers have developed adaptations of the instrument for particular research purposes (for example, Nunnally, Thistlethwaite, & Wolfe, 1963; Payne & Mansfield, 1973).

The Activities Index (AI), which might be regarded as a companion of the OCI for many research efforts, also comprises 300 items representing 30 scales. This instrument measures individuals' needs. Each item is a statement of an activity in which a person might engage. Respondents indicate whether they like or dislike each activity; and the answers are scored, again by computer in most studies, so as to yield scale scores that constitute a personality profile for each individual. These scores can be combined within organizations to determine whether people with similar needs congregate within organizations, or they may be treated separately in terms of individuals' personalities.

Several reliability and validity studies of the AI and the OCI (or its variants) have been conducted. Stern (1970) reported strong reliability findings for the AI and the CCI in terms of paired-item correlations and test-retest correlations. Pace (1960:24–25) also summarized CCI reliability findings, noting that response variation between schools is consistently greater than variation within schools and that college faculty members' responses generally correlate highly with students' responses. In a study of faculty and student responses to the preliminary draft of the CCI, Pace and Stern (1958) found high correlations between faculty perceptions and student perceptions, as well as substantial climate differences among the five institutions studied.

The question of whether the AI and the OCI or its variants are independent of each other or whether respondents' needs influence their perceptions of their environment has been of concern to several researchers, and the evidence on this question has not been conclusive. McFee (1961), in a study of 100 students at one university, correlated respondents' AI scale scores with their corresponding CCI scale scores and found no significant relationships. She also found that the objective CCI items elicited less response variation than did the subjective items and that the low-exposure items (aspects of the environment that respondents would not have much opportunity to observe) were more susceptible to influence by needs than were the high-exposure items. On the other hand, Mitchell (1968) studied high school students' personality characteristics (as determined by a variety of psychological inventories) in relation to students' perceptions of their high school climate as measured by the HSCI. He found high correlations between personality traits and perceptions of press and therefore concluded that students' personality characteristics do affect their perceptions (that is, that the AI and the HSCI are not independent measures). Similarly, Marks (1968) studied responses of beginning college freshmen at one institution to a variation of the CCI and their personality profiles. He found significant relationships between personality and climate perceptions, particularly for the more ambiguous climate items. When Saunders (1969) examined AI and CCI scores of over a thousand students at 23 assorted colleges, however, he found that factors made up of CCI scales exhibited far greater between-school variation than did factors comprising AI scales.

It seems likely that in studying one heterogeneous institution, relationships between needs and perceived press will emerge; but in studying many heterogeneous institutions, the influence of respondents' needs is less salient than is the influence of the setting. That is, although needs probably affect respondents' perceptions of climate to some degree, the respondents' needs within each organization vary more greatly than do their perceptions of press. Saunders (1969) found, further, that when the AI and CCI scale scores were factor-analyzed together, the AI scales for the most part clustered separately from the CCI scales, which supports the relative independence of the two measures.

Most of the published research on needs and press that has been generated by this climate framework has been conducted in school settings. Many of these studies focused on institutions of higher education. Fewer concerned public schools, particularly at the high school level.

Needs-Press Climate Research in Colleges and Universities

The climates of institutions of higher education have been of great interest to student personnel specialists and researchers concerned with such matters as attracting and retaining students, variations among colleges, and the effects of college life. The studies can be grouped in two categories for purposes of review: research on antecedents and effects of climate, and comparative studies of diverse institutions.

ANTECEDENTS AND EFFECTS OF CLIMATE

In general, the research indicates that aspects of an organization's structure and processes relate to participants' perceptions of the organization's climate. The climate in turn relates to some observable behavior patterns.

In a study of eight junior colleges, the presence of such faculty personnel policies as tenure, formal evaluation, and academic rank were found to relate to students' perceptions of the climate (Hendrix, 1965). In particular, students' aspiration-achievement, practicality, and sociability press factors differed in accordance with these personnel policies.

A study by Payne and Mansfield (1973) of business organizations might also be relevant to institutions of higher education. These researchers found that organizational size and degree of bureaucratization related to employees' perceptions of the environmental press. Size in particular was important, as it related directly to such press factors as science and technology, intellectualism, conventionality, and sociability.

The climate of an institution has been found to relate to some aspects of students' behavior. For example, Thistlethwaite (1960) found patterns of faculty press (as reported by students on the CCI) to be related to students' plans to seek advanced degrees in the sciences and humanities. He also found students' perceptions of faculty and student press to be related to the institutions' productivity of Ph.D. degrees (Thistlethwaite, 1959a; 1959b). Also, as reported by Standing and Parker (1964), students who left a college after one semester had greater discrepancies between preconceived college climate and perceived college climate than did students who remained at college (also see Lauterbach & Vielhaber, 1966).

In one of the very few studies of students' needs and environmental press in relation to observable behavior, Herr (1971) found that greater discrepancies between needs and press were associated with changes in the students' major fields of study. Discrepancies between preconceived and observed college climate were also associated with changes in majors.

In an unusual study of students' needs in relation to educational outcomes,

Stone and Foster (1964) found several need scales to be related both to predicted grade point averages and to obtained grade point averages after a semester. These researchers found in particular that the need for play was inversely related to the discrepancy between predicted and obtained grade point averages; that is, the greater the need for play, the greater the congruence between predicted and obtained grades.

COMPARATIVE STUDIES

Numerous research efforts have focused on comparisons between or among institutions in terms of their climates. In addition, various studies have dealt with needs-press combinations or organizational cultures characteristic of different types of colleges and universities. These comparative studies have consistently made use of the CCI to measure perceived environmental press.

Some climate differences between types of colleges or programs have been reported. Pace (1960), for example, identified five distinctive types of college environments on the basis of a study of 32 institutions: (1) intellectual with respect to humanism; (2) intellectual with reference to science and competitiveness; (3) practical; (4) socially supportive; and (5) aggressive and impulsive (see Pace & McFee, 1960). The social climate of a university apparently differs from that of a community college, as might be expected, with the university having greater press for high aspirations, intellectuality, self-expression, and group life (among other factors) and the community college having higher press for student dignity, academic organization, and vocational orientation (Campbell, 1964).

The climate of a college of business administration was found to differ significantly from the national norms for arts and science college climates (Lawlor, 1970). An innovative new campus was found to be similar in climate to its more traditional counterpart; and students' perceptions of the climate on both campuses differed substantially from faculty members' ideals (Schoen, 1966), suggesting that the perceived climate of an institution often differs radically from leaders' intentions. In an unusual study of students' perceptions, the perceived climate of a particular college was found to differ significantly from the imagined climates of rival colleges in the area (Cole & Fields, 1961). It appears that students' choice of an institution might be partly contingent on the climate reputations of a range of colleges.

In studies of departments of educational administration, the climates have been found to be very similar to each other (Steinhoff & Bishop, 1974; Bernstein, 1975), despite differences in size, location, sources of funding, and other demographic characteristics that could be expected to affect climate.

In comparative studies of needs based on AI data, some differences among groups have been identified. Teacher trainees, for example, were found to differ from the national norms for need patterns; and female trainees differed from males in some needs (Gillis, 1964). Community college students were also found to differ from university students in need patterns, the former having higher motivation and friendliness needs (Campbell, 1964). Educational administration students' needs were found to be related to their value orientations (Bernstein, 1975).

The differences among colleges in environmental press and students' needs, as illustrated earlier, suggest that young people having particular need patterns might be attracted to certain institutions in which they might find a compatible setting. Some studies of students' needs in combination with environmental press have indicated patterns that have been called college *cultures*. As Stern noted, each type of school "may be viewed…as an ecological niche for a particular kind of student" (Stern, 1970:86). He differentiated independent liberal arts colleges, business administration schools, and teacher training colleges as having distinctive needs-press configurations or cultures (Stern, 1970:86–92). In a similar vein, Cohen (1966) identified five distinctive college cultures in a study of AI and CCI scores in 55 institutions. These are: (1) nurturant (denominational colleges); (2) high self-expression (liberal arts colleges); (3) low self-expression (denominational colleges); (4) high collegiate (university-affiliated colleges); and (5) low collegiate (some denominational and some liberal arts colleges).

In summary, the research evidence suggests three major generalizations:

1. Organizational factors such as size, bureaucratization, and some staff personnel policies relate to perceived climate.
2. Perceived climate seems to relate in turn to such student behaviors as leaving school, changing majors, and planning to seek higher degrees.
3. Different types of institutions can be distinguished in terms of their perceived climates, students' needs, and need-press combinations or cultures.

Needs-Press Climate Research in Secondary Schools

The needs-press climate studies conducted in precollege institutions can best be reviewed in two general categories: studies of individual schools, and studies of many schools at once. For the most part, the single-school studies focused on relationships between students' characteristics and their perceptions of the environmental press. Most of the precollege research has used the HSCI in conjunction with other measures.

SINGLE-SCHOOL STUDIES.

The climate research focusing on individual high schools indicates that students' perceptions of the climate are influenced by such personal characteristics as their needs (Herr, Kight, & Hansen, 1969; Hansen & Warner, 1970); their academic adjustment (Hansen & Warner, 1970); and their achievement levels, IQ, and sex (Herr, 1965). One issue that should be kept in mind is that students having different attributes in terms of needs, IQ, achievement, and sex might actually experience different social forces due to instructional groupings and informal social interaction norms. In other words, it can be assumed that diverse *subcultures* exist within a school and that each subculture is characterized by a distinctive need-press configuration. Stated still differently, students' personal characteristics might affect not only their perceptions of climate but also the actual climates they inhabit.

MULTIPLE-SCHOOL STUDIES

The antecedents and effects of particular school climates are of special interest to educational administrators. Although research in these areas has not been extensive, some relationships have emerged from the few studies conducted in public schools.

Only one published study of antecedents of school climates was located. This was a study of five high schools having guidance programs and five matched schools having none (Kasper, Munger, & Myers, 1965). The schools with guidance programs had significantly higher press for adaptability, aggression, change, counteraction, dominance, scientism, sexuality, and succorance; the nonguidance schools had significantly higher affiliation, deference, and humanism press scores.

Another multiple-school study, this one concerning four high schools in Australia, dealt primarily with relationships between personal characteristics and perceptions of climate (Choo, 1976). Verbal IQ, quantitative IQ, home background, and sex were all found to be related to individuals' HSCI scores. Nevertheless, AI and HSCI scales did load on separate factors in the joint factor analysis; and climate differences among schools were identified despite demographically similar student populations. As noted earlier, students' personal and demographic attributes might affect the different group climates they actually experience.

Two studies of student achievement in relation to school climate are of interest. Hamaty (1967) found teachers' needs and their perceptions of the climate in 40 schools to have no bearing on student achievement; community socioeconomic status was the predominant predictor of achievement. On the other hand, McDill, Meyers, and Rigsby (1967) found school climate, as perceived by students as well as teachers in 20 schools, to be a significant predictor of student achievement. After controlling for student scholastic ability and community socioeconomic status, they found that climate retained significant predictive power, suggesting that school climate is related to student achievement, particularly in the middle-SES range (McDill, Rigsby, & Meyers, 1969).

Before summarizing the precollege climate research we should note the scarcity of published research in this area. The few reported studies suggest that particular features, such as guidance programs, have a bearing on school climate and that, despite individual differences in the perception of school climate, schools do seem to have distinctive climates that relate to student achievement. Because of the potential importance of the general tone of a school with respect to student outcomes, further research on school climate should be energetically pursued.

IMPLICATIONS OF THE NEEDS-PRESS CLIMATE FRAMEWORK FOR ENHANCING STUDENT LEARNING OUTCOMES

Many of the leading textbooks on school administration emphasize the importance of the instructional leadership role in education. However, few books can offer prescriptions for enacting that leadership role effectively. In this book we are seeking theoretical frameworks that might inform administrative practice in the domain of instructional leadership, the domain of enhancing student outcomes. Is climate theory a useful framework for considering student outcomes? More specifically, does Stern's need-press model offer a promising direction for generating knowledge about how to increase students' cognitive, affective, and psychomotor achievements?

Since the administrator's influence on students is usually indirect at best, a logical approach to this question might be to consider the climate that teachers experience and the potential impact of that climate on their professional performance. Theoretically, the best procedure for optimizing teacher performance would be to create an environment that both gratifies their personal expression needs and fosters the gratification of their psychological growth needs.

Some research indicates that teachers, at least during their training period, have needs that differ from the national norms. The findings by Gillis (1964), summarized in Table 9–2, indicate that teacher trainees tend to have lower intellectual needs, higher dependence needs, and other impulse expression needs than the norms for the college population. In the absence of more recent data or of research on need patterns of experienced practicing teachers, we can assume that school environments that support the gratification of these needs would be satisfying to most teachers. For example, environments that are not too intellectually demanding, that offer supportive group interaction, that are orderly and hierarchical while at the same time supportive, and that provide opportunities for emotional expression without risk would probably seem comfortable to most teachers.

On the other hand, environments that are high in development press have a somewhat different configuration, as summarized in Table 9–3. Development press scales that are congruent with teacher trainees' needs are indicated by a plus sign (+), and scales discrepant with teacher trainees' needs are highlighted by a minus sign (−).

Readers will recall, from Owens' factor analysis, that intellectual climate, achievement standards, practicalness, supportiveness, and orderliness are the

Table 9–2 TEACHER TRAINEES' NEEDS IN RELATION TO NEEDS OF THE COLLEGE STUDENT POPULATION

DOMAIN	SPECIFIC NEED SCALES	TEACHER TRAINEES' SCORES*
INTELLECTUAL NEEDS	Humanities interests	Lower
	Objectivity	Lower
	Understanding	Lower
DEPENDENCE NEEDS	Conjunctivity	Higher
	Abasement	Higher
	Affiliation	Higher
	Blame avoidance	Higher
	Deference	Higher
	Order	Higher
	Nurturance	Higher
IMPULSE EXPRESSION NEEDS	Aggression	Lower
	Dominance	Lower
	Impulsiveness	Lower
	Risktaking	Lower
	Emotionality	Higher
	Narcissism	Higher
	Sensuality	Higher
	Sexuality	Higher

SOURCE: From Gillis (1964).
NOTE: *Differences from national norms are significant beyond the .05 confidence level.

important dimensions of development press. How can a school administrator foster these types of social press without threatening the fulfillment of teachers' personal needs? More particularly, how can an intellectual climate and high achievement standards for teachers be fostered?

One strategy that could prove effective involves enacting a role that teachers might seek to imitate. An administrator who is intellectual, demonstrative, energetic, and achievement oriented is a model that many teachers and other staff members might try to emulate. Some examples of behavior patterns on the part of administrators that would be conducive to advancing a school's development press are as follows:

1. Wide reading in the arts, sciences, and humanities; attendance at cultural events; conversation about these readings and events; and genuine curiosity and thoughtfulness are some indicators of an intellectual bent. Such an intellectual demeanor on the part of the leader might be particularly important in schools that have been directed excessively toward athletics or discipline. A leader might cultivate these interests, or the central office administrator could consider assigning such persons to school leadership positions.

2. Emotional expressiveness, within reasonable limits, in terms of ready laughter, expressions of disappointment, clearly evident enjoyment, and other indicators of spontaneity can also be cultivated by those

Table 9–3 SCALES ASSOCIATED WITH HIGH DEVELOPMENT PRESS
AND HIGH CONTROL PRESS

Factor	Scales*

INTELLECTUAL
  CLIMATE
  PRESS
	High Humanities/social sciences (−)
	High Science interests
	High Reflectiveness
	High Understanding (−)
	High Fantasied achievement
	     Sensuality (+)
	High Ego Achievement
	     Exhibitionism
	     Change

ACHIEVEMENT
  STANDARDS
  PRESS
	High Counteraction
	     Energy
	High Achievement
	     Emotionality (+)
	High Ego achievement

PRACTICALNESS PRESS	Practicalness High Nurturance

SUPPORTIVENESS
  PRESS
	Assurance (−)
	     Tolerance (+)
	     Objectivity (−)
	High Affiliation (+)
	     Conjunctivity (+)
	     Supplication
	     Blame avoidance (+)
	     Harm avoidance (+)
	High Nurturance (+)

ORDERLINESS
  PRESS
	Order (+)
	High Narcissism (+)
	     Adaptability
	     Conjunctivity (+)
	     Deference (+)
	     Harm avoidance (+)

CONTROL
  PRESS
	Work
	     Prudishness (−)
	     Blame avoidance (+)
	     Deliberation (+)
	     Placidity (−)
	     Inferiority avoidance

NOTE: Reflected Intellectual Climate and Reflected Achievement Standards, not listed, are the converse of the corresponding Development Press factor scales.
*(+) indicates congruence with teacher trainees' deviations from national norms; (−) indicates incongruence.

leaders who tend to be more staid and reserved. Such behavior might help to loosen a school that has been rigid and repressive.

3. Leaders who are energetic—who move around a lot, are seen to be actively engaged in school events (with teachers and students), and are on hand to do the work—are often found in the most effective schools (see Edmonds & Frederiksen, 1978). Passive or sedentary individuals can develop a more active behavior pattern by intent and practice.

4. People who are achievement oriented often seek challenges to their abilities, take pride in their accomplishments, and overtly recognize other people's achievements. Leaders who set high standards for themselves and encourage others to do so can have great impact, particularly in a school that has had low standards and low expectations.

Apart from role model behavior patterns on the part of the leader, there are other strategies that might help to increase the development press of a school as experienced by teachers. Bearing in mind that practicalness, supportiveness, and orderliness are important aspects of development press and of teachers' need fulfillment, one can consider intellectual climate and achievement standards in terms of practices and structures that can enhance a faculty's development press.

Intellectual climate can be fostered by means of facilities and practices such as the following:

1. A professional library can be created within the school so that education research journals, books, and professional magazines are easily accessible. In conjunction with establishing this library, the leader(s) would begin to express clear expectations that teachers be familiar with the professional literature and have theory-based or research-based rationales for their classroom practices.

2. Some faculty meetings can be devoted to the exploration of pedagogical issues. Teachers as well as administrators would be expected to bring their readings to bear on these issues and to recommend particularly insightful publications to their colleagues.

3. Group cultural events such as theater parties, concert and opera outings, and excursions to art exhibits can be organized. Discounts for groups can often be arranged and travel expenses minimized. The linkage of such events to purely social activities (such as dinner before or a party after) might increase voluntary participation.

4. Teachers' art and craft products can be prominently exhibited in the school, and individual teachers with special talents can be asked to perform on a voluntary basis at social gatherings.

5. A faculty committee can be formed to consider the climate of the school and to generate strategies for raising the intellectual level of interactions. All possible efforts to implement the suggestions of such a committee should be made.

High *achievement standards* can be fostered in a school by some or all of the following strategies:

1. Public recognition can be given to teachers who attain outstanding success either personally or with students in the arts, humanities, or sciences. This recognition can be in the form of write-ups in the local newspapers, mention at parent and community group meetings, and memoranda to higher-level administrators and appropriate civic leaders.
2. Some faculty meetings can be devoted to specific strategies for improving student outcomes. Teachers who are especially successful with particular techniques—for example, individualizing instruction, maintaining healthy classroom order, or asking appropriate questions for stimulating students' higher-order reasoning—could be the organizers and major presenters at such meetings.
3. Teachers can be encouraged to be actively involved in changing school or district policies that detract from the achievement orientation of the school. Praise for being outspoken, critical, innovative, and active in promoting change is one way of encouraging such behavior; consultation or friendliness with faculty activists is another form of encouragement.
4. A faculty committee can be appointed to address problems of student achievement and develop plans for enhancing students' attitudes, skills, and knowledge. Committee suggestions for fostering higher achievement standards should, of course, be heeded to the fullest extent possible.

In striving to modify a school's climate as experienced by teachers, leaders must remain aware that organizational climate, like an individual's personality, is an enduring pattern that is difficult to change. Increasing the development press of a school would require both extensive time (perhaps a number of years) and consistent effort incorporating many different but interrelated tactics.

The needs-press theory suggests that teachers' behaviors will reflect both their personal needs and the social group's press. If the staff within a school is functioning in a growth-enhancing manner with respect to colleagues, it is probable that the staff will be helping to create a suitable environment for students. Additional efforts that are specifically directed toward students would be required, however. Educational features that seem likely to contribute to the *intellectual climate* of a school as experienced by students would include:

1. A strong extracurricular program emphasizing the arts, the humanities, and the sciences.
2. Exhibits of students' art and craft work throughout the school and perhaps outside the school.

3. Public recognition of students who achieve intellectual and artistic successes, with at least as much fanfare as athletic heroes and heroines enjoy.
4. Fairs and special exhibitions devoted to the sciences, mathematics, and the arts and crafts.
5. The encouragement of curiosity, independent exploration, creativity, and inventiveness in all curriculum areas.

Educational features that would likely contribute to raising the *achievement standards* of a school would include:

1. Clear and unambiguous expectations that students' achievements will be high.
2. Public recognition of outstanding student achievements (for example, students might present their original papers at student meetings or community group meetings).
3. Greater attention to achievement-oriented student behaviors than to disruptive student behaviors.
4. A genuine student self-government program with full representation of all student segments and real decision-making authority in some aspects of student life.

Although the strategies suggested here seem likely to have a favorable impact on the climate of a school and therefore on student outcomes, the paucity of research in this area makes it impossible to make predictions with certainty. Some of the many questions that remain for further empirical inquiry are:

1. Does the degree of congruence between teachers' needs and school social press relate to any behavior patterns of teachers? For example, do teachers' levels of effort, creativity, or participation in school events relate to their needs-press congruence?
2. Is there a relationship between the levels of development and/or control press in schools (as perceived by staff) and teachers' behavior patterns? For example, do teachers in schools having high development press invest more effort, display more creativity, or relate more closely to students than do teachers in schools with low development press?
3. Do students perceive the school's climate as teachers do? If not, which set of perceptions—students' or teachers'—is the more closely related to students' achievements?
4. Do different school climates relate favorably to student outcomes in different levels or types of schools? For example, is the best climate for a junior high school the same as that for an elementary or a high school? Is the best climate for a vocational school the same as that for an academic or general school?

5. Is there a relationship between school climate (as perceived by students) and student attitudes or achievements? Do the students' attainments of knowledge, attitudes, and motor skills relate differentially to school climates?

Although a tremendous amount of empirical research remains to be done, the available conceptual and empirical literature pertaining to needs and press offers a promising direction for the pursuit of knowledge about the improvement of student learning outcomes.

MASTERY QUIZ

To check your own understanding of the concepts and vocabulary of this climate theory, try to complete all the following sentences without reference to the preceding pages. Indicate the letter of the best completion for each item on a piece of scrap paper, and then check your answers against those in Appendix C, page 393.

1. According to Stern's theory, an individual's behavior results from the interaction of:
   a. development and control.
   b. organization and environment.
   c. personality and needs.
   d. needs and press.
2. The two major dimensions of an organization's climate are:
   a. Activities Index and Organizational Climate Index.
   b. development press and control press.
   c. personality and environment.
   d. needs and press.
3. The social environment in an organization is called:
   a. self-actualization.
   b. organizational climate.
   c. personality needs.
   d. an anabolic force.
4. The social forces acting on individuals within an organization are called:
   a. needs.
   b. personality.
   c. press.
   d. environment.
5. An instrument used to measure participants' needs is the:
   a. *High School Characteristics Index.*
   b. *Activities Index.*
   c. *Organizational Climate Index.*
   d. *College Characteristics Index.*
6. Of the two major dimensions (second-order factors) of organizational climate, the one more closely related to psychological growth is:
   a. development press.
   b. intellectual climate.
   c. achievement standards.
   d. control press.

7. All but one of the following are aspects of development press; the exception is:
   a. impulse control.
   b. orderliness press.
   c. supportiveness press.
   d. intellectual climate.

8. An organization in which participants' spontaneity and expressions of feeling are discouraged would likely have a high score for:
   a. intellectual climate.
   b. achievement standards.
   c. development press.
   d. control press.

9. Of the following pairs of terms, the one representing aspects of development press is:
   a. Activities Index and Organizational Climate Index.
   b. intellectual climate and reflected intellectual climate.
   c. practicalness press and supportiveness press.
   d. achievement standards and reflected achievement standards.

10. An educational leader attempting to strengthen the development press within a school would strive to:
    a. increase the orderliness press, increase the impulse control press, and increase the achievement standards.
    b. increase the supportiveness press, reduce the practicalness press, and increase the intellectual climate.
    c. increase the achievement standards, increase the supportiveness press, and reduce the impulse control press.
    d. reduce the practicalness press, reduce the orderliness press, and reduce the impulse control press.

EXERCISES

1. Think about one organization in which you have worked in terms of the social climate among staff members. Complete the following tasks with respect to that organization:
   a. For each of the five factors constituting the organization's development press, identify (in writing) one strength and one weakness of the organization. A strength would be a characteristic that increases the factor in question, and a weakness would be a characteristic that decreases that factor.
   b. For each of the five development press factors, consider the extent to which staff members' psychological needs were or were not generally gratified in the organization. Briefly discuss (in writing) staff need fulfillment with reference to each development press factor.

2. Regard yourself as the new principal of a school (elementary or secondary) that you consider to be extremely low in development press for faculty. You intend to change the atmosphere of the school over time by increasing

its development press measurably. After reviewing the five dimensions of development press, think of three (3) specific steps you could take to strengthen each dimension (total = 15 steps). Be sure none of your suggestions within one category contradicts or weakens those in any other category.

Examples for orderliness press:

1. Write complimentary notes (with copies to file) to teachers whose classrooms are neat and whose clerical work is prompt and neat.
2. In a friendly manner, ask chairpersons of faculty committees and departments for plans of their group's activities and for minutes of the meetings.

3. Still in your role as a principal who intends to intensify your school's development press, study the individual scales making up the intellectual climate and achievement standards factors. For each of these 13 scales, think of one step or action you could reasonably undertake in achieving your goal. Write the 13 action strategies so that you have them on hand for discussion.

4. Near the end of the chapter, five questions indicative of needed research in education were posed. Based on your understanding of the needs-press climate framework, generate one hypothesis for each of those questions. Be prepared to explain, if asked, your rationale (underlying reasoning) for each hypothetical prediction.

5. Carefully read the case study appearing in Appendix A (pages 383 to 387), and analyze it from the perspective of the needs-press climate theory. Include the following elements in your case analysis:

   a. A statement of the problem as it relates to this theory.
   b. An illustration of each major construct, with evidence from the case when possible (this might entail reading between the lines in some instances).
   c. A discussion of how a leading figure in the case situation might resolve the problem you identified based on a thorough understanding of this theory.

REFERENCES

Major Sources

Stern, G. G. Environments for learning. In N. Sanford (Ed.), *The American College.* New York: Wiley, 1962a, 690–730.

———. *People in context: Measuring person-environment congruence in education and industry.* New York: Wiley, 1970.

———. Self-actualizing environments for students. *School Review,* 1971, *80,* 2–25.

Related Conceptual Literature

Lewin, K. *A dynamic theory of personality.* New York: McGraw-Hill, 1935.

Murray, H. *Explorations in personality.* New York: Oxford University Press, 1938.

Owens, R. Organizational climate. *Organizational behavior in schools.* Englewood Cliffs, N.J.: Prentice-Hall, 1970, 167–194, chap. 8

————.Organizational climate. *Organizational behavior in education,* Englewood Cliffs, N.J.: Prentice-Hall, 1981, 189–231, chap. 7.

Stern, G. G. The measurement of psychological characteristics of students and learning environments. In S. J. Messick & J. Ross (Eds.), *Measurement in personality and cognition.* New York: Wiley, 1962b, 27–68.

————. Characteristics of intellectual climate in college environments. *Harvard Educational Review,* 1963a, *31, 5*–41.

Research in Colleges and Universities

Bernstein, W. B. Relationships among graduate students' value-orientations, personality needs and perceptions of organizational climate in New York State universities and colleges offering graduate programs in educational administration. Ph.D. dissertation, New York University, 1975.

Campbell, P. S. Personality needs of community college and university students and their perceptions of the press of their institutions: An experimental investigation. Ph.D. dissertation, Michigan State University, 1964 (Diss. Abstr. No. 64–9726).

Cohen, R. Students and colleges: Need-press dimensions for the development of a common framework for characterizing students and colleges. Ph.D. dissertation, Syracuse University, 1966 (Diss. Abstr. No. 67–12, 059).

Cole, D., & Fields, B. Student perceptions of varied campus climates. *Personnel Guidance Journal,* 1961, *39,* 509–510.

Gillis, J. W. Personality needs of future teachers. *Educational and Psychological Measurement,* 1964, *24,* 589–600.

Hendrix, V. L. Academic personnel policies and student environment perceptions. *Educational Administration Quarterly,* 1965, *1,* 32–41.

Herr, E. L. Student needs, college expectations, and "reality" perceptions. *Journal of Educational Research,* 1971, *65,* 51–56.

Lauterbach, C. G., & Vielhaber, D. P. Need-press and expectation-press indices as predictors of college achievement. *Educational and Psychological Measurement,* 1966, *26,* 965–972.

Lawlor, G. F. An analysis of institutional press in a college of business administration. *Journal of Experimental Education,* 1970, *38,* 48–53.

Marks, E. Personality and motivational factors in responses to an environmental description scale. *Journal of Educational Psychology,* 1968, *59,* 267–274.

McFee, A. The relation of students' needs to their perceptions of a college environment. *Journal of Educational Psychology,* 1961, *52,* 25–29.

Mitchell, J. V., Jr. The identification of student personality characteristics related to perceptions of the school environment. *School Review,* 1968, *76,* 50–59.

Nunnally, J. C.; Thistlethwaite, D. L.; & Wolfe, S. Factored scales for measuring characteristics of college environments. *Educational and Psychological Measurement*, 1963, *23*, 239–248.

Pace, R. C. Five college environments. *College Board Review*, 1960, *41*, 24–28.

Pace, C. R., & McFee, A. The college environment. *Review of Educational Research*, 1960, *30*, 311–320.

Pace, C. R., & Stern, G. G. An approach to the measurement of psychological characteristics of college environments. *Journal of Educational Psychology*, 1958, *49*, 269–277.

Payne, R. L., & Mansfield, R. Relationships of perceptions of organizational climate to organization structure, context, and hierarchical position. *Administrative Science Quarterly*, 1973, *18*, 515–526.

Saunders, D. R. A factor analytic study of the AI and the CCI. *Multivariate Behavioral Research*, 1969, *4*, 329–346.

Schoen, W. T., Jr. The campus climate: Student perception and faculty idealism. *Journal of Educational Research*, 1966, *60*, 3–7.

Standing, G. R., & Parker, C. A. The College Characteristics Index as a measure of entering students' preconceptions of college life. *Journal of College Student Personnel*, 1964, *6*, 2–6.

Steinhoff, C. R., & Bishop, L. K. Factors differentiating preparation programs in educational administration: UCEA study of student organizational environment. *Educational Administration Quarterly*, 1974, *10*, 35–50.

Stern, G. G. *Preliminary manual: Activities Index; College Characteristics Index.* Syracuse, N.Y.: Syracuse University, Psychological Research Center, 1958.

———. *Scoring instruction and college norms: Activities Index; College Characteristics Index.* Syracuse, N.Y.: Syracuse University, Psychological Research Center, 1963b.

Stone, L. A., & Foster, J. M. Academic achievement as a function of psychological needs. *Personnel Guidance Journal*, 1964, *43*, 52–56.

Thistlethwaite, D. L. College environment and the development of talent. *Science*, 1959a, *130*, 71–76.

———. College press and student achievement. *Journal of Educational Psychology*, 1959b, *50*, 183–191.

———. College press and changes in study plans of talented students. *Journal of Educational Psychology*, 1960, *51*, 222–234.

Research in Elementary and Secondary Schools

Choo, P. F. Factors related to student perceptions of the high school environment. *Journal of Educational Administration*, 1976, *14*, 199–210.

Edmonds, R. R., & Frederiksen, J. R. Search for effective schools: The identification and analysis of city schools that are instructionally effective for poor children. Cambridge, Mass.: Harvard University, Center for Urban Studies, 1978.

Hamaty, G. G. Some behavioral correlates of organizational climates and cultures. Ph.D. dissertation, Syracuse University, 1967 (Diss. Abstr. No. 68–5509).

Hansen, J. C., & Warner, R. W., Jr. Environmental press, student needs, and academic adjustment. *Journal of Educational Research*, 1970, *63*, 404–406.

Herr, E. L. Differential perceptions of "environmental press" by high school students. *Personnel and Guidance Journal,* 1965, *43,* 678–686.

Herr, E. L.; Knight, H. R.; & Hansen, J. C. The relation of student needs to their perceptions of high school environment. *Journal of Educational Research,* 1969, *61,* 51–52.

Kasper, E. C.; Munger, P. F.; & Myers, R. A. Student perceptions of the environment in guidance and nonguidance schools. *Personnel and Guidance Journal,* 1965, *7,* 674–677.

Kight, H. R.; & Herr, E. L. Identification of four environmental press factors in the Stern High School Characteristics Index. *Educational and Psychological Measurement,* 1966, *26,* 479–481.

McDill, E. L.; Meyers, E. D., Jr.; & Rigsby, L. C. Institutional effects on the academic behavior of high school students. *Sociology of Education,* 1967, *40,* 181–199.

McDill, E. L.; Rigsby, L. C.; & Meyers, E. D., Jr. Educational climates of high schools: Their effects and sources. *American Journal of Sociology,* 1969, *74,* 567–586.

Owens, R. C., & Steinhoff, C. R. A study of relationships between the Organizational Climate Index and the Organizational Climate Description Questionnaire. Paper presented at the New York State Educational Research Association annual meeting, Lake Kaimesha, New York, 1969.

Part VI
INDIVIDUALS
IN ORGANIZATIONS

An understanding of how individual human beings function in social settings such as organizations entails the blending of notions about people as psychological entities with ideas about organizations as societal phenomena. To explain human behavior either exclusively in terms of psychological dynamics or exclusively in terms of sociological regularities is to engage in a reductionism that defeats the purpose of thorough comprehension (see Tajfel, 1972). The merging of psychological and sociological perspectives, however, poses a dilemma that has intrigued scholars for several decades. The hybrid discipline of social psychology, a "complex and messy" field of inquiry (Weick, 1969), reflects scholars' efforts to come to grips with this dilemma.

In the literature on management and administration the primary interest of scholars during the first quarter of the twentieth century was in organizational phenomena such as span of control, unity of command, division of labor, and like matters associated with the "cult of efficiency" (Callahan, 1962). The bulk of scholarly interest in this field, however, shifted to the individual workers as psychological beings in the 1930s as the study of industrial psychology gained in stature. Theorists and researchers began to examine how the interests of individuals became integrated with those of the organization and its managers. This focus of attention was represented in a spate of volumes, of which the works of McGregor (1960), Argyris (1957), and Likert (1961) are only the most notable examples.

Two theoretical frameworks representing somewhat different perspectives on the matter of individuals in organizations are examined in Part VI. The first of these, a psychosocial perspective that can be considered a cornerstone of the discipline of social psychology, is called *social systems theory* and is examined in Chapter 10. Many regard this framework, which was developed by Jacob Getzels and Egon Guba (1957) after the seminal work of Talcott Parsons (Parsons & Shils, 1951), as the most fundamental theory in the field of educational administration. The second perspective treated in Part VI represents an information-processing approach to understanding the behavior of individuals in organizations. Conceptual systems theory, as developed by Harold Schroder and others (Schroder, Driver, & Streufert, 1967) after the work of O. J. Harvey (1966), focuses on the informational properties of organizations as human environments and on the information-processing styles of people in those environments. The theory is examined in Chapter 11. Both these frameworks seem to have important implications for administrative practice in schools. Both merit serious consideration.

REFERENCES

Argyris, C. *Personality and organization.* New York: Harper & Row, 1957.

Callahan, R. *Education and the cult of efficiency.* Chicago: University of Chicago Press, 1962.

Getzels, J. W., & Guba, E. G. Social behavior and the administrative process. *The School Review,* 1957, 65, 423–441.

Harvey, O. J. (Ed.). *Experience structure and adaptability.* New York: Springer, 1966.

Likert, R. *New patterns of management.* New York: McGraw-Hill, 1961.

McGregor, D. *The human side of enterprise.* New York: McGraw-Hill, 1960.

Parsons, T., & Shils, E. A. (Eds.). *Toward a general theory of action.* Cambridge, Mass.: Harvard University Press, 1951.

Schroder, H. M.; Driver, M. J.; & Streufert, S. *Human information processing.* New York: Holt, Rinehart and Winston, 1967.

Tajfel, H. Experiments in a vacuum. In J. Israel & H. Tajfel (Eds.), *The context of social psychology.* New York: Academic Press, 1972, 69–119.

Weick, K. E. Social psychology in an era of social change. *American Psychologist,* 1969, 24, 990–998.

Chapter 10
A Psychosocial Perspective

SOCIAL SYSTEMS THEORY

In an earlier chapter we considered the idea of a *system* as a set of
components that interact for a purpose within a boundary that filters
inputs and outputs. The image of the inner workings of a wristwatch
captures the intricate pattern of interactions among components in a mechanical system; one can readily picture the precision tooling of fine
gears, the minute springs and coils, the intricate balance of interconnections among the parts. In a mechanical system the form or structure of
each part determines the interrelations among the parts, which in turn
fulfill the functions of the whole system.

What about a social system—one in which many of the components
are human beings? Unlike the parts of a clockwork mechanism, human
beings have minds, drives, motives, and goals of their own. People are
potentially infinitely varied in their identities and expressions of self. Except in a dance, a wrestling match, or some equivalent physical encounter, their actions are not controlled physically by the other people in
the system. What is it that shapes, forms, or molds the behavior of
human beings so that they so often function in somewhat predictable
ways as components within systems?

The perspective provided by social systems theory, as illustrated by Getzels and Guba (1957), is that humans are both psychological and sociological beings. Their behavior in social situations is shaped by both their psychological uniqueness and their sociological identities as occupants of social positions in a system of social interrelationships. Stated differently, in a social system—that is, a system in which the components are people—each individual's behavior is shaped by two dimensions of the social reality: the sociological dimension and the psychological dimension. This can be illustrated as in Figure 10–1. Stated still differently, behavior is a function of social forces and psychological forces.

THE CORE OF SOCIAL SYSTEMS THEORY

Each social system is both a sociological and a psychological entity. That is, a social system is both a unit of the society as a whole and a collectivity of individuals. The behavior of each individual within the social system is a result of transaction between the sociological and the psychological features of the system (Getzels, 1952, 1958).

The sociological aspect of the system is called the *nomothetic dimension*. From the perspective of the sociologist, society as a whole is made up of subsystems called *institutions*. Each institution is a particular configuration of social positions called *roles*. Each role is associated with a particular set of *expectations* that people have about how someone occupying that role will behave.

The psychological aspect of the system is called the *idiographic dimension*. From the perspective of the psychologist, each person is a unique *individual*. Each individual is characterized by a distinctive *personality*. Each personality is defined as a unique set of *need-dispositions* that influence her or his behavior.

Both the nomothetic and the idiographic dimensions influence the behavior of each human component of the social system. Briefly, the theory

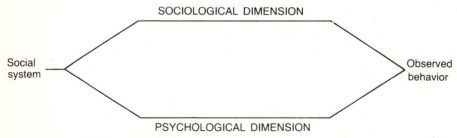

Figure 10–1   Human Behavior in a Social System

posits that in a social system the observed behavior of each person is a function of transaction between the nomothetic and the idiographic dimension of the system. The social system itself is any grouping of people in a socially prescribed unit; the grouping might be a small unit such as a nuclear family or an immense one such as the entire military establishment. In a social order of any size, human behavior reflects the interaction of nomothetic and idiographic influences.

Major Constructs in Social Systems Theory

NOMOTHETIC DIMENSION

The *nomothetic dimension,* as noted earlier, is the sociological aspect of the system; it includes the structural features of the system that enable the system to contribute to the functioning of the society as a whole. The word *nomothetic* refers to the making and transmission of laws. Thus the nomothetic dimension of the system is that which renders behavior lawlike, orderly, and predictable. This dimension, which ensures that behavior will conform to the norms of the society, is made up of three interrelated elements: institution, role, and expectations for behavior:

An *institution* is a pattern of social positions that has been established by society to ensure survival of the society. Institutions can be classified as those serving to maintain the pattern of norms and values, those established for attaining goals vis-à-vis the external environment, those directed toward adapting to changing circumstances, and those designed for integrating the many different parts of the society (Parsons & Shils, 1951; see also Hills, 1966). By this analysis, institutions such as the family and schooling might be regarded as pattern maintenance institutions.

Each institution is characterized by a particular arrangement of social positions. In the institution of family, for example, there are the positions of female parent, male parent, offspring, and perhaps—as in other societies— female and male parents of the parents and other kinfolk. As illustrated by the family institution, each position is a fixed location relative to other locations in the system of relationships. Each position is called a role.

A *role,* then, is a position within an institution. Like each gear in a clockwork mechanism, each role interconnects with other roles in complementary fashion so as to fulfill the functions of the institution. Each role is associated with a set of rights and obligations with respect to the other roles in the set.

A role is somewhat analogous to an office within a bureaucracy in that it entails rights and responsibilities; but *role* is a much broader construct than *office,* as it exists within any social system (not just formal organizations) and includes all the explicit and implicit reciprocal expectations associated with the position. For example, the *office* of teacher is associated with a job description of expectations regarding working hours, curriculum content, communication channels, and related matters. The *role* of teacher, on the other hand, includes both job descriptions and unspoken expectations regarding the speech patterns, modes of dress, expressions of attitudes and values, styles of movement, and all other aspects of the observable behavior of persons occupying the position of teacher. In brief, a role is a set of expectations about how any occupant of a given position in an institution will behave.

Expectations are preconceptions people have about how anyone in a particular position will or should behave. These conceptions are held by the role occupants themselves, by people occupying other roles within the institution, and by people outside the institution. They encompass all aspects of the behavior of persons in a given social position. They evolve as a result of observing, experiencing, and hearing about the role in the course of living in a social order.

To summarize, the nomothetic dimension of social systems comprises the societal institution, which is an arrangement of roles, each of which is a position bearing a set of expectations for behavior. If the nomothetic dimension existed alone, each collectivity of people would function like the precision mechanism of the wristwatch mentioned earlier—each role finely honed to interconnect with the other roles to fulfill the goals mandated by society. The nomothetic dimension represents order, regulation, and rational progression toward a goal. The nomothetic dimension exists only as a set of sociological abstractions, however; the social system always includes people.

IDIOGRAPHIC DIMENSION

The *idiographic dimension,* as noted earlier, is the psychological aspect of the system; it refers to the idiosyncratic or individualistic features of the human inhabitants of the system. The word *idiographic* refers to uniqueness and inimitability. Thus the idiographic dimension of the system is that which renders behavior unpredictable, divergent, and particularistic. This dimension, which ensures that individuals' unique identities will find expression, comprises three interrelated elements: individual, personality, and need-dispositions.

The *individual,* of course, is a single human being who is different from all others in physiological and psychological characteristics. The individual is the basic component of the social system. Of interest in this theory are the psychological aspects of individuals: the internal patterns and structures that influence behavior but are not directly observable. Although each individual differs from others, each exhibits a degree of consistency, regularity, or predictability that has led psychologists to posit the existence of an internal structure called a personality. Each individual is defined and differentiated from others by a distinctive personality.

A *personality* is a psychological structure internal to each individual. It is a particular configuration of psychological traits or characteristics that represent the individual's unique orientations toward the world external to self. That is, each individual perceives and responds to the world in a somewhat distinctive way, depending on the perceptual patterns, needs, habits, capacities, values, beliefs, and knowledge that individual possesses. This constellation of characteristics can be regarded as the personality of the individual; a personality, then, is a unique configuration of need-dispositions.

Need-dispositions, a compound word representing the diverse elements of a personality, are individual psychological traits that combine to yield an integrated personality. Need-dispositions are orientations toward social objects and tendencies to behave in a particular way toward those objects (Parsons & Shils, 1951:114–115). Since they are psychological attributes that constitute one's personality, they are relatively enduring over time.

The integral connection between needs and dispositions that warrants the unification of those concepts as the need-dispositions construct can be illustrated with refrence to some traits noted by psychologists. Some individuals are said to have a need for dominance, whereas others seem to need deference or subservience. The dominance-needing individual would tend to perceive other people as potential objects of dominance, to behave in a dominating manner, and to avoid others who also seek dominance. The need is closely related to the individual's way of perceiving others and to the individual's tendencies toward action vis-à-vis others—hence the compound term *need-dispositions*.

In sum, the idiographic dimension of social systems comprises individuals, each with a unique personality that is a particular set of need-dispositions. If the idiographic dimension existed alone, each collectivity of people would be chaotically disordered as each individual sought self-expression and pursued private intentions without regard for others in a broader context. The idiographic dimension exists only as a set of psychological abstractions, however; the individual people always coexist in a social order.

Transaction between the two dimensions is the dynamic interaction whereby the nomothetic and idiographic aspects of the system are merged. People occupying various roles in the system have expectations for the behavior of those occupying other roles. As *role senders* (see Katz & Kahn, 1966:182–198), they express the expectations in their behaviors when interacting with others. The others perceive these behaviors, interpret them in terms of their own need-dispositions, and respond in ways that express expectations for how the senders should behave. Each time an individual behaves in relation to or in view of other people, that individual is a role sender transmitting expectations; each time an individual perceives others' behaviors, that individual is a *role receiver* interpreting others' expectations. Thus there is a constant dynamic interplay between expectations and need-dispositions (or between role and personality, or between institution and individual) throughout all human interactions.

Relationships Among Constructs

The sociological and psychological aspects of social systems are parallel, interactive dimensions of each system. On each dimension, each construct is defined in terms of a less global construct: an institution is distinguished from other institutions by its particular configuration of roles, and each role is distinguished from other roles by its particular set of expectations for behavior; an individual is differentiated from other individuals by a distinctive personality, and each personality is distinguished from other personalities by its particular constellation of need-dispositions. By virtue of the dynamic of transaction, the two dimensions combine to shape or influence each individual's behavior. This set of relationships among constructs can be illustrated, as Getzels and Guba (1957) have demonstrated, by a diagram as in Figure 10–2.

The perspective represented by social systems theory, integrating as it does the sociological perspective and the psychological perspective, can be regarded as the basic orientation of the relatively new hybrid discipline of social psychology. As Katz and Kahn (1966) pointed out, *role* is the smallest unit of analysis in the discipline of sociology, whereas *personality* is the largest unit of analysis in the discipline of psychology. The blending of these two key constructs, then, is the benchmark of the psychosocial perspective that characterizes much of the scholarship in the study of organizations.

A phenomenon of major concern in the study of organizations is *role conflict*. The social systems framework has been immensely useful in elucidating the range of types of role conflict that exist within organizations. With reference to Figure 10–2, it can be seen that role conflicts might be purely nomothetic, purely idiographic, or transactional in nature, as described briefly here.

1. *Nomothetic role conflicts* are of four types: (1) those in which different referent groups transmit differing and competing expectations; (2)

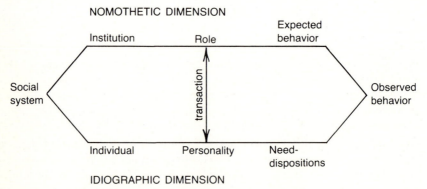

Figure 10–2   A Representation of Social Systems Theory

those in which an important individual transmits divergent or inconsistent expectations; (3) those in which the individual's expectations are discrepant with others' expectations; and (4) those in which the expected behaviors are impossible in the existing situation. These can be designated intersender, intrasender, self-other, and feasibility conflicts, respectively (Rizzo, House, & Lirtzman, 1970).

2. *Idiographic role conflicts* are those triggered by contrasting need-dispositions within an individual or by several individuals' clashing need-dispositions. In situations that evoke two or more equally important but divergent need-dispositions within a person, the individual experiences conflict with respect to how to behave. In addition, individuals can have psychological needs that clash with the needs of others.

3. *Transactional role conflicts* are those in which there is a disparity between the individual's personality (need-dispositions) and the institution's role (expectations). A need-disposition supporting assertiveness, for example, might be discordant with a role expectation supporting subservience.

The existence of role conflicts within social systems is virtually inevitable for a variety of reasons. First, social systems such as schools have a variety of goals, each of which implies a slightly different ordering of institutional roles in patterns that might not be congruent. A teacher, for example, is expected to be a facilitator of learning, an enforcer of rules, a parent substitute, and an emotional support in an institution intended for fostering learning, controlling youngsters, socializing people to the society at large, and enhancing children's mental well-being. Some of these goals are certain to bear contradictory expectations at times. Second, the human inhabitants of the system occupy a variety of roles in several social institutions, and there is necessarily some spillover across institutions. This can be illustrated in terms of the school principal who is also a member of a professional association, a spouse, a parent, a scout leader, a summer camp director, and a member of one sex. The expectations associated with those diverse roles will inevitably cause friction at times. Third, an individual's need-dispositions fluctuate somewhat in response to events and physical states. Therefore, received role expectations that are congenial at one time might not be so at another time; the expectations the individual sends will also vary as a reflection of mood or emotional state. Finally, the assorted role senders have varied agendas and intentions of their own that render their expectations for a particular role divergent. For example, middle-class parents, minority group leaders, federal or state agency personnel, principals, and teachers diverge as groups in their expectations regarding the superintendent's behavior. This can be anticipated because each group has its own interests at heart and its own goals to pursue.

In sum, social systems theory can be seen as the foundation of the discipline of social psychology and as a framework for explicating the nature and inevitability role conflict.

Major Propositions Associated with Social Systems Theory

Unfortunately, this theory was not stated originally as a formal theory with an explicit set of logically related propositions. Rather, it is a descriptive framework that offers one key message: *observed behavior is a function of the transaction between the nomothetic and idiographic dimensions of a social system.* The shorthand rendition of this statement is the formula, $B = f(R \cdot P)$: *Behavior is a function of Role in transaction with Personality.*

From the related conceptual literature on role and personality and from the research literature in which hypotheses were tested, some additional propositions can be inferred:

1. To the extent that the expectations for one's role and the need-dispositions of one's personality are both congruent with organizational goals, the individual experiences satisfaction in the organization (Getzels & Guba, 1957:433–435).
2. In situations of intersender role conflict, the individual's personality (need-dispositions) influences the strategies and directions of conflict resolution.

DISCUSSION OF THE SOCIAL SYSTEMS FRAMEWORK

The terms associated with this theory are used so widely in common parlance that it is easy to lose sight of the theory's uncluttered parsimony and elegant abstractness. The term *role*, for example, is used so extensively and in such varied contexts that one might easily forget that *role* is a sociological abstraction, a construct invented to explain an observable similarity in the behaviors of different people occupying similar social positions. *Personality* is another term so broadly used that its abstractness as a psychological construct can be mistakenly overlooked. Social systems theory is so basic to the psychosocial perspective, however, that the highly abstract nature of its terms should not be lost in the colloquial uses of those words.

Several features of the social systems model are of particular interest. In this section we will consider an expansion of the basic model, the dynamic nature of roles, and some theoretical frameworks that are closely related to social systems theory.

An Expanded Model

In recognition of the fact that each social system is embedded in a broader social context, Getzels and Thelen (1960) expanded the original model to demonstrate the importance of the *anthropological* dimension of behavior. As

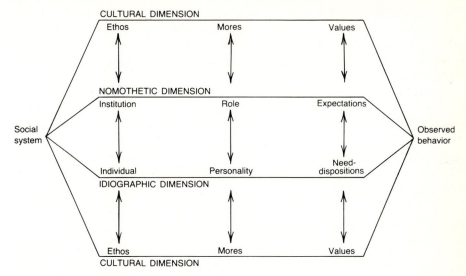

Figure 10–3   Expanded Social Systems Model

illustrated in Figure 10–3, the anthropological or cultural dimension is made up of the *ethos*, which is characterized by a unique set of *mores*, which in turn is a particular constellation of *values*. In traveling from one country to another, or even from one region to another within a country, one becomes aware of the striking differences in practically all aspects of life—language, clothing, architecture, and even the pace of living. The totality of a culture's distinctiveness is its *ethos*. Of special interest in this theoretical framework, however, is the particular set of *mores* (customs and folkways) characteristic of that ethos. Doing certain kinds of work at certain times, attending religious ceremonies in certain ways in designated places, and eating particular foods in certain ways at specified times are examples of some mores that make each culture unique. These mores are indicative of the *values* held dear by the inhabitants of the culture. Values are all the things, actions, or states of being that are favored by a people.

As indicated in the diagram, the anthropological dimension has impact on observed behavior at both the institutional level and the individual level. The society as a whole determines what institutions it will have and what the functions of those institutions will be. It is the culture that establishes norms for labor and leisure, artifacts (such as machinery and equipment) for work and play, and demands for products and services, to mention but a few examples of society's influence on institutions. The culture as a whole shapes the institutions within it and the roles and expectations that are intrinsic to those institutions. At the same time the culture as a whole has tremendous impact on the individuals—the language they speak and therefore their patterns of thought, the things they wear, the foods they eat, and the range of activities in which they engage. An individual's need-dispositions are always constrained by the options available in the society and by the values that others in the society express. Thus the society as a whole influences the personality of each of its individual participants.

The importance of the cultural context of each school has been emphasized either directly or indirectly in countless educational treatises and is probably apparent by now. Much of the variation among schools can probably be attributed to variations in the cultures or subcultures in which the schools are set. What should perhaps be emphasized here is that the cultural setting has direct impact on the school as a whole as well as on the individuals who participate in the school.

The Dynamic Nature of Roles

The role construct is of particular interest in the theory and in the related literature. As indicated in the discussion of transaction between the nomothetic and idiographic dimensions, role is a constantly evolving phenomenon, not a static given. Each role within a social system is cumulatively created and modified as a result of perpetual negotiation between the position occupant and other position occupants (Merton, 1957; Sarbin, 1954).

To illustrate this point, one might imagine a school in which one new teacher behaves in a manner that deviates from the prevailing expectations for teachers' behaviors. If the deviant behavior comes to be regarded by others as beneficial and therefore acceptable, the others might well begin to behave in a similar manner. Eventually, if a corps of teachers adopts the new pattern, the expectations for teacher behavior within that school change and an altered role is established. As the new expectations are communicated outside the school, they may begin to take root in other schools; over a period of time the entire institution of education might be affected.

The evolutionary nature of roles, then, is implicit in the *transaction* between dimensions. Every unit of overt or observable behavior serves three major functions: enacting a role, expressing a personality, and communicating expectations to others. Because of this perpetual transaction, roles have the potential for change over time.

Related Theories

So basic is this theory to the discipline of social psychology that it bears close affinity with many other theories emerging within that field. The most relevant are general system theory, the leader behavior framework, and the needs-press climate framework—all examined more extensively elsewhere in this book. These linkages will be explored briefly here.

A systems perspective is essential to a thorough grasp of social systems theory. Roles enable people to become system components interacting with other human components to accomplish social purposes—purposes that transcend the individuals' goals. By virtue of the somewhat unique role relationships that are specific to each particular social group, the system has an invisible boundary that separates it from its environment; thus the language, interaction styles, and affective ties among system members differentiate the system from its environment and serve to screen or filter inputs from the environment (see Katz & Kahn, 1966). The outputs from the social system are inputs to other social systems within the suprasystem that is the community or society as a whole. In brief, social systems theory can be regarded as a transposition of general systen theory to the human context (see Chapter 3).

Leader behavior in a variety of types of organizations has been studied extensively and successfully from the social systems perspective. Numerous researchers—most notably Halpin (1966)—have found that leader behaviors consistently exhibit two basic dimensions: behaviors directed toward maintaining the system as an ongoing unit (system-oriented behaviors) and those directed toward maintaining harmonious human relationships (person-oriented behaviors). System-oriented leadership emphasizes the nomothetic dimension of the social system, and person-oriented leadership emphasizes the idiographic dimension. As Brown (1967) has pointed out, leadership actions that foster integration of the two major dimensions can well be considered transactional leadership (see Chapter 6).

The idea of organizational climate has been treated in a variety of ways by theorists and researchers. In the conceptual framework explicated by Stern (1970), climate is viewed as a pattern of social forces that press on the individuals in the organization. *Press,* in other words, consists of the prevalent sets of expectations held by the collectivity regarding the behavior of individual members. It is of special interest in this climate framework that the group's expectations are construed in terms analogous to the needs that make up an individual's personality. Thus the patterns of press that prevail within an organization can be viewed as fostering the gratification of individuals' needs or impeding the gratification of these needs. Particularly pertinent to the social systems perspective is the notion that each individual's behavior is the result of the interplay between that person's needs and the organizational climate or press (see Chapter 9).

Summary

The major purposes of this section have been to caution readers not to mistake the elegant simplicity of social systems theory for simplistic thinking. Although it might strike some beginning scholars as practically self-evident that behavior reflects the interplay of personality and environment, explaining *how* that dynamic transaction occurs is no easy task. Both role and personality are highly abstract and abstruse theoretical constructs in the disciplines of sociology, psychology, and more recently social psychology. In addition, the discipline of anthropology cannot be overlooked, since the social system is an integral part of the culture in which it is found.

Recognizing that role is a dynamic rather than a static phenomenon and that the general system perspective is basic to understanding social interactions, scholars have built on the role-personality relationship as the cornerstone of numerous theoretical frameworks, of which the leader behavior literature and the needs-press climate literature are only two examples.

RESEARCH RELATED TO SOCIAL SYSTEMS THEORY

Research founded on the social systems model has taken a variety of directions and represented a wide range of methodologies. There are no standard instruments associated exclusively with this theory. Therefore, researchers have operationalized the major constructs in different ways, often using measures designed for their particular studies. Standardized psychological instruments such as personality profiles, need inventories, and projective tests have sometimes been used to operationalize variables representing the need-dispositions construct. Role expectations, however, have generally been ascertained by means of measures designed for particular studies. In much of the related research, as will be illustrated, the observed behavior construct was not operationalized. Instead, self-reports of behavior and attitude measures have often been used when behavior was of interest in the research.

The emphasis in the sample of studies reviewed in this section is on the role conflict phenomenon, but research on attitudes as well as on the socialization process has also been conducted. Studies in a variety of settings other than school systems are summarized first, and studies pertaining to education are then reviewed. This section concludes with some generalizations that can be drawn from the research related to social systems theory.

Social Systems Research in Varied Settings

The role conflict phenomenon as it occurs in work settings has attracted by far the greatest amount of research interest. The empirical studies in organizations other than school systems have focused on the antecedents of role conflict, its effects on attitudes or performance, and strategies for resolving or coping with role conflicts.

ANTECEDENTS OF PERCEIVED ROLE CONFLICT

Jacob Getzels and Egon Guba, leaders in the explication and illustration of the social systems framework, conducted extensive studies of air force school instructors, people likely to be exposed to conflicting expectations associated with their military status on the one hand and their academic status on the other. They found that the officer-instructors' personality characteristics affected the extent to which these individuals perceived role conflicts as stressful in their situation (Getzels & Guba, 1955a). More specifically, the respondents perceiving role conflicts as existing to a more stressful extent were those scoring higher in dogmatism, extrapunitiveness, and ego defensiveness but lower in impunitiveness and need persistence. They also found that the more academically oriented respondents—for example, those who held professional degrees, had pursued a professional career outside the military, and viewed their military service as temporary—perceived role conflict to exist to a greater degree than did the other officer-instructors (Getzels & Guba, 1954).

Corwin (1961), in a study of nursing students and practicing nurses, found that degree-holding nurses, as compared to diploma-holding nurses, experience greater role conflict. Corwin suggested that students in degree programs develop more professional and less bureaucratic role expectations than do those in diploma programs; therefore, they experience greater role conflict in the highly bureaucratic hospital setting.

Rizzo, House, and Lirtzman (1970) made a conceptual and operational distinction between role *conflict* and role *ambiguity*, the latter term referring to vagueness and indefiniteness of role expectations rather than competing expectations. They found that the supervisors' perceived initiating structure behaviors related inversely to subordinates' perceived role conflict and role ambiguity; that is, the more frequently the supervisors exhibited nomothetic leadership, the less role conflict and role ambiguity the subordinates reported. Using the same measure(s) of perceived conflict and ambiguity in a study of directors of community service agencies, Rogers and Molnar (1976) found that intraorganizational and interorganizational variables both related to the existence of role conflict and ambiguity. Greater role *conflict* was associated with organizational dependence on external agencies in combination with little interaction among agency directors. Greater role *ambiguity* was associated with similar interorganizational factors, as well as with internal features such as job formalization. Contrary to the researchers' expectations, more decision-making autonomy was associated with greater conflict and ambiguity. Interestingly, the within- and between-organization situational variables accounted for almost 50 percent of the variation in perceived role conflict and ambiguity; it might well be that respondent personality factors account for the other 50 percent of the variance.

To summarize briefly, role conflict and ambiguity can be regarded as dependent variables. It appears that personality factors (Getzels & Guba, 1955a); prior socialization (Getzels & Guba, 1954; Corwin, 1961); and situational factors within and between organizations (Rizzo, House, & Lirtzman, 1970; Rogers & Molnar, 1976) relate to the extent to which role conflict is perceived to exist. Since the Rogers and Molnar study was of boundary spanners specifically (of people who interact extensively with others outside as well as within the organization), it may well be that within-organization factors are more salient to personnel not occupying boundary positions.

EFFECTS OF PERCEIVED ROLE CONFLICT

In their series of studies of air force officer-instructors, Getzels and Guba (1954) found that performance effectiveness, as perceived by the subjects' peers, was negatively related to the reported existence of role conflict; the less role conflict an officer-instructor reported, the higher the rating by peers. In this study, performance in the teaching role but not performance in the military officer role was assessed by peers. As organizations, the purely military training schools (those emphasizing military technologies and tactics) had lower levels of perceived role conflict than did the more academic military schools (those emphasizing civilian content such as law and business management).

Researchers have distinguished between role *stress*—the extent to which competing expectations exist in the organization—and role *strain*—the extent to which job tension and discomfort exist in the individual. In an interview study of almost six hundred persons occupying diverse job positions in varied organizations, Snoek (1966) found a curvilinear relationship between the diversity of persons in one's role set—that is, the range of persons with whom one interacts on the job—and the experiencing of job strain. Supervisors, who interact with a more diversified set of role incumbents than do nonsupervisors, were found to experience a significantly greater degree of job tension (role strain), regardless of organizational size. The curvilinearity of the relationship found in this study suggests that job strain increases to a point as the diversity of persons occupying complementary roles increases, but that role strain tapers off as the range of complementary role incumbents increases still further.

Using the perceived role conflict and ambiguity measure(s) cited earlier, Rizzo, House, & Lirtzman (1970) found both role conflict and role ambiguity to be directly related to job dissatisfaction, ambiguity being the better predictor of dissatisfaction. Role conflict and ambiguity were also significantly but only slightly related to job anxiety (strain) and a propensity to leave.

Beehr (1976) examined situational variables that intervene in the association between role ambiguity and role strain in a study of over six hundred persons occupying diverse roles in five organizations. His three findings are of interest:

1. Although greater role ambiguity is generally associated with lower self-esteem, this is less true for members of cohesive groups.
2. Although greater role ambiguity is generally associated with lower job satisfaction, this is less true for those having considerable job autonomy.
3. For members of cohesive groups, greater role ambiguity was closely related to lower job satisfaction.

In other words, group cohesiveness seems to reduce the negative association between role uncertainty and self-esteem but to increase the negative relationship between role uncertainty and job satisfaction.

In sum, when role conflict and ambiguity have been treated as independent variables, they have been found to relate to role strain (Snoek, 1966; Beehr, 1976); job dissatisfaction; and propensity to leave the job (Rizzo, House, & Lirtzman, 1970).

ROLE CONFLICT RESOLUTION AND COPING

Researchers have used a variety of techniques for exploring how people cope with role conflicts and the effects of various coping strategies. In an elaborate experimental study, for example, in which new employees in the "supervisor" role in a simulated organization were confronted with conflicting expectations from superordinates ("managers") and subordinates ("workers"), Simmons (1968) found that the lowest-rated supervisors were the most conforming with superiors' expectations, and the average-rated supervisors were the most conforming with subordinates' expectations. Performance ratings, it should be noted, were assigned *before* the supervisors' interactions with subordinates took place. This brief experiment lasted only one hour, during which the experimental subjects might have thought they could change the manager's evaluations by conforming rigorously to their expectations. Over time, Simmons suggested, the lowest-rated persons would likely become the least conforming.

Hall (1972) conducted interviews with almost two hundred married women who were working and content-analyzed their responses concerning the role conflicts they were experiencing in terms of the resolution or coping strategies they used. He identified three pure types of coping strategies: actively changing other people's expectations, changing one's own orientations and expectations, and striving to meet all expectations better. The first type was found to be the most closely related to satisfaction, and the use of one or more of the strategies was found to be more satisfying than not using any coping strategy.

A participant-observation study was conducted in a psychiatric treatment/ research center (Perry & Wynne, 1959), where the conflict for professional staff members was between treatment success and research success. The authors identified two types of strategies for coping with this role conflict, both of which were employed either formally or informally. The *integrative* strategy of performing both roles, they suggested, leads to the establishment of a hierarchy of role expectations such that certain behaviors take priority over others but a range of types of behaviors is expected of each individual. The *split-relationship* strategy of selecting one or the other of the roles leads to increased role differentiation within the social system such that some individuals are expected to perform the research role and others to perform the clinical (treatment) role.

The role conflict resolution research, to recapitulate, suggests that situational factors affect which expectations will be fulfilled (Simmons, 1968); that some resolution strategies are more satisfying than others (Hall, 1972); and that within organizations role conflict coping strategies have differential effects on organizational structure (Perry & Wynne, 1959). Taken together, these studies illustrate indirectly how social systems generate differentiated role structures as people manage the conflicts inherent to their situations. It can be assumed that individuals' personalities influence the coping strategies they select and the degree of satisfaction they experience in relation to each strategy, although personality variables were not included in these studies. Other important studies of role conflict that should be of interest to students of organization were conducted by Ehrlich, Rinehart, and Howell (1962), Smith (1957), Stouffer and Toby (1951), Valenzi and Dessler (1978), and Whetten (1978).

Social Systems Research in Schools

Social systems theory has been used extensively as a conceptual framework for research in education. Of particular interest to educational researchers have been the linkage of role and personality to attitudes, the socialization phenomenon, and role conflict resolution or coping strategies.

ROLE AND PERSONALITY IN RELATION TO ATTITUDES

Teachers' job satisfaction and organizational commitment have been examined from the perspective of social systems theory in several studies. In one such study Allen, Hamelin, and Nixon (1976) found that teachers with a low need for structure were significantly more satisfied in open-climate programs than in closed-climate programs but less satisfied in open-space instructional settings than in self-contained classrooms. Thus both personality and role were related to satisfaction. Generally speaking, teachers working in self-contained classrooms reported greater satisfaction than did those working in open-space settings, which suggests a need on the part of teachers for privacy, autonomy, and independence in structuring class activities.

In a study of teachers' personality traits, demographic characteristics, and perceptions of role conflict or role ambiguity in relation to organizational commitment, Hrebiniak and Alutto (1972) found that perceived role ambiguity and years of experience interactively affected organizational commitment. As might be anticipated, briefer experience in combination with greater perceived role ambiguity were associated with lower levels of commitment. Job dissatisfaction and sex also were found to have interactive effects on commitment, with dissatisfied male teachers reporting the lowest levels of commitment. Teachers' levels of interpersonal trust were directly related to their organizational commitment in this study, and both job satisfaction and role ambiguity were inversely related to commitment.

Attitudes of students and of school board members have also been examined in the research literature. Using a semantic differential technique, Licata and Willower (1975) found that students were more favorably oriented toward (euphoric about) student acts of "brinksmanship" in schools having more custodial teachers than in schools having more humanistic teachers. This study suggests that students' need for power, a personality trait, expresses itself through humorous acts of subtle defiance (brinksmanship) and through appreciation of such acts, particularly in more controlling environments.

School board members' attitudes were studied by Abbott (1960), who found board members' confidence in the superintendent's leadership to be related to the degree of congruence between their own values and the superintendent's values. This study also revealed that both superintendents and school board members tend to project their own values onto others, assuming greater congruence in value orientations than actually exists.

Only one study was located in which behavior was examined in relation to role and personality. This was an experimental study by Liddell and Slocum (1976) in which a highly centralized communication system was established for the completion of a series of tasks. Wanting to be controlled and expressing control were the personality characteristics of interest; and groups were established so as to be compatible (controlling persons in controlling positions), incompatible (controlling persons in controlled positions), and random. As predicted, the compatible groups performed faster and with fewer errors than did the incompatible groups; the performance of the random groups was not significantly different from that of either extreme. The findings represent clear support for the proposition that role-personality congruence relates directly to performance.

By way of brief summary, the research indicates that role and personality factors affect both attitudes (Allen, Hamelin, & Nixon, 1976; Hrebiniak & Alutto, 1972; Licata & Willower, 1975; Abbott, 1960) and behaviors (Liddell & Slocum, 1976). Additional research on observable behavior seems to be needed.

ROLE SOCIALIZATION

The process of learning one's role has been of interest to some researchers. Cistone (1977), for example, found that the expectations of novice school board members regarding the role of the superintendent changed during their first years, converging toward the expectations of experienced board members rather than toward those of the superintendent. It appears that by associating with a particular group and identifying with that group, one learns and adapts to the expectations of that group. In a very small-sample study, Ferreira (1970) supported this conjecture. He found that administrative interns who had more frequent and more favorable interactions with teachers and students became more positively oriented toward teaching, whereas the interns who had more frequent and favorable interactions with administrators became less positively oriented toward teaching.

ROLE CONFLICT RESOLUTION AND COPING STRATEGIES

As in the noneducational settings, role conflict and its resolution have been of major interest to educational researchers. That educators do perceive role conflicts to exist has been amply demonstrated with reference to teachers

(Getzels & Guba, 1955b; Hrebiniak & Alutto, 1972); department heads in colleges and universities (Carroll, 1974); and other educators. How people in boundary-spanning positions cope with or resolve these conflicts is of prime interest. Boundary-spanning positions are those requiring extensive interaction with individuals outside the organization as well as those within it.

In the classic interview study by Gross, Mason, and McEachern (1958), the researchers identified three personality types among school superintendents: (1) the *moralists*, who tended to make judgments based on the legitimacy of the expressed expectations; (2) the *expedients*, who tended to base decisions on the sanctions associated with various courses of action; and (3) the *moral-expedients*, who tended to take both legitimacy and sanctions into consideration. When confronted with intersender role conflicts, the moralists most often expressed conformity with the expectations they perceived to be most legitimate, whereas the expedients most often expressed conformity with the expectations of the group holding the most power; the moral-expedients generally took both legitimacy and sanctions into consideration by generating compromise or avoidance solutions (see Gross, McEachern, & Mason, 1958). In a modified replication of this study that focused on principals, Sayan and Charters (1970) failed to replicate the findings; by querying principals about the legitimacy of each *group* in having expectations, however, in contrast to questioning them about the legitimacy of the *expectations* held by each group, these researchers seriously altered the nature of the original study.

A closely related study of principals' intersender conflict resolutions was conducted by Hatley and Pennington (1973). They used six role conflict vignettes, each having five resolution options; and they had respondents select a resolution option for each vignette. They also asked the principals to rate the legitimacy of each contender's expectations, indicate the degree of negative sanction they would tolerate, and state the reasons for their decision in each case. The researchers found that the principals more often sided with superordinates' expectations than with subordinates', regardless of the perceived legitimacy of those expectations; superordinates' expectations were also accorded more legitimacy than peers' or subordinates' expectations, and the respondents were more willing to tolerate peer or subordinate sanctions than superordinate sanctions. The study suggests that principals tend to be an expedient group, although independent action and compromise were the most frequently cited conflict resolution modes.

In sum, it appears that the conflict resolution modes of educators in boundary-spanning positions relate to aspects of the personality orientations of the role incumbents. More specifically, need-dispositions with respect to morality and to tolerance of sanctions seem to affect preferences in resolution modes. It should be noted, however, that the reported studies concerned actions the leaders *said* they would take in given conflict circumstances, not resolutions actually implemented. Thus there is considerable room for additional research on intersender role conflict coping behavior.

In general, the related research on educational and other organizations seems to substantiate the major proposition that observed behavior in a social system is a function of transaction between the nomothetic and idiographic dimensions of the system. Although the research used a range of methodologies and instruments, the findings consistently demonstrate the usefulness of social systems theory for understanding and predicting social behavior. As reported briefly in this section, both role and personality have been found to contribute to variations in perceived conflict, the effects of conflict on attitudes, conflict resolution strategies, and overt behavior. The last of these, observed or observable behavior, is the variable most greatly in need of further research based on the social systems perspective.

IMPLICATIONS OF SOCIAL SYSTEMS THEORY FOR ENHANCING STUDENT LEARNING OUTCOMES

As noted elsewhere throughout this book, our central theme is that educational administrators, in order to practice in a more professional manner, need a far more extensive body of knowledge than is currently available about how to enhance student learning outcomes. In addition to being directly applicable to administrative practice in school systems, moreover, this knowledge must be soundly based on theory drawn from the academic disciplines. Therefore, we now address the question of whether this particular theory, the foundation of the discipline of social psychology, has utility in generating the requisite knowledge. Is social systems theory a useful perspective for developing practical knowledge about improving student learning on a schoolwide basis?

A perspective that is closely analogous to the social systems framework and that has direct relevance to student learning at the individual youngster or classroom unit level has come to be known as aptitude-treatment interaction or ATI (see Cronbach & Snow, 1976). The ATI literature emphasizes the notion that student learning is the result of interaction between the youngster's personality and the instructional methods employed. More specifically, optimal learning is viewed as contingent on matching the style of instruction to the learning modality or proclivity of the student. There is a rapidly expanding body of evidence in support of this perspective—research findings that demonstrate that learning is increased by both aptitude and treatment in interaction (see, for example, Winne, 1977; Snow, 1976). Just as aptitude can be construed as students' need-dispositions with respect to learning, so treatment can be construed as both role enactment and role sending by the teacher.

The ATI research, though not studied in the context of school administration, appears to have clear implications for administrative practice. The implications seem pertinent to such administrative issues as student groupings, teacher assignments, and staff relations in general, each of which can be considered briefly here.

Despite the impressive findings of the aptitude-treatment interaction research, educators continue to interpret terms like *homogeneous grouping* and *heterogeneous grouping* with reference to students' scores on achievement tests. Rarely have students been grouped homogeneously in terms of learning styles. Stated differently, most classes that have been designated homogeneous might be quite heterogeneous with respect to students' learning modes. Social systems theory suggests, however, that homogeneous grouping of students by need-dispositions (for example, learning modes, aptitudes, interests, or conceptual structures), if instruction is offered in the appropriate style, would result in greater congruence between personality and role, which in turn might well result in increased learning.

By the same token, assignment of teachers to classes is most often done on the basis of seniority or of rotation without consideration of the instructional talents or propensities of the teachers. The social systems framework and the ATI research suggest, however, that teacher assignments based on teaching styles—that is, matching teaching styles with compatible homogeneously grouped classes—would likely be far more efficacious. Teachers with tendencies to teach in a particular fashion could be assigned to classes in which students learn best from that approach. From the point of view of social systems, such matching would serve not only the students but the teachers as well, since teachers would be performing an instructional role that is most closely congruent with their own tendencies or personalities and would have a higher probability of success and therefore greater satisfaction than they might now be experiencing. This innovation in administrative practice would, of course, require the accurate identification of teaching modalities or repertoires, an area that Bruce Joyce and others have studied extensively (see Hunt & Joyce, 1967).

Apart from the teaching-learning sphere of interest, social systems theory seems to have broad implications for the school as a whole, for relationships between administrators and teachers in the entire spectrum of school activities. Teachers are, of course, individuals with unique personalities and need-dispositions. To the extent that their roles can be individualized to conform to their differentiated personalities, the theory suggests, their behavior will be less conflict laden and more satisfying. This suggests that nonteaching assignments, reward systems, and even styles of interpersonal relating can and should be tailored to enable teachers to express their distinctive personalities fully in the course of achieving school goals.

In an attempt to render teachers' roles more nearly compatible with their individual need-dispositions, innovative administrators could consider a variety of strategies (see Trusty & Sergiovanni, 1966). The following are illustrative:

1. For extracurricular assignments such as activity programs, school duties, and clerical assignments, enable staff members to volunteer for

those tasks they prefer. Rotation systems can be set up for tasks that several people select or for those none select.

2. Curricular assignments can be made in similar fashion, with students homogeneously grouped according to learning styles or interest areas (if electives within curricular areas are made available) or with classes greatly varied in size and with teachers opting for the classes they both prefer and teach successfully. Again, rotation schemes could apply when several or no teachers select particular class assignments.

3. The encouragement of diversity and individuality in teaching patterns would enable teachers to experiment and to build on those teaching techniques with which they feel most comfortable. Diversification in teaching approaches, in other words, allows individual teachers to actualize their own need-dispositions in the classroom context. Individualistic instructional patterns could be encouraged as long as they result in desired student outcomes.

4. Supervision of instruction, evaluation and reward systems can also be tailored to individuals' need-dispositions by sensitive and creative administrators. For example, a variety of assessment plans could be made available, and staff members could select the ones they prefer as individuals. Assessments of classroom instruction could be tied to teachers' instructional strengths and particular aims (as well as to assessments of school goal-related student outcomes), rather than to perceptions about classroom decorum or appropriate teacher behaviors. Reward can even be individualistically allocated according to the apparent needs and preferences of staff members.

Social systems theory suggests that all these strategies and others designed to reduce role conflicts could serve to enhance student learning outcomes on a schoolwide basis. There is still little empirical evidence, however, to support or reject these conjectures that have been inferred from social systems theory.

A variety of implicit questions have been posed that would merit investigation by researchers. More explicitly:

1. In heterogeneously grouped classes, is there a relationship between the learning modes of individual students and the instructional styles of the teachers? Specifically, do students learn more (or more rapidly) when their aptitudes are congruent with the instructor's treatment?

2. Do classes that are homogeneous with respect to students' learning modes achieve more, on the average, than do heterogeneous classes? For such homogeneous classes, does the teacher's instructional style affect the average rate of learning in the class?

3. Do schools vary in the extent to which teachers perceive role conflicts to exist? If so, is there a relationship between school productivity (such as student outcomes on a schoolwide basis) and the extent of perceived

role conflict in the school? Do particular types of role conflict bear closer relation to student outcomes than do other types of role conflict?

4. Is there a relationship between the extent to which individual teachers experience role conflict and the rate of learning on the part of their students?

5. What administrative behaviors or patterns of behavior on the part of the principal are associated with reduced role conflict as perceived by teachers? If such behaviors or behavior patterns can be identified, are they associated with school effectiveness in terms of student outcomes?

These are only some of the empirical questions suggested by social systems theory that are directly relevant to student learning outcomes. It is important to bear in mind that the outcomes with which we must be concerned pertain not only to students' knowledge as a purely cognitive function but to their attitudes and motor skills as well. The social systems framework does, indeed, appear to be a useful perspective for generating knowledge about effective school administration. The usefulness of this perspective, however, remains to be tested by an array of empirical questions that demand further research.

MASTERY QUIZ

Without reference to any of the preceding pages, identify the best completion for each of the following sentences. The answers can be found in Appendix C, page 393.

1. According to social systems theory, observed behavior results from the transaction between:
   a. the nomological and the ideological dimensions.
   b. the nomothetic and the normative dimensions.
   c. the idiographic and the nomothetic dimensions.
   d. the numerological and the idiosyncratic dimensions.

2. The psychological aspect of the system is called:
   a. the nomothetic dimension.
   b. the sociological dimension.
   c. the transactional dimension.
   d. the idiographic dimension.

3. The elements making up the nomothetic dimension are:
   a. institution—role—need-dispositions.
   b. individual—personality—need-dispositions.
   c. expectations—role—institution.
   d. need-dispositions—personality—individual.

4. The term that refers to a socially endorsed set of interacting roles is:
   a. personality.
   b. social system.
   c. expectations.
   d. institution.

5. The result of transaction between the two dimensions is:
   a. personality.
   b. social system.
   c. observed behavior.
   d. the nomothetic dimension.
6. The term that refers to individuals' internal characteristics is:
   a. personality.
   b. social system.
   c. expectations.
   d. institution.
7. The psychological dimension of a social system is comprised of:
   a. personality—role—ideology.
   b. personality—individual—need-dispositions.
   c. personality—expectations—need-dispositions.
   d. cognitive—affective—psychomotor domains.
8. From the perspective of this theory, conflicts can be classified as:
   a. internal, interpersonal, and interinstitutional.
   b. sociological, psychological, and anthropological.
   c. social, political, and economic.
   d. transactional, idiographic, and nomothetic.
9. A situation in which an individual's needs clash with the superior's expectations is an illustration of:
   a. a psychological conflict.
   b. an idiographic conflict.
   c. a sociological conflict.
   d. a transactional conflict.
10. Nomothetic role conflicts include all of the following:
    a. Different groups have divergent expectations; one role sender communicates inconsistent expectations; one's needs contradict one's dispositions.
    b. The expected behaviors are not feasible in the situation; the supervisor transmits inconsistent expectations; two important groups express competing expectations.
    c. The expected behaviors are not congruent with one's needs; other persons' expectations are not congruent with one's own; the other role incumbents have inconsistent needs.
    d. Differing groups have similar expectations; a significant other communicates contradictory expectations; one's own expectations coincide with others' expectations.

EXERCISES

1. Each of the following situations represents one of the three types of role conflict—nomothetic, idiographic, or transactional. Indicate on the line to the left of each thumbnail sketch the type of conflict represented. The intended answers are listed in Appendix C, page 393.

———————————————— 1. Timothy Markham, a third-grade student, has a tremendous urge to go to the toilet, but he knows he's supposed to wait until the hall pass is available.

————————————— 2. Pat Windham, the high school principal, was acutely embarrassed when some influential visitors noticed many students wearing paint-splattered jeans and commented on the laxity of standards in today's schools. District policy, however, prohibited dress codes in the schools.

————————————— 3. Roger Jones was assigned to teach music appreciation in a classroom that didn't have an electrical outlet.

————————————— 4. Little Margie Watson had been an isolate in the school she recently left and now craved friends. At the same time she had an unusually strong sense of morality. Should she report, as the teacher was now demanding, that she knows who took the five dollar bill from Tommy's coat pocket?

————————————— 5. The pet rabbit in the third grade class was about to give birth, and the children clustered in the nature study area were awed and excited. Just then the principal entered and indignantly demanded that the children take their seats and pay attention to her important message. What should the teacher do?

————————————— 6. The superintendent, Mary Arthur, had a dilemma. The school board members insisted that the expensive bilingual program be discontinued to reduce costs. At the same time the vocal Aspira members were clamoring for expansion of the bilingual program to accommodate the influx of immigrants to the district.

————————————— 7. Bob Thompson had been the principal for five years and felt gratified by the way the teachers and students really "jumped to" when he came by. Now here was this professor telling him he should let the teachers participate in important decisions!

————————————— 8. Bill Schmidt was one of the most creative teachers in the school, his students thoroughly enjoying the teacher's spontaneity and unusual projects. How could he cope with this new curriculum mandating month-by-month coverage of specified material?

_____ 9. Theresa Miller is an impulsive young teacher with some strong views about how education should take place. Now here was her dearest friend and supporter saying something ridiculous at the faculty meeting. Should Terry blurt out her reaction?

_____ 10. The principal was in a bind. The union members were insisting that strict seniority be used in appointing the acting department head, and the women's interest group members were circulating the affirmative action guidelines!

2. Think of a role conflict that you are currently experiencing or have experienced in the past. Then complete the following tasks:
   a. Write a brief description (one or two paragraphs) of the situation in which you experienced role conflict.
   b. Identify the type of conflict (nomothetic, idiographic, or transactional) you described.
   c. Consider some actions a person in that situation could undertake to resolve the conflict. Think of at least three different strategies, and for each one specify how that action might serve to dispel the conflict.

3. To gain a clear understanding of the complementarity and reciprocity of roles within an institution, develop a chart like the following and list in the left-hand column five to ten individuals with whom you interact in the course of your work. The people listed should represent different roles in the organization. Then complete the chart by indicating one or two expectations each individual has for your behavior and one or two expectations you have for that person's behavior. Be as honest and realistic as you can. If possible, think of an action whereby each expectation (yours and others') was communicated.

OTHERS IN ROLE SET	OTHERS EXPECT OF ME	I EXPECT OF OTHERS

4. Think of a subordinate in your organization whose behavior has not been entirely to your liking. The subordinate may be a student or a staff member, depending on your own position in the organization. To gain some insight into that individual's behavior: first, briefly describe the behavior or behavior pattern that displeases you; then, develop a two-column chart with "Need-Dispositions" on the left and "Others' Expectations" on the right. List all the possible causes of the behavior you can think of in the appropriate columns. The challenge in this exercise is to identify as many items for the right-hand column as for the one on the left.

5. Select three of the studies that were cited in the section on related literature. From the scant information given about the studies, state what the hypothesis guiding each one might have been. For each hypothesis, indicate the study to which you are referring, and underscore all the variables. If you are especially ambitious, find one or more of the studies in the library, and see how close you came to the actual research hypotheses.

REFERENCES

Major Sources

Getzels, J. W. A Psycho-sociological framework for the study of educational administration. *Harvard Educational Review*, 1952, *2*, 235–246.

Getzels, J. W., & Guba, E. G. Social behavior and the administrative process. *The School Review*, 1957, *65*, 423–441.

Parsons, T., & Shils, E. (Eds.). *Toward a general theory of action*. Cambridge, Mass.: Harvard University Press, 1951.

Related Conceptual Literature

Brown, A. F. Reactions to leadership. *Educational Administration Quarterly*, 1967, *3*, 62–73.

Cronbach, L. J., & Snow, R. E. *Aptitudes and instructional methods*. New York: Halsted Press, 1976.

Getzels, J. W. Administration as a social process. In A. W. Halpin (Ed.), *Administrative theory in education*. Chicago: Midwest Administration Center, University of Chicago, 1958, 150–165.

Getzels, J. W., & Thelen, H. A. The classroom group as a unique social system. In A. B. Henry (Ed.), *The dynamics of instructional groups*. Chicago: National Society for the Study of Education, 1960, 53–82.

Halpin, A. W. How leaders behave. *Theory and research in administration*. New York: Macmillan, 1966, 81–130, chap. 3.

Hills, J. Some comments on James G. Anderson's "Bureaucratic Rules—Bearers of Organizational Authority." *Educational Administration Quarterly*, 1966, *2*, 243–261.

Hunt, D. E., & Joyce, B. R. Teachers trainee personality and initial teaching style. *American Educational Research Journal*, 1967, *4*, 253–259.

Katz, D., & Kahn, R. L. *The social psychology of organizations*. New York: Wiley, 1966.

Merton, R. K. The role-set. *British Journal of Sociology*, 1957, *8*, 106–120.

Sarbin, T. R. Role theory. In G. Lindzey (Ed.), *Handbook of Social Psychology*. Reading, Mass.: Addison-Wesley, 1954, 223–258.

Snow, R. E. Research on aptitude for learning: A progress report. In L. S. Shulman (Ed.), *Review of Research in Education* (Vol. 4). Itasca, Ill.: F. E. Peacock, 1976.

Stern, G. G. *People in context: Measuring person-environment congruence in education and industry*. New York: Wiley, 1970.

Winne, P. H. Aptitude-treatment interactions in an experiment on teacher effectiveness. *American Educational Research Journal*, 1977, *14*, 389–409.

Related Research: General

Beehr, T. Perceived situational moderators of the relationship between subjective role ambiguity and role strain. *Journal of Applied Psychology*, 1976, *61*, 35–40.

Corwin, R. G. The professional employee: A study of conflict of nursing roles. *American Journal of Sociology*, 1961, *66*, 604–615.

Ehrlich, H. J.; Rinehart, J. W.; & Howell, J. C. The study of role conflict: Explorations in methodology. *Sociometry*, 1962, *25*, 85–97.

Getzels, J. W., & Guba, E. G. Role, role conflict, and effectiveness: An empirical study. *American Sociological Review*, 1954, *19*, 164–175.

———. Role conflict and personality. *Journal of Personality*, 1955a, *24*, 74–85.

Hall, D. A model of coping with role conflict: The role behavior of college educated women. *Administrative Science Quarterly*, 1972, *17*, 471–486.

Perry, S. E., & Wynne, L. C. Role conflict, role redefinition, and social change in a clinical research organization. *Social Forces*, 1959, *38*, 62–65.

Rizzo, J. R.; House, R. J.; & Lirtzman, S. I. Role conflict and ambiguity in complex organizations. *Administrative Science Quarterly*, 1970, *15*, 150–163.

Rogers, D. L., & Molnar, J. Organizational antecedents of role conflict and ambiguity in top-level administrators. *Administrative Science Quarterly*, 1976, *21*, 598–610.

Simmons, R. G. The role conflict of the first-line supervisor. *American Journal of Sociology*, 1968, *73*, 482–495.

Smith, E. E. The effects of clear and unclear role expectations on group productivity and defensiveness. *Journal of Abnormal and Social Psychology*, 1957, *55*, 213–217.

Snoek, J. D. Role strain in diversified role sets. *American Journal of Sociology*, 1966, *71*, 363–372.

Stouffer, S. A., & Toby, J. Role conflict and personality. *American Journal of Sociology*, 1951, *56*, 395–406.

Valenzi, E., & Dessler, G. Relationships of leader behavior, subordinate role ambiguity, and subordinate job satisfaction. *Academy of Management Journal*, 1978, *21*, 671–678.

Whetten, D. A. Coping with incompatible expectations: An integrated view of role conflict. *Administrative Science Quarterly*, 1978, *23*, 254–267.

Related Research: Education

Abbott, M. G. Values and value-perceptions in superintendent-school board relationships. *Administrator's Notebook*, 1960, *9*, no. 4, 1–4.

Allen, D. I.; Hamelin, R.; & Nixon, G. Need for structure, program openness and job satisfaction among teachers in open area and self-contained classrooms. *Alberta Journal of Educational Research*, 1976, *22*, 149–153.

Carroll, A. B. Role conflict in academic organizations: An exploratory examination of the department chairman's experience. *Educational Administration Quarterly*, 1974, *10*, no. 2, 51–64.

Cistone, P. J. The socialization of school board members. *Educational Administration Quarterly*, 1977, *13*, no. 2, 19–33.

Ferreira, J. L. The administrative internship and role change: A study of the relationship between interaction and attitudes. *Educational Administration Quarterly*, 1970, *6*, no. 1, 77–90.

Getzels, J. W., & Guba, E. G. The structure of roles and role conflict in the teaching situation. *Journal of Educational Sociology*, 1955b, *29*, 30–40.

Gross, N.; Mason, W. S.; & McEachern, A. W. *Explorations in role analysis: Studies in the school superintendency role.* New York: Holt, Rinehart and Winston, 1958.

Gross, N.; McEachern, A. W.; & Mason, W. S. Role conflict and its resolution. In Maccoby, Newcomb, & Hartley (Eds.), *Readings in social psychology*, 3rd ed. New York: Holt, Rinehart, and Winston, 1958, 447–459.

Hatley, R. V., & Pennington, B. R. Role conflict resolution behavior of high school principals. *Educational Administration Quarterly*, 1973, *11*, no. 3, 67–84.

Hrebiniak, L. G., & Alutto, J. Personal and role-related factors in the development of organizational commitment. *Administrative Science Quarterly*, 1972, *17*, 555–573.

Licata, J. W., & Willower, D. J. Student brinkmanship and the school as a social system. *Educational Administration Quarterly*, 1975, *11*, no. 2, 1–14.

Liddell, W. W., & Slocum, J. W., Jr. The effects of individual-role compatibility upon group performance: An extension of Schutz's FIRO theory. *Academy of management Journal*, 1976, *19*, 413–424.

Sayan, D. L., & Charters, W. W., Jr. A replication among school principals of the Gross study of role conflict resolution. *Educational Administration Quarterly*, 1970, *6*, no. 2, 36–45.

Trusty, F. M., & Sergiovanni, T. J. Perceived need deficiencies of teachers and administrators: A proposal for restructuring teacher roles. *Educational Administration Quarterly*, 1966, *2*, no. 3, 168–180.

Chapter 11
An Information-Processing Perspective

CONCEPTUAL SYSTEMS THEORY

Two people who participate in a particular event sometimes interpret that event and describe it in vastly different ways. Two school principals attending a districtwide meeting, for example, might come away from that conference with very different interpretations of what transpired and how the other participants behaved. Similarly, two people who participate in a particular event sometimes behave in radically different ways in response to that event. For example, two teachers facing a noisy and disorderly class might respond very differently to the situation, even when the same group of students is involved.

Why do people interpret experiences differently and behave differently in apparently similar situations? What is it that varies about persons, situations, and behaviors?

One perspective for viewing persons, situations, and behaviors in relation to each other is that of information processing. From this perspective each situation can be viewed as a source of stimuli (signals) that are available for people to perceive. People are receivers and processors of stimuli; they perceive signals that are available in the environment, and they classify and interrelate these signals so as to render them meaningful. From this perspective, behaviors are interpreted as the results or manifestations of individuals' information processing. The essential feature of the information-processing perspective is that it provides a common rubric—degree of complexity—for viewing situations, people, and behaviors in interaction.

Conceptual systems theory, as developed by Schroder and others (Schroder, Driver, & Streufert, 1967; Schroder & Suedfeld, 1971), offers a framework for interrelating people, situations, and behaviors in terms of information processing. In other words, it offers an information-processing basis for explaining why and how people interpret situations in divergent ways, why and how their behaviors differ in response to situations, and how situations differ from each other.

THE ESSENCE OF CONCEPTUAL SYSTEMS THEORY

The focus of conceptual systems theory is interpersonal relations. The theory represents an information-processing approach to understanding human behavior in terms of people or groups in interaction: individuals are considered in terms of their processing of stimuli coming from other people; situations or environments are the human settings in which individuals find themselves; and behaviors are actions directed toward other people. In brief, conceptual systems theory deals with differences in the ways individuals perceive their varied interpersonal environments and respond to those environments.

People are more or less complex in the ways they process stimuli or signals from interpersonal situations; they have more or less complex *conceptual systems.* Interpersonal situations are more or less complex in the stimuli they provide; they vary in degrees of *environment complexity.* Finally, conceptual systems interact with environment complexity to yield behavior that is more or less complex; actions (behaviors) differ in their degrees of *behavioral complexity.* The interaction of these three major constructs is illustrated in Figure 11–1, which shows that as an individual's conceptual system becomes more complex and as her or his environment becomes more complex, the individual's behaviors generally increase in complexity.

Major Constructs in Conceptual Systems Theory

CONCEPTUAL SYSTEM

A person's *conceptual system* is the pattern of information processing that an individual uses to interpret interpersonal stimuli. One's conceptual system, also known as one's cognitive structure, is a mental pattern—a habitual way of dealing with stimuli. This pattern is analogous to a computer program, which controls how the data from the researcher will be treated in order to yield the

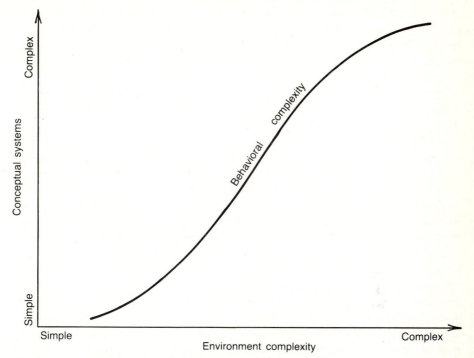

Figure 11–1   Relationships Between Individual Complexity and Environment
Complexity Resulting in Behavioral Complexity

printout; an individual's conceptual system controls how stimuli from the interpersonal environment are processed to yield behavior.

People's conceptual systems can range from very simple to highly complex, depending on three aspects of information processing: the degree of *differentiation* among stimuli; the degree of *discrimination* among stimuli; and the degree of *integration* among dimensions of stimuli (Schroder, Driver, & Streufert, 1965; Driver & Streufert, 1969). These three facets of conceptual systems can be described as follows:

Differentiation refers to the way(s) in which stimuli are dimensionalized by the perceiver's conceptual system. A dimension is a characteristic that other people in the environment are perceived to have—a mental or conceptual device for differentiating stimuli. For example, people can be perceived as differentiated in terms of height, sex, intelligence, friendliness, competence, and many other attributes, each of which represents a dimension. Some individuals use few dimensions for differentiating other people, whereas others use many differentiating dimensions.

Discrimination refers to the refinement of differentiations along any given dimension. Degrees of refinement can range from dichotomous discriminations through categorical discriminations to highly refined gradations of discrimination. For example, consider the intelligence dimension. One perceiver might classify people as simply "smart" or "stupid"—a dichotomous discrimination. Another might mentally classify people as very bright, above average, average, below average, and very dull—a categorical discrimination. A third perceiver might not classify people at all but instead might perceive each person as having a unique degree of intelligence on a highly refined scale. Virtually any attribute on which people are differentiated can range from dichotomous or grossly categorical to highly refined.

Integration refers to the extent to which the various perceived dimensions are interrelated—the degree to which varied perspectives, combinatory rules, or schemata are used for combining differentiations and discriminations among people. At one extreme is the individual who has one dominating perspective, so that he or she consistently assigns other people to the same positions on the various dimensions and does not see the dimensions as related to each other. For example, some persons in the environment are consistently viewed as smart, friendly, and competent, whereas others are perceived consistently as stupid, unfriendly, and incompetent. At the other extreme is the individual who has a broad range of perspectives: other people are not perceived consistently in the same positions on dimensions, but their positions change somewhat as each situation calls forth a different perspective. To illustrate in terms of one dimension, intelligence: people might be perceived as having certain degrees of intelligence when intelligence is interpreted in terms of creativity, different scores when intelligence is construed as a fund of knowledge, still different ratings when intelligence is considered in terms of a sense of humor, and so forth. At this extreme each dimension is interpreted in terms of all the other dimensions, depending on which integrative perspectives are being employed. At the other, more simplistic, extreme, each dimension is interpreted in a fixed way at all times; there are no different perspectives or schemata for perceiving the interpersonal world.

To summarize, each person's conceptual system is characterized by a degree of differentiation, a degree of discrimination, and a degree of integration. Simple conceptual systems are characterized by few dimensions, gross discriminations, and little integration. Complex conceptual systems are characterized by many dimensions, fine discriminations, and much integration. Multiple dimensions and some refinement of discriminations are necessary but not sufficient for integration to occur, and increased integration has the effect of increasing the differentiation and discrimination within a conceptual system. The various types of conceptual systems will be described and illustrated more fully later in the chapter.

ENVIRONMENT COMPLEXITY

An individual's *environment complexity* refers to the nature of the stimuli (signals) that are generated by people in an interpersonal situation. A person or group with whom an individual is interacting constitutes the individual's interpersonal environment. This person or group generates signals in the form of actions, statements, facial expressions, and postures, all of which are signals that are available to be perceived (or not perceived) by other participants in the situation. The degree of complexity of the interpersonal environment depends on the rate at which signals are emitted, the load of signals emitted, and the diversity of signals emitted by persons in the individual's environment. These aspects of environment complexity can be defined and described as follows:

The *rate* of signals refers to the speed or rapidity with which signals are sent within any given unit of time. The rate of signals is unique to each situation. For example, a class might be regarded as a teacher's interpersonal environment. When the students are all sitting quietly and reading a passage, the signals the students emit are slow or occasional; when an orderly discussion is in progress, the signals are faster as each student speaks and others react; in an exciting discussion, when students are interrupting each other, calling out, and competing for attention, the signals are still more rapid. The greater the rate of signals, the more complex the interpersonal environment.

The signal *load* refers to the total number of signals emitted by persons in the environment over a period of time. The signal load or total number of signals, like the signal rate, is unique to each situation. Rate and load are related, since faster signals result in a greater total number in any time span. The greater the load of signals, the more complex the environment.

The *diversity* of signals refers to the variation of signals within a time period, the changeability of signals, their unexpectedness or surprise value. The diversity of signals is unique to each situation. For example, in a classroom situation such as a roll call or an oral vote, there is little variation among signals, and each signal is relatively predictable; when an exciting argument is in progress, on the other hand, and the students are making conflicting statements, reacting in diverse emotional ways, and making seemingly irrelevant comments, there is wide variability of signals and great unpredictability or surprise value to any particular signal. The greater the diversity of signals, the more complex the environment.

In summary, an individual's interpersonal environment in any given time period is characterized by a particular rate of signals, a specific load of signals, and a degree of diversity of signals. Simple environments are those in which signals are infrequently emitted, small in number, and relatively unvaried. Complex environments are those in which signals are rapid, great in number, and widely varied or conflicting.

BEHAVIORAL COMPLEXITY

Behavioral complexity varies to the degree that behaviors require or show evidence of differentiation, discrimination, and integration on the part of the behaving individual. Classes of behaviors such as decision making, communicating, and problem solving can represent relatively few or many differentiations and integrations in the conceptual system of the person who is behaving. Variations in the complexity of behavior patterns can be illustrated with reference to three classes of behaviors, as follows.

Decision making can vary in complexity depending on the range of information used, the amount of conflicting information incorporated in the decision, and the certainty or authoritativeness with which the decision is rendered. Relatively simplistic decision making entails little search for information, quick closure or arrival at a decision, exclusion of conflicting or discrepant information, and high certainty that the decision was correct. Complex decision making entails a broad search for information; absence of complete closure (that is, no final, irrevocable decision is reached); inclusion of conflicting or discrepant information; and uncertainty about the correctness of the decision (see Suedfeld & Streufert, 1966).

Communication can vary in complexity depending on the extent to which messages sent are categorical, authoritarian, similar or predictable, and generalizable as rules. Relatively simple communication patterns are characterized by categorical, authoritarian, predictable, and rule-bound statements. Complex communication patterns, at the other extreme, include statements that are conditional, speculative, varied or unpredictable, and sensitive to the particular audience.

Problem solving is a class of behaviors that can vary in complexity depending on the range of alternative solutions sought, the degree of rigidity in combining bits of information, and how programmed or predetermined the solutions are. Simplistic problem solving is characterized by consideration of few alternative solutions, rigidity (conformity with habitual patterns) in combining pieces of information, and programmed (predictable) solutions. Complex problem solving, on the other hand, entails considering a broad range of alternative solutions, combining pieces of information flexibly (in many different ways), and inventing novel or unexpected solutions.

In sum, behavior patterns can vary in complexity in accordance with the degree of differentiation, discrimination, and integration of stimuli they entail or represent. Illustrations of variations in behavioral complexity can be found in decision making, communication, and problem solving.

At this point a general review is in order. We have explored the three major constructs in conceptual systems theory, an information-processing framework for understanding individuals' interpretations of and responses to interpersonal situations. Each individual has a *conceptual system* that is more or less complex depending on the stimulus differentiation, discrimination, and integration it encompasses for interpreting situations. Responses to situations are in the form of behaviors, which are more or less complex patterns of action. *Behavioral complexity* is a reflection of the differentiation, discrimination, and integration constituting the conceptual system of the person who is behaving in response to the situation. Finally, the situation itself is the interpersonal environment in which the perceiver/behaver exists. *Environment complexity* is a function of the rate, load, and diversity of signals available to be perceived and responded to.

Relationships Among Constructs in Conceptual Systems Theory

Before examining the ways in which conceptual systems, environment complexity, and behavioral complexity interact, some further explanation of the nature of conceptual systems would be helpful. As noted earlier, conceptual systems vary along a continuum from very simple to very complex. Although each individual has a conceptual system that is unique in its precise degree of complexity, four pure types of cognitive structures along the continuum can be distinguished. These can be described briefly as follows:

1. A *simple conceptual system*—also called low integrative complexity, a low integration index, or concrete functioning—is characterized by very few differentiating dimensions, dichotomous or grossly categorical discriminations, and one fixed perspective (one combinatory rule or schema) for integrating dimensions.
2. A *moderately simple conceptual system* is characterized by few dimensions, somewhat categorical discriminations, and few alternative perspectives for interrelating dimensions. These perspectives represent alternative viewpoints (either-or conditions), not integrated perspectives.
3. A *moderately complex conceptual system* has many differentiating dimensions, quite refined discriminations, and interrelated perspectives for interpreting interpersonal situations. The diverse perspectives can be used simultaneously in perceiving people.
4. A *complex conceptual system* is characterized by very many dimensions, highly refined discriminations, and multiple interrelated perspectives for integrating dimensions. People having this complex conceptual system—also called high integration index, high integrative complexity, or abstract functioning—have a theoretical outlook on life; they can create new generalizations about situations they experience, so that other persons are perceived according to dynamically changing patterns of thought.

People develop habitual patterns of thinking over time as a result of their learning experiences, particularly during childhood. Thus a person's conceptual system can be regarded as a personality *trait*, an enduring characteristic that persists over time and across situations. At the same time, conceptual systems can be affected by the situations in which people find themselves: simple situations call forth simple conceptual systems for processing information, whereas complex situations evoke more complex cognitive structures for processing information. Thus a person's conceptual system can be regarded as a personality *state,* a changeable characteristic that varies over time and across situations. The trait feature of conceptual systems is the maximum integrative complexity a person can achieve in processing information. The state feature of conceptual systems is the particular complexity an individual has in a given situation.

At this point the relationships among the major constructs can be stated more precisely. As environments increase in complexity, they evoke the individual's conceptual complexity to its maximum; as the environment continues to increase in complexity beyond the individual's information-processing capacity, however, the person's conceptual system progressively decreases in complexity. Furthermore, the complexity of an individual's conceptual system is reflected in the behavior patterns the individual exhibits. Therefore, a person's behavioral complexity increases progressively and then decreases progressively as the environment changes from very simple to very complex.

These relationships can be depicted as in Figure 11–2, an expansion of Figure 11–1. Behavioral complexity, a reflection of one's conceptual system, increases to a peak and then tapers off as the environment increases in complexity. Environment complexity that is too great—that exceeds the individual's information-processing capacity—reduces conceptual and behavioral complexity.

Propositions Constituting Conceptual Systems Theory

1. Cognitive structures of people in general reach a maximum level of conceptual complexity at some optimal level of environmental complexity; increasing or decreasing environment complexity simplifies the conceptual system, as indicated by a reduction in the level of information processing involved in behavior. This was illustrated in Figure 11–2.

2. The optimal level of environment complexity for any individual is a range of degrees of complexity rather than a precise point. Decreases in environment complexity below the lower boundary of the optimal range reduce conceptual (and behavioral) complexity—as in stimulus deprivation situations. Increases in environment complexity above the upper boundary of the optimal range reduce conceptual (and behavioral) complexity—as in stress or information overload situations. This is represented by the braces at the bottom of Figure 11–3.

3. People differ in their conceptual system traits. People having simple conceptual systems reach their maximal conceptual (and behavioral)

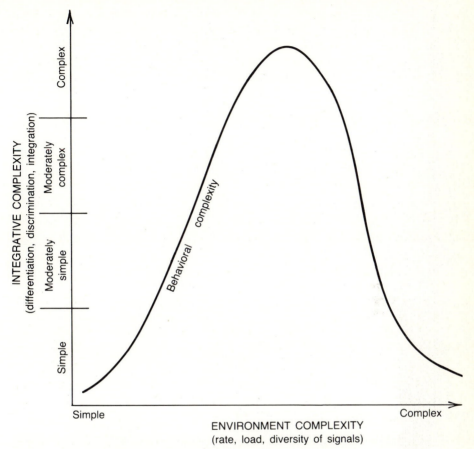

Figure 11–2   Relationships Between Conceptual Systems and Environment
Complexity as They Affect Behavioral Complexity

complexity in simpler environments than do people having complex
conceptual systems. This is depicted in Figure 11–3 by the two
behavior complexity curves.

4. In very simple and highly complex environments, people have
similarly simple conceptual systems and exhibit similarly simple
behavior patterns. In environments that are moderately complex,
particularly in the optimal range for complex conceptual systems,
people's conceptual systems and their behaviors are most highly
differentiated. This is depicted in Figure 11–3 by the dot-dash lines
between the two curves.

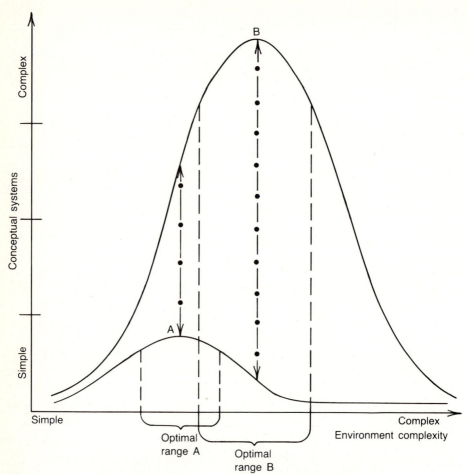

Figure 11–3   Relationships Among Integrative Complexity, Environment Complexity, and Behavioral Complexity for Persons of Different Conceptual Systems

DISCUSSION OF CONCEPTUAL SYSTEMS THEORY

Conceptual systems theory has been treated by several theorists who have emphasized different aspects of the theory in their writings. O. J. Harvey (1963, 1964, 1966), for example, stressed the developmental aspects of the theory and the behavioral manifestations of the four conceptual systems. Also prominent are James Bieri (1955, 1966, 1971), who emphasized the differentiation and discrimination features of the theory, and David Hunt (1966, 1975), who dealt with the applications of the theory to education. The theorist most closely identified with conceptual systems theory is Harold M. Schroder. He and his colleagues have generally emphasized the integration feature of conceptual structures and have explored group interactions extensively (Schroder, Driver, & Streufert, 1967; Harvey, Hunt, & Schroder, 1961; Schroder, 1971).

The integration concept is the most elusive feature of the theory. As noted earlier, integrations can be called perspectives, combinatory rules, or (most commonly) schemata. *Schemata* are mental devices or constructs for combining previously discrete or discrepant units of thought. Perhaps this notion can best be clarified with reference to Piaget (1954), whose work is in some ways a precursor to conceptual systems theory. In studying how children deal with the problem of conservation of matter, for example, Piaget noted that youngsters in the "preoperational" stage of development perceive variously shaped beakers of water as separate phenomena. Even after seeing the water poured from one beaker to another, the child perceives the tall, thin beaker as holding a lot of water and the short, squat one as holding little. At some point, however, a flash of insight occurs: the child perceives the relatedness of the two beakers; the separate dimensions (shape of beaker and quantity of water) have become interrelated by a mental device—a construct or schema that is born in the mind of the child, enabling the child to perceive that the quantity of water remains constant. The child does not have a name for this new insight, which Piaget calls "conservation"—only a new mental tool (a construct) for perceiving relationships. This construct is an example of a schema, a combinatory rule, a perspective, an integration. It enables the child to construe his or her surroundings in a more complex way. It is an example of the numerous schemata or constructs people generate in the course of their daily lives.

Theoretical constructs are analogous to personal constructs (schemata), except that they are imbedded in theories. Each theoretical construct represents an integration of what were formerly discrete ideas, just as the *conceptual system* construct is an integration of the formerly discrete ideas of differentiation, discrimination, and integration. Stated differently, each theoretical construct is a schema, and each theory is an integration of schemata. Thus the theories in this book are intended to provide new and different schemata for the reader—fresh and distinctive integrative perspectives for construing reality.

One of the major difficulties associated with conceptual systems theory is that of operationalizing its constructs. The measurement of environment complexity is one example of this problem. In a laboratory situation it is relatively easy to control the environment complexity of each subject by systematically varying the rate, load, and diversity of stimuli in experiments. In field research, however, there is virtually no way to capture how many stimuli are being emitted, how rapidly they are being generated, or how diverse they are. In fact, the precise nature of a stimulus (or signal) is not known. Is a word, a phrase, a sentence, or a paragraph a signal? Is a raised eyebrow, a facial expression, a gesture, or an entire body stance the stimulus? Karl Weick's (1969) interpretation of perception as a "bracketing" or "punctuating" of the flow of experience suggests that there are no objective criteria for identifying stimuli, only the perceiver's constructions (construct formations) for stimuli.

The measurement of behavioral complexity presents a similar problem of specifying units of behavior. We do not yet have a tool for determining when an act (a unit of behavior) begins and ends. An additional problem is that the behavioral complexity construct is not independent of the conceptual system construct. That is, behavior patterns are considered complex if they reflect conceptual systems that are complex; there is no independent taxonomy or metric in this theory for quantifying behavioral complexity.

Perhaps the most confounding measurement problem is that of quantifying conceptual complexity. Cognitive structures are, after all, internal to each individual; they are "black boxes" that cannot be measured directly, only inferentially. This is, of course, a problem with all psychological variables. The conceptual systems construct has spawned a formidable array of instruments; however, the relationships among them or between each instrument and the construct itself remain somewhat elusive.

Despite the fact that testing of this theory has been seriously hampered by measurement problems, the theory has attracted widespread attention, particularly among education researchers. Although conceptual systems theory is seldom included in administration and management textbooks, it appears to have relevance for educational leadership, as demonstrated in the research sections and further discussion that follow.

RESEARCH RELATED TO CONCEPTUAL SYSTEMS THEORY

The theory treated in this chapter has been of special interest to educators and has been used as the conceptual framework for a wide range of studies conducted in schools, colleges, and universities. In fact, the bulk of the research has drawn on student samples either to test theoretical ideas or to investigate school system functioning. The studies selected for review in this section have been grouped according to whether the research focus was on the theory and related ideas or on educational organizations. The section begins with an overview of the instruments used to operationalize the conceptual system construct and concludes with some generalizations that can be drawn from the body of related research.

Instruments

Of the three major constructs in the theory, *conceptual system* is the one that has commanded the most research interest. Whereas there are no widely used measures of behavioral or environmental complexity, there is a proliferation of instruments for measuring conceptual levels. In this section the most frequently used instrument, the Paragraph Completion Test (PCT), will be described in some detail; some of the other measures will be noted briefly.

The Paragraph Completion Test, sometimes called the Sentence Completion Test, was developed by Schroder and his colleagues specifically to measure individuals' integrative ability, their capacity to interrelate concepts at a relatively simple (concrete) or complex (abstract) level. It consists of five or more stimulus words or phrases connoting conflict or ambiguity—for example, "When someone disagrees with me . . ." and "Confusion . . ." Respondents write two or three sentences about each of these within strict time limits of 100 or 120 seconds.

In scoring the PCT, each paragraph is rated separately on the basis of whether it exhibits one sole perspective or absolutism (scored 1); two alternative but not integrated points of view (scored 3); an integration or compromise between two divergent viewpoints (scored 5); or a highly abstract, theoretical viewpoint (scored 7). Even-numbered scores represent transitions between the pure types of conceptual systems. Because of the somewhat subjective nature of the scoring, the scorers (raters) must be trained extensively so that they understand the theory and can interpret the written paragraphs in terms of the theory. Generally, two or more raters are employed, and respondents whose between-rater congruences are high are often those selected as research subjects. Each respondent's score is the sum or average of his or her two highest paragraph scores. The instrument and its scoring are described in Schroder, Driver, and Streufert (1967, Appendix II) and Phares and Schroder (1969). Some reliability and validity data were reported by Gardiner and Schroder (1972).

A precursor of the PCT is the This I Believe test (TIB) developed by Harvey (see Harvey, Hunt, & Schroder, 1961), an instrument similar in format and scoring to the PCT but including religious overtones. Because of the difficulties inherent in subjectively scored instruments, Harvey also used typical simple, moderately simple, moderately complex, and complex responses to the TIB to develop an objective measure he called the Conceptual Systems Test (see Harvey et al., 1966)—a set of rating scales on which respondents indicate the extent to which each statement represents their own point of view about each of six topics. Another objective instrument, this one based on typical PCT responses, was developed by Tuckman and named the Interpersonal Topical Inventory (Tuckman, 1966). Neither of the objective measures, however, has demonstrated the relatively consistent predictive validity that the PCT and the TIB have evidenced.

The search for objective measures of integrative complexity has touched on diverse measurement techniques, including object-sorting tasks (Scott, 1962; Gardner and Schoen, 1962); impression formation tasks (Gollin, 1958); interpersonal construct indicators (Bieri, 1955); and ratings of one's least-preferred coworker (Mitchell, 1970; Mitchell et al., 1970; Silver & Hess, 1981). These techniques, discussed in some detail by Schroder, Driver, and Streufert (1967, Appendix I), generally measure the differentiation and/or discrimination aspects of cognitive complexity rather than its integration aspect. Nevertheless, they have been widely used in research on conceptual systems.

Studies of Conceptual Systems Theory

The research designed to test this theory and related hypotheses has included experimental and quasi-experimental studies conducted in laboratory settings as well as descriptive-correlational studies in field settings. Central themes in the body of research have been tests of hypotheses deduced from the major propositions and the search for personality and behavioral correlates of subjects' levels of integrative complexity.

TESTS OF MAJOR PROPOSITIONS.

The most comprehensive body of research on the theory as a whole—research incorporating environment, personality, and behavior variables—was conducted by Schroder and his associates and reported in *Human Information Processing* (Schroder, Driver, & Streufert, 1967: 54–105). This experimental research used a set of simulated international decision and negotiation exercises with computer data bases (see Streufert et al., 1965; Karlins, Streufert, & Schroder, 1965) to examine students' conceptual and behavioral complexity under varying conditions of stimulus rate, load, and diversity. Hypotheses based on the theoretical propositions were generally supported. Briefly summarized, when either individuals or groups were the subjects of study, their integrative communicating and decision-making behaviors increased to a maximum as stimulus rate, load, and diversity increased; but subjects' integrative behaviors decreased progressively as the stimuli continued to increase in complexity. Also lower-conceptual-level individuals and groups, as identified by the PCT, reached optimal functioning in conditions of lower complexity than did higher-conceptual-level subjects. An added feature of this research is that stimulus unpleasantness (noxity) and pleasantness (eucity) were included in some of the manipulations of environment complexity.

Other reported experimental studies of students generally supported hypotheses deduced from the theory. For example, compared with low-complexity subjects, high-complexity persons were found to solve more ambiguous problems and use more clues in problem solving (Suedfeld & Hagen, 1966); to be less influenced by propaganda in environments of unnaturally low complexity (Suedfeld, 1964); and to use information more efficiently (Schneider & Giambra, 1971).

Unfortunately, relatively little of the research flowing from conceptual systems theory incorporates all three major variables. As noted, there are no standard measures of environment complexity; hence, this construct is often bypassed in the research. The bulk of research attention has been directed toward integrative complexity in terms of its measurement, its relation to other psychological traits, and its effects on behavior.

PERSONALITY AND BEHAVIORAL CORRELATES

A number of studies of personality characteristics involved administering several tests and analyzing the intercorrelations among scores. Of particular interest in the context of this chapter are findings that level of integrative complexity is related directly to the following: cognitive flexibility (Scott, 1962); grouping of disparate concepts together (Scott, 1963); comfort with discrepant information (Harvey & Ware, 1967; Menasco, 1976); original thinking and tolerance of stress (Bottenberg, 1969; and creativity (Tuckman, 1966). Although researchers have not consistently found the psychological relationships suggested by the theory (see, for example, Gardner & Schoen, 1962; Vannoy, 1965; Stewin & Anderson, 1974; Stewin, 1976), conceptual systems have generally related to other traits in predicted ways.

Research on behavior patterns associated with the various conceptual systems has indicated that people with higher levels of integrative complexity, in contrast to their conceptually simpler counterparts, engage in less dissonance reduction (Harvey & Ware, 1967; Menasco, 1976; Harvey, 1965); form more complex impressions and enact more roles effectively (Wolfe, 1964); do less stereotyping (Mcnasco, 1976); predict other people's behaviors more accurately (Bieri, 1955); and seek more diversified information in decision making (Karlins, 1967; Sieber & Lanzetta, 1964, 1966). In an interesting study of group behaviors, Stager (1967) found that the higher the proportion of high-complexity members in the group: the more flexible the group's role structure; the greater the interpersonal conflict within the group; the greater the constructive use of discrepant information; and the greater the search for novel information.

Although these studies of student samples used varied measures of conceptual systems, the psychological and behavioral predictions from the theory were generally supported.

Studies of Educational Organizations

Research on schools from a conceptual systems theory perspective can be classified roughly into two categories: studies of teaching or teacher-student interactions and studies of administration or administrator-teacher interactions.

RELATED RESEARCH ON INSTRUCTION

In the relevant studies of teaching, the conceptual levels of teachers have often been found to be related to teachers' classroom behaviors. For example, integratively complex teachers were found to be more resourceful and task oriented as well as less dictatorial and less punitive than integratively simple teachers (Harvey et al., 1966, 1968). Conceptually complex teachers, more than conceptually simple ones, tend to help students theorize, help them express themselves, and encourage them to search for information (Murphy & Brown, 1970). More complex teachers also project a reflective teaching pattern—one that facilitates students' explorations of ideas (Hunt & Joyce, 1967; Joyce, Lamb, & Sibol, 1966).

David Hunt conducted an unusual exploratory study in which some ninth-grade students were grouped homogeneously by conceptual levels to form three classes (Hunt, 1966). The classes were perceived both by observers and by their teachers to differ markedly in behavior patterns: the presimple class was very disorderly and easily confused and distracted; the simple conceptual-level class was attentive, hard working, competitive, and credulous of authorities; and the moderately simple conceptual-level group was resistant to authority, curious, self-reliant, and assertive. The differences can be seen to have implications for teaching as well as for advancing students' conceptual levels.

RESEARCH ON EDUCATIONAL ADMINISTRATION

Only one published study of schools was located in which all three major constructs were operationalized. Although the curvilinear relationships posited by the theory were not found in this study, elementary school principals' conceptual levels were found to be related to the complexity of their interpersonal environments and to the frequency of their person-oriented leadership behaviors (Silver, 1975). That is, the more conceptually complex principals had more functions performed in their schools, more professionally oriented faculty members and more frequent interactions with faculty; they also exhibited greater tolerance of uncertainty and freedom, greater consideration for teachers, and greater predictive accuracy.

There is contradictory evidence on the behavior patterns of leaders having different conceptual levels. Although the studies tend to confirm that more complex leaders are more frequently person oriented in behavior (Silver, 1975; Burrus, 1979; Streufert, Streufert, & Castore, 1968), some research reveals no differences between groups of leaders in system-oriented behaviors (Silver, 1975; Burrus, 1979), whereas other research reveals less complex leaders to be the more system oriented in behavior (Streufert, Streufert, & Castore, 1968). In an indirectly related study, Croft (1965) found "open-minded" principals to be no better than "closed-minded" principals at predicting others' perceptions of their behaviors. In the one remaining study of administrators' behaviors, conceptually simple superintendents regarded fewer, more concrete, and more authoritarian negotiation roles as suitable, compared with their more complex counterparts (Moellenberg & Williams, 1969). An ancillary finding in the studies of educational administrators was that the large majority of them have simple or moderately simple conceptual systems.

In summary, it can be said that the reported research has tended to confirm predictions based on conceptual systems theory. Integrative complexity has generally correlated significantly with personality traits that are theoretically relevant, and behavior patterns have generally correlated with integrative complexity as posited in the theory. An overview of the research findings cited in this chapter is presented in Table 11–1, which displays some psychological and behavioral correlatives of conceptual systems.

A major shortcoming of the descriptive research, especially in studies of

Table 11–1 SOME PSYCHOLOGICAL AND BEHAVIORAL CORRELATIVES OF CONCEPTUAL SYSTEMS

PSYCHOLOGICAL CORRELATIVES	BEHAVIORAL CORRELATIVES
Cognitive flexibility (Scott, 1962)	Communication complexity (Schroder, Driver, & Streufert, 1967)
Acceptance of discrepant information (Harvey & Ware, 1967)	Decision-making complexity (Schroder, Driver, & Streufert, 1967)
Originality (Bottenberg, 1969)	Problem-solving complexity (Suedfeld & Hagen, 1966)
	Immunity to propaganda (Suedfeld, 1964)
Tolerance of stress (Bottenberg, 1969)	Information utilization efficiency (Schneider & Giambra, 1971)
	Impression formation (Wolfe, 1964)
Creativity (Tuckman, 1966)	Predictive accuracy (Bieri, 1955)
	Group flexibility, conflict, novelty (Stager, 1967)
Resourcefulness (Harvey et al., 1966)	Helpfulness in theorizing and self-expression (Murphy & Brown, 1970)
Task orientation (Harvey et al., 1966)	Reflective teaching (Hunt & Joyce, 1967)
	Person-oriented leadership (Silver, 1975)

schools, is that the environment complexity construct has been insufficiently examined in relation to situation participants' cognitive structures and behavior patterns. The only studies in which the posited inverted U-curve relationships were found were the experiments based on the international simulation; there are no field-based studies in which the theory as a whole has been verified. Such descriptive research would demand a great deal of ingenuity, but it would fill an unfortunate gap in the available knowledge.

IMPLICATIONS OF CONCEPTUAL SYSTEMS THEORY FOR ENHANCING STUDENT LEARNING OUTCOMES

Student achievement as measured by a variety of standard tests has been declining consistently for many years, according to numerous reports. At the same time the public has been increasingly vociferous in its demands for school accountability, return to the "basics," competency testing, and the like. It has become undeniable that the school administrator's primary focus of attention must be on improving student achievement; all other functions and responsibilities must be regarded as secondary. Likewise, it has become imperative that researchers, working cooperatively with school personnel, generate knowledge that will be helpful in resolving this pressing problem. Is conceptual systems theory a useful foundation for generating knowledge about how to improve student achievement?

Some consideration of what constitutes student achievement might help to clarify the issue. The reader is probably familiar with the taxonomy of learning objectives developed by Benjamin Bloom (1956), in which cognitive, affective, and psychomotor goals are classified in terms of increasingly higher-order learning. In the cognitive domain, for example, objectives for learning range from simple factual recall, through more complex application and synthesis, to evaluation. A parallel between these learning objectives and conceptual systems is apparent: the higher-order cognitive objectives demand higher-order conceptual functioning on the part of students.

Unfortunately, research on the cognitive domain of learning has indicated that both instruction and achievement testing are most often directed toward the lower-order objectives; the higher-order objectives are often ignored. This suggests that teachers tend to strive for memorization and repetition rather than for deeper understanding, integration, and creative utilization of the curriculum content. It suggests also that teachers generally function at a relatively low conceptual level—one that relates to encouraging answers more than questions, conformity more than deviance, repetition more than creation.

In applying conceptual systems theory to education, some theorists have conjectured that *process* learning rather than *content* learning—emphasis on *how* to think rather than on *what* to think—would increase students' levels of conceptual complexity (Schroder, Karlins, & Phares, 1973) and that instructional programs can be designed that would systematically enhance students' conceptual systems (Hunt, 1966).

Instruction geared toward advancing students to higher levels of integrative complexity might entail grouping students homogeneously by conceptual systems and designing for each group learning experiences that challenge current modes of thinking and reinforce the next higher level of thinking (Hunt, 1964; McLachlan & Hunt, 1973). For conceptually complex students, particularly in secondary schools, the learning environments would have to be highly complex so as to foster abstract theoretical thinking. Such environments clearly would require higher-order functioning on the part of teachers.

How can teachers' cognitive structures be enhanced so that they will be able to create such instructional situations? The theory suggests that an answer might lie in administrators' enrichment of the environment in which teachers function. Schools, as human environments, can be made more complex by such strategies as increasing the diversity of functions performed, increasing the frequency of interactions among teachers, fostering the expression of divergent viewpoints, diversifying the faculty in terms of personality types and pedagogical orientations, increasing student participation in school decisions, and the like. That is, administrators can theoretically enhance the school's complexity by increasing the rate, load, and diversity of signals available there; such increased environment complexity theoretically would help to increase teachers' conceptual complexity or at least evoke the highest order of cognitive functioning of which the teachers are capable. This higher-order functioning would in turn be reflected in classroom techniques, especially if ample professional development opportunities were available for learning to enrich classroom environments.

Clearly, such development of the school environment would be somewhat contingent on high conceptual complexity on the part of school principals, which in turn depends to some extent on high-level complexity on the part of district administrators. Karl Weick (1978) has compared the organizational leader to an engineer's contour gauge, a tool for registering and reflecting the shape of a piece of material. By this metaphor he suggested that the greater the "requisite variety" within the leader—that is, the more discrete but interconnected concepts and constructs in the mind of the leader—the more accurately the leader can recognize the convoluted contours of the environment and the more sensitively she or he can respond to that environmental complexity. Stated in terms of the theory in question, the more integratively complex the educational administrator, the more accurately the school can be perceived and acted on in the interest of enriching the school's complexity for teachers and students.

Conceptual systems theory appears to be a useful framework indeed for generating knowledge about what administrators can do to improve school effectiveness, particularly when *effectiveness* refers to students' higher-order cognitive achievements. The applicability of the theory can be summarized by means of a series of questions that need to be addressed by means of empirical research.

1. Do the conceptual levels of administrators correlate with the complexity of the environments these administrators create for teachers?
2. Is there a relationship between the environment complexity of the school and teachers' levels of conceptual complexity?
3. Do school environment complexity and teacher integrative complexity interact to affect teachers' classroom behaviors?
4. Is there a relationship between classroom environment complexity and the hierarchical position of students' learnings (in Bloom's taxonomy)?
5. In district, school, or classroom settings, do participants' behaviors reflect maximum complexity in optimally complex environments and relative simplicity in suboptimally or superoptimally complex environments?

Since few of these questions have been addressed in the available research literature, much work lies ahead for inventive researchers. Major challenges include the need to develop valid measures of environment complexity and behavioral complexity in schools. The research issues are important enough, however, and the orientation toward schools interesting enough, to warrant the effort.

MASTERY QUIZ

For each of the following items, write the best sentence completion. Use a separate sheet of paper for your answers. The answers can be found in Appendix C, page 393.

1. The three major constructs associated with conceptual systems theory are:
   a. conceptual system, differentiation, and environment complexity.
   b. behavioral complexity, integration, and conceptual system.
   c. conceptual system, behavioral complexity, and environment complexity.
   d. environment complexity, discrimination, and information diversity.
2. The three concepts associated with the conceptual system construct are:
   a. differentiation, diversity, and integration.
   b. integration, discrimination, and differentiation.
   c. information rate, load, and diversity.
   d. discrimination, communication, and diversity.
3. The three concepts associated with the environment complexity construct are:
   a. integration, discrimination, and differentiation.
   b. discrimination, communication, and diversity.
   c. information load, diversity, and rate.
   d. information processing, discrimination, and information load.
4. Attributes or characteristics by which people are differentiated are called:
   a. dimensions.   c. categories.
   b. schemata.   d. combinatory rules.
5. Integrations of dimensions of information are called:
   a. discriminations.   c. schemata.
   b. dimensions.   d. diversity.
6. Levels of conceptual complexity are manifested in:
   a. environment.   c. differentiation.
   b. schemata.   d. behavior.
7. Another term for complex conceptual system is:
   a. high integration index.   c. behavioral complexity.
   b. absolutism.   d. refined discrimination.
8. All of the following are synonyms for simple conceptual systems except:
   a. concrete functioning.   c. combinatory rules.
   b. low integrative complex-   d. low integration index.
      ity.
9. All of the following are concepts associated with conceptual system except:
   a. categorization.   c. integration.
   b. discrimination.   d. differentiation.
10. An individual's behavioral complexity is affected by that person's:
   a. conceptual complexity and environment complexity.

b. problem-solving and information diversity.

c. integrative complexity and combinatory rules.

d. differentiation and discrimination of information.

EXERCISES

1. Think of a problem that confronts many school principals. Then consider how that problem might be handled by one principal having a simple conceptual system and by another principal having a complex conceptual system. Write a one- or two-page essay setting forth the problem, describing the two principals' responses, and explaining how the principals' conceptual systems would foster the reactions you described.

2. An assortment of words follows. As an exercise in stretching your own imagination and in divergent thinking, complete each of the tasks indicated following the list of terms.

ceremony	hammer	process
lipstick	gyroscope	banana
bulldog	bathtub	tank
match	drill	diamond
comet	horoscope	willow

a. Classify the words according to as many different classification schemes as you can think of. For each classification system, write the basis of classification and all the categories in the system. Each classification scheme must encompass all the words, but the words need not be listed each time.

b. For each of the first five words (those listed in the first column), list as many uses as you can for the item indicated.

c. Consider all possible pairs of the second five terms (those listed in the second column), and write one *similarity* and one *difference* between the items in each pair.

d. Explain the relevance of the foregoing three tasks, either individually or collectively, to conceptual systems theory.

3. Select one of the major propositions of conceptual systems theory. Deduce from that one proposition three testable hypotheses, and write the hypotheses on a sheet of paper. For each hypothesis indicate the variables of interest.

4. Select one of the hypotheses you generated in answer to exercise 3. Think through how you could test that hypothesis empirically. Prepare a one- or two-page outline of the study, including the following information: sample, instruments (invent them if necessary), data analysis (describe verbally if the specific statistics are not known), expected results of data analysis, and findings that would support your hypothesis.

REFERENCES

Major Sources

Schroder, H. M.; Driver, M. J.; & Streufert, S. *Human information processing.* New York: Holt, Rinehart and Winston, 1967.

Schroder, H. M., & Suedfeld, P. (Eds.). *Personality theory and information processing.* New York: Ronald, 1971.

Related Conceptual Literature

Bieri, J. Cognitive complexity and personality development. In O. J. Harvey (Ed.), *Experience structure and adaptability.* New York: Springer, 1966, 13–37.

————.Cognitive structures in personality. In H. M. Schroder & P. Suedfeld (Eds.), *Personality theory and information processing.* New York: Ronald, 1971, 178–208.

Bloom, B. S. *Taxonomy of educational objectives: The classification of educational goals.* New York: David McKay, 1956.

Driver, M. J., & Streufert, S. Integrative complexity: An approach to individuals and groups as information-processing systems. *Administrative Science Quarterly,* 1969, *14,* 272–285.

Harvey, O. J. (Ed.). *Motivation and social interaction: Cognitive determinants.* New York: Ronald, 1963.

————.System structure, flexibility and creativity. In O. J. Harvey (Ed.), *Experience structure and adaptability.* New York: Springer, 1966, 39–65.

Harvey, O. J.; Hunt, D. E.; & Schroder, H. M. *Conceptual systems and personality organization.* New York: Wiley, 1961.

Hunt, D. E. A conceptual systems change model and its application to education. In O. J. Harvey (Ed.), *Experience structure and adaptability.* New York: Springer, 1966, 277–302.

————.Person-environment interaction: Challenge found wanting before it was tried. *Review of Educational Research,* 1975, *45,* 209–230.

Piaget, J. *The construction of reality in the child.* New York: Basic Books, 1954.

Schroder, H. M. Conceptual complexity and personality organization. In H. M. Schroder & P. Suedfeld (Eds.), *Personality theory and information processing.* New York: Ronald, 1971, 240–273.

Schroder, H. M.; Driver, M. J.; & Streufert, S. *Information processing in individuals and groups.* New York: Holt, Rinehart and Winston, 1965.

Schroder, H. M.; Karlins, M.; & Phares, J. *Education for freedom.* New York: Wiley, 1973.

Weick, K. What is the "environment"? *The social psychology of organizing.* Reading, Mass.: Addison-Wesley, 1969, 27–29.

————.The spines of leaders. In M. U. McCall, Jr., & M. M. Lombardo (Eds.), *Leadership: Where do we go from here?* Durham, N. C.: Duke University Press, 1978, 37–61.

Related Research

Bieri, J. Complexity-simplicity and predictive behavior. *Journal of Abnormal and Social Psychology*, 1955, *51*, 263–268.

Bottenberg, E. H. Instrument characteristics and validity of the Paragraph Completion Test (PCT) as a measure of integrative complexity. *Psychological Reports*, 1969, *24*, 437–438.

Burrus, D. D. The relationships of conceptual complexity of elementary school principals and teachers to the perceived leader behaviors of principals. Ph.D. dissertation, University of Tulsa, 1979.

Croft, J. C. Dogmatism and perceptions of leader behavior. *Educational Administration Quarterly*, 1965, *1*, 60–69.

Gardiner, G. S., & Schroder, H. M. Reliability and validity of the Paragraph Completion Test: Theoretical and empirical notes. *Psychological Reports*, 1972, *31*, 959–962.

Gardner, R. W. & Schoen, R. A. Differentiation and abstraction in concept formation. *Psychological Monographs: General and Applied*, 1962, *76*, 1–21.

Gollin, E. S. Organizational characteristics of social judgment: A developmental investigation. *Journal of Personality*, 1958, *26*, 139–154.

Harvey, O. J. Some cognitive determinants of influencibility. *Sociometry*, 1964, *27*, 208–221.

———. Some situational and cognitive determinants of dissonance resolution. *Journal of Personality and Social Psychology*, 1965, *1*, 349–355.

Harvey, O. J.; Prather, M.; White, B. J.; & Hoffmeister, J. K. Teachers' beliefs, classroom atmosphere, and student behavior. *American Educational Research Journal*, 1968, *5*, 151–165.

Harvey, O. J., & Ware, R. Personality differences in dissonance resolution. *Journal of Personality and Social Psychology*, 1967, *7*, 227–230.

Harvey, O. J.; White, B. J.; Prather, M. S.; Alter, R. D.; & Hoffmeister, J. K. Teachers' belief systems and preschool atmosphere. *Journal of Educational Psychology*, 1966, *57*, 373–381.

Hunt, D. E. Homogeneous classroom grouping based on conceptual systems theory in an educational enrichment project. Paper presented at the Annual Meeting of the American Educational Research Association, 1964.

———. A conceptual systems change model and its application to education. In O. J. Harvey (Ed.), *Experience structure and adaptability*. New York: Springer, 1966, 277–302.

Hunt, D. E., & Joyce, B. R. Teacher trainee personality and initial teaching style. *American Educational Research Journal*, 1967, *4*, 253–259.

Joyce, B. R.; Lamb, H.; & Sibol, J. Conceptual development and information processing: A study of teachers. *Journal of Educational Research*, 1966, *59*, 219–222.

Karlins, M. Conceptual complexity and remote-associative proficiency as creativity variables in a complex problem-solving task. *Journal of Personality and Social Psychology*, 1967, *6*, 264–278.

Karlins, M.; Streufert, S.; & Schroder, H. M. *A controlled input program for a tactical war game*. American Documentation Institute, Auxiliary Project, Library of Congress, No. 8621, 1965.

Larson, L. L., & Rowland, K. M. Leadership style and cognitive complexity. *Academy of Management Journal,* 1974, *17,* 37–45.

McLachlan, J. F. C., & Hunt, D. E. Differential effects of discovery learning as a function of student conceptual level. *Canadian Journal of Behavioral Science,* 1973, *5,* 152–160.

Menasco, M. B. Experienced conflict in decision-making as a function of level of cognitive complexity. *Psychological Reports,* 1976, *39,* 923–933.

Mitchell, T. R. Leader complexity and leadership style. *Journal of Personality and Social Psychology,* 1970, *16,* 166–173.

Mitchell, T. R.; Biglow, A.; Orken, G. E.; & Fiedler, F. E. The Contingency Model: Criticism and suggestions. *Academy of Management Journal,* 1970, *13,* 253–267.

Moellenberg, W. P., & Williams, J. D. Conceptual Systems Theory and the superintendent in teacher negotiations. *The ISR Journal* (New York University), 1969, *1,* 64–78.

Murphy, P. D., & Brown, M. M. Conceptual systems and teaching styles. *American Educational Research Journal,* 1970, *7,* 529–540.

Phares, J. O., & Schroder, H. M. Structural scoring manual for Paragraph Completion Test. Unpublished manuscript, Princeton University, 1969 (mimeo).

Schneider, G. A., & Giambra, L. M. Performance in concept identification as a function of cognitive complexity. *Journal of Personality and Social Psychology,* 1971, *19,* 261–273.

Scott, W. A. Cognitive complexity and cognitive flexibility. *Sociometry,* 1962, *25,* 405–414.

————. Cognitive complexity and cognitive balance. *Sociometry,* 1963, *26,* 66–74.

Sieber, J. E., & Lanzetta, J. T. Conflict and conceptual structure as determinants of decision making behavior. *Journal of Personality,* 1964, *32,* 622–641.

————. Some determinants of individual differences in predecision information processing behavior. *Journal of Personality and Social Psychology,* 1966, *4,* 561–571.

Silver, P. Principals' conceptual ability in relation to situation and behavior. *Educational Administration Quarterly,* 1975, *11,* 49–66.

Silver, P. F., & Hess, R. The stability of administrators' conceptual structures across interpersonal domains. *Educational and Psychological Research,* 1981, *1,* 31–47.

Stager, P. Conceptual level as a composition variable in small group decision-making. *Journal of Personality and Social Psychology,* 1967, *5,* 152–161.

Stewin, L. L. Integrative complexity: Structure and correlates. *Alberta Journal of Educational Research,* 1976, *22,* 226–236.

Stewin, L. L., & Anderson, C. C. Cognitive complexity as a determinant of information processing. *Alberta Journal of Educational Research,* 1974, *20,* 233–243.

Streufert, S.; Clardy, M. A.; Driver, M. J.; Karlins, M.; Schroder, H. M.; & Suedfeld, P. A tactical game for the analysis of complex decision making in individuals and groups. *Psychological Reports,* 1965, *17,* 723–729.

Streufert, S.; Streufert, S. C.; & Castore, C. H. Leadership in negotiations and conceptual structure. *Journal of Applied Psychology,* 1968, *52,* 218–223.

Suedfeld, P. Attitude manipulation in restricted environments: I. Conceptual structure and response to propaganda. *Journal of Abnormal and Social Psychology,* 1964, *68,* 242–247.

Suedfeld, P., & Hagen, R. L. Measurement of information complexity: I. Conceptual structure and information pattern as factors in information processing. *Journal of Personality and Social Psychology*, 1966, *4*, 233–236.

Suedfeld, P., & Streufert, S. Information search as a function of conceptual and environmental complexity. *Psychonomic Science*, 1966, *4*, 351–352.

Tuckman, B. Integrative complexity: Its measurement in relation to creativity. *Educational and Psychological Measurement*, 1966, *26*, 369–382.

Vannoy, J. S. Generality of cognitive complexity-simplicity as a personality construct. *Journal of Personality and Social Psychology*, 1965, *2*, 385–396.

Wolfe, R. The role of conceptual systems in cognitive functioning at varying levels of age and intelligence. *Journal of Personality*, 1964, *31*, 108–123.

Part VII
INDIVIDUALS' ORIENTATIONS TOWARD WORK

The inner life of human beings—a realm of existence that defies scrutiny by others and perhaps even by the self—has been a subject of deep fascination to philosophers, artists, and scholars for time immemorial. Since the origin of such ideas as the human mind, the spirit, and emotions, thinkers have sought to understand the nature of the internal reality that serves as the fountainhead of human experience.

In Part VII we move to the most microscopic level of analysis: aspects of individuals. Here our interest is not divorced from a concern with the social context of individuals' lives. Rather, our emphasis is on how the individual experiences the social context, particularly the context of the workaday world.

Psychologists and social psychologists have enumerated various constructs pertinent to individuals' ways of construing the world. Some personalistic constructs—such as needs, need-dispositions, leadership styles, and conceptual systems—have been treated elsewhere in this book. Other constructs pertaining to individuals' internal lives but not treated directly in this book include people's values, belief systems, levels of moral reasoning, locus of control, psyche, attitudes, emotions, and attributions of causality. All these constructs can be subsumed within the broad category called *orientations* toward objects external to self (or toward self as an objectified entity).

Our focus in Part VII is on a small segment of the literature on individuals' orientations. Specifically, our concern is with two related aspects of people's orientations: their attitudes toward or feelings about work and their motivation to work. This emphasis is not meant to suggest that other dimensions of individuals' orientations are unimportant, but rather to serve as an introduction to ideas about how people might experience their surroundings.

The first framework selected for examination here is Frederick Herzberg's (1966) theory of job satisfaction, which is considered in Chapter 12. Herzberg identified two distinct categories of events that typically transpire in the work setting and demonstrated that only one of these categories serves as a source of feelings of satisfaction for employees. Victor Vroom's (1964) theory of motivation, as treated in Chapter 13, focuses on the dynamics of motivation as a force within individuals. This force or drive, he maintained, is shaped by the individuals' subjective interpretations of their experiences. Whereas Herzberg views satisfaction and dissatisfaction as the results of job-related events (that is, as dependent variables), Vroom views satisfaction and dissatisfaction as the springboards of motivation to act (as independent variables). Both frameworks appear to have profound implications for administrative behavior in school systems.

REFERENCES

Herzberg, F. *Work and the nature of man*. New York: World, 1966.
Vroom, V. H. *Work and motivation*. New York: Wiley, 1964

Chapter 12
Employees' Job Attitudes
THE MOTIVATION-HYGIENE THEORY

Are feelings of satisfaction on the job and feelings of dissatisfaction opposite sides of the same coin—or are they different phenomena altogether? Do the job features that cause feelings of satisfaction when present also cause feelings of dissatisfaction when absent—or are the satisfying features of a job different in kind from the dissatisfying features?

In common usage, *dissatisfaction* is considered the antonym of *satisfaction;* the two words are regarded as opposite aspects of the same noun. Because of this feature of English syntax, we tend to think of feelings of satisfaction and dissatisfaction as opposite extremes of one emotion. Frederick Herzberg's insights about job attitudes challenge this assumption, however.

Herzberg (1966) maintained that feelings of satisfaction are different in kind from feelings of dissatisfaction: that the opposite of satisfaction is *no satisfaction* and that the opposite of dissatisfaction is *no dissatisfaction.* He drew this conclusion from a broad range of research findings indicating that the job characteristics that result in employees' feelings of satisfaction differ in type from those that result in employees' feelings of dissatisfaction.

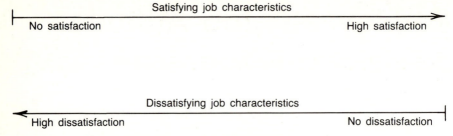

Figure 12–1   Major Categories of Job Characteristics

If you think for a moment about a job you have held, you will realize that it had many attributes that made it unique—a particular set of tasks, a particular work setting, a particular set of co-workers, a particular supervision, and so forth. The motivation-hygiene framework highlights the notion that the various features of a job situation are classifiable in two separate and distinct categories: those resulting in feelings of satisfaction and those resulting in feelings of dissatisfaction. Figure 12–1 illustrates the two-dimensional nature of job characteristics and emphasizes the idea that satisfaction and dissatisfaction are two separate dimensions of work experience.

THE TWO-DIMENSIONAL THEORY OF JOB ATTITUDES

All human beings have two basic types of needs: the need to avoid pain—a need that people share with other animals—and the need for psychological growth—a need that is distinctly human.

Pain-avoidance needs are those associated with physical drives. They include the needs to avoid hunger, cold, illness or malfunction, and danger. Psychological-growth needs, on the other hand, are those associated with mental development. They include the needs to acquire knowledge, perceive interrelationships among events, express creativity, experience individuality, and function well in ambiguous situations. In brief, the pain-avoidance needs pertain to physical well-being, whereas the psychological-growth needs foster self-actualization.

People seek to fulfill both types of needs in all situations, including employment situations. Every work setting potentially offers opportunities to gratify both pain-avoidance needs and psychological-growth needs. However, some aspects of the job enable employees to fulfill pain-avoidance needs, whereas other aspects of the work situation permit the fulfillment of psychological-growth needs.

The essence of the motivation-hygiene model is that the various features of a job can be classified according to the type of needs to which they relate. Job elements that can gratify employees' psychological-growth needs cause feelings of satisfaction when present and adequate; these job elements are called *motivation factors*. Job features that can gratify employees' pain-avoidance needs cause feelings of dissatisfaction when absent or inadequate; these job elements are called *hygiene factors*. The two types of factors will be defined below and the particular job aspects making up each type specified.

Major Constructs in the Motivation-Hygiene Theory

MOTIVATION FACTORS

Motivation factors are the aspects of a job situation that can, when present, fulfill employees' needs for psychological growth. They tend to be intrinsic to the work associated with the job; they pertain to the content of the job. When present, adequate, and positive in a job situation, these elements cause feelings of satisfaction in employees; when absent, inadequate, or negative, however, they do *not* generally cause feelings of dissatisfaction. The six motivation factors are:

1. *Achievement:* successful or unsuccessful completion of a job; solution or nonsolution of problems; seeing or not seeing the results of one's work.
2. *Recognition:* notice in the form of praise or blame from another person (a superior or manager, a client, a peer, a professional colleague); personal acknowledgment by management; reward or punishment that is directly related to task accomplishment.
3. *Work itself:* the nature of the tasks to be accomplished on the job. The tasks themselves might be routine or varied, creative or stultifying, interesting or boring, difficult or easy.
4. *Responsibility:* presence or absence of autonomy in carrying out job assignments; increase or decrease in authority over others; accountability for task accomplishment.
5. *Advancement:* actual change in status within the organization as a result of performance; promotion, lack of expected promotion, or demotion related to performance.
6. *Possibility of growth:* changes in the work situation such that advancement is more or less likely and opportunities to learn are increased or decreased.

HYGIENE FACTORS

Hygiene factors are the aspects of a job situation that can, when present and adequate, fulfill employees' pain-avoidance needs. They tend to be extrinsic to the work itself; they pertain to the context in which the work is performed.

When absent, inadequate, or negative in a job situation, these elements cause feelings of dissatisfaction; but when present, ample, and positive they do not generally cause feelings of satisfaction. The ten hygiene factors are:

1. *Company policy and administration:* adequacy or inadequacy of company management, including such elements as clarity of communication and adequacy of resources for task accomplishment; overall harmful or beneficial personnel policies, such as salary increment policies, promotion policies, and fringe benefits.
2. *Supervision (technical):* competence or incompetence, fairness or unfairness, and efficiency or inefficiency of superordinates.
3. *Salary:* wage and compensation features, such as pay increase expectations unfulfilled or exceeded, early or late salary adjustments, and adequate or inadequate pay.
4. *Interpersonal relations (superior):* pleasant or unpleasant interactions with superordinates that are or are not directly relevant to task accomplishment.
5. *Interpersonal relations (subordinate):* pleasant or unpleasant interactions with persons at a lower level in the organizational hierarchy.
6. *Interpersonal relations (peer):* pleasant or unpleasant interactions with co-workers (persons at the same level in the organization).
7. *Working conditions:* the physical conditions of work, such as the amount of work or the facilities available; heat, light, space, and ventilation; tools, equipment, and supplies.
8. *Status:* signs, symbols, or appurtenances of position within the organization, such as privileges, support staff, work space size and location, work space decor, and so on.
9. *Job security:* objective signs of the presence or absence of job security, such as tenure, company stability, and assurances of or threats to continued employment.
10. *Effects on personal life:* aspects of the job that have impact on personal life, such as work shifts, travel requirements, geographic location, and entertainment requirements.

Relationships Among Constructs in the Motivation-Hygiene Theory

The motivation factors and the hygiene factors tend to represent two different classes of experience. Feelings of satisfaction are generally associated with motivation factors, whereas feelings of dissatisfaction are usually associated with hygiene factors. Stated differently, when people describe episodes during which they felt particularly good, happy, or satisfied with their jobs, they usually mention the positive aspects of achievement, recognition, work itself, responsibility, advancement, and/or possibility of growth, but *not* the positive aspects of the hygiene factors. On the other hand, when people describe episodes during which they felt particularly bad, unhappy, or dissatisfied, they generally mention the negative aspects of company policy and administration, supervision, salary, interpersonal relations, working conditions, status, job security, and/or effects on personal life, but *not* the negative aspects of the motivation factors.

Although people usually mention motivation factors when describing especially satisfying job-related events and hygiene factors when describing particularly dissatisfying events, they do not always do so. Sometimes hygienes are mentioned in conjunction with satisfying episodes; and sometimes motivators are mentioned in connection with dissatisfying sequences of events. However, when motivation factors are associated with happy events, the feelings of satisfaction generally last longer than when hygiene factors are mentioned. Similarly, when hygiene factors are mentioned in connection with unhappy events, the feelings of dissatisfaction usually last longer than when motivation factors are so mentioned.

The motivation factors are so named because the six elements—successful achievement, favorable recognition, interesting work, sufficient responsibility, upward advancement, and increased possibility of growth—are far more often associated with increased effort (motivation to work harder) than are the positive aspects of the hygiene factors. Conversely, lack of accomplishment, unfavorable recognition, boring work, insufficient responsibility, absence of advancement (or demotion), and reduced possibility of growth are associated with decreased effort (motivation to produce less).

The relationships among the major constructs as well as the two-dimensional nature of satisfaction/dissatisfaction can be depicted by expanding on the diagram presented earlier, as in Figure 12–2.

Major Propositions of the Motivation-Hygiene Theory

1. When motivation factors are present and in a positive direction in a job situation, employees will experience feelings of satisfaction; when the motivation factors are absent or negative in direction, employees will not experience feelings of satisfaction.
2. When hygiene factors are absent, inadequate, or negative in a job situation, employees will experience feelings of dissatisfaction; when hygiene factors are present, adequate, and positive in direction, employees will not experience feelings of dissatisfaction.
3. Absent or negative motivation factors do not result in feelings of dissatisfaction on the part of employees, and adequate or positive hygiene factors do not result in feelings of satisfaction on the part of employees.

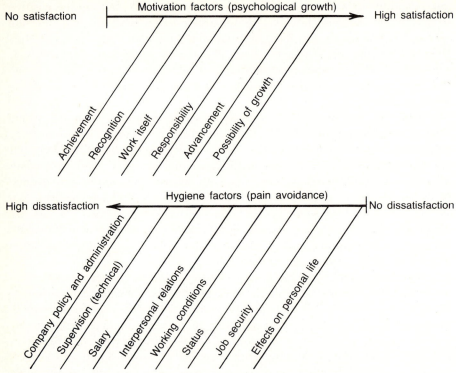

Figure 12–2   Motivation and Hygiene Factors in Job Situations

4. The presence and positive direction of motivation factors result in increased effort on the part of employees, whereas the adequacy and positive direction of hygiene factors do not result in increased effort.
5. The absence or negative direction of motivation factors results in decreased effort on the part of employees, whereas the inadequacy or negative direction of hygiene factors does not result in decreased effort.

DISCUSSION OF THE MOTIVATION-HYGIENE FRAMEWORK

The motivation-hygiene theory of job attitudes has been applauded by many for the novelty of its approach to understanding workers' feelings and for its implications for job design, management practices, and research. It has its critics, however (for example, Hinrichs & Mischkind, 1967; House & Wigdor, 1967; Lindsay et al., 1967), who view the theory as simplistic and based on faulty assumptions. The purposes of this discussion are to clarify some of the unique features of the model, to explore some of the critical issues raised by its detractors, and to consider some conceptualizations related to this theory.

Clarification of Aspects of the Theory

Although the sixteen factors encompassed by the motivation-hygiene framework have been classified into two categories, each factor individually can be regarded as a continuum having a negative and a positive pole. The motivation factor, *achievement*, for example, can range from failure to accomplish a relatively easy task to success in accomplishing a very difficult task. Similarly, the hygiene factor, *supervision (technical)*, can range from very ineffectual and hindering supervisory behavior to very effective and facilitating supervisory actions. Thus, when people describe pleasing events, they sometimes mention an example of excellent supervision (a hygiene factor); when describing unpleasant events, people sometimes mention being criticized by the boss (a motivation factor). What is important in this theoretical framework is that people mention positive examples of motivation factors *significantly more often* than hygiene factors when describing particularly pleasing experiences. Likewise, people mention negative hygiene factors *significantly more often* than negative motivation factors when describing especially dissatisfying job experiences.

Another distinctive feature of this framework is that it does not pertain to overall job satisfaction or dissatisfaction but to job-related episodes in which unusually good or especially bad feelings are evoked. The fact that Herzberg (1966) and others (Herzberg, Mausner, & Snyderman, 1959) used the phrase *job satisfaction* has been misleading to some researchers and some critics; nowhere in their original research did Herzberg or his colleagues measure employees' feelings about their work situations in general. Whitsett and Winslow (1967), who generally support Herzberg's approach, explored this issue thoroughly in their critique of some of the research based on Herzberg's work. As Behling, Labovitz, and Kosmo (1968) noted, there might be no such thing as "over-all job satisfaction" except in the minds (and measurement devices) of researchers; it may well be that job-related feelings are *only* episodic, related to specific events that transpire in the course of the working day. Whether or not general job attitudes exist, the motivation-hygiene model pertains to feelings about events, not about jobs in general.

Criticisms of the Theory

A major criticism that has been leveled at the motivation-hygiene theory is that it is method-bound. Several scholars maintain that the theory is supported by one method of research alone and that the research method yields findings that would not emerge from other methods. First, implicit in the interview method used by Herzberg and his followers is an assumption that feelings within an individual are caused by events external to the individual. Respondents are asked to think of a time when they felt especially good (or bad) about their job and then to describe the events associated with that feeling. Thus respondents are primed to attribute their feelings to job-related events. Second, as

Dunnette, Campbell, and Hakel (1967) and Salancik and Pfeffer (1977) noted, this method might result in a kind of reconstructed logic—a pattern of reasoning that follows rather than precedes a conclusion. It might be that the interviewee's awareness of a feeling makes particular aspects of the job salient; that is, the feeling might cause the events to be remembered rather than the events causing the feelings. Finally, although Herzberg, Mausner, and Snyderman (1959) considered the respondents' narrations to be renditions of objective events, critics such as Dunnette, Campbell, and Hakel (1967) and Vroom (1964) have suggested that one's recollections of past events tend to be highly subjective and that people tend to interpret their experiences in an ego-defensive manner. Respondents might well tend to attribute good feelings to their own accomplishments and bad feelings to circumstances beyond their control.

An alternative viewpoint is that the interview technique associated with the motivation-hygiene model has some decided strengths. For one thing, the open-ended interview questions allow respondents to mention all the aspects of the situation that seem relevant—and *only* those aspects. Furthermore, just as recollections of good (or bad) feelings might act as a screen filtering the types of events remembered, one's feelings during or preceding an episode might similarly screen one's perceptions and interpretations of the events as they are occurring. Thus, whether feelings cause or are caused by events, they seem to be associated with events in the minds of the persons being interviewed; it is this association that is pertinent to the theory. Finally, it can be argued that it is people's subjective interpretations of their experiences, not the objective reality of the events, that shape their later behaviors. The fact that the interview protocols have yielded two distinct sets of responses—one for satisfying events and one for dissatisfying ones—is in itself theoretically interesting.

Another criticism of the theory is that there is not much empirical evidence that the six factors associated with job satisfaction actually result in increased (or decreased) effort to perform well. Interview respondents tend to perceive relationships between the motivation factors and their own effort. There is little evidence, however, to support Herzberg's contention that providing recognition, interesting work, possibilities for growth, and so on actually results in increased effort on the part of employees. Whether satisfying events are also motivating events remains an empirical question.

Related Conceptualizations

One of the theorists with whom Herzberg's work has been associated is Abraham Maslow, whose theory of motivation was discussed briefly in Chapter 1. Readers will recall that Maslow (1962) posited a hierarchy of five types of needs that individuals seek to gratify in the various situations they encounter (or seek). Some scholars have recognized an affinity between Maslow's categories of need and Herzberg's categories of job factors, noting that the hygiene factors relate to the first four Maslovian levels of need, whereas the motivation factors relate to the fifth or highest order of needs, self-actualization (Hoy & Miskel, 1978:106).

Maslow's rationale for linking needs to motivation is more clearly stated or at least more explicit than Herzberg's reasoning. Maslow regarded needs as organismic deficiencies that generate tension within the individual. This tension is the source of energy that propels or motivates the organism into its environment to seek gratification. Herzberg's reasoning is rooted primarily in biblical and other literary references, with Adam and Abraham, respectively, representing the physiological (pain-avoidance) and psychological (pleasure-approach) drives. More scientific origins of the Herzbergian viewpoint may be available, however, in neurological theories of reinforcement. Some research on motor behavior in relation to brain areas seems to suggest that approach behaviors and avoidance behaviors are stimulated by different brain areas and neurological patterns (Glickman & Schiff, 1967) and that approach behaviors are related to pleasurable stimulation, whereas withdrawal or avoidance behaviors are related to aversive stimulation (Levine, 1975:440). Thus there appears to be some physiological foundation for a two-factor theory of motivation such as Herzberg postulated.

In summary, the motivation-hygiene conceptualization offers a new and interesting way of thinking about workers' feelings about their jobs. The model's two-dimensional nature represents a novel conceptualization, and the interview method from which it was generated is a refreshing departure from the rating-scale techniques that still dominate attitudinal research. The conceptual issues to be highlighted are: (1) that the motivation factors and hygiene factors are not exclusively but only predominantly associated with satisfaction and dissatisfaction, respectively; and (2) that feelings of satisfaction and dissatisfaction, as treated in the model, are related to episodes rather than to the job as a whole. The framework has been challenged on the basis of its underlying assumptions, methodological constraints, and questionable data base. Nevertheless, it has yielded a useful classification system for job-related events, stimulated sophisticated thinking about the nature of one's work experience, and generated a tremendous body of research designed to test its major propositions. Although the conceptual origins of the theory are not completely clear, the two-dimensional approach appears to be related to other frameworks, both psychological and physiological. Many of the conceptual and operational issues remain to be resolved, but it is undeniable that the theory is a major contribution to the field.

RESEARCH RELATED
TO THE MOTIVATION-HYGIENE THEORY

As suggested earlier, the large body of research on employees' job attitudes—particularly workers' positive or negative orientations toward their jobs—can be roughly divided into two categories: replications of Herzberg's interview technique and paper-and-pencil studies using rating scales. A representative sample of the studies is reviewed in this section following an overview of the interview procedures used by some researchers. Inquiries in a variety of settings other than schools are considered first, and a review of the research conducted in schools, colleges, and universities follows. This section concludes with some generalizations that can be inferred from the research findings to date.

Instruments

The data-gathering instrument most often associated with the motivation-hygiene framework is the semistructured interview protocol that Herzberg and his colleagues used in their original study. Employees are first asked to think of a time in the past when they felt especially good or especially bad about their jobs. After each respondent has thought of a particular time period and indicated whether his or her feelings were good or bad, the interviewer asks what events occurred at that time that caused the change in feelings. Interviewers are free to probe for information such as how long ago the sequence of events occurred, the circumstances in which the events occurred, how long the series of events lasted, how long the unusual feelings lasted, and what effects the events had on the respondent's feelings. After recording all the information, the interviewer asks the respondent to think of a time in the past when the opposite type of feeling was especially prevalent; the same questions are then asked about the second episode.

Transcripts are made of all responses, and all units of thought are marked on each transcript. A unit of thought is a phrase or sentence that represents one job-related event associated with the particularly good or bad episode being described. Each unit of thought is then coded by two or more raters according to a list of the sixteen factors and their definitions. High interrater agreements are necessary to ensure that the factor identifications are reliable. Analyses are then done to determine which factors are most frequently cited in good-feeling and bad-feeling sequences of events and which factors are associated with the longest-lasting feelings.

Many of the studies designed to test hypotheses deduced from the major propositions of the theory replicated this interview procedure. There is, however, a large body of related research using rating scales on which respondents could indicate degrees of satisfaction or dissatisfaction with various aspects of a job or with the job in general. The varied paper-and-pencil instruments will be reviewed briefly in conjunction with the reported research.

Research in Varied Settings

The research reviewed in this section has been grouped according to the methods employed. Replications of the interview studies are examined first, and rating-scale studies are then considered.

REPLICATION STUDIES

Herzberg himself reviewed ten of the studies, including his own, in which replications of the interview technique were used (Herzberg, 1966). Seventeen occupational groups had been studied, and a degree of support for the motivation-hygiene framework had been found in each group. Table 12–1 is a summary of the numbers of occupational groups in which motivators were cited significantly more often than hygienes in descriptions of pleasant episodes and in which hygienes were mentioned significantly more often than motivators in descriptions of unpleasant situations. In one occupational group (female professionals), interpersonal relations with peers and subordinates were mentioned more frequently as satisfiers than as dissatisfiers.

A noteworthy point about the information in Table 12–1 is that in many groups some motivators and some hygienes failed to differentiate between satisfying and dissatisfying episodes. For example, of the motivation factors, achievement was mentioned significantly more often in descriptions of satisfying events than in descriptions of dissatisfying situations in thirteen of the groups studied, but not in four of the groups. Similarly, recognition differentiated between types of episodes in eleven of the groups studied, but not in six of the groups. Support for the motivation-hygiene theory resides in the general finding that when job factors did differentiate between satisfying and dissatisfying sequences of events, they did so almost exclusively as predicted from the theory.

Table 12–1 NUMBERS OF OCCUPATIONAL GROUPS IN WHICH MOTIVATION AND HYGIENE FACTORS DIFFERENTIATED SATISFYING AND DISSATISFYING EVENTS

MOTIVATION FACTOR	NUMBER OF GROUPS*	HYGIENE FACTOR	NUMBER OF GROUPS*
1. Achievement	13	1. Company policy and administration	15
2. Recognition	11	2. Supervision (technical)	11
3. Responsibility	9	3. Working conditions	7
4. Work itself	5	4. Interpersonal relations (superordinate)	5
5. Advancement	5	5. Interpersonal relations (peer)	4
6. Possibility of growth	1	6. Personal life	3
		7. Interpersonal relations (subordinate)	2
		8. Status	1
		9. Security	1
		10. Salary	1

SOURCE: Condensed from Herzberg (1966: 124).
*Only groups in which the statistical significance of the difference had been established are included in this table.

RATING-SCALE RESEARCH METHODOLOGY

Some researchers have interpreted Herzberg's theory to mean that motivation factors would relate to general job satisfaction more closely than would hygiene factors, and that hygienes would relate to general job dissatisfaction more closely than would motivators. King (1970) identified five different interpretations of the theory, all involving general job satisfaction and dissatisfaction. In such studies, measures of satisfaction and dissatisfaction with various aspects of the job were used, and scores for those facet-satisfaction scales were analyzed in relation to overall satisfaction and dissatisfaction scores.

Just as the semistructured interview procedures can be criticized, so can the rating-scale methods. First, Herzberg did not assert that motivation or hygiene factors relate to general measures of job attitudes. An individual's estimate of overall job satisfaction or dissatisfaction, particularly after completing a series of job facet rating scales, can be assumed to involve a complex mental calculus whereby satisfying and dissatisfying job features are weighted according to their relative importance to the individual (see Whitsett & Winslow, 1967). That is, in their attempts to be rational and to appear rational to researchers, respondents might well review and compare their own ratings on the individual scales and then provide an overall satisfaction/dissatisfaction rating that is compatible with those scale responses.

A second shortcoming of the rating-scale studies is that any single bipolar general satisfaction/dissatisfaction scale, such as used for the criterion measure (dependent variable) in some studies, is a contradiction of the basic underlying meaning of the motivation-hygiene model, as Whitsett and Winslow (1967) argued in detail. In single-scale measures of job satisfaction/dissatisfaction, even when a zero point or neutral point is evident to the *researcher* as the midpoint of the scale, respondents might mentally convert such a scale to one in which zero (no satisfaction) is at one extreme end and the other extreme represents very high satisfaction. That is, if Herzberg's theory is correct in maintaining that satisfaction and dissatisfaction are separate spheres of emotion, then using a single scale forces the respondent to disregard one of those spheres.

A third problem apparent in the rating-scale studies is that they concern varied and not necessarily equivalent job factors as identified by the various researchers. Nuances of wording in scale items and directions to respondents seem to affect the findings in unanticipated ways. In other words, the terms used in rating scale items have different shades of meaning to researchers and respondents. The resulting diversity of job factors studied—factors that are often not clearly specified in the reported research—and the variations in the language used in the instruments underscore the need for a precise definition of the phrase *job factor* and for a genuine taxonomy of job factors to undergird research.

Finally, as argued convincingly by Herzberg himself (1966) and by Whitsett and Winslow (1967), the rating scale studies require that respondents express an attitude toward each and every job factor (each instrument item)—even factors that may have had no bearing on the especially pleasant or unpleasant incident being considered. An advantage of the interview method is that it enables respondents to mention only the job features that are salient to them; respondents are not primed either to consider other aspects of their job or to rate any features of their job.

RATING-SCALE STUDIES

A sample of the rating-scale studies will be reviewed briefly in terms of the methodologies used and relationships found. Although the various researchers used diverse terms to classify the variables they studied—terms such as *satisfiers/dissatisfiers, intrinsic/extrinsic factors,* and *content/context factors*—these have been translated into motivators and hygienes in this review for purposes of consistency.

In several of the reported rating-scale studies, feelings about aspects of the job and about the job as a whole were compared by means of several items or scales representing the independent variables (job factors) and a single satisfaction, dissatisfaction, or dissatisfaction/satisfaction scale for the dependent variable (general job attitude). In these studies several researchers used the Job Description Index (Hulin et al., 1963), a five-factor measure of facet satisfaction, to measure the independent variables. General satisfaction and general dissatisfaction typically failed to differentiate motivators from hygienes (Ewen et al., 1966; Graen, 1966, 1968; Graen & Hulin, 1968; Waters & Waters, 1969); that is, both motivation items and hygiene items correlated at a significant level with overall job attitude scores. In some rating-scale studies using instruments other than the Job Description Index, motivators generally were found to relate more strongly to overall job satisfaction than did hygienes (Halpern, 1966; Armstrong, 1971; Weissenberg & Gruenfeld, 1968). In some studies both motivators and hygienes were found to correlate with overall satisfaction (Brenner, Carmack, & Weinstein, 1971; Waters & Waters, 1969).

A generalization that can be drawn from the research reviewed up to this point is that when the interview method was used, the two-dimensional nature of job attitudes was relatively consistently supported; but when rating scales were used, the distinction between motivators and hygienes was quite consistently rejected.

An unusually interesting test of Herzberg's theory was designed by Wernimont (1966) for a study of accountants and engineers. Wernimont developed one instrument comprising 50 pairs of positively worded statements for describing especially satisfying events and another instrument consisting of 50 pairs of negatively worded statements for describing particularly dissatisfying events. Each pair of statements included one motivation and one hygiene factor. Respondents were instructed to think of an exceptionally good (or bad) job-related episode and to mark the statement within each pair (on the appropriate form) that best describes that episode. The respondents were then to follow a parallel procedure with reference to an especially bad (or good) sequence of events. On the basis of his findings, Wernimont rejected the Herzberg model, since both groups of respondents checked significantly more motivators than hygienes in describing *both* good and bad episodes. However, Whitsett and Winslow (1967:401–403), as well as Herzberg (1966:150–152), noted a variety of flaws in that study. They argued that the requirement to answer all 50 items on each form forced the respondents to mark many statements that had no bearing on the episodes being described. Furthermore, although the events were to have been dramatic episodes, the items were worded blandly and in present tense. The Wernimont study, they maintained, did not discredit the two-dimension framework because it was inherently flawed.

There was a free-choice component in the Wernimont (1966) study in which respondents were asked to check the ten most accurately descriptive statements from each set of 50 statements already checked. The analysis of this portion of the study revealed that motivators were checked significantly more often than hygienes for both good and bad experiences; however, the discrepancies were significantly greater for happy episodes than for unhappy ones. The findings suggest that there is some kind of difference between motivation factors and hygiene factors.

In another unusual study, this one based on a factor analysis of scale responses by Dunnette, Campbell, & Hakel (1967), motivation items generally had higher mean scores for satisfying situations than for dissatisfying ones; hygiene items generally had the higher mean scores for the dissatisfying situations. Thus there has been some tentative support for the motivation-hygiene theory even in rating-scale studies.

The studies of relationships between job facet attitudes and other variables have yielded an interesting array of findings. For example, motivators were found to correlate significantly with job involvement, whereas hygienes did not (Weissenberg & Gruenfeld, 1968). Motivators were found to be the more important factors for engineers, whereas hygienes were the more important ones for assemblers (Armstrong, 1971). Motivation factors were valued more by white-collar than by blue-collar workers, but hygiene factors were the more highly valued by the blue-collar group (Centers & Bugental, 1966). Finally, the higher the respondent's occupational level, the more consistently were the motivators valued (Centers & Bugental, 1966).

Wernimont and some coresearchers directed a sample of respondents to rank-order 17 job factors twice, first in order of the degree to which they relate to effort and then in order of their relationship to job satisfaction (Wernimont, Toren, & Kapell, 1970). Some factors were perceived to relate significantly more strongly to effort than to satisfaction, and other factors were related more strongly to satisfaction than to effort; but the motivation-hygiene dichotomy was not found to be helpful in predicting the differences. This conclusion was supported in an experimental study by Umstot, Bell, and Mitchell (1976) in which it was found that job enrichment (a motivator) was significantly related to increased satisfaction but not increased effort, and that goal setting and feedback (possibly hygienes) were related to increased effort and productivity but not satisfaction. These two studies cast some doubt on the validity of Herzberg's assumption that satisfying factors are related to performance and that the intrinsic job factors can legitimately be called motivation factors.

Research in Schools and Colleges

University undergraduate and graduate students as well as campus employees are convenient subjects for academic research. That is why they are so often sampled for descriptive or experimental studies. In research on job attitudes, work values, and related areas, however, these groups might be more representative of their campus norms and social values than of those of the business and corporate world. Since studies of these groups might shed more light on campus life than on other aspects of our culture, they are treated here in the context of research on education. Tests of the theory using student samples can be distinguished from studies of employees' attitudes in education systems.

TESTS OF THE THEORY
One replication of Herzberg's interview procedure was done on a sample of undergraduate students (Hinton, 1968) to determine whether the data obtained by such procedures are reliable. When the data gathered at one time were analyzed, the motivation-hygiene model was generally supported; aspects of student life that were associated with satisfying experiences were generally not associated with dissatisfying ones, and conversely. However, when interview data were gathered from the same students six weeks later and combined with the first set of data, the dichotomy between satisfying and dissatisfying factors disappeared. Hinton concluded that such interview data do not demonstrate test-retest reliability.

Several rating-scale studies were conducted on college or university campuses. A problem with these studies is that they all pertain to what subjects think would affect their job feelings rather than to actual job experiences. Both motivators and hygienes were found to correlate at significant levels with both general satisfaction and general dissatisfaction, but satisfaction was the more readily predictable feeling (Friedlander, 1964; Ondrack, 1974; Lahiri & Srivastva, 1967).

The factor-analytic studies of attitude rating scales appear to have yielded mixed results. In some studies the factors generated by factor analysis were mixtures of motivation and hygiene items (Levine & Weitz, 1968; Burke, 1966), whereas in other studies the resulting factors consisted of predominantly motivation or predominantly hygiene items (Malinovsky & Barry, 1965; Dunnette, Campbell & Hakel, 1967). Because these studies incorporated varied sets of items and diverse wordings of items, firm conclusions cannot be drawn.

STUDIES OF EDUCATORS' JOB ATTITUDES

Only two studies of public school systems were located that have direct relevance to the motivation-hygiene framework. In Schmidt's (1976) replication of the interview method with 74 high school administrators, Herzberg's model was consistently supported: motivators were mentioned significantly more often in conjunction with satisfying sequences of events than with dissatisfying ones, and the hygienes were the more often cited in connection with dissatisfying sequences; furthermore, motivators were perceived to be more closely associated with effort than were hygienes. In another replication study of schools, this one by Sergiovanni (1967), satisfying factors tended to be differentiated from dissatisfying ones for secondary school teachers, but the factors associated with satisfying experiences were not consistently Herzberg's motivation factors. Specifically, work itself and advancement were not often cited in conjunction with either satisfying or dissatisfying sequences.

In summary, the research findings associated with this theory represent a confusing and often contradictory assortment of approaches, interpretations, and findings. To simplify matters somewhat, Table 12–2 was designed as a means of displaying the findings from the varied studies concisely. The far left column lists the factors studied, and the remaining columns identify each piece of research by its author and the occupational group studied. The plus signs (+) indicate instances in which the given factors related to general satisfaction or dissatisfaction as predicted from the theory; minus signs (−) denote factors that correlated in a direction opposite to that predicted from the theory; and zero (0) indicates no significant correlation between the factors and feelings of satisfaction or dissatisfaction.

Table 12–2 suggests that the motivators have been found to be more consistently related to generalized job feelings than have the hygienes and that motivators tend to predict both general satisfaction and general dissatisfaction. The motivators, in other words, appear to be the stronger forces in generating general job attitudes.

Because of the divergent research findings, Hoy and Miskel (1978:108–113) proposed a three-dimensional model of job attitudes for the field of education. They suggested that the motivation factors and hygiene factors be retained but that a third category, called ambient factors, be added. This category would include those job aspects that correlate with satisfaction and dissatisfaction about equally. The ambients would include salary, growth possibility, risk opportunity, relationships with superordinates, and status.

It is clear that there is room for further research on job attitudes for purposes of resolving the contradictions in the findings, identifying the intervening factors that influence workers' perceptions of job aspects as either

Table 12–2 SUMMARY OF RESEARCH FINDINGS: RELATIONSHIPS BETWEEN JOB FACTORS AND JOB ATTITUDES

RESEARCHERS / GROUPS STUDIED →	EWEN ET AL., 1966 (BUS. & INDUST. ORGS.)	GRAEN, 1966 (BUS & INDUST. ORGS.)	GRAEN/HULIN, 1968 (MALE/FEMALE EMPLOYEES)	WATERS/WATERS, 1969 (FEMALE CLERICAL WORKERS)	HALPERN, 1966 (NONSUPERVISORY CLERICAL)	ARMSTRONG, 1971 (ENGINEERS/ASSEMBLERS)	WEISSENBERG/GRUENFELD, 1968 (MALE CIVIL SERVICE EMPL'S)	BRENNER ET AL., 1971 (ACCOUNTANTS)	WERNIMONT, 1966 (ENGINEERS/ACCOUNTANTS)	DUNNETTE ET AL., 1967 (SIX OCCUPATIONS)	FRIEDLANDER, 1964 (COLLEGE STUDENTS)	ONDRACK, 1974 (MBA STUDENTS)	LAHIRI/SRIVASTVA, 1967 (INDIAN MIDDLE MANAGERS)	SCHMIDT, 1976 (SCHOOL ADMINISTRATORS)	SERGIOVANNI, 1967 (SECONDARY SCHOOL TEACHERS)
JOB FACTORS															
RELATIONSHIP TO SATISFACTION															
1. Achievement	+			+	+	+	+	+/−	+/−	+	+	+	+/−	+	+
2. Recognition	+		+/−	+			+	+/−	+/−	+	+		+/−	+	+
3. Work itself		+	+/−	+	+	+	+	+/−	+/−	+	+	+	+/−		
4. Responsibility		+		+	+	+	+	+/−	+/−	+		+	+/−		+
5. Advancement				+	+	+	+	+/−	+/−	+	+	+	+/−	+	+
6. Possibility of growth													+/−		
RELATIONSHIP TO DISSATISFACTION															
1. Relations (superordinate)				+/−		0	−			+	−		+/−	+	
2. Relations (peer)	0		−	+	0	0	−	+/−	+/−	+	−		+/−	+	
3. Relations (subordinate)														+	
4. Supervision (technical)	0		−	+	0	0	−	+/−	+/−	+	−		+/−	+	
5. Policy/administration				+/−	0	+	−	+/−	+/−	+	−		+/−		
6. Working conditions				+	0	0	−	+/−	+/−	+	−		+/−		
7. Personal life							−					−			
8. Salary	0		−	+/−		0	−	+/−	+/−	+/−			+/−		
9. Status						0				+			+/−		
10. Security						0	−				−		+/−		

satisfying or dissatisfying, and determining whether satisfying events foster increased motivation on the part of employees.

IMPLICATIONS OF THE MOTIVATION-HYGIENE THEORY FOR ENHANCING STUDENT LEARNING OUTCOMES

Educational administrators perform such a wide variety of tasks and fulfill such a broad range of functions that it is easy occasionally to lose sight of their primary purpose: to help students acquire knowledge, values, and skills. Beneath the welter of administrative details, at the very core of administrative practice, is the key issue of enhancing learning outcomes for all students. Similarly, research in educational administration has addressed such a wide variety of questions and employed such diverse techniques of inquiry that one can forget that its major purpose is to produce knowledge for the improvement of administrative practice. Researchers, in partnership with practitioners, must strive toward a useful knowledge base to inform practice. Does the motivation-hygiene theory of job attitudes represent a useful foundation for producing knowledge about how school administrators can enhance student achievement?

If it is true that certain aspects of teaching and administration jobs contribute to feelings of satisfaction but other job features do not, and if it is true that teachers and administrators are more highly motivated and hence invest more effort in their work during or immediately following satisfying episodes, then district and building administrators would do well to increase the frequency of satisfying experiences for their staff members by manipulating aspects of the employees' jobs. For example, providing more interesting and challenging tasks for subordinates, recognizing subordinates' accomplishments in handling complex tasks successfully, and providing opportunities for advancement that are based on accomplishments might increase the frequency with which subordinates (teachers, supervisors, other administrators) experience feelings of satisfaction. Theoretically, this increased satisfaction will lead to greater effort to enhance student learning outcomes.

This is not a call for artificial ceremonies such as a Teacher Recognition Day or an end-of-year letter for teachers' files. Rather, it is a suggestion that administrators keep themselves genuinely attuned to outstanding efforts and the demanding challenges that subordinates surmount successfully. The motivation-hygiene model suggests numerous meaningful rewards that creative administrators can provide for excellent work.

Four key questions remain unanswered or insufficiently treated in the body of research in educational settings:

1. Are the aspects of a teaching or supervisory job that contribute to feelings of satisfaction different in kind from the aspects that contribute to feelings of dissatisfaction?

2. If there are consistent differences, are the job features that contribute to administrators' and supervisors' feelings of satisfaction similar to those that contribute to teachers' feelings of satisfaction?
3. Do employees' feelings of satisfaction actually correspond to periods of increased effort on the part of those employees?
4. Does increased effort by employees result in improved performance on their part? If so, what kinds of effort are most closely related to satisfaction and to performance?

These are fertile fields for research on educational organizations. These questions have not often been confronted by educational researchers; they demand creative research designs, perhaps including observational and experimental studies.

At another level of analysis—that of students' attitudes toward learning in school—the unanswered questions are similar. Benjamin Bloom (1976) theorized that pupils' attitudes toward school and learning, along with their knowledge when encountering a new learning task, have direct bearing on the affective and cognitive outcomes of the learning experience. However, Bloom did not posit a taxonomy of learning-task features toward which student attitudes are directed; he did not provide a framework for determining which aspects of the learning situation relate to favorable attitudes or to increased cognitive learning. It is here that the Herzberg two-dimensional approach might offer a major breakthrough. First, perhaps the aspects of school that are associated with students' feelings of satisfaction are different in kind from those that correspond to students' feelings of dissatisfaction. Second, perhaps satisfying episodes but not dissatisfying ones correspond to periods of increased effort on the part of students. In brief, it appears that the motivation-hygiene framework has important implications for student learning as well as for teacher performance.

The motivation-hygiene framework for viewing school effectiveness might be considered in terms of a chain of events whereby each level of the school system hierarchy is linked to the next lower level. That is, at each level in the hierarchy, individuals can provide satisfying or dissatisfying circumstances for persons at the next lower level. Theoretically, if the circumstances are satisfying, the employees will be motivated to exert more effort to improve their own performance. This conceptualization is illustrated in Figure 12–3.

In summary, it appears that the motivation-hygiene theory might have the potential to contribute to a knowledge base on what administrators can do to increase school effectiveness. Before the utility of the model can be verified, however, a body of research is needed. Essentially, the necessary research would pertain to each link in the causal chain suggested in Figure 12–3. The ultimate question is whether actions on the part of higher administrators are related to student learning outcomes; and the motivation-hygiene framework offers a perspective whereby this question might be addressed.

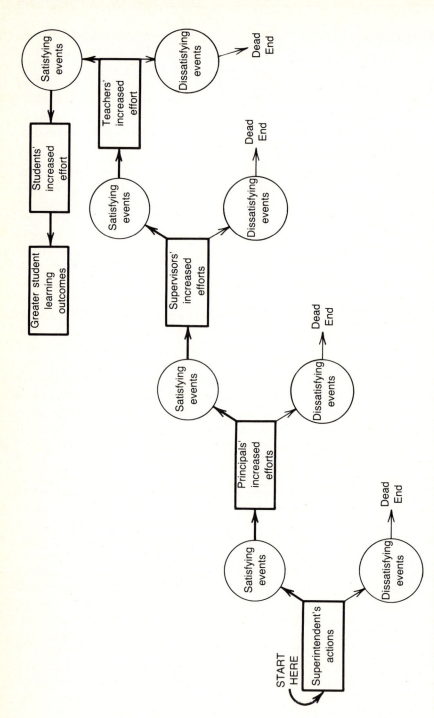

Figure 12–3 The Motivation-Hygiene Linkage of Administrative Actions to Pupil Learning Outcomes

MASTERY QUIZ

For each item that follows, indicate the best sentence completion by writing the letters of the answers on a separate sheet. Correct answers appear in the Appendix, page 393.

1. The two major constructs associated with this theory are:
   a. motivation factors and satisfaction factors.
   b. motivation factors and dissatisfaction factors.
   c. motivation factors and hygiene factors.
   d. motivation factors and psychological-growth factors.
2. According to this theory, motivation factors help employees:
   a. fulfill psychological-growth needs.
   b. fulfill achievement needs.
   c. fulfill pain-avoidance needs.
   d. fulfill interpersonal needs.
3. The motivation factors include all of the following except:
   a. advancement.   c. recognition.
   b. interpersonal relations. d. work itself.
4. All of the following are hygiene factors except:
   a. company policy.   c. working conditions.
   b. work itself.   d. effects on personal life.
5. The motivation factors include:
   a. achievement, interpersonal relations, and recognition.
   b. responsibility, status, and supervision.
   c. advancement, recognition, and achievement.
   d. work itself, interpersonal relations, and recognition.
6. The hygiene factors include
   a. interpersonal relations, supervision, and salary.
   b. working conditions, advancement, and status.
   c. job security, work itself, and supervision.
   d. salary, working conditions, and risk opportunity.
7. According to this theory, providing more recognition to employees:
   a. reduces dissatisfaction.   c. increases dissatisfaction.
   b. increases satisfaction.   d. fulfills pain-avoidance
                                      needs.
8. Improving employees' working conditions has the effect of:
   a. increasing dissatisfaction.
   b. fulfilling psychological-growth needs.
   c. increasing employee satisfaction.
   d. decreasing employee dissatisfaction.
9. To reduce employee dissatisfaction, an administrator should provide:
   a. more recognition and more responsibility for employees.
   b. better working conditions and better supervision for employees.

  c. better salaries and more interesting work for employees.

  d. better supervision and more opportunities for advancement.

10. The major propositions suggest that:

  a. improving working conditions increases employees' motivation.

  b. improving working conditions has no effect on employees' motivation.

  c. improving working conditions increases employees' job satisfaction.

  d. improving working conditions has no effect on employees' job attitudes.

EXERCISES

1. Think of 3 actions a school principal could realistically undertake to increase teacher satisfaction with respect to each of the motivation factors (18 actions in all). In addition, select 5 of the hygiene factors and, for each, think of 3 actions a principal could undertake to reduce faculty dissatisfaction (15 actions in all). List these 33 actions on a separate page.

2. Read the case study appearing in Appendix A. Analyze the case from the perspective of the motivation-hygiene theory according to an outline such as the following:

  a. Select a focal person from the case, and state that person's problem as it pertains to this theory.

  b. Cite evidence of low satisfaction with reference to as many of the motivation factors as possible.

  c. Cite evidence of high dissatisfaction with reference to as many of the hygiene factors as possible.

  d. Indicate how the focal person might resolve the problem you identified through a thorough understanding of this theory.

3. Based on your experiences and your understanding of this theory, generate three testable hypotheses that you can deduce from this theory.

  a. Beneath each hypothesis, identify the variables and indicate the direction of their relationship(s).

  b. Select one of the hypotheses, and think through how you could test it empirically; be prepared to describe your research design if asked.

REFERENCES

Major Sources

Herzberg, F. *Work and the nature of man.* New York: World, 1966.

Herzberg, F.; Mausner, B.; & Snyderman, B. *The motivation to work.* New York: Wiley, 1959.

Related Conceptual Literature

Behling, O.; Labovitz, G.; & Kosmo, R. The Herzberg controversy: A critical reappraisal. *Academy of Management Journal,* 1968, *11,* 99–109.

Bloom, B. S. *Human characteristics and school learning.* New York: McGraw-Hill, 1976.

Glickman, S. E., & Schiff, B. B. A biological theory of reinforcement. *Psychological Review,* 1967, *74,* 83–87.

Hinrichs, J. R., & Mischkind, L. A. Empirical and theoretical limitations of the two-factor hypothesis of job satisfaction. *Journal of Applied Psychology,* 1967, *51,* 191–200.

House, R. J., & Wigdor, L. A. Herzberg's dual factor theory of job satisfaction and motivation: A review of the evidence and a criticism. *Personnel Psychology,* 1967, *20,* 369–389.

Hoy, W. K., & Miskel, C. G. *Educational administration: Theory, research and practice.* New York: Random House, 1978.

King, N. Clarification and evaluation of the two-factor theory of job satisfaction. *Psychological Bulletin,* 1970, *74,* 18–31.

Levine, F. M. (Ed.). *Theoretical readings in motivation: Perspectives on human behavior.* Chicago: Rand McNally, 1975.

Lindsay, C.; Marks, E.; & Gorlow, L. The Herzberg theory: A critique and reformulation. *Journal of Applied Psychology,* 1967, *51,* 330–339.

Maslow, A. H. *Toward a psychology of being.* Princeton, N.J.: Van Nostrand, 1962.

Salancik, G. R., & Pfeffer, J. An examination of need-satisfaction models of job attitudes. *Administrative Science Quarterly,* 1977, *22,* 427–456.

Vroom, V. H. *Work and motivation.* New York: Wiley, 1964.

Whitsett, D. A., & Winslow, E. K. An analysis of studies critical of the Motivation-Hygiene Theory. *Personnel Psychology,* 1967, *20,* 391–415.

Related Research: General

Armstrong, T. B. Job content and context factors related to satisfaction for different occupational levels. *Journal of Applied Psychology,* 1971, *55,* 57–65.

Brenner, V. C.; Carmack, C. W.; & Weinstein, M. G. An empirical test of the Motivation-Hygiene Theory. *Journal of Accounting Research,* 1971, *9,* 359–366.

Centers, R., & Bugental, D. E. Intrinsic and extrinsic job motivation among different segments of the working population. *Journal of Applied Psychology,* 1966, *50,* 193–197.

Dunnette, M. D.; Campbell, J. P.; & Hakel, M. D. Factors contributing to job satisfaction and job dissatisfaction in six occupational groups. *Organizational Behavior and Human Performance,* 1967, *2,* 143–174.

Ewen, R. B.; Smith, P. C.; Hulin, C. L.; & Locke, E. A. An empirical test of the Herzberg two-factor theory. *Journal of Applied Psychology,* 1966, *50,* 544–550.

Graen, G. B. Addendum to "An Empirical Test of the Herzberg Two-Factor Theory." *Journal of Applied Psychology,* 1966, *50,* 551–555.

————. Testing traditional and two-factor hypotheses concerning job satisfaction. *Journal of Applied Psychology,* 1968, *52,* 366–371.

Graen, G. B., & Hulin, C. L. Addendum to "An Empirical Investigation of Two Implications of the Two-Factor Theory of Job Satisfaction." *Journal of Applied Psychology,* 1968, *52,* 341–342.

Halpern, G. Relative contributions of motivation and hygiene factors to overall job satisfaction. *Journal of Applied Psychology,* 1966, *50,* 198–200.

Hulin, C. L.; Smith, P. C.; Kendall, L. M.; & Locke, E. A. Cornell studies of job satisfaction: II. Model and method of measuring job satisfaction. Ithaca, N.Y.: Cornell University, School of Business, 1963 (mimeo).

Umstot, D. D.; Bell, C. H., Jr.; & Mitchell, T. R. Effects of job enrichment and task goals on satisfaction and productivity: Implications for job design. *Journal of Applied Psychology,* 1976, *61,* 379–394.

Waters, L. K., & Waters, C. W. Correlates of job satisfaction and job dissatisfaction among female clerical workers. *Journal of Applied Psychology,* 1969, *53,* 388–391.

Weissenberg, P., & Gruenfeld, L. W. Relationship between job satisfaction and job involvement. *Journal of Applied Psychology,* 1968, *52,* 469–473.

Wernimont, P. F. Intrinsic and extrinsic factors in job satisfaction. *Journal of Applied Psychology,* 1966, *50,* 41–50.

Wernimont, P. F.; Toren, P.; & Kapell, H. Comparison of sources of personal satisfaction and of work motivation. *Journal of Applied Psychology,* 1970, *54,* 95–102.

Related Research: Education

Burke, R. J. Are Herzberg's Motivators and Hygienes unidimensional? *Journal of Applied Psychology,* 1966, *50,* 317–321.

Friedlander, F. Job characteristics as satisfiers and dissatisfiers. *Journal of Applied Psychology,* 1964, *48,* 388–392.

Hinton, B. L. An empirical investigation of the Herzberg methodology and two-factor theory. *Organizational Behavior and Human Performance,* 1968, *3,* 286–309.

Lahiri, D. K., & Srivastva, S. Determinants of satisfaction in middle-management personnel. *Journal of Applied Psychology,* 1967, *51,* 254–265.

Levine, E. L., & Weitz, J. Job satisfaction among graduate students: Intrinsic versus extrinsic variables. *Journal of Applied Psychology,* 1968, *52,* 263–271.

Malinovsky, M., & Barry, J. Determinants of work attitudes. *Journal of Applied Psychology,* 1965, *49,* 446–451.

Ondrack, D. A. Defense mechanisms and the Herzberg theory: An alternative test. *Academy of Management Journal,* 1974, *17,* 79–89.

Schmidt, G. L. Job satisfaction among secondary school administrators. *Educational Administration Quarterly,* 1976, *12,* 68–85.

Sergiovanni, T. Factors which affect satisfaction and dissatisfaction of teachers. *Journal of Educational Administration,* 1967, *5,* 66–82.

Chapter 13
Employees' Motivation

THE EXPECTANCY THEORY

When educators think about motivation, they usually think in terms of youngsters in classrooms and the teacher's function of motivating students. Motivation, however, can be considered in terms of teachers and other personnel in a school as well as in terms of the principal's function of motivating staff—or, for that matter, in terms of the superintendent's function of motivating principals.

To think of motivation in terms of adult behavior is to raise the question of whether one can motivate someone to do something or whether motivation is internal to each individual and affected only indirectly, if at all, by other people.

Consider for a moment the school or office in which you work; consider specifically what the various staff members do during their free time at work. Their activities probably vary. Some individuals might congregate in the lounge or staff room to relax and converse, whereas others may stay at their workplaces preparing lessons, grading papers, or catching up on desk work. Some might be reading the newspaper or doing the crossword puzzle, others studying for courses they are taking or drawing up plans for a leisure-time activity. Would it be reasonable to say that some of these staff members are motivated and others are not—or that all are motivated but to do different things? Why are the staff members so diversely occupied?

Most contemporary theorists addressing the motivation question would agree in this case that all the staff members are motivated, but that they are motivated to invest their energies in varied actions. That is, all behavior can be regarded as the result of motivation to perform particular acts. Most would also agree that the extent to which people are motivated to engage in an activity has something to do with the effects or outcomes people anticipate as a result of having performed an act.

Since people place different values on the outcomes of actions, they are motivated to engage in diverse actions. For example, teacher A and teacher B might anticipate similar results from the acts of preparing lessons, but they might place different values on those results. Teacher A might value the results of preparing lessons more highly than teacher B does; therefore, teacher A is the more likely to invest time in preparation.

But imagine that both teachers, A and B, value good lessons and the effects of good lessons equally. Will they then invest equal time and energy in preparing to have good lessons? Not necessarily. Teacher A might believe that the lessons are as good as lessons can be and that additional effort will not improve them, whereas teacher B believes his lessons can be improved by the expenditure of additional time and energy. In this case teacher B is the more likely to invest effort in preparation, even though both teachers value good lessons and the effects of good lessons equally.

The unique and fascinating feature of the motivation theory articulated by Victor Vroom (1964) is the fine distinction between people's expectations regarding the results of their own actions and the perceived utility of those results for attaining or avoiding other outcomes. In other words, motivation can be conceptualized as the combination of two major elements: one's *expectancy* that an action will have a particular outcome; and the *instrumentality* of that outcome in relation to other valued outcomes. The relationships among these elements can be illustrated as in Figure 13–1. Motivation to perform an act is a combination of one's expectations that the action will have a particular outcome and the perceived utility of that outcome in relation to other outcomes.

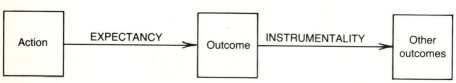

Figure 13–1   Relationships Between Expectancy and Instrumentality in the Expectancy Theory of Motivation

THE ESSENCE OF THE EXPECTANCY THEORY

All human (and animal) behavior can be regarded as the result of a state of arousal or internal tension that serves as an energy source or springboard for action. When this energy is channeled in a particular direction—that is, focused toward a particular objective—it is called a *drive*. A drive, then, has a degree of intensity depending on the amount of energy it incorporates; it also has a directionality depending on the object(s) toward which it points. Thus a drive is a more or less intense force to perform particular acts (acts directed toward particular objects).

Motivation is another name for force to perform. Motivation, then, has a degree of intensity and a directionality. The direction of the motivational force or drive is toward attractive objectives and/or away from repellent objects or outcomes. The intensity of this force is determined by the degree of attractiveness/repulsiveness of the outcomes of action: highly attractive outcomes generate greater force than do mildly attractive outcomes, and grossly repellent outcomes generate greater force than do mildly unpleasant outcomes.

Both the direction and the intensity of a person's motivation are influenced by two factors: (1) the person's perceptions of self—that is, of one's own capabilities for action; (2) the person's perceptions of the world external to self—that is, of the extent to which the results of actions yield rewards (attractive outcomes) and/or penalties (unpleasant outcomes).

People are viewed in this theory as basically hedonistic. At any given moment or in any situation they seek to maximize pleasure and minimize displeasure or pain. Thus their actions are intended to bring about outcomes that will yield maximum pleasure and/or minimum pain. In this respect the theory represents people as rational. Their rationality, however, is based on subjective assessments of their own capabilities and of the rewards and penalties associated with the results of actions. According to this theory, people are subjectively rational even when their actions do not seem rational to observers.

In brief, the expectancy theory posits that motivation is a force or drive within a person. This force varies according to two factors: expectancy and instrumentality. Expectancy is a perceived relationship between action and its direct outcomes. Instrumentality is a perceived relationship between direct outcomes and indirect outcomes of action. Both expectancy and instrumentality are influenced by the *valences* (attractiveness/repulsiveness) of outcomes.

Major Constructs in the Expectancy Theory

FORCE
Force to perform an act or to engage in action is synonymous with motivation to perform an act. It is internal energy or arousal that has direction and intensity. An individual in a low state of arousal is not motivated to act. On the other hand, an individual in a high state of arousal requires a channel or directionality

for action. This channeled or focused energy is a force to perform a particular act as opposed to other acts. Thus, a force can be regarded as a proclivity or propensity toward a particular action. The direction and intensity of this force are determined by the valences of the direct outcomes of the act and the expectancy that the act will result in particular direct outcomes.

VALENCE

Valence is the degree of perceived attractiveness or repulsiveness of an object—the extent to which objects are desired or rejected by an individual. Valence, in other words, refers to one's *affective orientation* toward an object, one's feelings about or attitudes toward an object. Something that is very attractive to or strongly desired by an individual has a high positive valence to that individual. Something toward which the individual feels indifferent has no valence (zero valence) to that individual. An object toward which a person feels repulsion or intense displeasure has a high negative valence to that person. Valence is a subjective phenomenon since individuals differ in their orientations toward any one object. Being fired, for example, might be extremely unpleasant to one person, a matter of indifference to another, and a very pleasant or attractive outcome for a third individual.

EXPECTANCY

Expectancy is a momentary belief concerning the probability that a particular action will result in a particular outcome or set of outcomes. Expectancy is a perceived action-outcome relationship that can vary in strength from certainty that the act *will* result in the outcome to certainty that the act *will not* result in the outcome. In the example presented earlier, teacher B had a strong expectancy that the action of preparing for classes would result in the direct outcome of good lessons. Teacher A, on the other hand, had a weak or zero expectancy that preparation would yield good lessons.

An important feature of this theory is that actions can have a variety of possible outcomes. The act of studying for an exam, for example, can have the direct outcomes of a high grade, a moderate grade, or a disastrously low grade. The force on a person to perform the act of studying, then, is a function of the valences of the various outcomes (in this case, grades) and the person's expectancies (probability estimates) regarding the relationship between studying and each of those outcomes. (Note that for some individuals, knowing the material is considered the direct outcome of studying, and grades considered indirect outcomes; for others, however, the studying is directed toward the grades.)

Since people often believe that their effort has no bearing on the results (for example, that studying has no bearing on grades), an individual's expectancy regarding the outcome of an action is not at all obvious to others. Similarly, just as some people would find receiving a very high grade a distinctly unpleasant experience, the valence of an outcome to an individual is not at all obvious to others. Both valence and expectancy are purely subjective assessments.

OUTCOMES

Outcomes are the perceived results of actions or of other results. They are the objects toward or away from which people direct their actions. Virtually any result of action that an individual can imagine is a potential outcome of action. Therefore, it might be helpful to differentiate direct outcomes from indirect outcomes.

Direct outcomes, sometimes called first-level outcomes (Galbraith & Cummings, 1967) or performance (Lawler, 1970), are the more immediate results of actions—the results that the actions themselves were directed toward or intended to accomplish. For example: the act of buying an item has ownership of the item as its direct outcome; the act of applying to a particular school would have the direct outcome of acceptance by the school or rejection by the school; the preparation of a lesson can result directly in a good lesson, a mediocre lesson, or a poor lesson.

Indirect outcomes, sometimes called second-level outcomes (Galbraith & Cummings, 1967) are the more remote results of actions—the perceived consequences of direct outcomes. For example, the consequences of a good lesson (a direct outcome), as perceived by an individual teacher, could include attentive students, learning on the part of students, disapproval of some co-workers, and self-respect. These consequences, then, would be the indirect outcomes of the action of preparing a lesson.

A direct outcome is desirable or undesirable to the extent that it is perceived to relate to indirect outcomes that are desirable or undesirable. More specifically, a direct outcome takes on valence as it is perceived to be instrumental in attaining desired indirect outcomes and/or avoiding unpleasant indirect outcomes.

INSTRUMENTALITY

Instrumentality, then, is the expected utility or usefulness of a direct outcome for the attainment or avoidance of other outcomes. It is the perceived relationship between direct and indirect outcomes. To the extent that a direct outcome of an act is useful (has perceived utility) in acquiring pleasurable indirect outcomes and avoiding displeasurable ones, it is instrumental to the individual's hedonism. The instrumentality construct highlights the notion that direct outcomes of action can be viewed as means toward the accomplishment of goals or ends. That is, direct outcomes are the ends of particular actions but may also be the means (instrumentalities) for attaining other ends. Whether an outcome is an end in itself or a means toward other ends is solely a matter of individual perceptions.

ACTION

Action is overt behavior—a doing of something. Action entails physical movement as well as cognitive content and emotional tone. The expectancy theory presupposes a repertoire of actions available to each individual. Any particular motor or psychomotor activity in which a person engages is an action that has been selected from the repertoire of possible actions.

Relationships Among Constructs in the Expectancy Theory

With these definitions in mind, the relationships among constructs can now be clarified. Motivation, as noted earlier, is a force that is generated within an individual and represents the channeling of energy in a particular direction.

The intensity and direction of the force are influenced by two elements in combination: (1) the valences of the direct outcomes of action; (2) the expectancies that the actions will result in those outcomes. In combining these elements to estimate an individual's force to perform an action, the valence of the preferred direct outcome is multiplied by the expectancy that the action will yield that outcome.

To illustrate: for teacher A in the example cited earlier, a good lesson has a high valence (say, about $+8$ on a scale of 10); but this teacher has a low expectancy that the act of planning would yield a better lesson (say, about .30 on a scale of 1.00); thus for teacher A the force to perform the act of planning equals $8 \times .30 = 2.40$. For teacher B a good lesson has an equally high positive valence ($+8$), but this teacher has a high expectancy that planning will result in a good lesson (perhaps .85 on a scale of 1.00); for teacher B, in contrast to teacher A, the force to perform the act of planning equals $8 \times .85 = 6.80$. By this analysis, teacher B is the more highly motivated to perform the act of planning a lesson.

The valence of a direct outcome also comprises two elements in combination: (1) the valences of indirect outcomes; and (2) the instrumentalities of the direct outcome in relation to the indirect outcomes. To combine these elements, the valence of each perceived indirect outcome is multiplied by the perceived relationship between possible direct outcomes and that indirect outcome, and these products are summed to provide an estimate of the valence of the direct outcome.

This can also be illustrated with reference to teachers A and B, as in figure 13–2. Note that both teachers had assigned the same valence to good lessons in the example cited earlier. The teachers, however, perceive different indirect outcomes, both desirable and undesirable, as related to good lessons. Although teacher B might have considered fewer instrumentalities, this teacher's expectancy, as computed earlier, rendered him or her more highly motivated.

These relationships among constructs represent a two-stage process for estimating force to perform—first the estimate of direct outcome valence, then

Teacher A				**Teacher B**			
Perceived indirect outcomes of good lesson	Valences	Instrumentalities	Cross-products	Perceived indirect outcomes of good lesson	Valences	Instrumentalities	Cross-products
Personal satisfaction	+7.0 ×	.85 =	+5.95	Supervisor's good rating	+9.0 ×	.60 =	+5.40
Appreciative students	+6.5 ×	.60 =	+3.90	Orderly classroom	+5.0 ×	.52 =	+2.60
Self development	+5.0 ×	.30 =	+1.50				
Student learning	+4.0 ×	.50 =	+2.00				
Higher student expectations	−5.6 ×	.95 =	−5.32				
		$\Sigma V_{ind} \times I =$	+8.03			$\Sigma V_{ind} \times I =$	+8.00

Figure 13–2   Estimation of the Valence of a Direct Outcome of an Act

the estimate of action-outcome relationships. The two-stage nature of this perspective can be illustrated as in Figure 13–3.

Major Propositions

There are two major propositions constituting this theory, each positing mathematical relationships among constructs. Therefore, each proposition is explained following its statement.

1. *The valence of a direct outcome of an act is a function of the summed products of the valences of the indirect outcomes and the perceived instrumentalities of the direct outcome in relation to the indirect outcomes.* This proposition, which pertains to the interrelations of parts B, D, and E in Figure 13–3, can be expressed in the formula:

$$V_{dir} = f[\Sigma(V_{ind} \times I)]$$

Stated differently, the valence of a direct outcome (V_{dir}) is equal to the sum of products of the indirect outcomes (V_{ind}) times their instrumentalities (I). This computation was illustrated in Figure 13–2. Instrumentality is viewed in this theory as a perceived correlation between direct and indirect outcomes; thus instrumentalities can range from −1.00 to +1.00.

2. *The force on a person to perform an act is a function of the summed products of the valences of its direct outcomes and the expectancies that the act will result in the direct outcomes.* This proposition can be represented by the formula:

$$F_{act} = f[\Sigma(V_{dir} \times E)]$$

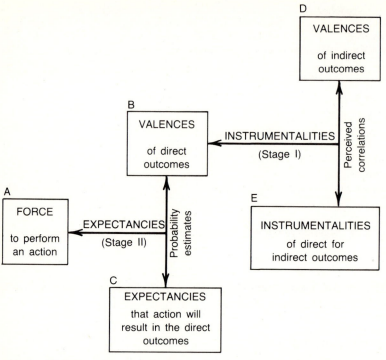

Figure 13–3   Relationships Among Major Constructs in the Expectancy Theory
of Motivation

Whereas instrumentalities (in Proposition 1) are perceived *correlations*, expectancies (in Proposition 2) are perceived *probabilities*. Thus the range of expectancies is from 0 to 1—from no possibility that an act will be followed by a particular direct outcome ($p = 0.0$) to certainty that the act will result in the outcome ($p = 1.0$).

To summarize, the two major propositions constituting the expectancy theory of motivation are:

1. $V_{dir} = f\Sigma(V_{ind} \times I)$: the valence of a direct outcome is a function of the summed valences times instrumentalities with reference to *indirect* outcomes.
2. $F_{act} = f\Sigma(V_{dir} \times E)$: the force to perform an act is a function of the summed valences times expectancies with reference to *direct* outcomes.

The theory does not, of course, suggest that people actually develop these complex charts and tables when making decisions. Vroom does maintain, however, that people consciously or unconsciously perform analogous mental computations, sometimes very rapidly, while they engage in action. A moment's thought will confirm that the theory, despite its esoteric language and complex implicit computations, makes good common sense. In nontheoretical language, it means simply that people want to do what they think they can best do that will yield them the greatest gains and the smallest losses.

EXPECTANCY THEORY APPLICATIONS
TO ADMINISTRATION AND MANAGEMENT

Although the expectancy theory is a psychological theory—one pertaining to dynamics within individuals—its applicability to the administration and management of organizations has been noted and studied extensively. The essence of the theory's relevance to administration is that levels of employee performance can be regarded as the direct outcomes of the actions of trying to perform well. Thus either employee effort or employee performance can be viewed as related to the valences of the indirect outcomes of various performance levels and the instrumentalities of performance levels for attaining these outcomes.

As noted in Chapter 12, administrators and supervisors have a degree of control over the rewards and penalties (indirect outcomes) available to employees. For example, supervisors and administrators can allocate praise, recognition, some privileges, and opportunities for growth (all rewards), as well as criticism, disapproval, and tedious tasks (all penalties). Thus administrators control many of the indirect outcomes of employees' actions (see Hackman & Oldham, 1976).

A major implication of the theory for administrative practice, then, is that leaders can have some impact on employees' motivation by influencing employees' expectancies and their perceived instrumentalities. Although employees' assessments of their own capacities (expectancies) and of the relationships among outcomes (instrumentalities) are subjective, the employees can be assumed to have developed these assessments on the basis of their experiences. Thus, by providing a different set of experiences for employees, administrators and supervisors can, over time, affect the employees' expectancies and subjective instrumentalities.

In a school setting, for example, where some teachers have low expectancies regarding their own capacity to teach well, a principal or department head might: (1) explicitly recognize good performance on the part of those teachers at frequent intervals; (2) specify in unambiguous terms some of the achievable teaching behaviors that constitute excellence in teaching; (3) provide genuine training so that those teachers will begin to perceive that they have the requisite skills; and (4) articulate a reasonable structure for the tasks of teaching, rather than leaving the idea of excellence in the realm of mysterious talent or artistry. Theoretically, the less secure and less confident teachers will realize eventually that the behaviors making up excellent teaching are within their repertoire of behaviors. That is, they will perceive a greater probability of success through effort: their expectancies will be raised.

In that same school setting, where some teachers perceive that excellence of teaching is not instrumental for attaining desired outcomes or delimiting distasteful outcomes, a principal or department head might: (1) consistently allocate rewards and penalties on the basis of quality of teaching performance; (2) become aware of the wide range of rewards and penalties potentially available in a school, even a school constrained by fixed salary, promotion, and class assignment policies; (3) consider seriously and realistically the kinds of outcomes each undermotivated teacher would regard as attractive or unattractive, and allocate them accordingly while keeping them contingent on quality of teaching. Theoretically, the teachers who have in the past been rewarded (or penalized) for behaviors irrelevant to quality of teaching or who have been rewarded (or penalized) at random will eventually begin to perceive that the attractive outcomes are contingent on good teaching and the unattractive ones contingent on poor teaching. That is, they will perceive a greater correlation between quality of teaching and attractiveness of outcomes: the subjective instrumentality of excellent teaching will be increased.

In summary, the expectancy theory, though essentially psychological in orientation, bears important implications for administrative practice. By systematically enhancing employees' self-confidence and making attractive and unattractive outcomes depend on performance quality, administrators can, in time, affect the expectancy and instrumentality assessments employees make. By thus increasing employees' motivation to perform well, they substantially increase the likelihood that the employees will in fact perform well.

It should be noted here that high motivation and good performance are related but certainly not synonymous. Motivation is a necessary but insufficient condition for excellent performance, but actual performance depends on the ability of the worker (such as talent, skill, and knowledge) and the circumstances of the job (such as appropriate materials and supplies), as well as on motivation. Vroom did acknowledge the importance of ability, noting that performance is a function of force to perform times ability, as represented by the formula:

$$P = f(F \times A)$$

However, he did not emphasize this aspect of behavior in his theory.

Figure 13–4, an expansion of the diagrams presented earlier, illustrates the dynamics of motivation and its relationship to ability as well as some implications for administrative practice.

FURTHER DISCUSSION OF THE EXPECTANCY THEORY OF MOTIVATION

The expectancy theory has generated tremendous interest on the part of theorists and researchers in social psychology and management. It has stimulated a range of interpretations and spawned an array of elaborations as

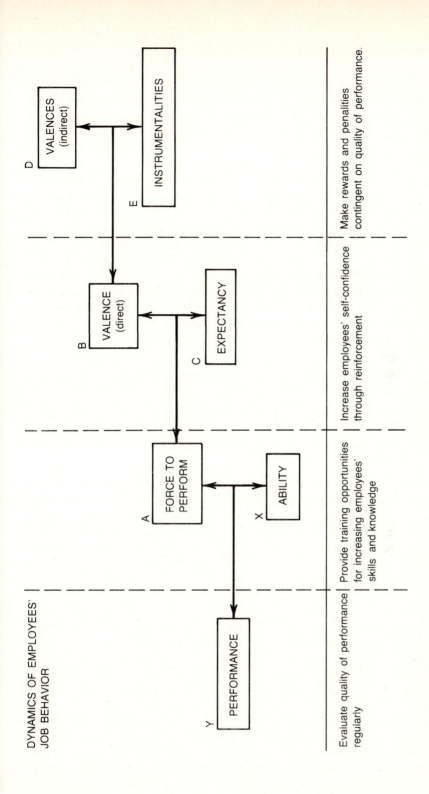

DYNAMICS OF EMPLOYEES'
JOB BEHAVIOR

IMPLICATIONS FOR
ADMINISTRATIVE
PRACTICE

Figure 13–4   Applications of Expectancy Theory to Administrative Practice

scholars have contemplated its relation to other theories and tested its validity in field and laboratory settings. In this section we will examine some modifications of the theory and some of its relationships to other theories.

Modifications of the Theory

There are two reasons for the development of alternative interpretations of the theory and elaborations on its original major propositions. First, the wording of the propositions is somewhat ambiguous. Second, the theory has two types of focus: particular actions and constellations of actions. These two aspects of the theory and the resulting elaborations will be treated in this section.

INTERPRETATIONS OF THE THEORY

One of the sources of divergent interpretations of the theory is that Vroom, in his statements of the propositions, did not differentiate types of outcomes. The original phrasing of the two major propositions is as follows:

> *Proposition 1.* The valence of an outcome to a person is a monotonically increasing function of the algebraic sum of the products of the valences of all other outcomes and his conception of its instrumentality for the attainment of these other outcomes [Vroom, 1964: 17].

> *Proposition 2.* The force on a person to perform an act is a monotonically increasing function of the algebraic sum of the products of the valences of all outcomes and the strength of his expectancies that the act will be followed by the attainment of these outcomes [Vroom, 1964: 18].

This ambiguity in phrasing has led some scholars to believe that the two propositions are similar to and independent of each other. Other scholars have interpreted the propositions as mutually related.

House, Shapiro, and Wahba (1974) regard the propositions as mutually independent and bearing on the two distinct phenomena of satisfaction and motivation. In this view, Proposition 1 pertains to satisfaction with an object such as a job: satisfaction with a job is a function of the extent to which the job is perceived by the employee to be instrumental in providing desired outcomes (or precluding aversive outcomes) for the employee. Proposition 2, in this view, pertains to motivation to invest effort in performing on the job. Motivation, from this perspective, is analogous to satisfaction but concerns orientations toward actions rather than toward outcomes: motivation to perform is influenced by the extent to which the actions involved in performance are perceived to lead to desired outcomes (or preclude aversive outcomes) for the employee.

Other scholars, such as Mitchell and Beach (1976) and Behling and Starke (1973), interpret the propositions to be mutually related as in this chapter. In this interpretation, force (motivation) is influenced by a two-stage process: first one's assessment of the valences of the possible outcomes (their instrumentality) and then one's assessment of the expectancy related to each direct outcome. To differentiate types of outcomes, as required for this interpretation, Galbraith and Cummings (1967) introduced the term *first-level outcomes* to refer to performance levels (what we have called direct outcomes) and the term *second-level outcomes* to refer to the rewards and penalties associated with different levels of performance (what we have called indirect outcomes).

FOCAL POINTS OF THE THEORY
It is clear that the alternative foci of the theory have contributed to this divergence in interpretations of the theory. When the theory is used to understand or predict choices among single acts—such as buying product A or product B, or selecting textbook A, B, or C—either proposition, without the other, would be useful. When the theory is used to understand or predict complex constellations of choices, however—such as performing well or poorly at work, using the phonics approach or the Initial Teaching Alphabet to teach reading, or pursuing a career—the two propositions used conjointly seem to provide a richer basis for analysis.

The latter focus of attention—complex combinations of actions—has led to several modifications of the theory. For example, Galbraith and Cummings (1967) elaborated the theory by distinguishing between intrinsic and extrinsic outcomes and explicating their differential effects on "force to perform." Lawler (1969) built on this distinction by suggesting horizontal and vertical job enlargement as a strategy for increasing motivation, since employees with more varied tasks and greater participation in decision making have increased opportunity to give themselves intrinsic rewards.

Lawler offered other alterations of the theory as well. Regarding the two propositions as interrelated, he posited effort-to-performance expectancies $(E \rightarrow P)$ and performance-to-outcome expectancies $(P \rightarrow O)$ as substitutes for the second and the first propositions, respectively (Lawler, 1969). This modification reduces all the perceptual elements to subjective probabilities, eliminating the subjective correlations in the original theory. Porter and Lawler (1968) further modified the theory by maintaining that "accuracy of role perception" is an important intervening variable influencing the relationship between motivation $[(E \rightarrow P) \times (P \rightarrow O)]$ and actual quality of performance. This intervening variable would be particularly important, of course, when performance quality is measured by superiors' or peers' ratings; it probably would be less important when there is an objective standard of measurement for performance.

Perhaps the most fully developed elaboration of the expectancy theory is what has been called the path-goal model of motivation (Georgopoulos, Mahoney, & Jones, 1957; House, 1971). The essence of this perspective is that a person's job performance at a given level is a path toward that person's goals. Goals are more or less salient to the individual depending on her or his particular needs. Thus a high need of particular type would render those outcomes that fulfill the need highly attractive. The need, in other words, generates the drive toward action, which then proceeds along a path to the goal of fulfilling the need. The fewer the hindrances or impediments along this path, the more directly will the individual be able to reach the goal. Therefore, if excellent performance is a path toward need-fulfilling goals (that is, is instrumental for attaining attractive outcomes), as the path-goal model explicitly assumes to be true for most people, then obstacles interfering with excellent performance should be removed by managers. House (1971) demonstrated both conceptually and empirically how the leader's behaviors (see Chapter 6) affect employees' orientations with respect to intrinsic and extrinsic relationships in the path-goal model of motivation.

In sum, expectancy theory has been interpreted in two ways: one viewing the propositions as unrelated and the other viewing them as interrelated. The latter view, particularly as applied to analyses of job performance, has stimulated a variety of modifications of and elaborations on the original theory. Of those elaborations, the most comprehensive appears to be the path-goal model of employee motivation.

Expectancy Theory in Relation to Other Theories

Consideration of this theory in relation to some other theories might help to clarify the meaning of the theory and underscore some of its distinctive features. To these ends we will briefly examine this theory's relationship to decision theory, to some cognitive theories in psychology, and to the motivation-hygiene theory of job satisfaction.

DECISION THEORIES

The theory most closely allied to the expectancy framework is a normative theory of decision making known as the theory of subjective expected utilities. This decision theory is normative in that it specifies the conditions for maximally rational decisions. This approach to analyzing choice behavior is, according to Behling and Starke (1973), a set of precise mathematical formulations dealing with outcome valences or weighted valences, subjective utilities (analogous to perceived instrumentalities), and probabilities. These authors severely criticized Vroom's expectancy theory for being less precise than decision theory and for being based on underlying assumptions (called postulates) that have not been supported empirically.

To clarify the distinction between a psychological theory of motivation and a mathematical theory of decision, it should be noted that motivation, in Vroom's framework, is construed as a momentary pheonomenon, a fleeting state that changes as people's transient needs and objects of attention shift. The expectancy model is a descriptive one rather than a normative one. From a psychological point of view, one's expectancies need bear no relationship to actual capabilities or realistic projections of possible outcomes, and one's perceptions of probabilities and correlations need not correspond to objective relationships. In fact, the very outcomes toward or from which one acts may change their nature and configuration as individuals' conceptions of the world change. In brief, as Mitchell and Beach (1976) noted, a psychological theory of motivation is not intended to be as precise as a mathematical theory of decision.

COGNITIVE THEORIES

The psychological or subjective nature of expectancies and instrumentalities brings the theory into alignment with other psychological theories of cognition. Of these, theories about locus of control, attribution of causality, dissonance reduction, and conceptual systems are particularly pertinent.

The core of the locus-of-control theory (Rotter, 1973) is that people differ in their perceptions of the causes of events such as success or failure and rewards or penalties; some individuals tend to perceive themselves as the causal agents of results (through effort or skill), whereas others generally perceive external forces or people (such as luck or others' kindness) as causal agents. People's locus-of-control orientations would certainly affect their expectancies, since "internals" would tend to discern greater action-outcome relationships than would "externals."

Similarly, individuals' patterns of attribution would affect their expectancies as well as their subjective instrumentalities. As Frasher and Frasher (1980) concluded on the basis of their review of the attribution research, there are systematic biases (based on asymmetrical perceptions, ego enhancement, mental computational processes, and other factors) in people's perceptions of the causal relationships among events. Thus many psychological factors—such as ego involvement, stereotypic thinking, general optimism and self-concept— are likely to affect not only individuals' expectancies regarding the outcomes of their own actions but their perceptions of instrumentalities as well.

One of the cognitive phenomena noted by Festinger (1957) is that after making a difficult decision, people experience *cognitive dissonance*, which they seek to reduce by various means such as lowering the valences of the possible outcomes of the rejected choice and raising the valences of the outcomes of the selected choice. This suggests that expectancies and instrumentalities will vary in relation to sequences of decisions. In other words, valences of outcomes cannot be expected to remain perfectly consistent but will fluctuate as a psychological mechanism for dissonance reduction.

Finally, conceptual systems theory (see Chapter 11) bears implications for motivational expectancies and instrumentalities. According to this theory (Schroder, Driver, & Streufert, 1967), individuals differ in the extent to which they are able to differentiate, discriminate, and interrelate stimuli (such as objects or people) in their environment. This suggests that people with more complex conceptual systems will perceive more complex and more finely differentiated possible outcomes of their actions, more numerous and more highly interrelated indirect outcomes, and more complicated causal interdependencies than will those with simpler conceptual systems. That is, conceptual complexity is likely to affect the number of elements relevant to an individual's motivation.

Vroom specified that his theory is ahistorical (Vroom, 1964:14); he was explicitly not concerned with the origins or development of one's valences, expectancies, or instrumentalities. Thus many of the psychological factors that researchers have suggested as important intervening variables are not strictly relevant to the theory as posited by Vroom. Virtually any cognitive theory can help to explain how or why individuals' expectancies and perceptions of instrumentalities vary; what is important in expectancy theory is that the expectancies and "cognized instrumentalities," regardless of how they originated, affect motivation.

SATISFACTION THEORIES

Whereas the expectancy theory focuses on the internal dynamics of motivation and of satisfaction, the motivation-hygiene theory of job satisfaction (Herzberg, Mausner, & Snyderman, 1959) provides a useful classification of the indirect outcomes usually perceived to be relevant to job performance. The two theories can be viewed as complementary, with the expectancy framework emphasizing the *processes* of motivation and the motivation-hygiene framework emphasizing the *contents* of motivation. The array of job factors provided in the Herzberg, Mausner, and Snyderman framework would be a useful list of the types of indirect outcomes by which to assess employees' valences and instrumentalities.

The expectancy theory, as noted earlier, can also be seen to have some bearing on Maslow's theory of motivation and need gratification (see Chapter 1). Depending on the level of need most important to an individual at a given time (Maslow, 1962), the indirect outcome having the greatest potential for gratification would likely have the highest valence and thus influence action most strongly.

Interesting critical analyses of the expectancy theory and its related research have been provided by Heneman and Schwab (1972), Mitchell (1974), and Sheridan, Richards, and Slocum (1975). These would be well worth reading for those planning to do research based on Vroom's theory.

In summary, the expectancy theory is essentially a psychological theory and, as such, need not entail the degree of mathematical precision that theories of purely rational decision making entail. Several psychological theories of cognition—such as those concerning locus of control, attribution, cognitive dissonance, and conceptual complexity—help to explain why or in what ways individuals' perceptions differ; but the expectancy theory is concerned primarily with the impact of these differences on motivation. Finally, the motivation-hygiene model and the needs hierarchy might be viewed as concerning the contents of motivation, whereas expectancy theory pertains more to the dynamics or processes of motivation.

RESEARCH RELATED TO THE EXPECTANCY THEORY

The numerous studies based on the expectancy theory and its variants have been diverse in emphasis and design, since there are no standard measures associated with this framework. In this section we shall review the most widely used methodologies and some criticisms of them, as well as representative samples of the research conducted in varied settings and in educational institutions.

Research Methods

Typically, researchers studying work motivation, effort, or satisfaction from the perspective of the expectancy theory have provided their respondents with lists of what we have called indirect outcomes of jobs. The lists have been varied in length, and the indirect outcomes have often been only those presumed to be positive in valence—for example, supervisor's supportiveness, salary increase, or promotion. Usually respondents have been asked to rate each outcome for importance or desirability on a three-, five-, seven-, or nine-point scale as a measure of outcome valence. Then respondents have been asked to indicate for each outcome how likely it is that good performance (or effort) will yield the outcome; this is a measure of the instrumentality. The researcher then multiplies each outcome valence by the instrumentality figure and sums these products for an estimate of *force to perform.* This is the methodology that was illustrated in Figure 13–2.

There are several problems associated with this methodology. One of them, as noted by Reinharth and Wahba (1975) and others, is that the lists generated by researchers are likely to include many outcomes that are not perceived to be relevant to individual respondents in their daily orientations toward their job. In addition, these lists probably lack many of the perceived outcomes that *are* relevant to individual workers. Particularly salient is the absence of negatively valent outcomes in most of the field studies, even though avoidance motivation is clearly as important as approach motivation in the theory. This method appears to force respondents into a superficial rationality as they attempt to appear consistent in their responses to questions; at the same time it may overlook the more compelling rationality of their real subjective assessments.

Another problem inherent in this methodology is that the outcomes listed on the questionnaires might not be independent of each other in the minds of individual respondents. In the minds of respondents the items might well form clusters that would likely differ from one individual to the next. Therefore, simply summing the products of valences and instrumentalities probably builds redundancy into the final score or gives excessive weight to some items. The mathematical legitimacy of multiplying item scores has been questioned by Schmidt (1973); it seems that summing the products is questionable as well.

A solution to some of the operational dilemmas might be to have respondents generate their own lists of perceived outcomes and to rate them for valence as well as for importance, so that more important outcomes can be assigned greater weight in the summation. This method entails the risk that less articulate respondents might not be able to verbalize all the indirect outcomes that are relevant to them; on the other hand, it increases the likelihood that the outcomes listed will be independent of each other and that the outcomes named will truly be relevant to the respondents. An alternative approach would be to provide lists of possible indirect outcomes, as has often been done, but to have respondents indicate which outcomes are interrelated and which, of each cluster, is the most important; then only the important items could be summed and their subsidiaries omitted from the analyses.

A variety of measures for the criterion or independent variables associated with the theory have been used in the research. These include self-reports of satisfaction, effort, or performance; supervisors and peers' ratings of effort or performance; and objective performance indicators such as number of items sold or number of products produced.

Expectancy Research in Varied Settings

Many of the studies designed to test hypotheses derived from one or both of the major propositions in organizations of various types have yielded some support for the theory, despite the methodological problems that have been noted. For example, Goodman, Rose, and Furcon (1970) found that the productivity of scientists and engineers, as measured both objectively and in terms of supervisors' ratings, was significantly related to the summed valences-times-instrumentalities of various work-related behaviors. Hackman and Porter (1968) found that telephone service representatives' performance, particularly effort (as measured in several ways) was directly related to the summed valences-times-instrumentalities of "working hard." Lawler and Porter (1967) found that effort on the part of managers in five types of organizations was related to the summed valences-times-instrumentalities of six behaviors. In this study, instrumentality-times-valence was found to be a better predictor of quality of performance than instrumentality alone or effort alone, and effort was found to be more readily predictable than quality of performance; both these findings support Vroom's theory. Additional supportive findings were reported with reference to nurses (Schneider & Olson, 1970; Sheridan, Richards, & Slocum, 1975) and operators in a manufacturing company (Galbraith & Cummings, 1967).

In these studies the correlations between the independent variable (summed valences of outcomes times instrumentality of action) and the dependent variable (effort or performance) were generally low but statistically significant. This means that the valence and instrumentality measures used in the research systematically accounted for some, but only a small amount, of the variation in performance or effort. It might be that an alternative methodology, such as suggested earlier, would yield stronger support for the theory.

In some studies, hypotheses deduced from the major propositions were not supported. For example, Reinharth and Wahba (1975) studied 348 sales representatives from four companies and found that in only one company did summed valences-times-instrumentalities relate significantly to performance. This study was unusual in that negatively valent outcomes were included in the valences-times-instrumentalities instrument, and respondents were invited to add indirect outcomes to the list. The researchers determined, however, that all the additions were simply repetitions of items already on the list (although they might have been perceived by the respondents as different and important constructs) and excluded them from the analyses. The researchers found that the negatively valent outcomes did not add to the predictive power of the independent variable. These findings concur with some of those in the Galbraith and Cummings (1967) study already cited, in which supervisors' supportiveness and money were the only indirect outcomes that were related to objective measures of productivity; the other indirect outcomes were not found to be predictive at a statistically significant level. It appears that when objective performance measures are used as the dependent variables, a valid ability measure as well as more rigorous expectancy and instrumentality measures are needed for further tests related to the theory.

Several studies have been designed with the intent of expanding on the theory by examining the effects of additional variables. In one such study, Gavin (1973) found that for high-self-esteem managerial candidates in an insurance company, but not for low-self-esteem candidates, the summed valence-times-instrumentality scores related to supervisors' ratings of effectiveness as much as a year after the data for the independent variables were collected. In another such study, Lawler and Porter (1967) found that inner-directedness was more closely related to perceived effectiveness for welfare administrators with high valence-times-instrumentality scores than for administrators with low valence-times-instrumentality scores; that is, degree of inner-directedness was found to be an intervening variable in the instrumentality-performance relationship. In a study of naval aviation officers, Mitchell and Albright (1972) found that job satisfaction, effort, performance, and retention in the military were all more closely related to valence-times-instrumentality scores for intrinsic outcomes than to such scores for extrinsic outcomes. These findings are congruent both with the motivation-hygiene framework (Herzberg, Mausner, & Snyderman, 1959) and with the path-goal model (House, 1971).

Lawler and Suttle (1973) studied department managers in retail stores and found that summed expectancy-times-instrumentality scores related more highly than did expectancy or instrumentality measures alone to effort and that effort, intelligence, and accuracy of role perceptions combined was the best predictor of objectively measured performance effectiveness. Role perception accuracy was interpreted in this study as the perceived importance of other-directedness (as opposed to inner-directedness); intelligence, an ability measure, was determined by IQ test scores; and the objective performance indicator was department sales figures standardized across departments. Thus the study offers strong support for the expectancy theory and for Lawler's elaboration of the theory.

An observation that should be made here is that the research cited in this section represents a variety of interpretations of the expectancy and instrumentality constructs. Many of the authors used the term *expectancy* to refer to what Vroom called *instrumentality*, and some of the authors blurred the distinction between expectancy and instrumentality by having respondents rate the "instrumentalities" of behaviors (actions). In none of the studies located was the two-stage procedure illustrated in Figure 13–3 tested. Thus there appears to be ample need for research to test hypotheses related to the theory with more rigorous methods.

Expectancy Research in Education Settings

As is often the case, the relevant research that has been conducted in schools, colleges, and universities can be classified into two broad categories: studies in which students were a convenient sample for testing hypotheses deduced from the theory; and studies designed to examine some dynamics of education systems. These general categories will be treated separately in this section.

STUDIES USING STUDENT SAMPLES

An area in which expectancy theory has received a great deal of attention is that of occupational choices and preferences. Vroom himself emphasized this area in his conceptual and empirical work (see Vroom, 1964, 1966; Vroom & Deci, 1971), and many researchers have pursued this domain of inquiry.

The research indicates rather consistently that students select jobs (Vroom, 1966), courses of study (Holstrom & Beach, 1973; Muchinsky & Fitch, 1975), and occupations (Mitchell & Knudsen, 1973; Wanous, 1972) on the basis of the perceived valences of indirect outcomes and instrumentalities for attaining those outcomes.

Some interesting tangential findings were obtained in these and related studies. For example, Wanous (1972) found that the MBA students in his sample had a fairly realistic perception of the instrumentalities of various occupations for the high-salary indirect outcome. Mitchell and Knudsen (1973) found that business and psychology students are similar in the types of indirect outcomes they value and that for both groups the extrinsic outcome instrumentalities-times-valences were better predictors of occupational choice than were intrinsic outcomes; also, perceived instrumentality alone was a better predictor of occupational choice than was valence alone, although a combination of both was the best predictor. Vroom and Deci (1971), in a follow-up study of students (see Vroom, 1966) immediately after, one year after, and three and a half years after they started working at their chosen jobs, found that there is considerable disillusionment—as reflected in changed attractiveness of outcomes and changed perceptions of instrumentalities—after working at a job site. The authors attributed the changes in orientations to inflated recruitment propaganda and to dissonance reduction.

Two experimental studies to test assumptions underlying expectancy theory might serve to illustrate the efficacy of laboratory approaches to testing ideas related to this theory.

In one experiment, Liddell and Solomon (1977a, 1977b) tested the consistency (called *transitivity* in many studies) of valence ratings by having subjects repeatedly select the preferred outcome from a set of all possible pairs of 14 indirect outcomes. Out of a possible 3,472 inconsistencies, they found only 94 instances of inconsistency; of these 94, all but 13 were probabilistically consistent. That is, all but 13 of the few inconsistencies found dealt with outcomes toward which the respondents were indifferent.

In a fascinating experimental study to test theory-related hypotheses and judge the realism of people's perceptions, Peters (1977) manipulated the instrumentality variable (performance was or was not related to the indirect outcome) and the expectancy variable (effort was or was not related to quality of performance). He also controlled for the valence variable (subjects liked or disliked the indirect outcome, a record album prize) for an experimental task of identifying misspelled words in rows of words. His findings represent strong empirical support for the theory on several grounds: first, students in the high expectancy and high valence conditions spent significantly more time on the task than did all other subjects, and those in the low expectancy and low valence conditions spent significantly less time on task; second, students in the high expectancy/instrumentality/valence condition had significantly higher *force* scores (subjective expectancy-times-instrumentality-times-valence) than did other subjects; finally, force scores correlated highly ($p = < .001$) with time on task (that is, effort) but not with number of correct answers (that is, quality of performance), which correlated with spelling ability.

To summarize, the studies of students' occupational and academic choices indicate rather consistent confirmation of the theory. In addition, some experimental studies using college students as subjects lend further support to the theory and one of its underlying assumptions. The experimental studies indicated that outcome valences are relatively consistent (Liddell & Solomon, 1977a, 1977b) and that subjective assessments are closely related to real conditions (Peters, 1977).

STUDIES OF EDUCATIONAL SYSTEMS

Few studies were found in which the theory was tested with reference to teacher, student, or administrator performance or effort in schools. In only two of the studies located was the theory tested explicitly, but some other published studies have indirect bearing on the theory.

Henson (1976) found that for a group of college freshmen, the valences of the listed indirect outcomes of studying times the instrumentalities of getting good grades for attaining those outcomes was related to the amount of time the students reported themselves to spend studying; also, this valence-of-good-grades measure and ability, as measured by previous grade point average (GPA) and Scholastic Aptitude Test (SAT) scores, were related to subsequent GPA, the ability measures being the better predictors. In this study both self-esteem and locus of control affected the degree of relationship between valence-of-good-grades and reported effort, which supports the theoretical proposition that expectancy, along with outcome valence, affects force to perform (in this case, force to perform the act of studying).

Miskel, DeFrain, and Wilcox (1980) found that for the secondary school and college teachers in their sample, the valence of effective teaching (that is, valences of indirect outcomes times instrumentalities of effective teaching for attaining them) times the expectancy that effort will yield effective teaching was related to teachers' satisfaction and to supervisors' perceptions of the teachers' effectiveness. No differences were found between extrinsic and intrinsic outcomes in their effects on satisfaction or perceived effectiveness. In this study the statistically significant but low correlation between teachers' motivation and supervisors' effectiveness ratings might be explained by the fact that for teachers, effectiveness was considered in terms of student achievement, whereas for supervisors, teaching effectiveness was considered in terms of behavior patterns such as originality, empathy, and sociability. If the two groups of respondents had been considering equivalent effectiveness criteria, the resulting correlations might well have been higher.

In a study indirectly related to the theory, Spuck (1974) found that the rewards of community support/recognition and agreement with school goals and policies (that is, the reward of self-confirmation) were inversely related to teacher absenteeism, and that in schools characterized by pride in workmanship, positive social interactions, poor physical environment, and low influence on district policy, the teacher turnover rate was lowest. In this study the data were, of course, aggregated by schools, indicating that schools differ in the extent to which intrinsic and extrinsic rewards are perceived to be available to teachers.

In another study indirectly related to this theory, Miskel, Glasnapp, and Hatley (1975) found that for teachers and educational administrators, the discrepancy between desired and available rewards was significantly related, but to a small extent, to job satisfaction. The degree to which education was central to respondents' life interests was a significant intervening variable mediating the relationship between reward desirability/accessibility discrepancies and satisfaction, which might indicate that indirect outcomes of job-related work are more highly valent to those for whom the job is more important.

In the remaining indirectly relevant study, Stephens (1974) found that innovative and traditional schools were differentiated in the degree to which innovative behaviors (such as creativity) were perceived to be instrumental for

attaining extrinsic rewards. Furthermore, the innovative schools were characterized by higher perceived extrinsic rewards for innovative behaviors but not
by more innovative perceived norms than were traditional schools. Stephens
concluded that perceived norms may be less relevant to teaching behavior in
schools than are extrinsic rewards because teaching is usually done in privacy
and isolation with respect to other teachers. In expectancy theory terms,
teaching behaviors are not generally perceived to be instrumental for attaining
peer-related indirect outcomes (such as approval, friendly interactions, or
esteem); on the other hand, teaching behaviors might be perceived as
instrumental for attaining school-controlled indirect outcomes, since teaching
is usually observed by superordinates (if by anyone).

   To summarize, although the theory has not been tested extensively as a
way to describe, explain, or predict educators' motivation or performance,
there is some evidence to indicate that the theory is relevant to school systems.
Specifically, it has been found somewhat useful in explaining college students'
effort and performance; teachers' satisfaction and perceived effectiveness; and
teachers' behaviors in terms of absenteeism, turnover, and innovativeness.
Support for the theory is more extensive in the occupational choice studies in
which course, job, and occupational choices were found to relate to expectancy,
valence, and instrumentality factors. Most substantial support for the theory,
however, is found in the corporate, military, and service organization
literature.

IMPLICATIONS OF THE EXPECTANCY THEORY FOR ENHANCING STUDENT LEARNING OUTCOMES

School administrators, confronting growing public scrutiny and scathing
criticisms of education in the media, have been increasingly concerned about
their own image in the eyes of the public. A theme throughout this book is that
in the long run the surest way to enhance the image of administrators is to
establish a demonstrably reliable body of professional knowledge to inform
practice. The theme, in other words, is that administrators and researchers
must engage cooperatively in efforts to generate knowledge that will be truly
applicable to creating optimally effective schools. Therefore, the question we
now face is whether the theory reviewed here is a useful framework for
generating the relevant knowledge. Is the expectancy theory an appropriate
framework for knowledge production in the interest of improving student
learning outcomes?

   Since the effects of administrators' actions on student learning are indirect
at best, we would do well to consider the question first in terms of teachers'
motivation and then in terms of the possible impact of administrators' actions
on teacher motivation. Our strategy will be to analyze teachers' motivations in
terms of force, expectancies, valences, and subjective instrumentalities, and

then to examine whether administrators might have impact on those motivations.

A substantial and growing body of research on teachers' classroom behaviors provides increasingly convincing evidence that specific actions and patterns of action practiced by teachers have effects on the amount of learning students achieve (see Borich, 1977; Peterson & Walberg, 1979). Significant classes of behaviors include allocations of reinforcement, techniques of control, styles of questioning students, and patterns of provision for students' time on task (Centra & Potter, 1980). A related body of research—on Pygmalion effects (Rosenthal & Jacobson, 1968) or self-fulfilling prophecy—indicates that teachers' expectations regarding student achievement affect the achievement levels students attain. In addition, teachers' differential expectations regarding the achievements of groups of youngsters—minority group children and majority group children, middle-class children and poor children, female children and male children—result in differential achievements of those groups (Rist, 1970; Berman and Serbin, 1977), not because of a mystical transference of beliefs from teacher to student but because teachers systematically behave differently toward different groups of students (Cooper, 1979; Achilles et al., 1975). In brief, it appears that teachers' actions vis-à-vis students affect student achievements in general and that teachers direct their actions toward students in groups differentially.

The expectancy theory would lend us to believe that teachers' actions are, at least in part, the result of the forces to perform these actions. Furthermore, the theory maintains that the forces to perform certain actions (such as delimiting time on task, withholding reinforcement, and posing restrictive questions) are greater for a proportion of teachers than are the forces to perform other actions (such as increasing time on task, lavishing reinforcement, and posing appropriate questions). According to the theory, these forces are the results of teachers' expectancies, outcome valences, and the instrumentalities of direct outcomes in relation to indirect outcomes.

To analyze teachers' behaviors from the perspective of this theory, we can consider each of the major constructs and their interrelationships in sequence. The actions with which we are concerned are those associated with increasing students' achievements.

Valences of High, Moderate, and Low Student Achievement Levels

The valences of these possible direct outcomes of teachers' efforts are, according to the theory, a function of the valences of the indirect outcomes and the instrumentalities of student achievement levels for attaining these outcomes. Some teachers perceive that their own feelings of satisfaction, which have high positive valence, are directly correlated with levels of student achievement; many teachers, however, do not perceive their own satisfaction as related to student achievement. For the former group, high student achievement is instrumental in attaining satisfaction; but for the latter group, high student achievement is not instrumental in attaining satisfaction. Whereas in some schools there are rewards for teachers (such as recognition or supervisors' approval) and penalties for teachers (such as criticism or supervisors' disapproval) associated with student achievement, in most schools the rewards and penalties are not associated with student achievement. For teachers in the former schools, high student achievement is instrumental for attaining extrinsic rewards and avoiding extrinsic penalties; for those in the latter schools, however, high student achievement is not instrumental with respect to extrinsic outcomes. We are left with the conclusion that only those teachers who derive satisfaction from student achievement in itself and those in the few schools in which meaningful extrinsic outcomes are associated with student achievement would be likely to find high student achievement significantly more positively valent than moderate or low student achievement.

Forces to Perform Actions Directed
Toward High Student Achievement

This motivational force is, according to the theory, a function of the valences of the direct outcomes and teachers' expectancies with respect to the results of their actions. Some teachers believe that they have the skills requisite for good teaching and that, if they act on those skills, there is a strong probability that high student achievement levels will be the direct outcome of their efforts. Many teachers, however, believe that they lack the requisite skills (or do not know what those skills might be) or that there is scant possibility that high student achievement levels will be a direct outcome of their actions. These teachers believe that some students are either dull or recalcitrant, that home conditions or the students' cultural and socioeconomic backgrounds have limited their learning potential, or that the students do not want to learn and therefore will not respond to the teacher's efforts. We must conclude that, of the segment of the teaching staff who perceive high student achievement to be more positively valent than other levels of student achievement, only a subsegment will have a strong force to expend effort toward that goal.

If we carry the analysis one step further, to consider excellent teaching performance, it becomes clear that only a subset of the highly motivated teachers actually teach well, since many who believe they have the requisite knowledge and skills do not actually possess the relevant abilities. Thus, as shown in Figure 13–5, the theory suggests that the teachers who do teach well would be some sub-subset of the total teaching population; the proportional size of this segment is not known.

As noted earlier, the theory bears important implications for administra-

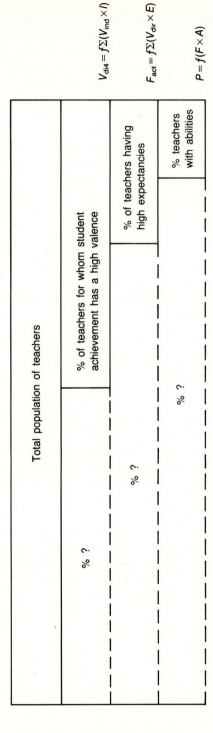

$$V_{di4} = f\Sigma(V_{ind} \times I)$$

$$F_{act} = f\Sigma(V_{dir} \times E)$$

$$P = f(F \times A)$$

NOTE : Percentages in each subset are unknown. The illustration shows about 50 percent of each preceding category, which might be an optimistic or a pessimistic representation.

Figure 13–5 Expectancy Theory Analysis of Teaching Performance

346

tive and supervisory practice at the building or department level. There are implications for practice, it appears, at each layer of the analysis depicted in Figure 13–5. The implications can be illustrated as follows:

1. At the $P = f(F \times A)$ level, it seems clear that providing effective staff development programs (not just topical lectures and discussions but bona fide skill-, attitude-, and knowledge-learning programs) can increase the number of motivated teachers who have the requisite abilities. Also, removing the obstacles from the path of teachers who are willing and able to perform well can increase the number of teachers who do perform well.

2. At the $F = f\Sigma (V_{dir} \times E)$ level, both training programs and recognition of successful performance can increase the number of teachers who believe their effort will relate to student outcomes. Recognition of successful teaching can serve to help some teachers understand the linkage between their own behaviors and students' attainments.

3. At the $V_{dir} = f\Sigma (V_{ind} \times I)$ level, the conscious and consistent allocation of rewards and penalties to teachers on the basis of their students' achievement gains would, in time, increase the number of teachers who perceive high student achievement as instrumental in maximizing their own gains. By allocating rewards and penalties on the basis of specific classroom behaviors that are correlated with student achievement, administrators and supervisors can increase the perceived instrumentality of those behaviors; that is, extrinsic rewards can become the direct rather than indirect outcomes of teacher behaviors.

By extension of this analysis, the theory bears implications for administrative practice at the executive level, for it would be incumbent on superintendents and central office executives to increase principals' motivation to behave in such a way as to increase teachers' motivation and performance levels. Some of the actions that principals and supervisors must experience a force to perform are: becoming aware of the teacher behaviors that relate to student achievement; observing teaching, with special attention to those behaviors (and with skill in recognizing them); distributing positive and negative extrinsic outcomes on the basis of teachers' performance efforts and successes; aggregating student achievement gains by classes; and providing feedback to teachers whose students do gain appreciably. Increasing the likelihood of forces within principals to perform these actions, of course, would require affecting principals' abilities, expectancies, performance level valences, and instrumentalities at the district level.

As indicated in the foregoing research section, there have been very few studies of school personnel motivation based on the expectancy theory. By logic, the theory holds promise for informing administrative practice with reference to enhancing student learning outcomes. Empirical verification of our analysis is lacking, however. Some of the questions that remain to be answered through empirical research are:

1. Is the attractiveness to educators of various performance levels related to the summed valences of indirect outcomes times perceived instrumentalities of performance levels?
2. Is the motivation educators have to perform effectively related to the summed valences of performance levels and the educators' expectancies that their actions will or will not yield those performance levels?
3. Do schools differ in the extent to which indirect outcomes are contingent on educators' performance levels? If so, do educators' degrees of intensity of the force to perform well differ by schools in accordance with indirect outcome contingencies?
4. Is there a relationship between teachers' levels of motivation and the quality of their performance?
5. Finally, is there a relationship between teachers' levels of motivation and their students' achievement gains?

In summary, the expectancy theory of motivation seems to have bearing on the production of knowledge about effective administrative practice. The essence of the theory's relevance to administrative practice is that administrators can, to some extent, control the indirect outcomes of teachers' behaviors; thus they theoretically can have an impact on teachers' expectancies and instrumentalities, and hence on their motivational forces. What remains is for inventive and imaginative researchers to discover, by means of experimental as well as descriptive studies, whether the theory does describe and explain personnel behaviors in schools and, if so, which indirect outcomes within the administrators' sphere of control have the greatest impact on teacher motivation.

MASTERY QUIZ

Select the one best completion to each of the following sentences without reference to the preceding text. Answers are given in Appendix C, page 393.

1. Motivation is equivalent to
   a. the summed instrumentalities of outcomes.
   b. the expectancy that one can perform well.
   c. the force to perform an act.
   d. the force to perform times the valence of the outcome.
2. Expectancy can be defined as
   a. the perceived correlations among outcomes.
   b. the perceived probability that an act will be followed by an outcome.

c. the perceived correlation between actions and outcomes.

d. the summed products of instrumentalities and valences.

3. Valence can be defined as
   a. the perceived utility of an action.
   b. the attractiveness or repulsiveness of an outcome.
   c. the attractiveness or repulsiveness of an action.
   d. the perceived utility of an outcome for attaining other outcomes.

4. Instrumentality can be defined as
   a. the perceived utility of an action.
   b. the attractiveness or repulsiveness of an outcome.
   c. the perceived probability that an outcome will lead to other outcomes.
   d. the perceived correlations between an outcome and other outcomes.

5. The two elements that comprise force to perform an act are
   a. the valence of the direct outcome and expectancy.
   b. the valence of the direct outcome and instrumentality.
   c. the valences of the indirect outcomes and instrumentality.
   d. the valence of the direct outcome and its utility.

6. The two elements that comprise valence of a direct outcome are
   a. the valences of the indirect outcomes and expectancy.
   b. the valence of the direct outcome and its utility.
   c. the valences of the direct outcomes and expectancy.
   d. the valences of the indirect outcomes and the utility of the direct outcome.

7. Expectancy can best be defined as
   a. a perceived action-outcome relationship.
   b. a perceived outcome-outcome relationship.
   c. a perceived valence-instrumentality relationship.
   d. a perceived force to perform an action.

8. The formula that most concisely defines motivation is:
   a. $P = f(F \times A)$. c. $V = F(V \times I)$.
   b. $F = f(V \times E)$. d. $F = f(V \times I)$.

9. The formula that most concisely defines the valence of a direct outcome is
   a. $P = f(F \times A)$. c. $V = f(V \times I)$.
   b. $F = f(V \times E)$. d. $F = f(V \times I)$.

10. To estimate the valence of a direct outcome, one would
    a. sum the valences of all the indirect outcomes and multiply that sum by the instrumentality.
    b. sum all the negative valences and all the positive valences, and subtract the negative total from the positive total.
    c. multiply the valence of each direct outcome by its perceived probability, and sum all the products.
    d. multiply the valence of each indirect outcome by its perceived correlation with the direct outcomes, and sum all the products.

(Running header)

EXERCISES

1. Think of a decision you face now concerning some action in the near future. This can be a relatively trivial decision or a serious one. Identify the action alternatives relevant to the decision. Then use the expectancy theory as a basis for analyzing your present feelings (that is, force to perform) about the options. Develop the appropriate tables, as in Figure 13–3, to compute the valences, instrumentalities, and expectancies. Try to include in your analysis all the indirect outcomes that are relevant to you.

2. Imagine that you are a principal newly assigned to a school (elementary or secondary) in which teaching performance—and student outcomes—have been notoriously low for some period of time. Without reference to the contents of the expectancy theory chapter, think of three (3) strategies you could use to enhance teachers' performance with respect to each of the following:
   a. improving teachers' *abilities*.
   b. raising teachers' *expectancies*.
   c. increasing the *instrumentality* of good teaching.
   d. increasing the range of positively valent *indirect outcomes*.
   Your total list should have 12 discrete items.

3. After reading the case description appearing in Appendix A, imagine that you are the principal of the school facing the decision as to which teacher to transfer. Use the expectancy theory as a basis for your analysis by developing tables such as those in Figure 13–3, and reach a conclusion about what you, as the principal, are likely to do. Be prepared to justify your conclusion if asked.

4. Several questions were posed toward the end of the chapter to suggest some directions for needed research. Refer to those questions in completing the following tasks:
   a. Based on your understanding of the theory, convert each of the questions into a testable hypothesis.
   b. Select one of those hypotheses and consider how it might be tested in a school setting. Jot an outline of the study so as to be able to describe it if asked.

REFERENCES

Major Source

Vroom, Victor H. *Work and motivation*. New York: Wiley, 1964.

Related Conceptual Literature

Behling, O., & Starke, F. A. The postulates of expectancy theory. *Academy of Management Journal*, 1973, *16*, 373–386.

Borich, G. *The appraisal of teaching: Concepts and process.* Reading, Mass.: Addison-Wesley, 1977.

Centra, J. A., & Potter, D. A. School and teacher effects: An interrelational model. *Review of Educational Research*, 1980, *50*, 273–291.

Cooper, H. M. Pygmalion grows up: A model for teacher expectation communication and performance influence. *Review of Educational Research*, 1979, *49*, 389–410.

Festinger, L. *A theory of cognitive dissonance.* Standford, Calif.: Stanford University Press, 1957.

Frasher, J., & Frasher, R. The verification of administrative attribution theory. Paper presented at the American Educational Research Association annual meeting, Boston, 1980.

Heneman, H. G., III, & Schwab, D. P. An evaluation of research on expectancy theory predictions of employee performance. *Psychological Bulletin*, 1972, *78*, 1–9.

Herzberg, F.; Mausner, B.; & Snyderman, B. *The motivation to work.* New York: Wiley, 1959.

House, R.; Shapiro, H. J.; & Wahba, M. Expectancy theory as a predictor of work behavior and attitude: A reevaluation of empirical evidence. *Decision Sciences*, 1974, *5*, 481–506.

Lawler, E. E., III. Job design and employee motivation. *Personnel Psychology*, 1969, *22*, 426–435.

Maslow, A. H. *Toward a psychology of being.* Princeton, N.J.: Van Nostrand, 1962.

Mitchell, T. R. Expectancy models of job satisfaction, occupational preference, and effort: A theoretical, methodological, and empirical appraisal. *Psychological Bulletin*, 1974, *81*, 1053–1077.

Mitchell, T. R., & Beach, L. R. A review of occupational preference and choice research using expectancy theory and decision theory. *Journal of Occupational Psychology*, 1976, *49*, 231–248.

Peterson, P. L., & Walberg, H. J. *Research on teaching: Concepts, findings and implications.* Berkeley, Calif.: McCutchan, 1979.

Porter, L. W., & Lawler, E. E. *Managerial attitudes and performance.* Homewood, Ill.: Irwin-Dorsey, 1968.

Rist, R. C. Student social class and teacher expectancies: The self-fulfilling prophesy in ghetto education. *Harvard Educational Review*, 1970, *40*, 411–451.

Rosenthal, R., & Jacobson, L. *Pygmalion in the classroom.* New York: Holt, Rinehart and Winston, 1968.

Rotter, J. B. Generalized expectancies for internal versus external control of reinforcement. *Psychological Monographs*, 1973, *80*, 38–88.

Schmidt, F. L. Implications of a measurement problem for expectancy theory research. *Organizational Behavior and Human Performance*, 1973, *10*, 243–251.

Schroder, H. M.; Driver, M. J.; & Streufert, S. *Human information processing.* New York: Holt, Rinehart and Winston, 1967.

Sheridan, J. E.; Richards, M. D.; & Slocum, J. W., Jr. Comparative analysis of expectancy and heuristic models of decision behavior. *Journal of Applied Psychology*, 1975, *60*, 361–368.

Related Research: General

Galbraith, J., & Cummings, L. L. An empirical investigation of the motivational determinants of task performance. *Organizational Behavior and Human Performance*, 1967, *2*, 237–257.

Gavin, J. F. Self-esteem as a moderator of the relationship between expectancies and job performance. *Journal of Applied Psychology*, 1973, *58*, 83–88.

Georgopoulos, B. S.; Mahoney, G. M.; & Jones, N. W. A path-goal approach to productivity. *Journal of Applied Psychology*, 1957, *41*, 345–353.

Goodman, P. S.; Rose, J. H.; & Furcon, J. E. Comparison of motivational antecedents of the work performance of scientists and engineers. *Journal of Applied Psychology*, 1970, *54*, 491–495.

Hackman, J. R., & Oldham, G. R. Motivation through the design of work. *Organizational Behavior and Human Performance*, 1976, *16*, 250–279.

Hackman, J. R., & Porter, L. W. Expectancy theory predictions of work effectiveness. *Organizational Behavior and Human Performance*, 1968, *3*, 417–426.

House, R. J. A path-goal theory of leader effectiveness. *Administrative Science Quarterly*, 1971, *16*, 321–338.

Lawler, E. E. Job attitudes and employee motivation: Theory, research and practice. *Personnel Psychology*, 1970, *23*, 223–237.

Lawler, E. E., III, & Porter, L. W. Antecedent attitudes of effective managerial performance. *Organizational Behavior and Human Performance*, 1967, *2*, 122–142.

Lawler, E. E., & Suttle, J. L. Expectancy theory and job behavior. *Organizational Behavior and Human Performance*, 1973, *9*, 482–503.

Mitchell, T. R., & Albright, D. W. Expectancy theory predictions of satisfaction, effort, performance and retention of naval aviation officers. *Organizational Behavior and Human Performance*, 1972, *8*, 1–20.

Reinharth, L., & Wahba, M. A. Expectancy theory as a predictor of work motivation, effort expenditure, and job performance. *Academy of Management Journal*, 1975, *18*, 520–537.

Schneider, B., & Olson, L. K. Effort as a correlate of organizational reward system and individual values. *Personnel Psychology*, 1970, *23*, 313–326.

Related Research: Education

Achilles, C. M.; Crump, H. B.; Woodbury, R.; & French, R. L. Verbal and nonverbal behaviors of teachers analyzed by teacher/pupil sex and race. *The Educational Catalyst*, 1975, *3*, 121–130.

Berman, L. S., & Serbin, L. A. Observer expectations of a child's performance as a function of sex. Paper presented at the Annual Midwest Conference on Research on Women in Education, Milwaukee, Wisconsin, 1977.

Henson, R. Expectancy beliefs, ability, and personality in predicting academic performance. *Journal of Educational Research*, 1976, *70*, 41–44.

Holstrom, V. L., & Beach, L. R. Subjective expected utility and career preferences. *Organizational Behavior and Human Performance*, 1973, *10*, 201–207.

Liddell, W. W., & Solomon, R. J. A total and stochastic test of the transitivity postulate underlying expectancy theory. *Organizational Behavior and Human Performance*, 1977a, *19*, 311–324.

―――――. A critical reanalysis of a test of two postulates underlying expectancy theory. *Academy of Management Journal*, 1977b, *20*, 460–464.

Miskel, C.; DeFrain, J.; & Wilcox, K. A test of expectancy work motivation theory in educational organizations. *Educational Administration Quarterly*, 1980, *16*, 70–92.

Miskel, C.; Glasnapp, D.; & Hatley, R. A test of inequity theory for job satisfaction using educators' attitudes toward work motivation and work incentives. *Educational Administration Quarterly*, 1975, *11*, No. 1, 38–54.

Mitchell, T. R. & Knudsen, B. W. Instrumentality theory predictions of students' attitudes toward business and their choice of business as an occupation. *Academy of Management Journal*, 1973, *16*, 41–52.

Muchinsky, P. M., & Fitch, M. K. Subjective expected utility and academic preferences. *Organizational Behavior and Human Performance*, 1975, *14*, 217–226.

Peters, L. H. Cognitive models of motivation, expectancy theory, and effort: An analysis and empirical test. *Organizational Behavior and Human Performance*, 1977, *20*, 129–148.

Spuck, D. W. Reward structures in the public high school. *Educational Administration Quarterly*, 1974, *10*, 18–33.

Stephens, T. Innovative teaching practices: Their relation to system norms and rewards. *Educational Administration Quarterly*, 1974, *10*, 35–43.

Vroom, V. H. Organizational choice: A study of pre- and postdecision processes. *Organizational Behavior and Human Performance*, 1966, *1*, 212–225.

Vroom, V. H., & Deci, E. L. The stability of post-decision dissonance: A follow-up study of job attitudes of business school graduates. *Organizational Behavior and Human Performance*, 1971, *6*, 36–49.

Wanous, J. P. Occupational preferences: Perceptions of valence and instrumentality and objective data. *Journal of Applied Psychology*, 1972, *56*, 152–155.

Part VIII
ENHANCING RESEARCH AND PRACTICE

Chapter 14
Review and Synthesis
of Theories

A day in the life of an educational administrator is typically a hectic one. In the flow of daily events—mail, meetings, phone calls, visitors, interruptions, crises that are usually minor but occasionally shattering—there is rarely the time to sit back and analyze. The administrator reacts spontaneously, often making important decisions at a moment's notice. One could scarcely expect the harried administrator to halt the flow of action, reach for a theory handbook to seek an appropriate framework for interpreting this situation, and weigh the alternative courses of action dispassionately. Of what use, then, is an array of theories dreamed up by scholars in their ivory towers?

The fact is that even when the job is at its most demanding and frenetic, there are occasions—perhaps at home or during an occasional interlude at work—when calm, solitary reflection is possible. These are times for introspection and retrospection as well as for planning for some future events. These are times for interpreting the recent past and projecting into the near future, times when particular theories can be selected and used intentionally as tools for expanding one's understanding of the world of action.

In all probability the spontaneous actions and responses that busy administrators generate in the course of events derive from deeply held beliefs about people and principles of practice they developed over time on the basis of experience. Argyris and Schön (1974) called these personalistic generalizations *theories-in-use*—sets of basic assumptions and precepts that guide everyday action. By integrating more scientific frameworks based on other people's insights into this corpus of theories-in-use, active administrators can add coherence to their understandings and enhance their repertoire of responses. In other words, scientific theories, if studied in the light of one's own experiences, can become integral to one's world view and thereby help to guide action without conscious deliberation.

We have examined twelve theories, each representing a way of viewing organizations or interpreting events that transpire in organizations. It is hoped that these perspectives will add richness and coherence to administrators' theories-in-use by becoming integrated with long-held beliefs and assumptions and by adding to them more refined differentiations of experiences. To reinforce the understandings gained in earlier chapters, a review of the major elements of the theories is provided here. Then, for purposes of further integration, some ways of interrelating theories are suggested. The chapter concludes with an exploration of some functions of synthesis in research and practice.

REVIEW OF THEORIES

The 12 frameworks examined in this volume were arranged, somewhat arbitrarily, according to the scope of the phenomena of interest—from the more global or macroscopic phenomena, total organizations, to the more delimited or microscopic phenomena, attitudes of people within organizations. This arrangement of theories is certainly not inclusive of all relevant conceptualizations and is not the only possible system of ordering them. It offers an overview of numerous perspectives on organizations, however—particularly those perspectives generated in the disciplines of sociology and social psychology—and a sort of cognitive armature on which to attach additional viewpoints as they are encountered.

Whole Organizations

Organizations as entities have been viewed in various ways by thinkers and scholars through the ages. A *structural* view—one emphasizing the arrangement of positions and the results of that arrangement—is represented by Jerald Hage's *axiomatic theory* of modern formal organizations. Hage focused on the structural dimensions of complexity, centralization, formalization, and stratifi-cation as they relate to such outcomes as organizational adaptiveness, production, efficiency, and employees' job satisfaction. Specific predictions about the impact of structure on outcomes were made in this theory in the form of 8 axioms and 21 corollaries (Hage, 1965).

A *process* view of organizations—one emphasizing the dynamic interplay and constant interchange among parts, is represented by Ludwig von Bertalanffy's *general system theory*. Organizations are viewed from this perspective as equivalent to other living or open systems, which are sets of components interacting purposefully within a boundary that filters inputs and outputs (Bertalanffy, 1968; Berrien, 1968). The inputs of energy and informa-tion are used in the interactions among components to bring about intended changes in the throughput; these changes along with some waste and some noise, are the outputs of the system. In this framework, interaction is the exchange of energy and information among components.

These two frameworks for viewing organizations, though vastly different from each other, are not contradictory. One can readily interpret the structural features of organizations as constraints on the interactions among their components. Most of the outcomes of the constrained interactions among components, then—specifically, production, efficiency, and job satisfaction—can well be interpreted as the outputs of the system. From a systems point of view, adaptiveness would be seen in terms of system openness—the degree of flexibility the interacting parts have in responding to new input.

Power in Organizations

One of the important phenomena found in all organizations is power: the dominance of some people over others. One type of power, legal authority, is viewed in terms of its ramifications in organizational structure and outcomes in Max Weber's *bureaucracy theory*. The characteristics of bureaucracy—hierarchy of offices, rules and regulations, task specialization, impersonality, documentation, full-salaried personnel, and organizational control of re-sources—are seen to be prevalent in organizations based on legal authority and to contribute to the efficiency and rationality such organizations exhibit (Weber, 1963; Gerth & Mills, 1958).

Although authority is the predominant form of influence in most formal organizations, it is by no means the only type of power used. Three types of power as they combine with three types of participant orientations are considered in Amitai Etzioni's *compliance theory*. Here the clients or employees of the organization, who may feel an alienative, a calculative, or a moral involvement in the organization, are viewed as the lower participants. The types of power used by those in positions of dominance are coercive, remunerative, or normative. Thus organizations can be classified into nine compliance categories based on power uses and lower participants' involvement; of these, the coercive, utilitarian, and normative compliance types have congruent power and involvement (Etzioni, 1975).

Though representing contrasting views of organizations, these two theories are not incompatible. As the Weberian notion of authority (willing and unquestioning obedience to directives) suggests, a fully bureaucratic organization would be regarded as a normative type in Etzioni's scheme: the employees in a bureaucracy conform because they are ideologically committed to the values for which the bureaucracy stands—that is, morally involved. From the Weberian perspective, obedience for reasons of being paid to conform, as in calculative involvement, constitutes a loss of legitimate authority. It should be noted that many of the organizations that are considered coercive in the Etzioni typology are only coercive with respect to their "clients" (such as prisoners, delinquents); for the employees the authority structure tends to be normative-bureaucratic.

Leadership in Organizations

Among the most widely studied of organizational and small-group phenomena, leadership has been conceptualized in numerous ways. A *behavioral* approach to leadership research was initiated by Andrew Halpin and others at the Ohio State University as the *leader behavior description framework*. Two major dimensions of behavior were found, through much empirical research, to be exhibited by people occupying leadership positions in organizations: the person-oriented dimension, including tolerance of uncertainty, tolerance of freedom, consideration, demand reconciliation, integration, and predictive accuracy; and the system-orientation dimension, including production emphasis, initiating structure, representation, role assumption, persuasiveness, and superior orientation. Both aspects of behavior are viewed as essential for effective leadership (Halpin, 1966a; Stogdill, 1974).

A *situational* view of leadership—one emphasizing the impact of circumstances on the leader's effectiveness—is Fred Fiedler's *contingency model*. In this framework the leader's personality or leadership style—task oriented or relationship oriented—is of prime importance, as is the degree of favorableness of the group-task situation. Three aspects of the group-task situation—leader-member relations, task structure, and leader position power—are combined to determine the degree of situation favorableness, and the performance of the group is viewed as dependent on the matching of leadership style and situation favorableness. More specifically, task-oriented leadership matched with very favorable or unfavorable situations is said to yield optimal group performance; similarly, relationship-oriented leadership matched with moderately favorable situations yields optimal group performance (Fiedler, 1967).

These two approaches to leadership research concern different aspects of organizational interaction, but they can be seen as complementary perspectives. The leader with a given personality (task oriented or relationship oriented) interacts with a group in a particular social setting (situation favorableness) and, as a result, exhibits a distinctive pattern of behavior (person oriented and system oriented). This behavior pattern in turn stimulates the group toward greater productivity or hampers the group's productive efforts. One cannot assume that a task-oriented leader will behave in a system-oriented manner or that a relationship-oriented leader will exhibit person-oriented behavior. Instead, one can assume that a given situation will affect a task-oriented leader's behavior in one way and a relationship-oriented leader's behavior in another. Stated differently, the leader's behavior as it influences the group's efforts can be viewed as emerging from the combined effects of the leader's personality and situation.

Climate in Organizations

Though a somewhat elusive notion, the atmosphere or unique flavor of each organization has been an object of great interest to scholars, who have approached the matter in diverse ways. A *descriptive* orientation to climate research is the Andrew Halpin and Donald Croft *organizational climate description framework*, which focuses on principals' and teachers' interactive behavior patterns. In this conceptualization the principal's behavior with respect to aloofness, production emphasis, thrust, and consideration, in combination with teachers' group behaviors in terms of disengagement, hindrance, esprit, and intimacy, is found to yield six different types of climate. These have been called open, autonomous, controlled, familiar, paternal, and closed (Halpin, 1966b). Clearly implied in this framework is the desirability of an open climate for maximizing teachers' professional performance.

A completely different strategy for studying organizational climate—this one a more *psychological* approach—is represented in George Stern's *needs-press theory*. Using 30 dimensions of personality (that is, needs) as the foundation for the research, he found two major social forces that act on participants' personalities in organizations. These have been named development press (a growth-enhancing force) and control press (an expression-inhibiting force). Aspects of development press are intellectual climate, achievement standards, practicalness, supportiveness, and orderliness. Aspects of control press are reflected intellectual climate (antiintellectualism), reflected achievement standards (low expectations), and impulse control. A strong development press is viewed in this theory as representing a highly desirable climate for learning (Stern, 1970).

The two conceptualizations of climate, though divergent in theoretical orientation, are not mutually exclusive. From the Stern point of view, the individual's psychological needs in combination with the organization's social press or climate result in observable behavior. If one considers the principal and each teacher as an individual with psychological needs subject to social press, the result is behavior of the group, which can be described in Halpin-

Croft terms as ranging from open to closed climate. In other words, in the needs-press framework, climate is equivalent to group expectations for behavior; in the descriptive framework, climate is equivalent to observed behaviors.

Individuals in Organizations

The problem of explaining the dynamics of how or why individuals function in group settings such as organizations has been the most basic issue in social psychology. Two systems approaches have been selected for this volume. A *psychosocial* perspective is represented by the *social systems model*. As explicated by Jacob Getzels and Egon Guba, human behavior is the result of transaction between the sociological or nomothetic dimension of the system and the psychological or idiographic dimension. The nomothetic view is that each social system represents an institution, which is a unique arrangement of roles, each of which is made up of expectations for the behavior of occupants. The psychological view is that each social system is made up of individuals, each of whom has a distinctive personality, which is a constellation of need-dispositions. Each person's need-dispositions, in transaction with the expectations for the role that person occupies, generate that person's behavior (Getzels & Guba, 1957).

An *information-processing* approach to understanding individuals' functioning in organizations is represented by Harold Schroder's *conceptual systems theory*. People are viewed in this framework as having particular levels of integrative complexity as defined by the ways in which they differentiate, discriminate, and integrate stimuli (information or signals) in their environments. The environments themselves are more or less complex as defined by the rate, load, and diversity of signals being emitted. The behavior a person exhibits (which can vary from simple to complex) is viewed as resulting from the combined effects of environment complexity and integrative complexity. When the environment is highly complex, it evokes a high level of integrative complexity in persons who have the capacity for abstract thinking; their behavior in such areas as decision making and problem solving is consequently more complex. In a simpler environment the same people would function at a lower level of complexity and would therefore exhibit simpler behavior (Schroder, Driver, & Streufert 1967).

Again, the two conceptualizations, though different, are quite congruent. The need-dispositions of an individual refer to all the aspects of the individual's personality, and one aspect of a personality in its level of integrative complexity. The expectations associated with the role a person occupies are communicated in the behavior of others within and beyond the organization, and these communications can be seen as signals in the environment of the role occupant. Finally, observed behavior can have many dimensions, including appropriateness, spontaneity, and orientation (toward the system or toward people); one of those dimensions is complexity. Thus conceptual systems theory can be seen as elucidating an aspect of social systems theory. The relevance of conceptual systems to social systems can perhaps best be seen in the matter of role conflict, where conflicting and competing sets of expectations bombard the individual role occupant. These divergent messages constitute a highly complex environment for the individual, and that individual's capacity to integrate or reconcile the competing demands is clearly a function of the person's level of integrative complexity.

Motivation of Individuals

The problem of motivating employees to strive for excellence has long been of interest to industrial psychologists and is of growing interest to educational leaders. Of the many approaches to an understanding of human motivation, a more *external* orientation is represented by Frederick Herzberg's *motivation-hygiene theory,* which focuses on aspects of the job and its setting. According to this theory, the many individual events that transpire over time in an organization can be classified into two broad categories: motivation factors and hygiene factors. The motivation factors, which pertain to qualities of the job, are achievement, recognition, work itself, responsibility, advancement, and growth possibility. The hygiene factors, which pertain to the setting in which the job is performed, are company policy and administration, technical supervision, salary, relations with supervisors, relations with subordinates, relations with peers, working conditions, status, security, and effects on personal life. Whereas the hygiene factors can cause employee dissatisfaction if inadequate and do not affect employee motivation, the motivation factors can cause great satisfaction when present and also can influence employee motivation (Herzberg, 1966).

A more *internal* or psychological approach to the study of motivation is represented by Victor Vroom's *expectancy theory.* From this perspective one's interest is in the employees' orientations toward self and toward the environment more than in the actualities of the job. Motivation is viewed as an internal force or drive. The intensity and direction of this force are shaped by two elements: the individual's expectancy that particular actions will result in given (direct) outcomes, and the instrumentality of the outcomes for attaining other desired (indirect) outcomes. The instrumentality of a direct outcome (such as excellent performance) depends on the valences of the indirect outcomes (such as praise and advancement) and the perceived correlation between the direct and indirect outcomes (the relationship between quality of performance and praise, for example). One's expectancy regarding the likelihood of achieving a desired direct outcome such as excellent performance depends on one's self-assessment; for example, if I try, can I succeed in producing an excellent performance? Thus motivation is viewed as a result of psychological factors, one's self-appraisal of abilities and one's subjective assessment of the rewards and penalties associated with the results of actions (Vroom, 1964).

These contrasting conceptualizations of motivation are, again, highly congruent or complementary. The motivation and hygiene factors enumerated in Herzberg's theory can readily be seen as the possible indirect outcomes of action on the job. Such outcomes as achievement, recognition, interesting tasks, responsibility, advancement, and growth opportunity would have a very high positive valence to most employees. If these outcomes are forthcoming when workers perform well, then good work will be seen as instrumental in attaining desired outcomes. If, in addition, the employees are made aware that they have the knowledge and skills required for good work, they will have high expectancies that their effort will yield excellent performance. In brief, having the abilities and knowing that good work brings rewards are the essential elements of high motivation. What Herzberg's theory clarifies in relation to Vroom's theory is that the motivation factors are more attractive (have higher positive valence) when present and positive than do the hygiene factors when present and positive. Thus the motivation factors have greater impact on one's internal force or drive.

In sum, this book as a whole has addressed six broad topics, ranging from whole organizations, through phenomena within organizations and people in organizational settings, to an aspect of the people: their motivation. For each general topic two contrasting perspectives were explored in some detail. The brief summaries of the 12 theories were provided mainly as a review of the key terms associated with each perspective and the essence of each conceptualization.

SYNTHESIS OF THEORIES

The preceding section included brief discussions of the complementarities between pairs of theories treating the six central topics of the book. For example, the two leadership theories were shown to be different but compatible or complementary. These discussions were a step in the direction of interrelating and integrating divergent theoretical frameworks.

It is important to bear in mind that each theory represents a distinctive perspective but that the various perspectives are not mutually contradictory. Rather, each theory can be viewed as an expansion or elaboration of one or more other theories. It is, after all, one phenomenon—organization—that is being studied; and each theory is an effort to describe or explain human behavior within that enterprise called organization. Each theory affords insight into an aspect of organizational behavior, and each additional theory one encounters can enrich that insight by adding dimensions to one's prior understanding.

There is, of course, no one best way to interrelate diverse theories. Because synthesis is a cognitive activity that is shaped by each individual's unique understanding of the materials presented, there are as many different ways of integrating the theories as there are people thinking about them. A few integrative schemes—ways of interrelating clusters of theories—are provided in this section to stimulate thought about some interconnections among ideas. Readers are urged to generate their own syntheses as well and to add these to their store of conceptual capital for understanding organizational life in schools.

Individual-Organization Interaction

One feature common to many of the theories in this volume is the analysis of human behavior as the result of interaction between an aspect of the individuals and an aspect of the organization. This perspective is most directly expressed in the Getzels-Guba social systems model, in which observed behavior in general is seen as the outcome of transaction between the institutional role (expected behaviors) and the individual's personality (need-dispositions). Related perspectives, however, can be found in some of the other theories as well. These are illustrated in Figure 14–1, which is summarized in the next few paragraphs.

1. Social systems theory, as noted, posits that observed behavior is the outcome of transaction between the nomothetic or institutional dimension and the idiographic or individual dimension of the system. That is, it is the interactive effects of various people's expectations and the individual's unique need-dispositions that result in the individual's observable actions.

2. One way in which expectations are expressed by higher-echelon authorities is through their uses of power to reward or punish lower participants' actions. Thus power uses represent an expression of role expectations. The individual lower participants, on the other hand, have particular orientations toward the organization and its representatives' uses of power. That is, as individuals they have attitudes, which are a facet of their need-dispositions. Since certain types of power (coercive, remunerative, or normative) generate congruent attitudes (alienative, calculative, or moral, respectively), the lower participants are likely to develop somewhat similar attitudes; these, in combination with power uses, are expressed in the predominating compliance pattern of the organization. Compliance, then, can be seen as the typical behavior pattern of the organization as a whole.

3. As the organizational participants interact over time, they develop some similarities of attitudes and interests and some norms for behavior. These norms represent the group's expectations regarding the behavior of each member, and the expectations of the group as a whole become a powerful force or pressure on each individual to conform. Thus the dimensions of organizational climate (development press and control press, as well as their constituent

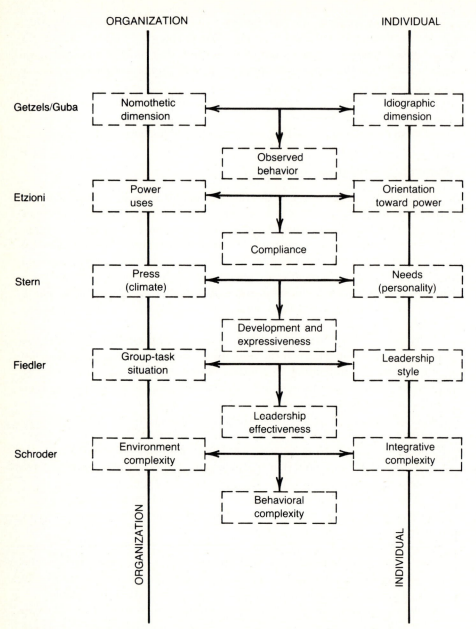

Figure 14–1   Behavior as a Result of Individual-Organization Interaction

press factors) are the group's generalized expectations. At the same time, the individual group member has a unique personality with needs related to self-development and self-expression. These psychological needs are an important component of the person's need-dispositions. Thus the participant attempts to develop and to express self in a context that either fosters or impedes these drives, and the result is the behavior that participant exhibits in the group setting.

4. When the individual participant is the leader of the group, it is the group's expectations in combination with the leader's need-dispositions that determine the leader's behavior and effectiveness. The group's expectations can be expressed with regard to three important dimensions of the group-task situation: the expressed attitudes of the members toward the leader (leader-member relations), the degree of specific direction they anticipate (task structure), and the power they attribute to the leader by virtue of position (position power). The leader while interacting with the group and perceiving its members' expectations, has a particular personality; the leader is relatively task oriented or person oriented. Thus leadership style can be viewed as an aspect of the leader's need-dispositions. The leader's effectiveness, then, is a function of the leader's personality and the group's expectations.

5. From the standpoint of conceptual systems theory, the group members' expectations are expressed as signals or messages to the individual, be it the leader or a group member. To the extent that those signals are harmonious or consistent and moderately paced, the individual's environment is moderately simple; to the extent that the signals (expressing expectations) are discordant or conflicting and rapid-fire, the individual's environment is more complex. At the same time, the individual perceiving those signals or messages from others has a unique capacity to interpret, understand, or integrate them. The participant's integrative complexity, in other words, is an important facet of that person's need-dispositions. Thus the behavior one exhibits, which itself varies in complexity, can again be seen as the outcome of individual and organization in interaction.

All five of the frameworks summarized here can readily be interpreted as illustrations of Kurt Lewin's classic formulation, $B = f(P \cdot E)$: Behavior is a function of Personality in interaction with Environment. When the environment the person is inhabiting is a formal organization, it can be conceptualized as the nomothetic dimension of a system, the power uses by superordinates, the organizational climate the group-task situation, or the source of signals, all of which have impact on each participant. The organization member's personality can also be conceptualized in a variety of ways: as the idiographic dimension of a system, an orientation toward power, a set of psychological needs, a leadership style, or a level of integrative complexity. Finally, aspects of behavior resulting from personality-environment interaction can be conceived as observed behavior, organizational compliance, psychological growth and expressiveness, leadership effectiveness, or behavioral complexity.

A Systems Approach

From the perspective of Bertalanffy's general system theory, an organization is viewed as an open system: a set of components interacting purposefully within a boundary that filters inputs to and outputs from the system. As illustrated in Figure 14–2, this perspective can be seen as a core around which several other theories can be integrated.

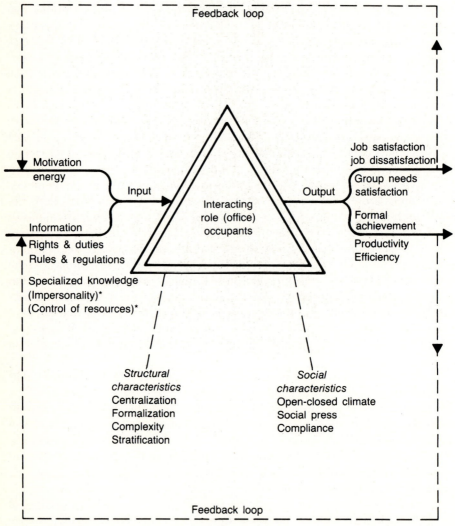

*Note that these items represent information that is systematically screened out of bureaucratic social systems.

Figure 14–2   A Systems Approach to Synthesis

1. The Getzels-Guba social systems model clarifies that the individuals, each having a unique set of need-dispositions, occupy institutional roles, each of which represents a set of societal expectations. Thus the human components of the organization are not simply people but role occupants. Their behavior as components within the system is constrained by both their personalities and their roles.

There are two types of inputs to this social system that is an organization: information inputs or encoded signals and energy inputs or encoded forces. Two theories help to clarify the nature of these inputs.

2. From the standpoint of Weber's theory of bureaucracy, the information inputs to the system are in the form of: (1) legislative mandates specifying the authority relationships among components; (2) job descriptions clarifying the rights, obligations, and duties associated with each role; and (3) the specialized knowledge needed to perform the differentiated tasks in fulfilling the system's purposes. Note that some information that is systematically filtered out of a bureaucratic system are personalistic emotions, biases and preferences (the role occupants are impersonal), and outsiders' dictates about resource allocations (the organization controls the sources). The information inputs are, of course, stored within the bureaucratic social system in the form of such memories as policy manuals, files, job descriptions, procedural guidelines, and human memories. Thus the information inputs signal the human components as to how and when to interact in fulfilling the bureaucracy's purposes. By virtue of the information inputs, the roles become offices: positions bound by explicit expectations concerning the occupant's rights and duties.

3. From the point of view of Vroom's expectancy theory, motivation can be seen as an important energy input to the system. Motivation is viewed as a force to perform, a drive that each person brings (in varying degrees of intensity) to the system, a psychological energy that propels one to act. The intensity and direction of this force are, according to this theory, shaped by each person's history of experiences both within and outside the system. Thus the rewards and penalties that have in the past been the indirect outcomes of certain actions influence the perceived instrumentality of those actions, and the quality of performance that has in the past been the direct outcome of an action influences the expectancies associated with that action. Both the instrumentality of an outcome and the expectancy of that outcome shape the direction and intensity of the psychological force one brings to the system. Along with the fuel energy that drives the material components and the caloric energy that permits human action, then, there is the psychological energy or motivation that shapes the intensity and direction of human action.

The uniqueness of each system can be defined in terms of the particular pattern of interactions among the components. Several social theories have been directed toward describing the pattern of interactions within organization systems. Some theories have emphasized the structural pattern, and others have stressed the social pattern.

4a. The structural characteristics of organizations—that is, the structural constraints on the ways in which the human components interact—can be described in terms of Hage's axiomatic theory of organizations. From this perspective the interactions are described in terms of the organization's complexity (degree of specialization), centralization (locus of decision authority), formalization (degree of codification or standardization), and stratification (degree of hierarchy or layering). One can readily see that the information inputs associated with bureaucracy affect the organization's interaction patterns and result in these structural characteristics. Organizations vary, of course, in their degrees of complexity, centralization, formalization, and stratification; and these features constitute greater or lesser constraints on when, how, and with whom or what the components may exchange information and energy. The other facets of the axiomatic theory will be summarized in a later section.

5. The social characteristics of organizations—that is, the sociocultural constraints on interactions among the human components—have been described in a variety of ways. One of these is in terms of the climate descriptions proposed by Halpin and Croft. This approach emphasizes aspects of the superordinate's behavior (in this case, the principal's), such as aloofness, production emphasis, thrust, and consideration, and aspects of the subordinates' behaviors (in this case, the teachers'), such as disengagement, hindrance, esprit, and intimacy. The results of these patterns of interaction among the human, role-enacting, office-holding components is described in terms of the openness or closedness of the climate.

From the standpoint of system theory it appears that the relatively more open climates—open, autonomous, and controlled—have comparatively more permeable boundaries; they permit more varied and more rapid input to the system. The more closed climates—familiar, paternal, and closed—would have comparatively more impermeable boundaries; they would screen out more information and energy that is potentially available in the environment.

The linkage of climate theory to system theory can be illustrated with reference to the two extreme types of climate. In an open climate the principal's thrust is evidence that much energy (and high motivation) is brought to bear on the system, and high consideration is indicative of enabling staff members to express their unique identities as information input. At the same time, high esprit on the teachers' part is indicative of high energy levels and sharing on their part. These three factors, then, point to greater information and energy input in open-climate systems. In the closed climate the principal's high aloofness indicates that information from individual teachers is screened out, and high production emphasis suggests that all information and energy not directly related to productivity are screened out. High hindrance on the teachers' part suggests that potentially useful information from some teachers is blocked or screened out by others (or by the principal), and high disengagement indicates that there is little motivational energy brought to the system.

These four factors, then, represent low input levels or a relatively impermeable boundary by closed-climate systems.

6. Another approach to describing the social interaction patterns within the system is Stern's climate framework, in which aspects of the group norms are conceived as environmental press. From the standpoint of this theory the social characteristics of the system are described in terms of participants' perceptions of the degree of development press and the degree of control press that are prevalent in the interpersonal interactions among components. A system characterized by high development press and low control press would be regarded as considerably more open than one with the opposite characteristics. The dimensions of development press, particularly the intellectual climate and achievement standards factors, suggest that participants express their growth needs (provide information input), invest considerable energy, and are receptive to change—all of which indicate system openness (permeable boundary). On the other hand, the dimensions of control press, especially the impulse control factor, suggest that a high score represents a filtering out of participants' potential inputs; the participants are relatively inactive and nonexpressive, and hence withhold energy and information about themselves.

7. A third approach to describing the pattern of interactions among system components is Etzioni's theory of compliance. Like the climate description framework summarized earlier (see item 5), the compliance model is a classification scheme for describing patterns of superordinate-subordinate interactions. In this instance, however, the emphasis is on superordinates' power uses and subordinates' involvement. Based on the types of resources used by superordinates to control the lower participants—that is, coercive (physical resources), remunerative (material resources), or normative (symbolic resources)—and the types of involvement the lower participants invest—that is, alienative (hostility), calculative (materialistic), or moral (ideological)—one can identify nine types of organizational social systems. Of these, the three congruent types are called coercive, utilitarian, and normative.

From the perspective of general system theory this classification is based not on the *amount* of system input but on the *types* of input. Certain types of resources are available for allocation by power holders: physical energy for coercion; money and material goods for remuneration; and symbolic goods (such as status, approval, values) for normative control. Other inputs of energy and information are brought in by the participants and reflect their orientations or motivations. Some bring the energic force of hostility; others bring the motivational drive of materialism; still others bring the energic forces of idealistic commitment and loyalty. Thus compliance theory can be viewed as a framework for describing the configurations of inputs and their deployment within the social system.

A system's outputs can also be conceptualized in a variety of ways. Basically, apart from waste and noise, a system's outputs are the results of the interpersonal behaviors of participants (interaction patterns of components) as these results relate to the purposes of the system. Berrien identified two types of social system outputs, the formal achievement outputs and the group needs satisfaction outputs. These can be further explicated with reference to other theories treated in this volume:

4b. Formal achievement outputs of a social system are the changes the system brings about in its material or human throughputs. The degree to which the desired changes are accomplished is the measure of goal attainment by the system. In accordance with Hage's axiomatic theory introduced earlier, the goal-related outputs of an organization can be described in terms of its production and its efficiency, as well as its adaptiveness and employee satisfaction. *Production* refers to the number of units of something (products, services, achievement gains in students, and so on) generated by the system; the production of intended products is a reflection of the rationality of the system. *Efficiency* refers to the expenditure of resources (material goods, time, energy, and so on) in generating the products. High efficiency would be a reflection of low noise output and low waste output in relation to the amount of input invested. From the standpoint of general system theory, adaptiveness might better be seen as a system characteristic than as a system output, since the organization's degree of adaptiveness (flexibility of interaction patterns) will influence its ability to produce outputs efficiently in a changing environment. The job satisfaction output, though mentioned in the axiomatic theory, is explicated more fully in another framework.

8. Group needs satisfaction outputs of a social system can be explicated in terms of Herzberg's theory of job satisfaction. As this framework points out, certain types of positive events in the interactions among system components generate feelings of satisfaction when present. When negative, these types of events—called motivation factors—have little impact on the participants' emotions. For example, success in a tough task (achievement), praise (recognition), an interesting challenge (work itself), accountability for results (responsibility), promotion (advancement), and further training (growth possibility) generate feelings of satisfaction, whereas their opposites—unsuccessful task completion, criticism, and so on—do not greatly affect one's feelings of satisfaction. Other types of positive events—called hygiene factors—have little impact on participants' feelings of satisfaction but, when they are negative, stir feelings of dissatisfaction. Thus such contextual events as encountering an unfair policy (company administration), receiving unsound instructions (technical supervision), having a dispute (interpersonal relations), being given a drafty or dingy room (working conditions), losing an assistant (status), being informed of staff cutbacks (security) or a pay cut (salary), and being transferred to the boondocks (personal life) generate intense feelings of dissatisfaction; but positive aspects of these types of events—for example, making use of a fair policy or receiving sensible instructions—typically do not stimulate feelings of satisfaction. According to this theory, it is the satisfying types of events, the

motivation factors, but not the dissatisfying types of events, the hygiene factors, that spark the motivational drive within people. In brief, feelings of satisfaction and dissatisfaction can be seen as system outputs generated by the episodes of interaction among human components.

This brings us to the matter of the feedback loops necessary to every open system. As depicted in Figure 14–2, it is readily apparent that the feedback the organization receives regarding its productivity and efficiency will serve to modify the rules, mandates, job descriptions, and other bureaucratic information inputs to the system. A discrepancy between the societal goals and the actual productivity and efficiency of the organization is evidence of irrationality; and the greater the perceived irrationality (that is, the more negative the feedback), the more this information is encoded into the bureaucratic mode. Feedback associated with the satisfaction-dissatisfaction output of the system clearly affects the motivational force that participants bring to bear on their work. As indicated earlier (see item 3), it is one's perceptions of what transpired in the past, as described in the motivation-hygiene theory, that shapes the direction and intensity of one's psychological energy in the future. Thus, if a teacher who invested effort performed well in the past and received some praise, advancement, or other attractive benefits for that excellence, the awareness of that reward is feedback to the teacher, who will then perceive excellent teaching as highly instrumental for obtaining benefits. Such a teacher's motivation to invest effort is thus intensified.

To recapitulate briefly, an organization can be viewed as an open social system having role incumbents as its human components. Certain types of information inputs, such as rules, mandates, and specialized knowledge, render the system bureaucratic, as evidenced by such structural characteristics as centralization, formalization, specialization, and stratification. Certain types of energy inputs, such as motivation, affect the system's social atmosphere, as evidenced by its climate (ranging from open to closed), its environmental press (development and control), and its compliance pattern (coercive, utilitarian, or normative). These patterns of interaction, in turn, yield system outputs both goal oriented (production and efficiency) and interpersonal (satisfaction and dissatisfaction). Information about the formal achievement outputs returns to the system in the form of modified information inputs, and information about the group needs satisfaction outputs returns to the system in the form of modified motivational drives. In this way the open system that is an organization can be seen as evolving continuously in cycles related to changes in the environment or suprasystem.

A Behavioral Approach

One additional integrative scheme might be of value primarily to demonstrate that the leader behavior framework, not mentioned in the other syntheses, need not stand in isolation. As illustrated in Figure 14–3, the behaviors of principals and teachers, and the origins of those behaviors, can be the focal point of an integrative view:

1. As the social systems model developed by Getzels and Guba clearly illustrates, each individual's behavior is the result of transaction between the nomothetic dimension (role) and the idiographic dimension (personality) of the system.

2. When the individual being considered is the leader, Fiedler's theory suggests, an important facet of the personality is the individual's leadership style, relationship oriented or task oriented. In this model the important facets of the leader's role are expressed in terms of the group-task situation—the group's attitudes, its anticipation of structure, and its attributions of position power. The leader's effectiveness, then, is contingent on the appropriate matching of leadership style and situation favorableness.

3. From a different point of view, however, the transaction between leadership style (need-dispositions) and group-task situation (role expectations) can be seen as yielding the leader's observed behavior pattern. The work of Halpin, Stogdill, and others in the famed Ohio State leadership research program demonstrates that this observed behavior has two basic dimensions, which have since come to be called *person-oriented* behavior and *system-oriented* behavior. A leader who stresses organizational goals and tasks above all else is said to have a system-oriented behavior style, whereas one who emphasizes the needs and comforts of the individual participants is said to have a person-oriented behavior style; those who manage to blend the two orientations in their everyday actions are considered to have a *transactional* behavior style.

4a. Another approach to describing the leader's observable behavior, particularly when the leader is a school principal, was developed by Halpin and Croft in conjunction with their work on organizational climate. In this framework the leader's behavior is described in terms of aloofness, production emphasis, thrust, and consideration. Like other facets of the leader's behavior, such as those described in item 3, these behavior patterns can be seen as the result of transaction between the principal's personality (task or relationship oriented) and role (group-task situation).

4b. When it comes to the teachers' observed behavior, this too can be seen as the result of transaction between teachers' individual personalities and the roles they occupy. The teachers' behavior with respect to their students might best be explained in terms of their individual leadership styles and the group-task situation of each class. An alternative perspective, however, is available in the Halpin-Croft descriptive framework. The behaviors of the teachers as a group tend to become similar over time. This is because those with salient ungratified needs are likely to leave the school, and those who remain are pressured by the group to conform. The general behavior patterns

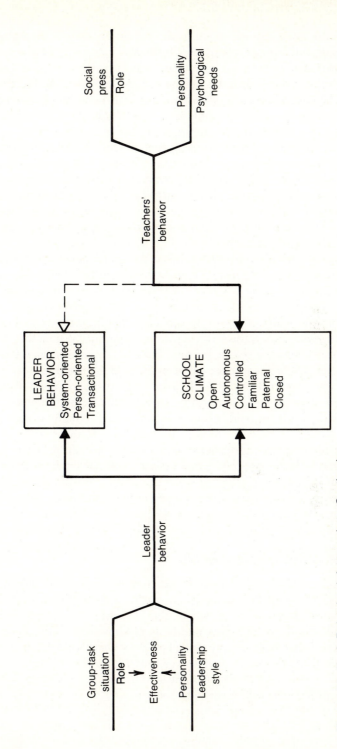

Figure 14–3 A Behavioral Approach to Synthesis

of the teachers as a group, then, can be described in terms of their disengagement, hindrance, esprit, and intimacy.

As the Halpin-Croft climate framework clarifies, these teacher behaviors in combination with the principal's behaviors (see 4a) constitute the climate of the school. The several types of climate range along a continuum from open to autonomous to controlled to familiar to paternal to closed, each type characterized by a different configuration of observed behaviors.

5. Another perspective for interpreting teachers' behavior patterns is available in Stern's needs-press framework. From this point of view the important idiographic characteristic of teachers is their psychological needs, and the important nomothetic characteristic of schools is their social press. Thus the observed behaviors of teachers as individuals can be seen as the result of transaction between their psychological needs and the environmental press they experience in the schools.

To summarize briefly, observable behavior can be viewed as the focus for an integration of several theories. When the observed behavior is the leader's, it can be described in terms of either the leader behavior framework or the climate description framework. In either case this behavior can be seen as emerging from the leader's need-dispositions (orientation) in transaction with the leadership role expectations (group-task situation). When the observed behavior is the teachers', it can be described in terms of either the leader behavior framework or the climate description model. In either case it can be seen as the outcome of transaction between the teachers' need-dispositions (psychological needs) and their role expectations (environmental press). Finally, the teachers' observed behavior patterns in combination with those of the principals yield a type of climate that can vary from open to closed.

These three examples of synthesis are certainly not all inclusive; they are simply illustrative of the integrative process and product. Each theory probably could serve as a core about which to view the others, and there are doubtless some overarching conceptions that could promote synthesis to a higher level of abstraction.

SOME FUNCTIONS OF SYNTHESIS

The art of synthesis is as individualistic and creative as that of theorizing—and just as vital to the growth and development of a field. For a field such as educational administration, synthesis of the available conceptualizations can add order and coherence to a disparate body of knowledge, indicate gaps and inadequacies in that knowledge, and point to the directions for needed conceptual work. In this section, however, our purpose is to explore some of the benefits of synthesis to individuals engaged in research about schools and to those in the practice of administrating schools.

Synthesis and the Research Process

In Chapter 1 of this book we examined the nature of theory and the relationship between theory and research. Theories were viewed as the foundations for research and the origins of hypotheses about reality. Many of the most compelling theories about human behavior, especially behavior in organizations, have scarcely been tested in school settings. Although some studies to test the applicability of behavioral theories to the field of education have been conducted, they have been too few and sometimes far too inadequate to tell us with any degree of certainty whether these theories are valid in schools. Therefore, questions remain to be answered by means of research—questions related to the individual theories and posed to test the validity of those theories in schools. If the theories are sound, they certainly suggest guidelines for administrative action in education. The questions suggested within each of the theory chapters might suggest hypotheses that merit testing through empirical research in schools.

Beyond the confines of any individual theory are additional questions that warrant research if a more comprehensive understanding of schools is to be gleaned. Since no one behavioral or organizational theory explicates all of social reality, only through integration and cross-fertilization of ideas will a richer, deeper comprehension emerge. Thus integrative thinking, once the individual perspectives have been grasped, will suggest research questions and hypotheses not embedded in any one theory alone.

One illustration might suffice to demonstrate this point. The expectancy theory of motivation (Vroom, 1964) maintains that the force to perform an action is a function of one's expectancies regarding the outcomes of the action and the instrumentalities of the outcomes for attaining other desired ends. Both expectancy and instrumentality are viewed as subjective assessments—one concerning one's ability (expectancy) and the other concerning the utility of possible outcomes (instrumentality). This is an interesting theory but one that has not been tested adequately in schools. The theory might lead one to expect that teachers' levels of motivations vary in accordance with the reward system of their school. On the other hand, we know that teachers within any one school, where a particular reward system is used for all, are likely to experience and exhibit different levels of motivation. What might account for these variations within a given school?

Conceptual systems theory (Schroder, Driver, & Streufert, 1967) maintains that people vary in their levels of integrative complexity—their cognitive ability to differentiate, discriminate, and interrelate the diverse stimuli available in their environment. This suggests that teachers with more complex conceptual systems might perceive a wider range of indirect outcomes of action as relevant to their interests than would teachers having lower levels of integrative complexity. That is, if asked to specify the positive and negative outcomes of using a given teaching method, for example, relatively complex teachers would likely generate longer lists than would their conceptually simpler colleagues and would probably make finer distinctions among the items on these lists. These perceptions of relevance, then, would influence the direction and intensity of the motivational force the teachers experience. Thus it is possible that the most obvious rewards and penalties in a school would have greater impact on the motivation levels of teachers with low integrative complexity than on those with higher conceptual complexity. Is this so? Only carefully designed empirical research can yield the answer.

The point here is that interesting research questions can evolve from the interrelating of theories as well as from individual theories, and the answers to such questions can be as vital to the field of practice as are the tests of particular theories. The integrations or syntheses of theories must occur in the mind of the researcher, however; it is from one's own understandings of the theories individually and one's own quest for interrelationships—not the thinking of others—that the provocative research questions will arise.

Synthesis and the Administrative Process

What about the practicing administrator confronting the heat of each moment in the engrossing and concrete world of experience? Generally, the leader at the front lines is not seeking questions for research or consciously contemplating hypotheses about the staff, the students, or the events to be encountered. More typically, she or he is actively resolving a real problem of relatively simple or complex dimensions; it would be unusual to stop and analyze the situation from one or more theoretical perspectives, even though each one could probably shed some light on the problem at hand.

One reason that scientific theories are not often evoked in the quick of the moment is that they are only superficially understood. The language of the theories, the specialized meanings of the terms, and the particular dynamics explicated seem foreign and unrelated to one's everyday vocabulary and thought processes. Thus the first step in coming to grips with a theory, as in any real learning, is to become so familiar with the ideas and their language that they become second nature. Initially, as in learning to ride a bicycle or to multiply large numbers, the application of ideas or principles to practice requires conscious, intentional repetition characterized by an awareness of each step. In the case of making theories useful in the concrete world of experience, this entails consciously applying the constructs and propositions in the analysis of one's own situations time after time, until they feel natural and even self-evident. At that point the theoretical notions and their vocabularies will be integrated with the rest of one's world view and thus will shape one's most basic perceptions of reality. This is the deepest level of synthesis—the thorough integration of new ideas into an established habit of thought.

Once a new theory (new to the user, that is) has become synthesized with previously established conceptualizations in one's mind, further reinforcement and richer understanding can be gained by consciously and repeatedly interrelating another "new" theory or two to the first one, until these additional frameworks too become integrated in a newly natural mode of thought.

Why should busy administrators take the time and trouble to engage in this intellectual drill? The answer is that it can serve to expand and enhance our most basic perceptions of events and situations; that eventually the need for conscious application will end and what remains will be spontaneity based on richer understandings; and that each theory projects an array of fine distinctions that most individuals would not conceptualize independently and that, when synthesized within one's own cognitive map of the experienced world, make for sensitive and fine-tuned responses to events.

The theme to be emphasized here is that individual theories memorized from a book are unlikely to be of real use to a busy administrator. Their utility in the spontaneous world of practice comes only after thoughtful study and the labor of repetitive use, when the conceptualizations and their terminologies become synthesized with each other and the rest of one's world view. At that point the active, involved administrator's very conceptions of events encompass more dimensions of the reality at hand, and her responses reflect that richer understanding.

SUMMARY AND CONCLUSION

The purposes of this chapter have been to review in brief the 12 theoretical frameworks treated in this book and to take some initial steps toward synthesis. The 12 theories were paired in terms of six broad topics:

1. *Whole organizations*—structure and process viewpoints.
2. *Power*—authority and compliance conceptions.
3. *Leadership*—behavioral and contingency approaches.
4. *Climate*—descriptive and psychological frameworks.
5. *Individuals in organizations*—psychosocial and information-processing perspectives.
6. *Motivation*—external and internal orientations.

Within the pairs of conceptualizations each framework represents a different perspective on the broader topic, but the two viewpoints should not be considered incompatible.

Steps toward integration beyond the scope of each general topic were taken in the form of three synthesizing schemata. The first of these, the organization-individual interaction scheme, highlights the fact that in many theories an aspect of human behavior is viewed as the result of transaction between a facet of the organization and a facet of the individual. The second integrative scheme, called a systems approach in this chapter, uses general system theory as the focal point and regards several other theories as elucidations of the system's inputs, interaction patterns, and outputs. The third synthesis, here called a behavioral approach, emphasizes the descriptions of behavior patterns and the influences on behavior as the bases for interrelating several theories. These schemata do not exhaust the possibilities for synthesis; they simply illustrate the feasibility of conceptualizing integrations of diverse theories.

Readers are encouraged to pursue the intellectual activity of synthesizing on their own. Not only does this activity reinforce one's understanding of the theories themselves and point to directions for needed research, but it also facilitates the integration of the ideas into one's own conceptual system so that they ultimately serve as a foundation for improved practice.

MASTERY QUIZ

For practice in thinking across theories rather than within theories, try to specify one *similarity* in meaning and one *difference* in meaning between the terms in each of the following pairs. Theorists' names are indicated in parentheses to indicate the context of each term. Since there are several possible correct responses for each item, answers are not provided in Appendix C. Instead, class discussion is recommended.

1. Component (Bertalanffy)—individual (Getzels-Guba).
2. Task-oriented style (Fiedler)—system-oriented style (Halpin/Stogdill).
3. Role (Getzels-Guba)—office (Weber).
4. Normative power (Etzioni)—authority (Weber).
5. Climate (Halpin-Croft)—compliance (Etzioni).
6. Needs (Stern)—need-dispositions (Getzels-Guba).
7. Motivation (Vroom)—satisfaction (Herzberg).
8. Involvement (Etzioni)—need-dispositions (Getzels-Guba).
9. Environment complexity (Schroder)—social press (Stern).
10. Productivity (Hage)—output (Bertalanffy).

EXERCISES

1. The following is a matrix with all the theoretical frameworks treated in this book listed along the horizontal and vertical axes. Each cell within the matrix represents a pair of theories. Can you think of a way in which the two theories in each cell are related, congruent, or compatible?

	Axiomatic	General system	Bureaucracy	Compliance	Leader behavior	Leadership effectiveness	Climate (open-closed)	Climate (needs/press)	Social systems	Conceptual systems	Motivation-hygiene	Expectancy
Axiomatic theory												
General system theory												
Bureaucracy theory												
Compliance theory												
Leader behavior												
Leadership effectiveness												
Climate (open-closed)												
Climate (needs/press)												
Social systems theory												
Conceptual systems												
Motivation/hygiene												
Expectancy theory												

2. Of the behavioral theories you may know that were not treated in this text—for example, Freudian theory, operant conditioning theory, Maslow's needs theory, an economic or political theory—select one and see if you can relate it to any one or more of the theories listed here. That is, identify in your own mind some points of tangency between the theory you know from elsewhere and those you know from this text. Be prepared to discuss your insights in class.

3. You may already be familiar with the case description appearing in Appendix A. For purposes of this exercise, it would be advisable to reread the case to refresh your memory. Then, with reference to the foregoing list of theoretical frameworks, identify *one* element in the case that is pertinent to each of the 12 theories. Stated differently, for each theoretical framework, pinpoint a relevant element in the case situation; the selected aspects of the case may differ with respect to each theory.

4. In some of the earlier chapters you were asked to generate hypotheses deduced from individual theories. At this point try to develop three hypotheses, each of which is derived from two (or more) theoretical foundations. Write a brief statement of the underlying reasoning for each hypothesis to clarify the relevance of the two or more theories to your conjecture.

REFERENCES

Argyris, C., & Schön, D. A. *Theory in practice: Increasing professional effectiveness.* San Francisco: Jossey-Bass, 1974.

Berrien, F. K. *General and social systems.* New Brunswick, N.J.: Rutgers University Press, 1968.

Bertalanffy, L., von. *General system theory: Foundations, development, applications.* New York: George Braziller, 1968.

Etzioni, A. *A comparative analysis of complex organizations,* rev. ed. New York: Macmilllan, Free Press, 1975.

Fiedler, F. E. *A theory of leadership effectiveness.* New York: McGraw-Hill, 1967.

Gerth, H. H., & Mills, C. W. (Eds. & trans.). *From Max Weber: Essays in sociology.* New York: Oxford University Press, 1958.

Getzels, J. W., & Guba, E. G. Social behavior and the administrative process. *The School Review,* 1957, 65, 423–441.

Hage, J. An axiomatic theory of organizations. *Administrative Science Quarterly,* 1965, 10, 289–320.

Halpin, A. W. How leaders behave. *Theory and research administration.* New York: Macmillan, 1966a, 81–130, chap. 3.

———.The organizational climate of schools. *Theory and research in administration.* New York: Macmillan, 1966b, 131–249, chap. 4.

Herzberg, F. *Work and the nature of man.* New York: World, 1966.

Schroder, H. M.; Driver, M. J.; & Streufert, S. *Human information processing.* New York: Holt, Rinehart and Winston, 1967.

Stern, G. G. *People in context: Measuring person-environment congruence in education and industry.* New York: Wiley, 1970.

Stogdill, R. M. *Handbook of leadership.* New York: Free Press, 1974.

Vroom, V. H. *Work and motivation.* New York: Wiley, 1964.

Weber, M. Bureaucracy. In J. A. Litterer. (Ed.), *Organizations: Structure and behavior.* New York: Wiley, 1963, 40–50.

Appendix A
Things That Go Bump
in the Blight: A Case Study

Jerry A. F. Jones
Paula F. Silver

History seemed to be repeating itself. Only two years before, Brenda March had "bumped" a special education teacher who had provided nine years of service at Kennedy Middle School. Although it had been Brenda's first year at Kennedy, she did have a few months' seniority in the district. The Kennedy faculty thought it unkind and unreasonable of her to demand her senior rights when changing schools caused their old friend such grief. Now Brenda herself faced a trim-off decision in which district seniority rules would probably be applied.

Mary Travail was Kennedy's other special education teacher. She had been at Kennedy for two years as a half-day traveling teacher. Mary and Brenda were required to work closely together since they were the only members of their department.

When the fall projections for enrollment came out in March, the principal announced that two and a half faculty members would be trimmed. *Trimming* does not mean termination, but it does mean involuntary transfer to another school where needed. Both Brenda and Mary were familiar with this discomfiting procedure since their respective schools had been closed because of declining enrollments just two years earlier.

After the faculty meeting one teacher made it public that she had already asked for a transfer; another was taking advantage of the early retirement "carrot" the district was offering. This left only a half-time position to be trimmed—and that, it seemed, would have to be in special education.

This turn of events set the stage for a series of episodes that were to have deep effects on the faculty at the Kennedy school for a long time to come.

During their two years at this school, Brenda had been on staff full time and Mary had worked half days at two schools. Some time during the second year, Brenda had begun to assume the team leader role, although no such official designation had been made. Mary, who was also an experienced teacher, resented being treated as a subordinate and began to wonder what had caused the change. She did not discuss it with the principal, however, because she feared that Brenda was being encouraged by Ms. Steele. After the trim-off announcement was made public, the strain on the two women's relationship became more and more pronounced.

Former friends, they now could occupy the same lunch table without exchanging a word or a glance. Whereas once they had worked in close cooperation in adjacent rooms, Brenda now began to close the double doors between them and work in a self-contained space. Mary felt that she was the soul of cooperation but that whenever she tried to renew cordial relations with Brenda, she was rebuffed.

Both teachers were in their mid-forties and had stable marriages and grown children. Brenda, who was black, was gregarious, fun-loving, and active in school and community social life. Mary was quieter and somewhat reserved but was said to be warm and friendly in small-group situations. Since her duties shuttled her back and forth between schools, her time to develop friendships was limited. She also happened to be white. Racial balance had not quite been attained at Kennedy Middle School, as white teachers were still in the majority.

To further stack the cards in Brenda's favor, Mary had gotten off on the wrong foot with the Kennedy principal, Ms. Steele, from the start. On her crucial first day of orientation, she had made the mistake of going to another school for the retirement party of an old friend. Arriving at Kennedy forty minutes after the back-to-school luncheon had started, she was greeted coolly by Ms. Steele, who suggested that her place was at her newly assigned building. Mildly flustered, Mary made an innocuous comment about old ties being hard to break. This did not seem to soothe Ms. Steele's ruffled feathers, and it laid the foundation for strained relations between them from then on.

Mary felt she had done nothing wrong and was hurt and resentful to be treated so gruffly by her new boss. Her solution to this unhappy situation was withdrawal. She avoided the principal whenever possible and could not bring herself to join in any of the lounge banter with her. Sensing Mary's rejection of her weak attempts toward reconciliation, Ms. Steele came to regard Mary as uncooperative and unfriendly.

Pat Steele pursed her lips ruefully as she drove back to her school from the district's Education Service Center one morning in April. Not only had the enrollment projections not changed, but two additional factors had come to light. First, Mary Travail was actually senior to Brenda March by two days. Second, a small delegation of black parents had made an appearance the previous day at the superintendent's office to insist that Brenda, who presumably had better rapport with the black students, be retained at Kennedy. Alice Vocal, the self-appointed spokesperson for the community, had made no specific threats, the superintendent reported; but she had made it clear that the issue of racial balance on the faculty was regarded as "cause for great concern" in the community.

Mary is a difficult person, Pat was thinking—hostile and withdrawn. But there's no denying she's a good teacher, and she's won the respect of several others on the staff. Brenda's a gem, though, and marvelous at linking with the minority groups. Maybe with more help in the classroom she'd function better. And there's no doubt about the super's views; he's a no waves administrator for sure! Maybe Mary could be induced to request a transfer....

Ms. Steele's coolness became unmistakable when she began reminding Mary of trivial responsibilities she rarely mentioned to other staff members and observing her frequently in the classroom. On the few occasions when Mary was detained at her morning school, Ms. Steele was invariably in the hall watching for her and looking ostentatiously at her wristwatch. Although Mary proffered legitimate reasons, the principal was never receptive to her explanations.

Meanwhile, Brenda's fine relationship with Ms. Steele was advertised by the exchange of gourmet recipes; inside jokes in the faculty lounge; and occasional calls to the office during class time, when Mary would be charged with overseeing both groups. When decisions about the big May special education field trip had to be made, Brenda was the only one consulted. Mary saw Brenda as increasingly favored.

As she endured the unsupportiveness of both the principal and her buddy-teacher, Mary's morale hit rock bottom. She felt she was losing control of the situation and was on the verge of dropping the graduate course she and four others on the Kennedy staff were taking. They had been car pooling to a university in another city for nearly two semesters, and Mary felt that their support and friendship were lifesavers in the stormy work atmosphere.

Another member of the car pool crowd was Mike Stark, who also happened to be the school's union representative. He was entirely sympathetic with Mary's point of view and on several occasions offered full union support if an unfavorable decision was made. "Not only are you senior," he once remarked heatedly, "but you're a much better teacher too!" Brenda had been absent frequently this year, and her classes were noisy and unruly, to the intense annoyance of the neighboring teachers. On more than one occasion

Mary had rescued a hapless substitute teacher by bringing Brenda's class to order and getting the kids working productively. Mike, fully aware of the history of difficulties, might almost have welcomed a contract violation on the principal's part as a chance to generate union interest and rally support. He urged Mary to drop the thoughts she'd been voicing about requesting a transfer for the following year.

As the hectic days of spring ground on toward school's end at Kennedy, the atmosphere was tense as the faculty waited to see how the trim-off stalemate would be resolved. Although Mary missed no school, it became known that she was seeing a doctor for nervousness and heart palpitations. She began to lose weight, rarely ate lunch in the faculty lounge, and was noticeably depressed.

During this strained time, Ms. Steele and Brenda seemed cozier than ever. Brenda maintained her breezy style and seemed confident that she would not be the one to go. Mary, however, was made to feel more like the unfavored stepchild.

By now the faculty had begun to polarize. The favoritism exhibited by the principal rallied some more teachers to Mary's side of the dispute. The teachers felt that a very unprofessional scenario was being played out. As they watched the performance from the wings, they were alarmed to realize that any one of them might be a main character in years to come.

Pat Steele's next visit to the central office, this one in early May, was no more rewarding to her than the previous one. The superintendent reiterated his interest in promoting racial balance at Kennedy and mentioned that the Parents Advisory Council was becoming more vociferous on this issue. He would offer no advice on the matter at hand, however. The director of personnel, whom she visited next, could find no loopholes in the seniority clauses of the teachers' contract that would enable the principal to exercise discretion.

Things were going downhill at the school, Pat felt. In subtle ways Brenda seemed to be taking advantage of her good relationship with the principal, and Mary appeared no more inclined to ask for a transfer than before. If anything, her position seemed to have solidified. Pat felt sure that Mary would request the presence of the union representative if the subject were broached directly. It could not have been a coincidence, moreover, that no members of Mary's growing circle of allies had volunteered to help chaperone the upcoming senior dance or to offer after-school tutorial help to students. Pat felt guilty and inept because of these events, but she was no closer to resolving her dilemma.

June had already arrived, and students and staff alike were restless and impatient for the year's end, when the situation came to a head. The story came out only disjointedly and in fragments—after Brenda's student, Diane Vocal, had been rushed off to the hospital for emergency stitches. Evidently there had been a fight between Diane and little Joannie Grimes from Mary's class.

Brenda had been out of her room "on urgent business," leaving her class unsupervised; Diane, according to her mother, simply went to get a drink of water when she was accosted by Joanie, who should have been kept in her room by "that awful teacher." Joanie, for her part, had a hall pass and insisted that Diane had intercepted her and demanded some money. Diane had pushed her, Joanie said; when she pushed back, Diane had slipped and hit her face on the water fountain. No witnesses came forward to verify either story.

That very afternoon a dozen parents, led by Alice Vocal, crowded into Pat Steele's office to demand better corridor patrol, to offer their own help in monitoring the hallways, and to insist that Mary Travail be released.

At the same time Mike Stark had assembled a group of teachers, including Mary, in the lounge to review a petition he had drafted to the effect that Brenda be transferred out and Mary put on full-time status. "Not only is it her seniority right," Mike maintained, "but it is in the best interests of the children as well."

With only two weeks of school left, Pat Steele could no longer postpone the decision.

Appendix B
Sample Analysis
of "Things That Go Bump
in the Blight"

ANALYTIC FRAMEWORK: MASLOW'S THEORY OF MOTIVATION

PROBLEM STATEMENT

Maslow's theory of motivation states that human needs are of five types, which are hierarchically ordered, and that motivational needs of a given type become salient only when the lower-order needs have been sufficiently satisfied. The types of needs, from the lowest to the highest order, are: physiological, security, affiliation, esteem, and self-actualization. Motivation is the desire to fulfill the salient needs at any given point in time.

The problem at Kennedy Middle School is that teachers' motivational levels have been reduced from high levels (self-actualization and esteem) to low levels (physiological and security). The *focal person* for this analysis is Mary Travail.

NOTE: Maslow's theory, which was discussed briefly in Chapter 1, is used as the framework for the sample analysis so as not to influence students' analyses based on the major theories treated in detail in this volume.

MAJOR CONSTRUCTS

Self-actualization: needs for personal growth to the maximum of one's potential. Evidence of Mary's attainment of that level is found in her having enrolled in graduate school and in hints that she was an excellent teacher. That she ceased to function at this level is suggested by her consideration of dropping out of graduate school. This was because lower-order needs that were no longer being satisfied became salient to her.

Esteem: needs for status, prestige, and respect from others. Mary's needs at this level were not being gratified, as she was hurt by Brenda's assuming the team leader role and by the principal's rebuffs. However, she was not motivated to reestablish her status, as she was preoccupied with lower-order needs.

Affiliation: needs for friendship and human contact. This type of need was salient to Mary, as indicated by her attempts to reestablish cordial relations with Brenda, her visiting the old school on the first day, and her relief that supportive friendships were developing with the car pool group. That this level of need was losing its motivational force, however, is suggested by her self-enforced isolation at the Kennedy school and her willingness to drop out of the graduate school car pool. Mary's affiliation needs might motivate her to try to retain her position at Kennedy Middle School since her friend Mike and several other teachers are encouraging this.

Security: needs for assurance that physiological needs will continue to be fulfilled in the future. This level of need was clearly threatened, as Mary became uncertain about whether and where she would be working the following year. Mary's security needs became the most salient, as much of her thinking and activity were directed toward securing her position.

Physiological: needs for the most basic requirements of life—food, air, a functioning body, and so on. This had become a salient need level to Mary, as evidenced by her failing health and visits to doctors. These needs had been fulfilled to some degree (she missed no school), but not completely; she still directed time and energy to physiological gratifications.

Summary: Although Mary Travail had the potential for functioning at the highest level (self-actualization), the situation at Kennedy had caused her lower-order needs to reemerge in importance.

CONCLUSION

If Mary had known this theory well, she might have been able to prevent the situation from getting out of hand by reminding herself that her teaching skills and contributions to helping exceptional youngsters (that is, her self-actualization) are her highest priorities and that it does not matter *where* she practices her art. Perhaps she would have recognized, too, that esteem and affiliation would be as accessible in another school and that she could win some respect by withdrawing from the Kennedy School with dignity.

Appendix C
Answers to Mastery Quiz Items and Some Exercise Items

Chapter 2, Mastery Quiz, page 43

1. c
2. b
3. d
4. a
5. b
6. d
7. a
8. c
9. c
10. b

Chapter 2, Exercise 1, page 44

1. positive
2. negative
3. negative
4. positive
5. negative
6. positive
7. positive
8. negative
9. negative
10. positive

Chapter 3, Mastery Quiz, page 66

1. b
2. c
3. d
4. b
5. b
6. d
7. a
8. d
9. c
10. c

Chapter 3, Exercise 1, page 67

1. e
2. m
3. h
4. b
5. j
6. o
7. a
8. g
9. l
10. c

Chapter 4, Mastery Quiz, page 91

1. c	4. c	7. d	10. c
2. a	5. b	8. b	
3. a	6. d	9. c	

Chapter 4, Exercise 1, page 92

1. f	4. b	7. e	10. o
2. m	5. j	8. i	
3. r	6. a	9. c	

Chapter 5, Mastery Quiz, page 116

1. d	4. b	7. c	10. c
2. b	5. d	8. a	
3. b	6. d	9. c	

Chapter 5, Exercise 1, page 117

1. utilitarian	4. coercive	7. coercive	10. normative
2. normative	5. normative	8. coercive	
3. utilitarian	6. normative	9. utilitarian	

Chapter 6, "Mastery Quiz," page 145

1. b	4. b	7. d	10. b
2. c	5. a	8. a	
3. c	6. d	9. b	

Chapter 6, Exercise 1, page 146

1. Superior orientation	6. Tolerance of uncertainty	11. Tolerance of uncertainty
2. Persuasiveness	7. Initiating structure	12. Tolerance of freedom
3. Role assumption	8. Integration	13. Production emphasis
4. Consideration	9. Demand reconciliation	14. Predictive accuracy
5. Representation	10. Role assumption	15. Persuasiveness

Chapter 7, Mastery Quiz, page 171

1. c	4. c	7. a	10. d
2. b	5. c	8. c	
3. d	6. b	9. d	

Chapter 7, Exercise 1, page 172

1. IV/R	4. II/T	7. III/T	10. VIII/T
2. VI/R	5. III/T	8. V/R	
3. VI/R	6. I/T	9. V) R	

Chapter 8, Mastery Quiz, page 200

1. b	4. d	7. a	10. c
2. b	5. b	8. c	
3. b	6. d	9. a	

Chapter 9, Mastery Quiz, page 233

1. d	4. c	7. a	10. c
2. b	5. b	8. d	
3. b	6. a	9. c	

Chapter 10, Mastery Quiz, page 262

1. c	4. d	7. b	10. b
2. d	5. c	8. d	
3. c	6. a	9. d	

Chapter 10, Exercise 1, page 263

1. transactional	4. idiographic	7. transactional	10. nomothetic
2. nomothetic	5. nomothetic	8. transactional	
3. nomothetic	6. nomothetic	9. idiographic	

Chapter 11, Mastery Quiz, page 288

1. c	4. a	7. a	10. a
2. b	5. c	8. c	
3. c	6. d	9. a	

Chapter 12, Mastery Quiz, page 317

1. c	4. b	7. b	10. b
2. a	5. c	8. d	
3. b	6. a	9. b	

Chapter 13, Mastery Quiz, page 348

1. c	4. d	7. a	10. d
2. b	5. a	8. b	
3. b	6. d	9. c	

Author Index

Subject Index

Research Instruments Index

DATE DUE

MAR 1 1 2001		
4/8/01		

DEMCO 38-297